Parental Psychiatric Disorder
Distressed Parents and Their Families

SECOND EDITION

Edited by

Michael Göpfert
Consultant Psychiatrist in Psychotherapy,
Webb House, Crewe

Jeni Webster
Family Therapist, Warrington

and

Mary V. Seeman
Professor Emerita, Department of Psychiatry,
University of Toronto

CAMBRIDGE
UNIVERSITY PRESS

PUBLISHED BY THE PRESS SYNDICATE OF THE UNIVERSITY OF CAMBRIDGE
The Pitt Building, Trumpington Street, Cambridge, United Kingdom

CAMBRIDGE UNIVERSITY PRESS
The Edinburgh Building, Cambridge CB2 2RU, UK
40 West 20th Street, New York, NY 10011–4211, USA
477 Williamstown Road, Port Melbourne, VIC 3207, Australia
Ruiz de Alarcón 13, 28014 Madrid, Spain
Dock House, The Waterfront, Cape Town 8001, South Africa

http://www.cambridge.org

First published 2004

Printed in the United Kingdom at the University Press, Cambridge

Typefaces Minion 10.5/14 pt., Formata and Formata BQ   *System* LATEX 2$_\varepsilon$ [TB]

A catalogue record for this book is available from the British Library

Library of Congress Cataloguing in Publication data
Parental psychiatric disorder : distressed parents and their families / [edited by] Michael
Göpfert, Jeni Webster, Mary V. Seeman. – 2nd ed.
    p.   cm.
  Includes bibliographical references and index.   -
  ISBN 0 521 53497 6 (paperback)
    1. Families of the mentally ill. 2. Children of the mentally ill. 3. Problem
families – Mental health services.   I. Göpfert, Michael, 1947–   II. Webster, Jeni.
III. Seeman, M. V. (Mary Violette), 1935–
[DNLM: 1. Mental Disorders – psychology. 2. Parenting – psychology. 3. Child of
Impaired Parents – psychology. 4. Mental Disorders – therapy. 5. Parent–Child Relations.
WM 140 P228   2003]
RC455.4.F3 P365   2003
616.89–dc21   2002036835

ISBN 0 521 53497 6 paperback

Every effort has been made in preparing this book to provide accurate and up-to-date
information that is in accord with accepted standards and practice at the time of publication.
Nevertheless, the authors, editors and publisher can make no warranties that the information
contained herein is totally free from error, not least because clinical standards are constantly
changing through research and regulation. The authors, editors and publisher therefore
disclaim all liability for direct or consequential damages resulting from the use of material
contained in this book. Readers are strongly advised to pay careful attention to information
provided by the manufacturer of any drugs or equipment that they plan to use.

To the memory of

Channi Kumar

Contents

Contributors

Gwen Adshead
Broadmoor Hospital
Crowthorne
Berkshire RG45 7EG, UK

Eia Asen
Marlborough Family Service
38 Marlborough Place
London NW8 0PJ, UK

Karen Baistow
Division of Psychological Medicine
KCL Guy's Campus
9th Floor, Capital House
42 Weston Street
London SE1 1UL, UK

Sandra Bilsborough
Barnados
24 Colquitt Street
Liverpool L1 4DE, UK

Colby C. Brunt
294 Washington Street, Suite 320
Boston, MA 02108, USA

David Clodman
Centre for Addiction and Mental Health
250 College Street
Toronto
Ontario M5T 1R8, Canada

Sue Conroy
Division of Psychological Medicine
De Crespigny Park
Denmark Hill
London SE5 8AF, UK

Alan Cooklin
Family Project
Camden & Islington
Mental Health & Social Care Trust
St. Pancras Hospital
4, St. Pancras Way
London NW1 0PE, UK

Vicki Cowling
Maroondah Hospital CAMHS
21 Ware Crescent
Ringwood East 3135
Victoria, Australia

John Cox
Harplands Hospital
Hilton Road
Harpfields
Stoke on Trent ST4 6TH, UK

Adrian Falkov
Consultant Child & Adolescent Psychiatrist
Department of Psychological Medicine
Childern's Hospital Westmead
Locked Bag 4001
Westmead 2145
Sydney, NSW, Australia

Michael Göpfert
Webb House Democratic Therapeutic
Community
Victoria Avenue
Crewe CW2 7SQ, UK

Gill Gorell Barnes
Tavistock Clinic
120 Belsize Lane
London NW3 5BA, UK

Alyson Hall
Emanuel Miller Centre for Families and
Children
The Health Centre
11 Gill Street
London E14 8HQ, UK

Sydney L. Hans
Department of Psychiatry, MC3077
The University of Chicago
5841 S Maryland Avenue
Chicago, IL 60637, USA

Jennifer Hearle
Queensland Centre for Schizophrenia
Research
Wolston Park Hospital
Wacol Q4076, Australia

Rachael Hetherington
c/o Karen Baistow
Division of Psychological Medicine
KCL Guy's Campus
9th floor, Capital House
42 Weston Street
London SE1 1UL, UK

Jonathan Hill
Child Mental Health Unit
Mulberry House
Royal Liverpool Children's Hospital
Alder Hey, Eaton Road
Liverpool L12 2AP, UK

Teresa Jacobsen
School of Social Work
University of Illinois
at Urbana-Champaign
1207 West Oregon Street
Urbana, Illinois 61810, USA

Clare Mahoney
National Institute for Mental Health
(England)
North-West Team
Hyde Hospital
Grange Road South
Hyde Cheshire SK14 5NY, UK

John McGrath
Queensland Centre for Schizophrenia
Research
Wolston Park Hospital
Wacol Q4076, Australia

Duncan McLean
Queensland Centre for Schizophrenia
Research
Wolston Park Hospital
Wacol Q4076, Australia

Julia Nelki
Seymour House
Seymour Terrace
Liverpool L3 5TE, UK

Christine Puckering
Department of Child and Adolescent
Psychiatry
Royal Hospital for Sick Children
Yorkhill
Glasgow G3 8SJ, UK

Heiner Schuff
Marlborough Family Service
38 Marlborough Place
London NW8 0PJ, UK

Mary V. Seeman
Centre for Addiction and Mental Health
250 College Street
Toronto
Ontario M5T 1R8, Canada

Neil Seeman
260 Heath Street West
Toronto
Ontario M5P 3L6
Canada

Gertrude Seneviratne
Division of Psychological Medicine
De Crespigny Park
Denmark Hill
London SE5 8AF, UK

Graham Thornicroft
Health Services Research Department
De Crespigny Park
Denmark Hill
London SE5 8AF, UK

Richard Velleman
Director of Research and
Development
3 East, 2.10
University of Bath
Bath BA2 7AY, UK

Jeni Webster
Psychological Therapies
Garven Place
Warrington WA1 1RH, UK

Amy Weir
115 Mount View Road
London N4 4JH, UK

Foreword

Graham Thornicroft

Institute of Psychiatry, London, UK

The joys of parents are secret, and so are their griefs and fears.

Francis Bacon (1625) Essays. Of Parents and Children.

This thoroughly revised second edition of *Parental Psychiatric Disorder*, following on so soon upon the heels of the first edition, shows both how important this book has become and how rapidly the field is changing. The first edition broke new ground by presenting a coherent range of contributions across the spectrum from primary research, through policy to clinical practice. The new edition takes the field a measured step further. One measure of the rapid maturation of this area is that discussion of the complex interactions between mentally ill parents and their families is now entering mainstream clinical practice in many countries. Until recently, at least in many adult services, the dominant mental health paradigm focused primarily upon the *individual* treatment offered by a clinician to a patient. The importance of this paradigm shift, towards seeing unwell parents in relation to their immediate and their wider family contexts, is of fundamental importance.

This more complex perspective necessarily means that many aspects of the conventional treatment approach have to be revised or completely rethought. A family-context perspective means less certainty for staff who will now need to take into account simultaneously many points of view. Such complexities include, for example (as this splendid volume clearly demonstrates) the need to balance the interests of the child and each of the parents. This focus upon unmet needs of families is especially important now, at a time when, in some economically developed countries, there is a wider cultural shift towards risk avoidance, and it is necessary to recognize that professional abilities to predict harmful activities, for example by parents towards their children, are imprecise at best.

The epidemiological context to this field is also of major importance. As several chapters show, the lifetime prevalence of mental disorders is such that in many cultures children are now more likely than not to live with a parent undergoing a period of mental illness at some time during their upbringing. The increasing rates of separation, and divorce are likely to make such exposure even more probable in the foreseeable future. Parental mental illness therefore poses a very substantial public health challenge to many communities. Given this, it is surprising that there is relatively little high-quality research addressing aetiology, prevention and treatment from a family perspective. This volume summarizes much of the published scientific investigations. Thus far, the social, psychological and psychotherapeutic traditions have only just begun to join forces with genetic and epidemiologic investigators, in order to bring the full rigour of a truly multidisciplinary approach to this field. Such an approach will lead to an understanding of the complex chains of causation of mental illness and distress among mentally ill parents, their children and their shared families. At the same time there is a need to apply the highest possible scientific standards to intervention studies for and with such families, including the use of randomized controlled trials more often in future.

This book presents a balanced, humane and expert source of knowledge. Tough issues are addressed head on: including complex ethical and legal issues, alongside a clear emphasis upon what has been learned from clinical practice, using vignettes and case histories to carefully illustrate the key points. The question of what does 'family' mean in times of separated and reconstituted relationships is addressed, as is the difficult area of blame (children blaming themselves, and also parents blaming themselves, for parental mental illness), a form of internalized stigma. From the many expert contributions in this volume, the second edition of this rich repository can only serve to advance our knowledge and practice in relation to parental psychiatric disorder.

Preface

Being asked to provide a second edition of 'Parental Psychiatric Disorder' meant that the initial edition had filled a perceived gap. We were pleased and caught by surprise by the response to the first edition, each of us now in new places and stages of life and career. We had moved on and so had the field. Like the previous edition, but perhaps more clearly so, the volume focuses on the parent with a psychiatric disorder while keeping in mind that the best interests of the child must be considered paramount, if service systems are to work coherently, so that child and adult services complement one another. This edition is completely rewritten bar one chapter by Roberts (Chapter 20), which because of its seminal value, was retained unchanged. Two other chapters (Hall, Chapter 3; Velleman, Chapter 13) were retained but revised and updated. The rest of the chapters are either completely rewritten, or are new, representing the changes in thinking, knowledge and service developments that have taken place since 1995. We made a conscious editorial decision not to republish material where no major change had occurred (e.g. eating disorders, psychosomatic disorders, learning disability). The first edition remains available as a resource and is referenced extensively in this volume.

Our own interests have made us more aware of some developments focusing on personality-disordered parents and their children. We therefore commissioned a new chapter (Adshead *et al.*, Chapter 15) and asked previous contributors to focus their rewritten chapter on personality-disordered parents and their families (Asen and Schuff, Chapter 10). Similarly, we felt that the voice of parents was not present enough in the literature. We therefore commissioned a chapter by Clare Mahoney (Chapter 23), and Vicky Cowling kindly agreed to collect data for the compilation of a chapter that could represent the voice of parents (Chapter 25).

Perhaps the most striking differences in this edition will be in the development of family-sensitive services in so many different countries. Some of these have had a major impact on the delivery of mental health services to women (e.g. Cowling, Chapter 25), or for women with specific disorders. Of course our own thinking and our work has developed further and this is reflected in a number of contributions.

It is difficult to summarize and convey the experience accumulated over decades of work with families and their mentally ill parents. Since the first edition, the literature and efforts in providing services for mentally ill and disordered parents and their families has expanded considerably and become much more diverse. This is reflected in the content of this edition although we are aware that we have omitted some important service developments (e.g. in Sweden and Holland), and other work in progress.

Acknowledgements

Bertram Cohler in Chicago, and Tara Weeramanthri in London, UK, have significantly helped to shape the current edition with advice and support. The other person without whom this book would not have been put together is Jenny Davenport at Webb House in Crewe, UK, who provided a stable centre of administrative solidity in the midst of our professional turbulence. Of course our families have had to share the burden of writing to varying degrees, and one of our children's birthday wish was that the book should be finished before their birthday! We therefore want to acknowledge Jayne Webster and Renée Webster Zempt, grandsons Ahron, Geoffrey and Ciara Seeman, the late Erna Nelki (Oma, mother and mother-in-law), and Anya, Max and Leo Göpfert. Our colleagues at times have also had to put up with the additional stress that editorial and writing work engenders, especially for full-time clinicians with little or no dedicated time to give to such tasks. The developments in our professional thinking come from many sources – our own family experiences, work with colleagues and friends, and the many families with whom we have worked.

Part I

Basic issues

What we want from adult psychiatrists and their colleagues: 'Telling it like it is'

Sandra Bilsborough

Barnados, Liverpool, UK

With Lynsey, Sue, Nikki, Tracey, Peter and Alan

Children and young people want professionals to listen to them, to talk to them and, above all, they want to be recognized as important to the parent they live with.

In November 1999 a small group of young people involved with Barnardos Action with Young Carers (AWYC) were invited to take part in a conference launching the report 'Keeping the Family in Mind' (Göpfert *et al.*, 1999; Mahoney, Chapter 23). The project, like other Young Carer projects, provides a service for children and young people who live with someone with a mental health problem, many of whom take on caring roles and responsibilities. All of the young people who participated care for a parent with mental ill health and receive support from staff at the AWYC's project. We know from research and consultations with children and young people that they value being listened to and drawing upon their own experiences (see Cooklin, Chapter 21). They have some very important messages for professionals and policy makers.

Introduce yourself, tell us who you are and what your job is

Young people report that they are often ignored by professionals. They are not given information about what is going on in the family and who and why professionals are visiting. The way in which professionals deliver their service to a family can have a direct effect on other family members.

Have you any idea what it feels like for a complete stranger to come into your home, ignores you and then blames you for your home situation?

Sometimes I remember coming home from school and walking into our living room to find someone I didn't know sticking a needle into my mum. They never introduced themselves but just continued to do what they were doing.

Tell us what is going to happen next

Young people do not always know where to go for services, get information or how they can be included in decision-making. They are unfamiliar with how agencies work and professionals need to take time to explain what is happening or the process and procedure required to make things happen. This helps allay anxieties and gives recognition of the young person's role within the family.

All the professionals would visit whilst I was at school. I would come home and her medication would have been changed. I was the one who had to make sure she was taking her tablets but no one explained what they were or what they were for.

Give us as much information as you can

Children and young people want to understand and make sense of their parents' ill health. First, it is important that the information given is age appropriate. Second, this can be written or given verbally by professionals who have some knowledge and understanding and are able to answer young people's questions.

I feel if I had had more information about my mum's illness at the time, it wouldn't have been so difficult for me. I might have been able to understand why she cried so much and why she said and did such strange things. I might not have worried so much that I would become like her.

Talk to us and listen to us — remember it is not hard to speak to us, we are not aliens!

Children and young people want to understand and be part of decisions made about their family. They want to be respected, included and acknowledged. Article 12 of the UN Convention on the Rights of the Child states children have a right to be listened to and have their views taken into account on matters that affect them.

I remember calling my mum's social worker and asking her to come to see my mum because she had started to become slightly manic. She came three hours later and by that time my mum's mood had changed again and she was calm. My mum's social worker came in and sat down. She didn't ask me what had gone on, she just asked my mum how she felt and my mum said 'fine'. By 3 a.m. the next morning the police and ambulance had been called by neighbours. My mum was taken to hospital and put on a 6 month section [a compulsory order].

Ask us what we know and what we think — we live with our parents, we know how they are behaving — ask us!

The recognition of the role and support given by other family members needs to be valued, whilst acknowledging that without accurate information children and young people may not talk freely for fear of being separated from their parents.

Children and young people are an important source of information about their parents' health. It is a two-way process. They can also assist professionals!

Before my mum went into hospital, it felt like we were hiding and keeping the situation in our family, locked away. When she went into hospital, it was like an explosion. There were lots of people around us. I felt frustrated and confused.

Keep on talking to us and keep us informed — tell us it is not our fault

If information about what is happening is not shared then, for some people, this can leave them feeling guilty and to blame for their parent's illness. The young people are often given the responsibility for caring, but are not given the opportunity to participate in the decision-making.

One time the doctor came to see my mum at home. I opened the door to him and tried to tell him that my mum wasn't well. He told me he wanted to speak to an adult in the family. There was only me and mum and she was ill in bed upstairs. He went to see her and when he came back down, he handed me all her tablets and told me not to let her have any of them.

Tell us if there is anyone we can contact

The provision of information and access to services is an important factor in supporting children in the family. Professionals need to make themselves aware of ways in which they can assist supporting the young people and their families and other services available in the area.

Most of my teachers understood my reason for being away from school, but some thought that just because my mum was depressed enough to lie in bed and cry all day or be manic and throw everything from clothes to furniture out of the window, I still did not have reason enough to miss their classes, although I did try my best to get good grades and keep up to date with lessons.

Please don't ignore us, remember we are part of the family and we live there too

A recurring theme from young people is that other family members need support. Changes in practice, that cost nothing, can make a significant difference to the lives of these children and young people.

Two people arrived and sat beside my mum and dad. They did not introduce themselves to me even though I was in the same room. I heard them talking about my mum. It was as if I was invisible. I was glad when they went.

Previous personal accounts (Roberts, Chapter 20; Marlowe, 1996) also told of acts of thoughtlessness by professionals. Children who had witnessed their parents' disturbed behaviour, added these experiences to their feelings of disregard. From the professional's point of view, these encounters often arise unexpectedly, either through routine interactions with a client with whom they already have a relationship, or while undertaking emergency duties without a previous relationship with the client. An individualized focus draws a boundary around the professional–client relationship which excludes the children, and therefore it is as if they are not present.

However, there is some evidence that some professionals use these momentary encounters to connect with children. Approved social workers in the UK have a statutory role under the Mental Health Act 1983. They must undertake a social assessment and consult the closest relatives, and explore the possibility of any alternative to a compulsory hospital admission. Sometimes children are present, and some approved social workers make a point of explaining their role and actions to children, although a minority thought that they 'were not allowed to speak to the children' (Webster *et al.*, 1999). The social workers most likely to speak to children were parents themselves.

Many booklets are now available to help professionals explain mental illness to children (Falkov, 1998; Sobkiewicz, 1996*a*, *b*), some of which emerge from local initiatives (Joint Consultative Committee, 1999). They provide formulae for adults to develop a personalized story and for groups in which children can share experiences. With minimal notice, it is possible to create a context in which children feel contained, such as when helping children in a residential setting deal with parental suicide (Ward, 1995).

Conclusion

These messages reinforce the view that the direct involvement of service users and their children is essential to improve the quality and range of support to families living with mental ill health. Family members have diverse needs, and the impact of living with mental illness must be recognized, and risks assessed. Many of the necessary changes are possible and some will demand resources. But what the young people highlight is the need for more fundamental changes of attitude and approach from services.

REFERENCES

Falkov, A. (1998). *Crossing Bridges*. London: Department of Health.
Göpfert, M., Harrison, P. & Mahoney, P. (1999). *Keeping the Family in Mind*. Liverpool: North Mersey Community NHS Trust, Barnardos and Save the Children.
Joint Consultative Committee (1999). *Young Carers' Mental Health Resource Pack*. Liverpool: Consumer, Carer & Public Information Unit.

Marlowe, J. (1996). Helpers, helplessness and self-help: 'Shaping the silence': a personal account. In *Parental Psychiatric Disorder*, ed. M. Göpfert, J. Webster & M. V. Seeman, pp. 99–106. Cambridge: Cambridge University Press.

Sobkiewicz, T. (1996*a*). *Our Special Dad*. Pittsburgh: University of Pittsburgh.

Sobkiewicz, T. (1996*b*). *Our Special Mom*. Pittsburgh: University of Pittsburgh.

Ward, A. (1995). The impact of parental suicide on children and staff in residential care: a case study in the function of containment. *Journal of Social Work Practice*, 9, 23–32.

Webster, J., Hatfield, B. & Mohamad, H. (1999). Assessment of parents by Approved Social Workers under the Mental Health Act 1983. *Practice*, 11, 5–18.

Parenthood and adult mental health

Mary V. Seeman[1] and Michael Göpfert[2]

[1] University of Toronto Centre for Addiction and Mental Health, Toronto, Canada;
[2] Webb House, Crewe, UK

Introduction

Because individuals and families seek relief from psychological distress from a number of different sources, confusion can arise as to the specific role of one professional versus another. Tugs of territorial war often exist among psychologists, social workers, child psychiatrists and adult psychiatrists, to mention only a few of the players. Each profession is armed with its own specialized weaponry of psychological interventions and rival factions not infrequently claim superiority. To some degree this has become a battleground for the distribution of limited resources. Statutory issues such as prescription rights cause bitter interprofessional disputes. The roles of mental health workers are not always sufficiently clearly delineated, nor can they ever be because human suffering knows no clear borders. So the professional field is rife with tensions, splits and competition while the needs of patients or service users go, at times, unmet. In our experience and in the opinion of others (Consumers' Association (UK), 2002), when the expertise of service users is recognized and when they are given a degree of power in the way services are designed and delivered, professional competition is reduced and interprofessional collaboration grows.

This book focuses on services for individuals with mental illness who are parents. In many systems of mental health service provision, the identity of the patient as a parent does not receive sufficient recognition (see Göpfert *et al.*, Chapter 5). This is true irrespective of the patient's diagnosis or type of service provided and, therefore, clearly reflects deficiencies of service design, training and professional role identity. As one family put it succinctly in one of our research projects: 'Psychiatric services are excellent when it is a question of treatment of symptoms but absolutely useless when it comes to family issues or anything beyond the symptoms of mental illness' (Göpfert, pers. obs.). It is with this consideration in mind that we outline the role of the psychiatrist and highlight pertinent issues that arise when a patient is a parent.

Perspectives of power and hierarchy in mental health services

For decades the power of the doctor resided in the particular expert knowledge and clinical skills that she or he was presumed to have. This is now increasingly being eroded, but for the time being the doctor still has a dominance among other health professionals that is based on the role of diagnostician and prescriber of medical treatment, and when all goes well, is validated by the quality of training and competence. In terms of the dynamics of the organization, this is a powerful position, containing anxiety for both patients and carers, and for other mental health professionals (see Göpfert *et al.*, Chapter 5), and shouldering risks that other mental health professionals might not yet be ready to accept. Therefore, for now, the medical member of the multidisciplinary mental health team may hold a particularly influential position that can define both the shortcomings of any service, but also its strengths. The mental health professional who carries out an assessment and decides on treatment has the power to allocate or withhold resources from the patient and the patient's family, and therefore the patient is in a somewhat dependent role.

The role of the psychiatrist attending adult patients is, first and foremost, to assess the complaint the patient presents and make a provisional diagnosis. The psychiatrist then rules out other possible diagnoses, considers comorbidities, and initiates a treatment plan. The prescribed treatment is subsequently monitored, both for effectiveness and for freedom from unwanted side-effects. The psychiatrist also provides the patient with information about the diagnosis and the treatment and offers a prognosis on how soon the patient is likely to be free of the present-ing complaint and ready to resume former activities. Since psychiatric problems invariably impact on those close to the patient, psychiatrists need also to make themselves available to family members. All patient–psychiatrist exchange happens in the context of a relationship, and the quality of that relationship, or therapeutic alliance, determines outcome to a significant degree.

There is a substantive body of evidence that shows psychiatric symptoms arise from early experience. That early experience is important to elicit because taking it into account will make treatment more successful. For instance, there is some emerging evidence that links the symptom of hallucinations in a proportion of peo-ple seen by adult psychiatrists to an early history of childhood sexual abuse (Bentall, 2003). On the other hand, hallucinations may be associated with traditional cul-tural beliefs in supernatural powers. Such considerations are of extreme relevance to treatment. Therefore, as part of a comprehensive assessment, psychiatrists ask their patients not only about symptoms but also about developmental history, ethnicity and culture, and religious faith, about the type of work they do, about financial security and medical status, about social relationships, where and with whom they live, and whether they have children at home for whom they are responsible. Surprisingly, the question about parenthood is often not asked or not recorded in the medical chart (Hearle *et al.*, 1999; White *et al.*, 1995). Especially important in this context is the ascertainment of single parent status and finances because these correlate strongly with the adequacy of parenting (McKie, 1993; McLanahan & Sandefur, 1994; Munroe-Blum *et al.*, 1988). Because psychiatric illness is, to a certain extent, linked to teenage pregnancy which, in turn, confers potential harm to children (Kessler *et al.*, 1997), the age at which the patient became a parent is important to know. Another important variable to monitor is the presence of domestic violence (Royal College of Psychiatrists, 2002), as this is common and of relevance to both the mental health of the parent and the healthy development of children.

Some psychiatrists argue that, as doctors, they should mainly be attentive to disorders of somatic origin, defining psychiatry essentially as neuro-psychiatry. Contextual and psychological issues, in their minds, belong to the domain of other professional groups. This reinforces the very issue of specialization which so clearly is one of the major barriers to appropriate service provision for families when one or both parents has a psychiatric disorder (Hetherington *et al.*, 2002) (Hetherington & Baistow, Chapter 26; Falkov, Chapter 27). It raises the old nature vs. nurture debate, with physicians attending to nature and non-physicians to nurture. In our opinion, the current evidence clearly supports the view that the effects and aetiological significance of genetic and neurophysiological factors can only be fully appreciated in the larger context not only of the whole person, but also of interconnected family and social networks (Leff, 2001; Lerner, 2001). For instance, adopted-away children at genetic risk for psychiatric disorder are persistently more likely to receive negative parenting from their adoptive parents than children who are not at risk. This suggests that the behaviour of these children elicits a negative response from their environment (O'Connor *et al.*, 1998). At the same time, significant aspects of parenting patterns create and reinforce enduring personality features in children as they grow into adulthood (Caspi *et al.*, 2002; Kendler 2001; Moffitt, 2002; Plomin *et al.*, 2001). Having a depressed parent is a strong risk factor for depression in children (Beardslee *et al.*, 1998) and in adults (Nomura *et al.*, 2002). Psychological intervention can help these children (Clarke *et al.*, 2001); so do family interventions. Psychological interventions alter biology and biological interventions alter psychology (Fishbein, 2000; Leff, 2001; Wykes *et al.*, 2002). Both genetic and shared environmental factors are essential ingredients of human development with varying and sometimes surprising effects in terms of directionality, interaction and power (Plomin *et al.*, 2001; see Reiss *et al.*, 2000 for a detailed analysis of the interconnectedness of genetic, shared and nonshared environmental factors in human development).

Children of mentally ill parents are being actively recruited into research studies specifically because they are known to be at risk. It is ethically important that they be viewed not only as subjects for research but as members of a family that can benefit from sophisticated understanding and intervention. Mentally ill parents may be in double jeopardy, attempting to raise children who are 'difficult' children because of genetic predisposition while, at the same time, struggling with their own mental health problems (Azar, 1997). The developmental lags of the children may be inappropriately attributed to poor parenting when, in fact, the parents are coping as best they can with temperamentally difficult children. They need help and understanding rather than misattribution.

For the psychiatrist, professional competence requires fluency in working in both the psychological and the biological domain, although personal preference will always dictate the specific focus of one's work. Psychiatrists need to be up-to-date with current developments in the biological understanding and treatment methods of their field. Equally, they need to be competent not only in the delivery of psychological treatment to individual patients but also in family intervention. This is especially necessary as public health considerations impose increasingly stringent requirements of preventive practice in mental health service provision. Since a psychiatrist is often the only professional with statutory responsibility for treating a mentally ill parent, considerations for the well being of the children of that parent fall squarely within the psychiatric remit. Among clinicians, they are the one professional group that holds the key for effective prevention and intervention not only for the parents but also for their children.

Why does it matter?

Some psychiatrists still argue that proportionally few of their patients are parents. The actual proportion varies from setting to setting but it is reasonable to assume that as many as half of all patients seen in adult facilities are parents with children at home (R. Haigh, pers. comm.; Poole, 1996). Although the bulk of the literature in this area deals with mothers with mental illness, the responsibilities and requirements of parenting, i.e. the social role of parent, are the same for fathers, except for the specifics of pregnancy and lactation (Abosh & Collins, 1996). First and foremost, it is the far-reaching consequences for children that make questions about parental status important to ask of all adults who seek help from psychiatrists. This is a unique opportunity for preventing problems that may lie ahead for these children and must not be missed. These families may have no other contact with services.

Additionally, for the sake of the adult, a psychiatrist–patient relationship must also go beyond symptoms to involve the whole person, including the person's parental role, one of the most important roles undertaken in adult life. No therapist can meaningfully relate to a parent of young children without acknowledging the children's important presence in the mental and emotional life of the parent. Parents often judge first encounters by the way people relate to them around the issue of children, and therapists are no exception. Relating to children within an adult mental health context means an acknowledgement and validation of the children's welfare. Such validation, even if seemingly small, is significant in the longer term – the child will often carry the memory of someone in authority, an important adult, who has shown an understanding of their predicament and a willingness to help.

Knowing whether patients are parents is therefore critical for primary prevention in psychiatry, for more profound understanding of the patient, and for optimal intervention. It is also crucial for a number of legal/ethical reasons and for humanitarian reasons, so that services can work together to promote a better quality of life for the whole family.

Prevention

A variety of psychiatric illnesses may, by the symptoms they induce, undermine an individual's parenting abilities and lead to suboptimal care of children (Appleby & Dickens, 1993; Goodman & Brumley, 1990; Orvachel *et al.*, 1980). The symptoms of a psychotic disorder, for instance, make it hard for parents to provide the support that infants need in order to regulate their physiological processes and to engage with the world. As they grow older, children need stimulation, teaching and discipline, and the presence of a significant adult who believes in them, encourages them and comforts them. Parents who are severely ill find it difficult to provide these necessities. In addition, the stress of adapting to a new child may well exacerbate a psychotic illness. Antipsychotic medications that control symptoms may, unavoidably, reduce responsiveness to children. The ability to tolerate frustration is undermined in severe psychiatric illness, as is the capacity to form ongoing relationships. These deficiencies interfere with parents being able to support their children's needs for education, recreation and socialization. Mood fluctuations, withdrawal, magical thinking, and unpredictable or inappropriate behaviour impair basic functions of daily living and consistent parenting. In the worst scenario, parents can pose a physical threat to the child if the child becomes embroiled in a parent's delusional belief.

Specific parental illnesses may impact differently on a child's development. Very florid symptoms bring about the rapid removal of the child from the parent's home, thus safeguarding the child's developmental needs, although introducing other problems in the wake of parent–child separation. In more chronic and less dramatic presentations of mental illness, especially if a parent is able to provide some

Table 2.1. Protective factors to be reinforced by mental health professionals

Knowledge that their parent(s) is ill and that they are not to blame
Help/support from family members
Stable home environment
Psychotherapy for the child and the parent(s)
A sense of being loved by the ill parent
A naturally stable and happy personality in the child
Positive self-esteem
Inner strength and good coping skills in the child
A strong relationship with a healthy adult
Friendships, positive peer relationships
Interest and success at school
Healthy interests outside the home for the child
Help from outside the family to improve the family environment (e.g. marital psychotherapy or parenting skills classes)

Source: Adapted from AACP, Facts for Families, No. 39.

care for the child, the impact on the personality development and psychological health of the child might, in fact, be worse because no immediate danger is seen and the status quo prevails for too long. The intermittent nature of many mental disorders is associated with 'intermittent parenting' (Anthony & McGinnis, 1978), an off and on phenomenon which presents problems for the child and a need for specialized interventions on the part of the psychiatrist and the mental health team.

The shame and stigma of mental illness, when severe, leads secondarily to the family's isolation and this subsequently imposes its own limits on the healthy development of children. Unfortunately, treatment for psychiatric conditions (removing the parent from the home, prescribing sedating medications, requiring frequent attendance at clinics, recommending treatment that impairs memory, initiative and energy) can also harm the child. Expert understanding, sound interventions and specialized services are urgently needed to stop preventable problems from being transmitted to the second generation. Working with psychiatrically ill adults who are parents requires creative child-monitoring procedures (Jellinek *et al.*, 1991; Silverman, 1989) and family supports (Garley *et al.*, 1997; Webster-Stratton, 1994). When working with young adults who are not yet parents, future parenting issues need to be anticipated and, if appropriate, preventive measures initiated (Beardslee, 1990; Institute of Medicine, 1994).

The American Academy of Child and Adolescent Psychiatry has proposed that a number of protective factors be addressed or reinforced by mental health professionals working with families with a mentally ill parent (Table 2.1).

Gender

Mental illness usually affects the two sexes somewhat differently and this difference changes with age. Boys have many more psychological problems than girls prior to puberty, after which virtually all the major officially recognized psychiatric disorders (with the exception of substance abuse, schizophrenia and impulse control disorders) become substantially more common in women than in men (Seeman, 1997a, 2000). Poverty may explain some of the difference. Mental illness is widely acknowledged as more prevalent in the context of poverty and economic hardship, and women all over the globe are financially disadvantaged relative to men. This is seen most dramatically in single mothers, who live in circumstances of marked financial constraint and who suffer high rates of mental illness. Friendship networks (larger in women than in men) are, in theory, buffers to stress. A contrary view is that women more than men pay the 'price of caring', their extended friendship circles and nurturant social roles putting them into closer contact with people whose diverse problems reverberate through the network. Family interactions have long been suspect as both triggers and buffers of psychiatric symptoms and are probably perceived and experienced differently by men and women. Married men have been found, time and time again, to be relatively shielded against psychiatric disease; the opposite being true for women. Marriage seems to put women's mental health at risk in that the rate of mental illness is higher among married than among single women; the reverse is true for men. Women are often at the receiving end of family violence. Most importantly, women continue to be the primary caretakers of children and of elderly parents and the emotional burdens of family life fall more severely on their shoulders (Seeman, 2002).

Regardless of specific diagnosis, women almost always express their psychological distress in ways that can be distinguished from those of men. Optimal treatment may also differ (Seeman, 1983). Interpersonal interventions are relatively more meaningful to women and, when it comes to pharmacological interventions, the effective dose range of a medication may not be the same in the two sexes. The side-effect profile may also be different. 'Standard' treatment, when applied, works less well for women than for men because it has largely been tested on male animals in the laboratory and on male research subjects in the clinic (Seeman, 1997b). The lesson from all this is that both men and women need to be treated as individuals and not as representatives of a group, whether it be a diagnostic group, an ethnocultural group, or a gender group.

Gender is particularly relevant when dealing with parenting issues. While there is no difference in the responsibility of fathers and mothers for their children, there *are* differences in how the two sexes approach the role of parent. Sex-specific services may be needed (Abel *et al.*, 1996) and this applies to parents with mental illness (Apfel & Handel, 1993).

Assessment

Asking about children is important not only for the sake of the children but also for the well-being of the parent, because the stresses of parenting may well be contributing to the onset or severity of the mental illness. Quite apart from the well-recognized postpartum depressions, the demands and responsibilities attendant upon parenthood contribute in many other ways to psychiatric illness in mothers and fathers (Cowan & Cowan, 1988; Joseph *et al.*, 1999; Murray *et al.*, 1996; Nicholson *et al.*, 1998, 1999). Our standard research data sets still require information about marital status, a demographic variable that has become increasingly less relevant to mental health issues. It is much more relevant clinically to enquire about parental status (lone parent, custodial parent, visiting parent, parent without access).

Intervention

When there are children at home, certain interventions may be contraindicated or need to be more carefully considered. Hospitalization is one such example because it separates parent and child and may require mental health professionals to collaborate with other agencies in order to ensure adequate care for the child and sufficient support for the parent in their role while an inpatient. Sedating drugs may be another. On the other hand, additional interventions such as marital counselling and family approaches are almost always needed (Blanch *et al.*, 1994; Judge, 1994; Mannion *et al.*, 1994; Miller, 1992; Nicholson & Blanch, 1995; Rolland, 1994). The evidence base related to issues of parental psychiatric disorder is limited, partly because research efforts over the decades have focused on genetic and aetiological questions. A number of questions need to be urgently explored, such as the value of service provision for the mental health of both parent and child.

Legal/ethical issues

The best interests of parents may not always conform with the best interests of the child (Table 2.2). Although parents with severe mental illness love their children and usually want to parent (Mowbray *et al.*, 1995), the interests of the child (sometimes the safety of the child) (Monahan & Steadman, 1994; Oates, 1997; Ramsay *et al.*, 1998) may require foster care placement or interruption of custody rights (Jacobsen *et al.*, 1997; Louis *et al.*, 1997). During pregnancy, although the best interests of the child-to-be-born may be that the mother abstain from drugs and alcohol, obtain testing for sexually transmitted disease, or receive treatment for psychiatric illness, the mother's right to autonomy usually trumps the welfare of the fetus. Breastfeeding while receiving therapeutic medication that is potentially unsafe for the infant is another difficult ethical territory.

Table 2.2. Legal/ethical issues for adult psychiatrists

Decisions about pregnancy termination and adoption
Parenting capacity assessments
Risk assessments
Child protection vs. maternal autonomy decisions
Child custody issues
Involuntary drug screen, HIV testing and treatment
   during pregnancy
Breast-feeding while on medication

Humanitarian issues

Knowing whether a patient is a parent also facilitates the organization of flexible approaches such as extended hospital visiting hours for children or longer weekend home passes for the patient, evening office hours, the provision of transportation or baby-sitting allowances, outreach mental health teams, financial coverage for infant day care and appropriate family housing, liaison with grandparents and other family members, suggestions around parent–child activities, parenting groups, summer camps, arrangements with community services and visiting nurses. Including the consideration of the patient's role as a parent and the consideration of the child as a significant stakeholder in the parent's treatment, even if they are not living together, can make a significant difference to the long-term outcome. Training curricula for mental health in the medical professions and in psychiatry need to explicitly address the importance of parenthood to the evaluation and treatment of psychiatric conditions.

Issues for the psychiatrist

An adult psychiatrist is not, by training, an expert in children's developmental needs nor in the assessment of parenting competence. In an environment of increasing litigation and emphasis on risk management, it is tempting to pay heed only to the symptoms of the presenting adult and to ignore the question of whether parenting responsibilities are being met and whether children's needs are attended to. There may also exist a powerful collective and unspoken assumption that mentally ill persons should not have children (for the sake of the children). This raises the whole spectrum of the power of the professional's beliefs and assumptions shaping the way treatments are delivered. As outlined at the beginning, the way our services are designed, the system bestows particular power on the psychiatrist. This, however, also implies particular responsibilities. Nobody can live and act consistently against their assumptions and beliefs. Parenthood, like race or gender, brings with it a whole host of beliefs and activates many of our basic assumptions. The psychiatrist therefore has a particular responsibility to examine those assumptions.

Confronted with the strong emotions that patients bring to therapy, a clinician may unconsciously identify with the child who they imagine is subjected to these same emotions. Fears for the child are reinforced by child protection requirements and it becomes easy, at times, to overreact. Furthermore, taking into consideration the best interests and needs of our patients' children is likely to make our professional lives much more complex and add to the work load. However, if the psychiatrist cannot incorporate the consideration of the children's and the family's needs into their work it will make it much more unlikely that within the foreseeable future the needs of our patients who are parents, and of their families will be adequately taken care of. The evidence (Hetherington *et al.*, 2002) suggests that collaboration between agencies and services is key to improving services for families with children. The ability to effectively collaborate is associated with the capacity to consider the needs of the family, which in some countries seems to be easier than in others. The 'Anglo' countries have higher levels of specialization and more difficulty in considering the family across adult and child mental health services (Hetherington *et al.*, 2002). Systemically speaking, even if there is considerable expertise in our children's services, by implication this will make others more reluctant to engage with the task unless they can develop their own expertise. It has been difficult to anchor the family perspective solidly in adult mental health service provision. This is partly a training issue, partly reflects our professional culture and our professional assumptions, and in part is the responsibility of those who fund and commission our services. 'Keeping the family in mind' is a task at all three levels.

The task of the psychiatrist is to look after the needs of the patient. A working definition of parental responsibility as *putting the interests of the child first*, helps both the psychiatrist and the parent to work collaboratively toward increasing the parent's health such that she or he can, indeed, put the needs of the children first (The Michael Sieff Foundation, 1997). Ignoring the patient's parental role helps neither parent nor child.

Conclusion

The consideration of the parental role and of the welfare of children constitutes an important aspect of comprehensive care on the part of the adult psychiatrist. It helps the parent to recover, protects the welfare of the child and enhances the quality of life for the family unit (Cowling, 1996; Hearle & McGrath, 2000, Nicholson *et al.*, 1993; Oyserman *et al.*, 1994; Zemenchuk *et al.*, 1995). Psychiatrists must work with other professions and with the patients they serve to develop a mental health intervention capacity that is responsive to family needs.

Acknowledgement

Brigitta Bende helped with valuable comments.

REFERENCES

Abel, K., Buszewicz, M., Davison, S., Johnson, S. & Staples, E. (1996). *Planning Community Mental Health Services for Women.* London: Routledge.

Abosh, B. & Collins, A. (ed.) (1996). *Mental Illness in the Family.* Toronto: University of Toronto Press.

American Academy of Child and Adolescent Psychiatry. Facts for families No. 39. Available via the AACP office (in the US: 800-333-7636 ext. 131, Nelson Tejada) or www.aacp.org/publications/ factsfam/parentmi/htm.

Anthony, E. J. & McGinnis, M. (1978). Counseling very disturbed parents. In *Helping Parents Help Their Children*, ed. L. E. Arnold, pp. 328–41. New York: Brunner and Mazel.

Apfel, R. J. & Handel, M. H. (1993). *Madness and Loss of Motherhood: Sexuality, Reproduction and Long-term Mental Illness.* Washington: American Psychiatric Press.

Appleby, L. & Dickens, C. (1993). Mothering skills of women with mental illness. *British Medical Journal, 306,* 348–9.

Azar, B. (1997). Nature, nurture: not mutually exclusive. Studies on twins have established that most traits and behaviors are partially influenced by genes. *APA Monitor,* May 1997, American Psychological Association.

Beardslee, W. R. (1990). Development of a clinician-based preventive intervention for families with affective disorders. *Journal of Preventive Psychiatry and Allied Disciplines, 4,* 39–60.

Beardslee, W. R., Versage, E. & Gladstone, T. (1998). Children of affectively ill parents: a review of the past 10 years. *Journal of the American Academy of Child and Adolescent Psychiatry, 37,* 1134–41.

Bentall, R. P. (2003). *Madness Explained: Psychosis and Human Nature.* Penguin, Harmondsworth.

Blanch, A. K., Nicholson, J. & Purcell, J. (1994). Parents with severe mental illness and their children: the need for human service intervention. *Journal of Mental Health Administration, 21,* 388–96.

Caspi, A., McClay, J., Moffit, T. E. et al. (2002). The role of genotype in the cycle of violence in maltreated children. *Science, 207,* 851–4.

Clarke, G. N., Hornbrook, M., Lynch, F. et al. (2001). A randomized trial of a group cognitive intervention for preventing depression in adolescent offspring of depressed parents. *Archives of General Psychiatry, 58,* 1127–34.

Consumers' Association (UK) (2002). 'Who are the experts, where is the expertise?' *Drugs and Therapeutics Bulletin, 40,* 55–6.

Cowan, P. A. & Cowan, C. P. (1988). Changes in marriage during the transition to parenthood: Must we blame the baby? In *The Transition to Parenthood: Current Theory and Research*, ed. G. Y. Michaels & W. A. Gildberg, pp. 114–54. Cambridge: Cambridge University Press.

Cowling, V. (1996). Meeting the support needs of families with dependent children where a parent has a mental illness. *Family Matters*, 45, 22–5.

Fishbein, D. (2000). How can neurobiological research inform prevention strategies? In D. Fishbein, ed. *The Science, Treatment, and Prevention of Antisocial Behaviors: Application to the Criminal Justice System*, ed. D. Fishbein, pp. 25–30. New York: Civic Research Institute, Inc.

Garley, D., Gallop, R., Johnstone, N. & Pipitone, J. (1997). Children of the mentally ill: a qualitative focus group approach. *Journal of Psychiatric and Mental Nursing*, 4, 97–103.

Goodman, S. H. & Brumley, H. E. (1990). Schizophrenic and depressed mothers: relational deficits in parenting. *Developmental Psychology*, 26, 31–9.

Hearle, J. & McGrath, J. (2000). Motherhood and schizophrenia. In *Women and Schizophrenia*, ed. D. J. Castle, J. McGrath & J. Kulkarni, pp. 79–94. Cambridge: Cambridge University Press.

Hearle, J., Plant, K., Jenner, L., Barkla, J. & McGrath, J. (1999). A survey of contact with offspring and assistance with child care among parents with psychotic disorders. *Psychiatric Services*, 50, 1354–6.

Hetherington, R., Baistow, K., Katz, I., Mesie, J. & Trowell, J. (2002). *The Welfare of Children with Mentally Ill Parents: Learning from Inter-country Comparison*. Chichester: John Wiley & Sons.

Institute of Medicine (1994). *Reducing Risks for Mental Disorders: Frontiers for Preventive Intervention Research*. Washington, DC: National Academy Press.

Jacobsen, T., Miller, L. J. & Kirkwood, K. P. (1997). Assessing parenting capacity in individuals with severe mental illness: a comprehensive service. *Journal of Mental Health Administration*, 24, 189–99.

Jellinek, M. S., Bishop, S. S., Murphy, J. M., Bederman, J. & Rosenbaum, J. (1991). Screening for dysfunction in the children of outpatients at a psychopharmacology unit. *American Journal of Psychiatry*, 148, 1031–6.

Joseph, J. G., Joshi, S. V., Lewin, A. B. & Abrams, M. (1999). Characteristics and perceived needs of mothers with serious mental illness. *Psychiatric Services*, 50, 1357–9.

Judge, K. A. (1994). Serving children, siblings, and spouses: understanding the needs of other family members. In *Helping Families Cope with Mental Illness*, ed. H. P. Lefley & J. Wasow. New York: Harwood.

Kendler, K. S. (2001). Twin studies of psychiatric illness: an update. *Archives of General Psychiatry*, 58, 1005–14.

Kessler, R. C., Berglund, P. A., Foster, C. L., Saunders, W. B., Stang, P. E. & Walters, E. E. (1997). Social consequences of psychiatric disorders. II Teenage parenthood. *American Journal of Psychiatry*, 154, 1405–11.

Leff, J. (2001). *The Unbalanced Mind*. London: Weidenfeld and Nicholson.

Lerner, R. M. (2001). Toward a democratic ethnotheory of parenting for families and policy-makers: a developmental systems perspective. *Parenting: Science and Practice*, 1, 339–51.

Louis, A., Condon, J., Shute, R. & Elzinga, R. (1997). The development of the Louis MACRO (Mother and Children Risk Observation) forms: assessing parent–infant–child risk in the presence of maternal mental illness. *Child Abuse and Neglect*, 21, 589–606.

Mannion, E., Mueser, K. & Solomon, P. (1994). Designing psycho educational services for spouses of persons with serious mental illness. *Community Mental Health Journal*, 30, 177–90.

McKie, C. (1993). An overview of lone parenthood in Canada. In *Single Parent Families – Perspectives on Research and Policy*, ed. J. Hudson & B. Galaway. Toronto: Thompson Educational Publishing.

McLanahan, S. S. & Sandefur, G. (1994). *Growing Up with a Single Parent: What Hurts, What Helps.* Cambridge, MA: Harvard University Press.

Miller, L. J. (1992). Comprehensive care of pregnant mentally ill women. *Journal of Mental Health Administration*, *19*, 170–7.

Moffitt, T. (2002). Quoted by C. Cookson in 'Variations in gene cause different reaction to abuse'. *Financial Times*, 2.8.2002, p. 4.

Monahan, J. & Steadman, H. J. (ed.) (1994). *Violence and Mental Disorder: Developments in Risk Assessment.* Chicago: University of Chicago Press.

Mowbray, C. T., Oyserman, D. & Ross, S. (1995). Parenting and the significance of children for women with a serious mental illness. *Journal of Mental Health Administration*, *22*, 189–200.

Munroe-Blum, H., Boyle, M. H. & Offord, D. R. (1988). Single-parent families: child psychiatric disorder and school performance. *Journal of the American Academy of Child and Adolescent Psychiatry*, *27*, 214–19.

Murray, L., Fiori-Cowley, A., Hooper, R. & Cooper, P. J. (1996). The impact of postnatal depression and associated adversity on early mother-infant interactions, and later infant outcome. *Child Development*, *67*, 2512–26.

Nicholson, J. & Blanch, A. (1995). Rehabilitation for parenting roles for people with serious mental illness. *Psychosocial Rehabilitation Journal*, *18*, 109–19.

Nicholson, J., Geller, J., Fisher, W. & Dion, G. (1993). State policies and programs that address the needs of mentally ill mothers in the public sector. *Hospital and Community Psychiatry*, *44*, 484–9.

Nicholson, J., Sweeney, E. M. & Geller, J. L. (1998). Mothers with mental illness I. The competing demands of parenting and living with mental illness. *Psychiatric Services*, *49*, 635–42.

Nicholson, J., Nason, M. W., Calabresi, A. O. et al. (1999). Fathers with severe mental illness: characteristics and comparisons. *American Journal of Orthopsychiatry*, *69*, 134–41.

Nomura, Y., Wickramaratne, P. J., Warner, V. et al. (2002). Family discord, parental depression and psychopathology in offspring: ten-year follow-up. *Journal of the American Academy of Child and Adolescent Psychiatry*, *41*, 402–9.

Oates, M. (1997). Patients as parents: the risk to children. *British Journal of Psychiatry*, *170*, 22–7.

O'Connor, T. G., Deater-Deckard, K., Fulker, D., Rutter, M. & Plomin, R. (1998). Genotype-environment correlations in late childhood and early adolescence: antisocial behavioural problems and coercive parenting. *Developmental Psychology*, *34*, 970–81.

Orvachel, H., Weissman, M. M. & Kidd, K. K. (1980). Children and depression: the children of depressed parents; the childhood of depressed patients; depression in children. *Journal of Affective Disorders*, *2*, 1–16.

Oyserman, D., Mowbray, C. T. & Zemenczuk, J. A. (1994). Resources and supports for mothers with severe mental illness. *Health and Social Work*, *19*, 132–42.

Plomin, R., Defries, J. C., McClearn, G. E. & McGuffin, P. (2001). Behavioural Genetics, 4th edn. New York: Worth Publishers.

Poole, R. (1996). General adult psychiatrists and their patients' children. In *Parental Psychiatric Disorder: Distressed Parents and their Families*, ed. M. Göpfert, J. Webster & M. V. Seeman, pp. 3–6. Cambridge: Cambridge University Press.

Ramsay, R., Howard, L. & Kumar, C. (1998). Schizophrenia and safety of parenting of infants: a report from a U.K. mother and baby service. *International Journal of Social Psychiatry*, *44*, 127–34.

Reiss, D., Neiderhiser, J. M., Hetherington, E. M. & Plomin, R. (2000). *The Relationship Code. Deciphering Genetic and Social Influences on Adolescent Development.* Cambridge, MA: Harvard.

Rolland, J. S. (1994). *Families, Illness and Disability: An Integrative Treatment Approach.* New York: Basic Books.

Royal College of Psychiatrists (2002). *Domestic Violence.* Council Report CR 102. London: Royal College of Psychiatrists.

Seeman, M. V. (1983). Schizophrenic men and women require different treatment programs. *Journal of Psychiatric Treatment and Evaluation*, *5*, 143–8.

Seeman, M. V. (1997*a*). Psychopathology in women and men: focus on female hormones. *American Journal of Psychiatry*, *154*, 1641–7.

Seeman, M. V. (1997*b*). CNS Clinical drug trials and women. In *The Handbook of Psychopharmacology Trials*, ed. M. Hertzman & D. E. Feltner, pp. 100–22. New York: New York University Press.

Seeman, M. V. (2000). Are gender differences in psychopathology due to hormones? *Primary Psychiatry*, *7*, 47–50.

Seeman, M. V. (2002). Schizophrenia: two sides of the mirror. *Queens Quarterly*, *109*, 191–205.

Silverman, M. (1989). Children of psychiatrically ill parents: a prevention perspective. *Hospital and Community Psychiatry*, *40*, 1257–65.

The Michael Sieff Foundation (1997). *Keeping Children in Mind: Balancing Children's Needs with Parents' Mental Health.* Report of the 12th annual conference hosted by the Michael Sieff Foundation, Flimwell, East Sussex, UK.

Webster-Stratton, H. M. (1994). *Troubled Families – Problem Children: Working with Parents: A Collaborative Process.* New York: John Wiley & Sons.

White, C., Nicholson, J., Fisher, W. et al. (1995). Mothers with severe mental illness caring for children. *Journal of Nervous and Mental Diseases*, *183*, 398–403.

Wykes, T., Brammer, M., Mellers, J. et al. (2002). Effects on the brain of a psychological treatment: cognitive remediation therapy. Functional magnetic imaging in schizophrenia. *British Journal of Psychiatry*, *181*, 144–52.

Zemenchuk, J., Rogosch, F. A. & Mowbray, C. T. (1995). The seriously mentally ill woman in the role of parent: characteristics, parenting sensitivity, and needs. *Psychosocial Rehabilitation Journal*, *18*, 77–92.

3

Parental psychiatric disorder and the developing child

Alyson Hall

Tower Hamlets, London, UK

This chapter reviews how mental illness affects parenting and influences the development of children. Topics covered in the chapter include abuse and neglect, the effects of separation and the risk of mental health problems in children.

Large numbers of children grow up with a mentally ill parent. A study of parental psychiatric histories of 850 twin pairs in Virginia found that only 26% of families had no lifetime history of psychiatric disorder in either parent (Foley *et al.*, 2001). Short-lived depression is the most frequently found mental illness in parents (see Puckering, Chapter 12). Relatively few children live with parents who are psychotic but many parents suffer from persistent problems such as personality disorder, alcoholism, learning difficulties or chronic depression.

The children of mentally ill parents have a substantially increased risk of childhood psychiatric disorder (Hare & Shaw, 1965; Richman *et al.*, 1982; Rutter & Quinton, 1984; Simonoff *et al.*, 1997).

Childhood disorder

Rutter & Quinton (1984) found that, over a 4-year period, a third of the offspring of consecutive new psychiatric cases exhibited a persistent disorder, a third had transient psychiatric difficulties and a third showed no emotional or behavioural disturbance. Controls from the same area showed comparable rates of transient disturbance but half the rate of persistent disturbance, such as conduct disorder.

In this inner London population, Rutter & Quinton (1984) identified risk factors associated with childhood disorder, all of which were more common among those whose parents had a psychiatric disorder: single parenthood (twice as common), separation, divorce, current marital discord (39 vs. 8%), admission to care, parental criminality, large family size, overcrowding and an unskilled or semi-skilled breadwinner. Children in the comparison group showed similar disturbance when exposed to the same risks. Persistent marital discord was the most significant risk factor, more so in boys, for childhood disorder. Rutter & Quinton concluded that greater psychosocial disadvantage experienced by psychiatrically ill parents accounted for increased rates of disorder in their children.

Many studies (Beardslee *et al.*, 1983; Beidel & Turner, 1997; Cytryn *et al.*, 1984; Rutter & Quinton, 1984; Watt *et al.*, 1984) agree that disorders in children are not tied to specific types of mental disorders in parents. In two-parent families where one parent is healthy, the only diagnosis that increases the rate of disturbance in children is personality disorder. Over half of the children with mentally ill parents in the Rutter & Quinton study had fathers with personality disorders (PD); one quarter had mothers with PD. When children with a parent with PD were exposed to hostile aggressive behaviour, as many as half developed persistent psychiatric disorder themselves. Rutter & Quinton considered exposure to hostile behaviour to be the major risk factor for the development of conduct disorder and they found this to be more frequent in families with mental illness than in the comparison families (Norton & Dolan, 1996) (see Adshead *et al.*, Chapter 15).

Recent research has been able to show some more specific links between child-hood disorders and types of parental illness, perhaps because the study populations were less disadvantaged than those in Rutter & Quinton (1984). The Virginia twin study (Foley *et al.*, 2001) looked at comorbidity and combinations of different dis-orders in mothers and fathers. They demonstrated an increase in depression and overanxious disorder in the children of depressed parents, particularly mothers. Girls were especially vulnerable. Rates of oppositional defiant disorder and con-duct disorder were increased in boys when both parents had psychiatric illness, especially the combination of a depressed mother and an alcoholic father. In a study of sibling pairs, Rende *et al.* (1999) found that anxiety in children, rather than depression, was associated with major depression in parents, although these children showed depressive and suicidal behaviour at 10-year follow-up. These investigators suggested that childhood depression could result from stressors such as domestic conflict and be independent of parental diagnosis.

Beidel & Turner (1997) found that the offspring of anxious parents were more likely to suffer from anxiety disorders whereas the children of depressed parents showed a broad range of disorders and frequent comorbidity. The Yale Family Study of Comorbidity of Substance Abuse and Anxiety (Merikangas *et al.*, 1998*a*) also showed strong familial aggregation for anxiety disorder and a weak one for conduct disorder and substance misuse. School-refusing children have been associated with parents suffering from simple and/or social phobia, panic disorder and agorapho-bia (Martin *et al.*, 1999). Children with obsessive-compulsive disorder have been reported likely to have a parent with obsessive-compulsive disorder (Thomsen, 1995).

When both parents misuse alcohol or drugs or when a psychiatrically ill parent is comorbid for substance misuse, their children can have higher rates of conduct disorder (Dierker *et al.*, 1999). Kuperman *et al.* (1999) found increases in both conduct disorder and attention deficit disorder. The children of opiate addicts on methadone maintenance were found to have cognitive and social impairment (Nunes *et al.*, 1998) and the same group (Weissman *et al.*, 1999*a*) found 60% of children of opiate- or cocaine-addicted mothers had a psychiatric disorder, major depression, conduct or oppositional defiant disorder, attention deficit disorder or substance misuse. Pollock *et al.* (1990) related the development of conduct disorders in the sons of substance-misusing men to physical abuse while Moss *et al.* (1995) suggest that this association is related to the fathers' reactivity to stress, alienation and aggression.

Studies generally support the view that conduct disorder in children develops as a result of experienced or witnessed aggression and violence (Davies & Windle, 1997; Frick *et al.*, 1992; Harnish *et al.*, 1995; Rutter & Quinton, 1984) as well as poor parenting practices (Kuperman *et al.*, 1999), both of which are more commonly seen among psychiatric patients than in the general population. Professionals often fail to make a connection between mental health problems and domestic violence (Humphries, 2000). Women rarely volunteer the extent of violence in their current relationships, particularly when they are fearful that their children may be taken into care. This is an area into which adult and child psychiatrists need to enquire routinely (Royal College of Psychiatrists, 2002*a*, *b*).

Although the Virginia twin study (Foley *et al.*, 2001), by taking comorbidity and the mental health of both parents into account, was able to demonstrate a specific association between childhood emotional disorders and parental depression, generally the literature suggests that the high rate of disturbance in children of psychiatric patients results more from the associated psychosocial disturbance in the family than from illness itself. The major contributors, especially to the development of conduct disorder, are hostility, aggression, marital discord and disruption (Emery *et al.*, 1982; Rutter, 1982).

Physical harm to children

Death

In England and Wales, a quarter of all homicide victims are children, most killed by their own parents (Gibson, 1975). Each year there are 200–300 deaths from abuse and neglect in England and Wales (Creighton & Gallagher, 1988; Wilczynski, 1994). In the United States, where the numbers are increasing, there are between 2000 and 5000 (Lung & Daro, 1996; US Advisory Board on Child Abuse and Neglect, 1995). Children under 2 years are particularly at risk (Durfee & Tilton-Durfee, 1995) and accounted for 78% of the deaths in a recent British study (Reder & Duncan, 1999). Relatively few children are on the child protection register at the time of their death, although the majority of their families have previously been referred to child protection agencies because of concerns about parenting (Falkov, 1996; Reder & Duncan, 1999). In the United States, relatively fewer families where a child death occurred had had previous contact with social services (Levine *et al.*, 1994).

Children are more likely to be killed by their mother's partner than by their natural father, but in 60% of cases the mother is responsible. D'Orban (1979) and Wilczynski (1997) found that the small group of women who kill, neglect or abandon their babies at birth do not usually suffer from mental illness. They tend to be young single immature women who have concealed their pregnancies and rarely seek antenatal care. A few totally deny the pregnancy while the majority have unresolved conflicts about pregnancy (Bonnet, 1993; Reder & Duncan, 1999).

The majority of fatal child abuse cases are the result of physical abuse, especially when a parent is misusing alcohol or drugs. D'Orban (1979) found that 40% of the women killed their children impulsively, in reaction to the child's behaviour, and 10% in retaliation against their spouse. One mother in this study killed her handicapped child to relieve suffering. Nine per cent of children in the series died from neglect. Neglect accounted for 26% of recent British deaths (Reder & Duncan, 1999) and an estimated 37% in the United States (Lung & Daro, 1996).

D'Orban found that 27% of women were mentally ill when they killed their children (puerperal psychosis (8%), schizophrenia, depression or personality disorder). Three recent British studies of statutory reviews of child deaths confirm the high prevalence of psychiatric illness in one or both of the child's caretakers: 44% in Reder & Duncan (1999), 50% in Wilczynski (1995) and 25% in perpetrators and 10% in partners (Falkov, 1996). Psychosis was the most common problem, occurring in 9–10% of the perpetrators. Puerperal illness was rare, perhaps because of early detection and intervention. Wilczynski found psychosis and depression in 24% of parents and substance misuse in 33% of perpetrators. Reder & Duncan (1999) also report high rates of depressive disorder (17%) and substance misuse (20%). Falkov found 5% of those who killed a child had a personality disorder and reported two cases of Munchausen by Proxy. International studies in Hong Kong (Cheung, 1986) and Australia (Wilczynski, 1997) show similar high rates while New York studies (quoted by Reder & Duncan, 1999) report especially high rates of substance misuse in addition to psychiatric illness.

Although the majority of the women in D'Orban's study were not considered mentally ill at the time they killed their children, 41% had previously received psychiatric treatment, a quarter had a parent with mental illness and 43% had a personality disorder. Most often, they killed their children impulsively during an outburst of temper. They came from disadvantaged backgrounds: 61% had been separated from one or both parents as a child and 21% had experienced abuse (D'Orban, 1979). Reder & Duncan (1999) found histories of parental discord, parental criminality and large family size in the parents of children who died and identified a group of mothers who had been sexually abused. They consider that unresolved problems with dependency, control and authority are central issues for women who kill their children. They conclude that conflict about care or dependency arise from experiences of abandonment, neglect or rejection in childhood, while difficulty with control and authority are based on experiences of inappropriate limit setting or helplessness in the face of physical, sexual or emotional abuse.

Risk factors for fatal child abuse (domestic conflict or violence, pregnancy or recent birth, housing and financial difficulties) are common in socially disadvantaged adults with mental health problems. Their presence should be taken into account in considering serious risk to any child in their care. Compared with women without psychiatric illness who killed their children, D'Orban (1979) found that severely ill women generally suffered less stress and social disadvantage. About half were attempting suicide and extended the suicidal act 'because there would be no one to care for the children'. They were more likely to attempt to kill all their children. D'Orban concluded that the deaths were a direct result of the illness, although the killing was rarely framed in the context of delusional ideas. Reder & Duncan (1999) found that some depressed or psychotic mothers had made previous threats to kill a child; many more had withdrawn from contact with professionals prior to the fatal act. Psychiatrists treating seriously depressed and psychotic women must be aware of these grave risks (Adcock, 1996; Seeman, 1996).

Child maltreatment

Just as in child death, unresolved conflicts with dependency, control and authority are also central to nonfatal injury, emotional abuse or neglect of children, particularly for individuals with personality disorders and those who have experienced abuse and separation. Parents with learning difficulties also have difficulty with control and dependency and frequently suffer psychiatric disorder and social disadvantage. Their children are more likely to experience physical abuse, sexual abuse or neglect and, as a result, to be removed from their care. Large family size and high intelligence in the child increase the risk of abuse, while effective support networks reduce it (Accardo & Whitman, 1990; Cameron et al., 1966; Holter & Friedman, 1968; Tsiantis et al., 1981; Whitman et al., 1987).

What is the contribution of psychiatric disorder to child abuse and neglect? In a prospective study, Browne found that parents with a history of mental illness or substance misuse were seven times more likely to abuse or neglect their children than controls (Browne & Herbert, 1997). The risks of abuse were greatest when there was a history of family violence, when parents were abused or neglected as children and when the parent was intolerant, indifferent or overanxious towards the child. Socio-economic problems and being a lone parent were important factors that contributed to parental stress. Taylor et al. (1991) examined the court records of 206 seriously abused children from Boston, Massachusetts. In 84% of cases one or both parents suffered from psychiatric disorder or had IQs less than 80. Sixty-four per cent of the mothers suffered from a psychiatric disorder, with major depression or schizophrenia accounting for 42% of the diagnoses. Fathers had high rates of schizophrenia, personality disorders and severe depression. More than half of the parents had received psychiatric treatment, 29% as inpatients. In Britain, high rates of depression, personality disorders, suicide attempts and substance misuse were found in the parents of children involved with child protection agencies (Falkov, 1997; Sheppard, 1997) and associated with emotional abuse (Glaser & Prior, 1997) but schizophrenia and severe psychiatric illness were less frequent. Oates (1997) reported children of seriously mentally ill parents were at greater risk of death or neglect but physical abuse was uncommon.

The high rates of psychosis in abusing parents in the Boston study could be related to the use of crack cocaine and amphetamines or could reflect different arrangements for statutory services and support systems across the Atlantic. In the UK, the Children Act (1989) requires courts to make decisions based on the principle of the best interests of the child. This is now complemented by the Assessment Framework for Children in Need (Department of Health, 2000), and local authorities are expected to undertake assessments and provide services for children and their families before child protection concerns are identified. In the United States, intervention is less likely prior to the detection of serious abuse or neglect, although informal arrangements are often made within the extended family. Permanent placement outside the family can be difficult to achieve as, in most states, the child must be returned when the natural parent is deemed 'fit' (see also Brunt, Chapter 18; Weir, Chapter 19).

In a deprived London borough, 64% of parents of neglected children were reported by health visitors and social workers to have a mental health problem compared with 30% of carers of control children (Adrian *et al.*, 2002). The study demonstrated high rates of mental health problems (30%) in parents of young children in the inner city but did not differentiate minor from more serious psychiatric illness. Learning difficulties (36%), drug misuse (43%), alcohol problems (29%) and becoming pregnant as a teenager (86%) were common in those parents who neglected their children and rare among the controls. Because of the chronic and insidious nature of neglect, timely intervention for children can be difficult, especially when working with vulnerable parents who are doing their best. To help social workers, health visitors and mental health professionals recognize and monitor neglect, the authors of this study have developed a Childcare and Development Checklist to record features associated with neglect, such as language delay and poor peer relationships.

Physical abuse, neglect, abandonment and exposure to extreme violence appear to be particularly common in families involved in crack cocaine use. Famularo *et al.* (1992) found 70% of parents whose children were removed for physical abuse misused alcohol and 51% used cocaine. In Boston, Murphy *et al.* (1991) found 43%

of parents before the courts were currently misusing alcohol or drugs and 70–80% of parents with substance abuse, low intelligence, psychosis, severe depression or personality disorders had their children removed compared with 22% of parents given a neurotic diagnosis. Substance misusers rejected court-ordered treatment more often than other parents, were more likely to have had previous charges of child maltreatment and were considered to pose a higher risk to their children. Of the cocaine or heroin misusers, 90% eventually had their children removed compared with 60% of those who misused alcohol, although they actually abused their children more frequently than the drug misusers. It is not clear whether other effects of drug misuse on children, such as neglect, influenced the courts or whether they were being more lenient with alcoholic parents (Gerada, 1996) (see Velleman, Chapter 13; Hans, Chapter 14).

Adult psychiatrists may be asked by social services to assess parents with psychiatric disorders and advise about prognosis in order to consider whether rehabilitation of a child with his family is feasible. This can bring with it a number of professional dilemmas (Poole, 1996; Webster & Huxley, 1996) (see Seeman & Göpfert, Chapter 2; Göpfert et al., Chapter 7; Clodman, Chapter 17). Jones (1987) reviews the characteristics of 'untreatable families', families in which it is unsafe to permit an abused child to live. Poor outcome was associated with treatment refusal, dropouts and denial of wrongdoing. Parents tended to suffer from sociopathy, grossly inadequate personalities, persistent addiction problems or learning difficulties. They had frequently been abused as children and were hostile, with little capacity to love, relate to others or to empathise with the child, who was viewed as a possession. Jones also suggests that, when the child becomes involved in a psychotic parent's delusional system, successful treatment is unlikely. A poor prognosis is likely after serious or deliberate injury, sadistic treatment, previous serious injury, nonaccidental poisoning, Munchausen's by Proxy or a child's severe failure to thrive.

Psychiatric illness and the developing child

Attachment and the quality of the mother–child relationship

Since the early work of Bowlby and Ainsworth (Ainsworth et al., 1978; Bowlby, 1969, 1973), attachment theory has developed to include the child's relationships with parents and substitute caregivers, adult attachment and the long-term effects of abuse and neglect on social development and relationships (Belsky et al., 1995; Cicchetti & Toth, 1995; Main, 1995) (see Hill, Chapter 4; Adshead et al., Chapter 15). Research has established clear associations between impairment of attachment in infants and specific types of psychiatric disorder in their parents. Children of mothers with psychiatric disorders are more likely to show anxious or avoidant attachment in the second year of life. The attachment may become secure if the child has the opportunity for an improved relationship later (Ainsworth *et al.*, 1978). Maternal depression in infancy is associated with long-term effects on the child's physical and psychological health, behaviour and academic performance (Murray *et al.*, 1999; Puckering, 1989). Murray (1992) showed that the infants of postnatally depressed mothers were more insecurely attached to their mothers, performed worse on object concept tasks and showed more mild behavioural difficulties. The effects were independent of the length of the mother's illness, suggesting that any intervention must focus on the mother–child relationship, not just on treating the mother. Infants who show avoidant attachment or the disorganized attachment behaviour associated with maltreatment, generalize this behaviour to other adults. Their social development is impaired, with serious implications for future relationships and for parenting (Cicchetti & Toth, 1995; Field *et al.*, 1988; Main, 1995).

Adult attachment

Specific aspects of parenting contribute to abnormalities of early attachment and lead to persistent difficulties, such as behaviour and learning problems (Cox *et al.*, 1987). Some parents with mental health problems may, as a result of their own faulty attachment, become dismissive, blocking off traumatic experiences in childhood and lacking the capacity for self-reflection. Other parents may become preoccupied, parents with eating disorders or obsessional symptoms for example (Main, 1995; Stein *et al.*, 1996). Manassis *et al.* (1995) found that 80% of children of mothers with anxiety disorders had insecure attachment. This high rate could be associated with the exacerbation of anxiety and obsessive-compulsive symptoms during pregnancy and the puerperium (Cohen *et al.*, 1994; Neziroglu *et al.*, 1992). The style of parenting when ill provokes responses in very young children and influences their development. Withdrawn depressed mothers had more vocal demanding children while the children of agitated intrusive mothers were often tense and withdrawn (Weissman & Paykel, 1974). Rodnick & Goldstein (1974) found young schizophrenic mothers with poor premorbid adjustment were apathetic and unresponsive to their child's needs. This early emotional deprivation was likely to contribute to long-term difficulties in the child's relationships. The children of paranoid schizophrenic mothers with good premorbid personalities, who recovered fast, did much better despite a period of rigid or erratic parenting.

Attachment and decisions regarding placement

When a child is separated from its mother in infancy because of her inability to parent, the length of time professionals should wait before permanent placement depends on the likelihood of an early recovery and her ability to maintain a relationship with the child during the first 12–18 months of life. If the infant has never developed a healthy attachment to its mother (s)he should only be returned to mother's care if she is very likely to provide adequate long-term care. Permanent substitute care should be arranged if the mother is unable to develop a satisfactory relationship with the child or when she clearly cannot meet the child's developmental needs in the long term. Later placement for adoption is more difficult for the child and his adopters, with greater risk of breakdown or permanent disturbance in the child (Department of Health, 1991; Howe, 1998). Children often wait for long periods in temporary care in order to assess whether rehabilitation with a mentally ill parent is feasible, only to experience further delays for legal proceedings and matching with adoptive parents. This may be reasonable for an older child. It should not occur for infants and young children who have not had the opportunity to form a healthy attachment and for whom delay in achieving permanent placement may be seriously damaging (Webster & Huxley, 1996) (see Göpfert *et al.*, Chapters 5 and 7; Clodman, Chapter 17).

The child is at serious risk of disturbance if rehabilitation breaks down and (s)he returns to foster care. The effects of repeated separations and loss of relationships with significant attachment figures, such as foster parents, is inevitably harmful, contributing to future difficulties for the child in forming healthy relationships even with high quality carers (Adam, 1982; Bowlby, 1969, 1973, 1980; Brown, 1982; Rutter, 1972). Early loss is particularly associated with depression in adulthood. Repeated disruption of attachments or care by multiple caretakers is associated with severe antisocial personality disorders in adulthood.

Distress

There is little information in the literature about the quality of life and experiences of children who show no obvious disturbance while living with a mentally ill parent. Child psychiatrists and other professionals may observe relatively subtle behavioural changes such as anxiety and fearfulness. Harder & Greenwald (1992) found that higher IQ, positive family interactions and good recovery of the mentally ill parent after hospitalization, protected sons from distress. A longitudinal study (Klimes-Dougan *et al.*, 1999) found children of depressed mothers were more likely to report suicidal thoughts or behaviour than children of mothers who were well. Beardslee *et al.* (1998) reported general difficulties in functioning, increased guilt and social difficulties in children of parents with affective disorder. In a small qualitative study over 10–15 years, Anthony (1986) looked at the effects on 12 siblings from three families with psychotic illness. Anxious children were more likely to experience posttraumatic stress that sometimes persisted. Children with existing poor relationships and those more involved in the parent's psychosis seemed especially vulnerable to poor adjustment, impaired relationships and adverse long-term outcome. They often remained close to the ill parent and denied the illness. Other children who were more successful socially and academically, showed increasing resilience as they became habituated to recurrent stress. They tended to distance themselves from the parent.

Many children are ashamed of their parent's illness and strive to keep their family life separate from their relationships outside the home. They may be torn by loyalty and concern for their parent in the face of criticism from others, while they feel guilty about their own feelings of resentment (Anthony & McGinnis, 1978). Unfortunately, many potentially supportive adults, teachers, relatives or neighbours, can be anxious about or unfamiliar with mental illness and avoid discussion with the child, increasing his isolation and anxiety. Clinical experience suggests that the stigma associated with intoxication or psychotic behaviour is particularly distressing and increases social isolation. Older children who can voice their feelings directly, may obtain relief from the opportunity to discuss the illness with a professional who can help them to understand the nature of the illness, answer their questions and reveal their fears. Unfortunately, children of parents with psychiatric illness, especially depression, who have been referred to child mental health services are more likely to drop out of treatment than other referred children (Dover *et al.*, 1994). This may be because of the child's responsibilities for caring for their ill parent and younger siblings or because they need a motivated parent to attend with them. The emotional development of children who care for a vulnerable parent for long periods may be impaired and their anxiety about their parent's welfare and loyalty may make both disclosure of concern and desirable separation difficult (Barnett & Parker, 1998). Professionals working with the parent need to support the family in seeking and continuing treatment for their children.

Clinical work shows that a particular child may be closely identified with an ill parent and may be afraid that his own feelings or symptoms are early signs of illness. The problem is reinforced if siblings or close family members also worry about the child, especially when (s)he shares personality characteristics with the ill individual. Social withdrawal, anxiety, emotional lability or oversensitivity could be symptoms of the child's distress or enduring personality traits exacerbated by their reaction to the parent's illness. The general public holds strong beliefs about the high heritability of mental illness and these concerns may not be allayed simply by provision of information about genetic risk. Bringing the issue out into the open with the child and his family may reduce these deep-rooted and persistent fears. Sometimes, of course, a young person presents with symptoms suggestive of the same mental illness present in a relative. Management of this situation may prove challenging, as diagnostic interviews and attempts to arrange treatment only reinforce the adolescent's fears that (s)he is 'mad', resulting in denial of symptoms and refusal of psychiatric care. More rarely, a submissive child who is very close to and identified with a psychotic parent may find it difficult to distinguish his own reality from that of the parent. In its most extreme form the two can present with a shared delusional state as a folie á deux psychosis (Anthony, 1970).

Case 1: Amanda

Amanda was 16 when she was referred to a child mental health clinic where she had attended briefly in childhood for behaviour problems. Her parents' concern that she might develop a manic-depressive illness like her grandmother because of her explosive outbursts, increased when she developed an obsessional preoccupation with her hair, spending hours before the mirror. After cutting a few strands she became extremely distressed and she remained convinced her hair would never grow even after reassurance from many local hairdressers. She was unwilling to see a psychiatrist until she lost her first job when she shouted and swore at a customer on her first day. She appeared tense with flat affect, inappropriate laughter and was anxious about her hair, her lost job and her outbursts.

When seen on her own, Amanda's major preoccupation was that her hair was going to fall out. She was aware that she smiled and laughed at strangers, which made them stare at her. She denied other symptoms apart from low mood and tearfulness at times. It was explained that the risk of developing a disorder like her grandmother was low and that her grandmother was very unusual in her lack of response to treatment. She was able to accept that her symptoms were not unusual in adolescents coping with leaving school and other life changes, reflecting her anxiety, insomnia and sensitivity in relationships. She agreed in principle, albeit reluctantly, to try medication if she could not control her symptoms herself. Meanwhile she kept a diary of her outbursts. After a few months she tried a small dose of an antipsychotic medication, with good response.

This case illustrates several issues:

- It is preferable for such adolescents to be referred to child psychiatry rather than adult services, where their relative may have been treated. The family doctor may then continue treatment.
- It is important not to talk to parents behind the young person's back. Parents may be bewildered by inexplicable behaviour but discussing underlying feelings may help to explain and normalize the adolescent's response. Talking about difficult feelings as exaggerated examples of common problems experienced by other young people helps to keep a distance from 'madness'.
- Proposing medication or, if required, admission, raises anxiety. It is preferable to delay initiating this if it is safe to do so, in order to give the adolescent a sense of control and partnership.

It is difficult to study the direct emotional effects of psychiatric illness on children as it may not be possible to separate them from indirect effects of the illness, such as marital disharmony, separations due to hospital admissions, unemployment and social disadvantage. In individual cases, the direct consequences for the child of a parent's behaviour can be identified. The child's response is often nonspecific, such as social withdrawal or poor concentration at school, and the long-term effects clearly vary according to the child's history, maturity and his social supports. The problems are more likely to be severe if the mother rather than the father is ill (Clausen & Huffine, 1979), especially if the illness is disabling and chronic.

Serious problems are more likely when a socially isolated parent with mental illness raises a child alone. A young girl became very distressed when her psychotic mother firmly believed she was being sexually abused at school. Her mother examined her daughter's underwear daily and frequently marched into school threatening the staff. The mother denied her own illness and refused treatment so, eventually, her daughter was received into care. In another family, a depressed mother who was terrified of their father concealed her children from the authorities for 2 years. Avoidance of professionals and children's loyalty to their parent can make interventions difficult. Depending on how a parent and child make sense of the parental illness (see Hill, Chapter 4), ongoing involvement of professionals can help contain the child's worry about a parent: the child expects treatment will make the parent better which helps reduce their anxiety and the child knows that (s)he can live elsewhere (e.g. respite foster care) if necessary and therefore does not need to keep the family together at all costs to ensure a functional home. The following case illustrates this.

Case 2: Stephen

Stephen was referred, aged 7, after his father, Rob, was compulsorily admitted to hospital with a first episode of psychotic illness. As his father had raised him alone since the age of 2 and he had minimal contact with his mother, he was placed with a foster family. Initially the direct effect of the illness was that Rob withdrew Stephen from school and completely isolated him. They became overinvolved with each other. The boy never admitted that his father neglected him despite the deterioration in his cleanliness, lack of food and state of their home at the time of his admission. Once Stephen trusted that he would return home after his father recovered, he acknowledged guardedly that his father was ill. His drawings reflected some of his fears: frightening faces and a crazy house in orange and black were recurring themes. Both he and his father had bright auburn hair. He began to talk about his father's 'funny ideas'. After he returned home to his father he lost ground academically and also showed uncharacteristic disruptive aggressive behaviour at school. He controlled his feelings at home until he began to feel increasingly confident in his father's recovery. Once he could take the risk of misbehaving at home his behaviour improved at school.

A year later Rob, who always denied he had been ill, discontinued his medication and relapsed. He withdrew Stephen from school again and isolated them both. Stephen was placed with the same foster family and this time was more open about his concerns about his father and refused to collaborate with his father's delusional religious behaviour. He confirmed his independence when he insisted on having his long hair cut in the style of his peers. This time his father had greater insight into his illness and was willing to continue his depot phenothiazines to avoid relapse. The increased openness and insight in both father and son may have been facilitated by continuity of the professionals involved in their care and trust that the goal was to reunite them. Supportive work with the boy alone and joint interviews from the time of the father's first admission, encouraged increasing age-appropriate independence. After the father's second admission he attended a psychiatric day centre for a few months, which helped him to be more relaxed with his son, who showed little disturbance at school when he returned home.

The effects of parental psychiatric disorder on the adult child

Over half of children of mentally ill parents had significant disturbance as adults, mainly affective disorders and substance misuse (Carlson & Weintraub, 1993). Many adult difficulties, such as teenage pregnancy, inadequate and disrupted relationships and problems with parenting are related to the indirect effects of parental illness such as poor parenting, social disadvantage and separations (Harris *et al.*, 1986, 1987). Beardslee *et al.* (1998) showed that children of a parent with affective disorder have a 40% risk of a major depressive episode by the age of 20 (see Puckering, Chapter 12). Approximately 10% of children of schizophrenics develop schizophrenia but assumptions about genetic aetiology are complicated by environmental factors (Mednick, 1973; Tienari *et al.*, 1994). Those most at risk show attention and interpersonal difficulties in childhood and lack of emotional rapport and cognitive problems in adolescence (Garmezy, 1974; Parnas *et al.*, 1982).

Adult personality disorder is associated with nonoptimal parenting, abuse and separations (Zeitlin, 1986). Antisocial personality disorder is almost always preceded by antisocial behaviour in childhood (Patterson, 1982) (see Adshead *et al.*, Chapter 15). Alcohol problems with antisocial behaviour were increased fourfold in the adopted offspring of parents with antisocial and alcohol problems (Cadoret *et al.*, 1989, 1995). As well as replicating the finding of a fourfold increased risk of alcoholism in the sons of alcoholics, in a large epidemiological study Greenfield *et al.* (1993) and Mathew *et al.* (1993) showed significantly raised rates of anxiety disorders, agoraphobia, antisocial disorders and marital instability in their adult offspring. Children of drug misusers have serious problems with conduct disorders, aggression and substance misuse (Merikangas *et al.*, 1998*a*; Moss *et al.*, 1995).

Developmental framework

The final section of this chapter will outline a developmental framework (Fig. 3.1) to help understand the interrelationship of risk variables in the development of the child, the emergence of disturbance and its modification. Clinically, this framework may assist with the developmental assessment of children.

The developmental process is central to the effects of adversity for any child. The age, the previous experience of the child, and the child's prior course of development, will contribute to his or her resilience/vulnerability in the face of adversity. The effects may be modified by constitutional factors, the age of the child and protective factors such as social support and professional intervention.

Constitutional factors

Constitutional (predisposing) factors are the child's endowment that puts him or her at advantage or disadvantage in life. They include genetic make-up,

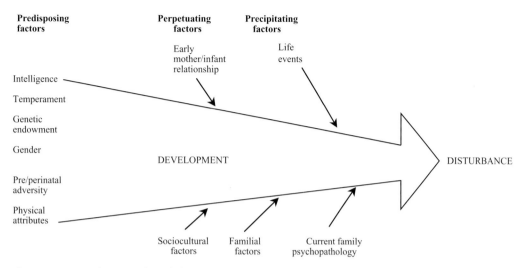

Figure 3.1   Developmental model.

temperament and associated emerging personality, gender, intelligence, physical attributes, disability and illness, whether congenital or acquired.

Children of higher ability who succeed at school may be protected against adversity such as parental mental illness (Harder & Greenwald, 1992). Children with lower IQ and socio-economic status are particularly susceptible to the cumulative effects of negative family qualities and life events (Masten *et al.*, 1988). They are more likely to become disruptive in school than more advantaged, brighter children, who may respond to stress by becoming disengaged in school.

Temperament

The temperament of a particular child may contribute to his risk of abuse. Thomas & Chess (1982), in their New York Longitudinal Study, identified a group of temperamentally difficult children who were irregular in their feeding and sleeping patterns, withdrew in new situations, showed poor adaptability, negative mood and intense reactions. The child's temperament interacts with the parents' ability to manage him, so that children who are difficult to handle are more likely to develop behaviour problems later in childhood. Babies suffering from narcotic withdrawal syndrome have difficult temperaments and remain very difficult to care for because of irritability, feeding and sleeping difficulties.

Certain temperamental characteristics, such as social responsiveness and activity, appear to protect children from adversity (Garmezy, 1984). The resilience of some children in the face of adversity is surprising and it is clear that the temperament of some children enables them to seek out and make greater use of social supports than others (Garmezy, 1984; Rutter, 1990). The Yale Family Study of Comorbidity of

Substance Abuse and Anxiety (Merikangas *et al.*, 1998*b*) showed that temperament remains associated with psychopathology throughout the life span. They found that children and adults with low scores on adaptability and approach/withdrawal were more likely to suffer from depression or anxiety, while low attention scores or high activity was associated with behavioural disorder or substance misuse. They suggest that socially fearful temperament is a precursor for overanxious disorder in childhood and social phobia in adolescence and adulthood.

Gender

Rutter & Quinton (1984) showed that boys with a mentally ill parent are more likely to develop conduct disorder, while girls require longer periods of exposure to adversity before developing problems. Children of the same gender as the ill parent are at greatest risk of disorder. There is a stronger association between maternal depression and the development of depression in girls than boys (Goodyer *et al.*, 1993). There is little evidence for difference between girls and boys in genetic influences, except for separation anxiety, where there is a large genetic effect in girls but not in boys (Eaves *et al.*, 1997). In general, girls are more likely to develop emotional disorders and boys, disorders of behaviour. In adolescence, girls are more likely to develop eating disorders or to self-harm, while boys may become aggressive, involved in delinquency or substance misuse.

Genetic endowment

Genetic propensity interacts with environmental factors, especially the quality of parenting (Tienari *et al.*, 1994), to determine whether a child will develop a disorder, its severity and course, as well as the timing of its onset. Rutter *et al.* (1990) conclude that there is little evidence for a major genetic contribution in child psychiatric disorders, apart from early-onset major depressive disorder (Price *et al.*, 1987; Puig-Antich *et al.*, 1989) and bipolar disorder (Akiskal *et al.*, 1985; Strober *et al.*, 1988). Unlike major depressive disorder in adulthood for which family and twin studies indicate significant genetic predisposition (Kendler & Prescott, 1999), few conclusions can be drawn as yet regarding the genetic contribution to depressive symptoms in childhood (Rice *et al.*, 2002). Because of its size, the Virginia Twin Study of Adolescent Behavioural Development (Eaves *et al.*, 1997) was able to demonstrate in 1412 twin pairs greater heritability than earlier studies for conduct disorder, oppositional defiant disorder and depression, as well as confirming the findings of others that reading ability, attention deficit hyperactivity disorder and impulsivity are highly heritable. Generally, individual genetic loading, particularly for impaired sociability, considerably compounds the adverse influences of parental psychopathology (Hill *et al.*, 1989; Rutter *et al.*, 1990) (see Seeman & Göpfert, Chapter 2; Seneviratne & Conroy, Chapter 9).

Prenatal and perinatal adversity

Prenatal adversity and perinatal complications are known to be associated with increased prevalence of child psychiatric disorders.

Mentally ill mothers are more likely to have unplanned pregnancies and little antenatal care compared with healthy parents. Twenty per cent gave birth to premature or ill babies compared with 2% of controls (Stewart & Gangbar, 1984) (see Seneviratne & Conroy, Chapter 9). Perinatal risk factors (smoking, poor diet, alcohol or drugs during the pregnancy) are associated with psychosocial adversity and maternal mental illness (Taylor, 1991). Smoking in pregnancy has recently been shown to carry independent long-term risks for conduct disorder in boys and drug dependence in girls (Weissman *et al.*, 1999*b*). Alcohol exposure in utero is associated with fetal growth retardation and hyperactivity in childhood. High levels early in pregnancy contribute to the more serious physical, intellectual and psychological impairment found in fetal alcohol syndrome (Von Knorring, 1991). Drug addiction in mothers is associated with its own specific risks (Gerada, 1996) (see also Hans, Chapter 14).

A growing concern in Western cultures is the effect of maternal eating disorders on young children (see Hall, 1996). Poor weight gain by the mother in pregnancy is associated with increased risk of low birth weight and prematurity in infants, as well as stillbirth (Brinch *et al.*, 1988; Stewart *et al.*, 1987). Bulimia nervosa and extreme preoccupation with weight, shape and diet are common and often undetected by professionals because of guilt and secrecy in women whose weight and fertility may appear normal.

Physical attributes

The physical appearance of a particular child, specific handicaps or chronic illness, may make him vulnerable in his family. The child may remind a parent positively or negatively of an absent partner. Handicap, illness or unattractiveness may contribute to criticism, rejection or even abuse by some vulnerable parents and affect the mother–child relationship.

Perpetuating factors

Early mother–infant relationships

When an infant remains in the care of a mother who is unable to provide adequate care, (s)he may show failure to trive, often with both developmental delay and retarded growth. A period in foster care may produce a rapid acceleration of growth and development as a result of a healthy relationship with the foster mother.

A secure attachment is an important protective factor and this may develop with a well functioning second parent or relative. Infants of mentally ill mothers are more likely to experience separations, as women are more vulnerable to psychiatric illness after childbirth than at any other time (Oates, 1997).

In families with eating disorders, time-consuming binges and vomiting mean that mothers are often physically and emotionally unavailable to their infants. The adverse effects on the mother–child relationship may be compounded by associated depression and maternal preoccupation with food and feeding. Mealtimes, particularly after weaning, may become a tense battleground for control rather than a pleasurable social experience (McFadyen et al., 1999). Stein et al. (1996) demonstrated effects on the growth of infants of mothers with eating disorders and more recently Stein et al. (unpublished data) showed daughters of bulimic and anorexic mothers were less able to initiate interaction with their peers and to see their perspective compared with controls. These findings may relate to a lack of sensitivity to their children's needs and developing autonomy on the part of mothers with eating disorders (Woodside & Shekter-Wolfson, 1990).

Socio-cultural factors

The effects of social disadvantage have been discussed throughout this chapter. Socio-cultural factors are also protective for the child with a mentally ill parent: a close extended family may provide stability, support and confiding relationships, especially in times of stress. Relationships with adults in the community as well as confiding friendships, especially in adolescence, influence ability to cope. In a longitudinal study in New Zealand, Lynskey & Fergusson (1997) found that friendship with nondelinquent peers in adolescence and good paternal care and support protected against the serious problems found in 80% of young adults who had been sexually abused.

Sensitive teachers and educational opportunities offer protection against adversity (Rutter, 1979; Quinton & Rutter, 1984; McKay & Pollard, 1996). If one excludes the effects of social disadvantage, rural life also offers some protection (Rutter, 1981). It may be that city life exposes the family to more stressors and less stability.

The effects of immigration may be stressful or protective for families of ethnic minorities. Families may escape war or persecution but traumatic experiences may bring an increased risk of psychiatric disorder. Some aspects of immigrant family life are protective for the child e.g. lower rates of single parenthood, strong extended family and concern for moral welfare and educational achievement amongst Asian families. On the other hand, where strong cultural values are in conflict with those of the indigenous population, children may experience more conflict, adding to the burden of racism and of having a mentally ill parent (see also Göpfert et al., Chapter 5).

Familial factors

Some families are more adaptable than others because of positive qualities such as warmth, closeness, flexibility, organization and ability to handle conflict. Warner *et al.* (1995) found that chaotic family environment was an independent predictor of mood and panic disorders in children of parents with major depression and panic disorders.

The Finnish adoption study has shown that the increased genetic risk for psychosis, borderline syndrome and severe personality disorder found in the adopted children of schizophrenics was only manifest in the presence of a disturbed family environment (Tienari *et al.*, 1994). Patterson (1982) showed that indifferent, uninvolved and neglectful parenting tended to increase aggression, low self-esteem, poor self-control and disturbed parent–child relationships in the children. Such families rarely had consistent rules. The parents tended to issue more commands while failing to follow through with discipline or praise good behaviour. This style of parenting is more likely to occur when a parent is ill and the effects on the child will depend on duration and the availability of another parent who handles the child effectively.

A number of studies of family interaction have looked at the effects of family communication on the developing child. High levels of negative expressed emotion and particularly critical comments by depressed or anxious parents are associated with a number of disorders, including depression, substance misuse and conduct disorder in children (Schwartz *et al.*, 1990; Hirshfield *et al.*, 1997) and, when pervasive, may be considered a form of emotional abuse (Hall, 2002). Communication through somatization is characteristic of some families (Livingston, 1993) and associated with reduced maternal warmth (Hodes *et al.*, 1999) and difficulty expressing negative feelings (Garralda *et al.*, 1999). Excessive preoccupation about children's health, often associated with overprotection, is harmful as most clearly shown for parents with Munchausen by proxy syndrome (Schreier & Libow, 1993).

Precipitating factors

Life events

Girls aged 11–16 years, whose mothers had a history of psychiatric disorder, especially depression, and who were exposed to one or more undesirable events, were especially at risk for depression (Goodyer *et al.*, 1993). Undesirable life events in the past year are associated with child psychiatric disorders of all types and occur in 60% of new cases. Events involving permanent separation or exit events are associated with severe anxiety, depression and somatic complaints (Goodyer *et al.*, 1985). Goodyer *et al.* (1988) found maternal distress and lack of confiding relationships considerably increased the risk of disorder in the child after a single stressful event. For children presenting with obsessive-compulsive disorder, over half reported precipitating events (Thomsen, 1995).

The interrelationships between psychosocial adversity and life events are complex (Goodyer, 1990). Several events occur more often in the offspring of mentally ill parents: separation from a parent, unemployment, marital breakdown, parental changes of partner and bereavement. A parent's suicide or murder by the ill partner is especially devastating. Alcohol and drug misuse are associated with high death rates from overdose, violence, suicide and accidents. Children who experience more negative life events have lower self-confidence, with differential effects on siblings that were not accounted for by temperamental differences (Beardsall & Dunn, 1992). The effects of multiple childhood adversities have been shown to persist into adulthood and are associated with increased risk of comorbid psychiatric disorder (Kessler *et al.*, 1997).

Current family psychopathology

Long-lasting changes in family functioning are likely in families with parental psychiatric disorder and include marital disharmony, marital violence, child sexual or physical abuse and substance abuse. The risk of disturbed child development is greatly increased by marital conflict. Apart from causing direct distress to the child, the parents may disagree in their views about child care, causing inconsistency and poor limit setting; they may show less affection to the child, and they may be poor role models for the child, for example in household tasks, decision making or conflict resolution.

An older child may become particularly embroiled in parental marital difficulties as a result of a close confiding relationship with one parent and may prematurely take on a parenting role with younger siblings.

The interaction of risk and protective factors

The above developmental model illustrates the complex interrelationship of risk and protective factors for child psychiatric disorder (Rutter, 1990). Many risk factors are more commonly experienced in children with a mentally ill parent. These children are also more likely to experience more undesirable life events and deterioration in family functioning, as well as the potent chronic effects of social disadvantage.

Child-rearing patterns, often already inadequate, may deteriorate further when a parent becomes ill. The effects of illness vary greatly depending on the developmental stage of the child and steps taken to reduce harm. For example, if the child of a severely chronically ill mother is placed in an adoptive family soon after birth, the outcome may be excellent compared with that for a child who is exposed to multiple caretakers and repeated separations in early childhood. The latter may prove very difficult to place in stable alternative care at a later stage because of the virtually irreversible effects on his or her ability to form relationships.

A short-lived puerperal psychosis may have few enduring effects for the child if the child is adequately cared for during the illness and subsequently. The effects of illness in an older child are reduced if the child has experienced a good relationship with his mother and, at this stage, peer and family support, as well as good individual adjustment, are protective. The effects of parental illness for an adolescent may be compounded if it coincides with public examinations, the establishment of intimate relationships or leaving home. The adolescent may get drawn back into the family to care for the parent or younger siblings.

The effect of illness in a father may be considerably less than that of a mother unless he is the main caretaker, but may exert potent effects by impairing the parenting of the mother, contributing to marital disharmony or loss of the relationship. Chronic problems, particularly violence, conflict, hostility or substance abuse are more likely to occur when he suffers from a personality disorder, and are especially harmful to sons.

The effects of multiple childhood adversities have been shown to persist into adulthood. The catalogue of risks for children of mentally ill parents described in this chapter emphasizes the need for skilful coordination of professionals involved with both the parents and the children. Adult psychiatrists, who only rarely consider the needs of the children of their patients (Reder *et al.*, 2000), refer relatively few families to child mental health services. It is vital that those involved in the mental health care of adults appreciate the risk to offspring and liase closely with family agencies. As has been shown, children of mentally ill parents experience more life events and adversity that are associated with increased risk of comorbid psychiatric disorder in adulthood (Kessler *et al.*, 1997). With appropriate and timely intervention, as well as adequate resources, the effects on the next generation may be reduced.

REFERENCES

Accardo, P. J. & Whitman, B. Y. (1990). Children of mentally retarded parents. *American Journal of Diseases of Childhood, 144*, 69–70.

Adam, K. S. (1982). Loss, suicide and attachment. In *The Place of Attachment in Human Behaviour*, ed. C. Murray Parkes & J. Stevenson-Hinde, pp. 269–94. London: Tavistock.

Adcock, M. (1996). A legal framework for child protection: the Children Act 1989 (UK). In *Parental Psychiatric Disorder: Distressed Parents and their Families*, ed. M. Göpfert, J. Webster & M. V. Seeman, pp. 312–24. Cambridge: Cambridge University Press.

Adrian, N., Hall, A., Harris, R. J. & Gold, J. A. (2002). *When is it Neglect? The Development of a Tool to Identify and Monitor Neglect*. Report to Tower Hamlets Area Child Protection Committee.

Ainsworth, M. D. S., Blehar, M. C., Waters, E. & Wall, S. (1978). *The Strange Situation: Observing Patterns of Attachment*. Hillsdale, NJ: Lawrence Erlbaum Associates.

Akiskal, H. S., Downs, J., Jordan, P., Watson, S., Daugherty, D. & Pruitt, D. B. (1985). Affective disorders in referred children and younger siblings of manic-depressives: mode of onset and prospective course. *Archives of General Psychiatry*, *42*, 996–1003.

Anthony, E. J. (1970). The influence of maternal psychosis on children – folie à deux. In *Parenthood*, ed. E. J. Anthony & T. Benedek. Boston: Little, Brown.

Anthony, E. J. (1986). Terrorising attacks on children by psychotic parents. *Journal of the American Academy of Child and Adolescent Psychiatry*, *25*, 326–35.

Anthony, E. J. & McGinnis, M. (1978). Counselling very disturbed parents. In *Helping Parents to help Their Children*, ed. L. E. Arnold, pp. 328–41. New York: Brunner and Mazel.

Barnett, B. & Parker, G. (1998). The parentified child: early competence or childhood deprivation. *Child Psychology and Psychiatry Review*, *4*, 146–55.

Beardsall, L. & Dunn, J. (1992). Adversities in childhood: siblings' experiences, and their relations to self-esteem. *Journal of Child Psychology and Psychiatry*, *33*, 331–59.

Beardslee, W. R., Bemporad, J., Keller, M. B. & Klerman, G. I. (1983). Children with parents with major affective disorder: a review. *American Journal of Psychiatry*, *140*, 825–32.

Beardslee, W. R., Versage, E. & Gladstone, T. (1998). Children of affectively ill parents: a review of the past 10 years. *Journal of the American Academy of Child Psychiatry*, *37*, 1134–41.

Beidel, D. C. & Turner, S. M. (1997). At risk for anxiety: I. Psychopathology in the offspring of anxious parents. *Journal of the American Academy of Child and Adolescent Psychiatry*, *36*, 918–24.

Belsky, J., Rosenberger, K. & Crnic, K. (1995). The origins of attachment security: 'classical' and contextual determinants. In *Attachment Theory: Social, Developmental and Clinical Perspectives*, ed. S. Goldberg, R. Muir & J. Kerr, pp. 153–84. New Jersey: The Analytic Press, Inc.

Bonnet, C. (1993). Adoption at birth: prevention against abandonment or neonaticide. *Child Abuse and Neglect*, *17*, 501–13.

Bowlby, J. (1969). *Attachment and Loss. Vol. 1: Attachment*. New York: Basic Books.

Bowlby, J. (1973). *Attachment and Loss. Vol. 2: Separation: Anxiety and Anger*. New York: Basic Books.

Bowlby, J. (1980). *Attachment and Loss. Vol. 3: Loss: Sadness and Loss*. New York: Basic Books.

Brinch, M., Isager, T. & Tolstrup, K. (1988). Anorexia nervosa and motherhood: reproduction pattern and mothering behaviour of 50 women. *Acta Psychiatrica Scandinavica*, *77*, 611–17.

Brown, G. W. (1982). Early loss and depression. In *The Place of Attachment in Human Behaviour*, ed. C. Murray Parkes & J. Stevenson-Hinde. London: Tavistock.

Browne, K. & Herbert, M. (1997). *Preventing Family Violence*. Chichester: John Wiley & Sons.

Cadoret, R. J., Troughton, E., Moreno, L. & Whitters, A. (1989). Early life psychosocial events and adult affective symptoms. In *Straight and Devious Pathways from Childhood to Adult Life*, ed. L. N. Robins & M. Rutter, pp. 183–214. Cambridge: Cambridge University Press.

Cadoret, R. J., Yates, W. R., Troughton, E. et al. (1995). Adoption study demonstrating two genetic pathways to drug abuse. *Archives of General Psychiatry*, *52*, 42–52.

Cameron, J. M., Johnson, H. R. M. & Camps, F. E. (1966). The battered child syndrome. *Medicine, Science and the Law*, 6, 2–21.

Carlson, G. A. & Weintraub, S. (1993). Childhood behaviour problems and bipolar disorder: relationship or coincidence? *Journal of Affective Disorders*, 28, 143–53.

Cheung, P. T. K. (1986). Maternal filicide in Hong Kong, 1971–1985. *Medicine, Science and the Law*, 26, 185–92.

Cicchetti, D. & Toth, S. L. (1995). Child maltreatment and attachment organisation: implications for intervention. In *Attachment Theory: Social, Developmental and Clinical Perspectives*, ed. S. Goldberg, R. Muir & J. Kerr, pp. 153–84. New Jersey: The Analytic Press, Inc.

Clausen, J. A. & Huffine, C. L. (1979). The impact of parental mental illness on children. In *Research in Community and Mental Health*, ed. R. Simmons, pp. 183–214. Greenwich, CT: JAI Press.

Cohen, L. S., Sichel, D. A., Sena, R., Henker, B. & Rosenbaum, J. F. (1994). Post-partum course in women with pre-existing panic disorder. *Journal of Clinical Psychiatry*, 55, 289–92.

Cox, A. D., Puckering, C., Pound, A. & Mills, M. (1987). The impact of maternal depression in young children. *Journal of Child Psychology and Psychiatry*, 28, 917–28.

Creighton, S. J. & Gallagher, B. (1988). *Child Abuse Deaths. Information Briefing No. 5*. London: NSPCC.

Cytryn, L., McKnew, D. W., Zahn-Waxler, C. & Gershon, E. S. (1984). Developmental issues in risk research: the offspring of affectively ill parents. In *Depression in Children: Developmental Perspectives*, ed. M. Rutter, C. R. lzard & P. B. Read. New York: Guilford Press.

Davies, P. T., & Windle, M. (1997). Gender specific pathways between maternal depressive symptoms, family discord and adolescent adjustment. *Developmental Psychology*, 33, 657–68.

Department of Health (1991). *Patterns and Outcomes in Child Placement: Messages from Current Research and their Implications*. London: HMSO.

Department of Health (2000). *Framework for the Assessment of Children in Need and their Families*. London: The Stationery Office.

Dierker, L. C., Merikangas, K. R. & Szatmari, P. (1999). Influence of parental concordance for psychiatric disorders on psychopathology in offspring. *Journal of the American Academy of Child and Adolescent Psychiatry*, 38, 280–8.

D'Orban, P. T. (1979). Women who kill their children. *British Journal of Psychiatry*, 134, 560–71.

Dover, S. J., Leahy, A. & Forman, D. (1994). Parental psychiatric disorder: clinical prevalence and effects on default from treatment. *Child: Care, Health and Development*, 20, 137–43.

Durfee, M. & Tilton-Durfee, D. (1995). Multi-agency child death review teams: experience in the United States. *Child Abuse Review*, 4, 377–81.

Eaves, L. J., Silberg, J. L., Meyer, J. M. et al. (1997). Genetics and developmental psychopathology: the main effects of genes and environment on behavioural problems in the Virginia Twin Study of Adolescent Behavioural Development. *Journal of Child Psychology and Psychiatry*, 38, 965–80.

Emery, R., Weintraub, S. & Neale, J. (1982). Effects of marital discord on the school behaviour of children of schizophrenic, affectively disordered, and normal patients. *Journal of Abnormal Child Psychology*, 10, 215–28.

Falkov, A. (1996). *Study of Working Together 'Part 8' Reports. Fatal Child Abuse and Parental Psychiatric Disorder. An Analysis of 100 Area Child Protection Committee Case Reviews Conducted under the Terms of Part 8 of Working Together under the Children Act 1989.* Department of Health. London: HMSO.

Falkov, A. (1997). *Parental Psychiatric Disorder and Child Maltreatment. Part II: Extent and Nature of the Association.* National Children's Bureau Highlight, No. 149.

Famularo, R., Kinscherff, R. & Fenton, T. (1992). Parental substance abuse and the nature of child maltreatment. *Child Abuse and Neglect, 16,* 475–83.

Field, T., Healy, B., Goldstein, S. et al. (1988). Infants of depressed mothers show 'depressed' behaviour even with non-depressed adults. *Child Development, 59,* 1569–97.

Foley, D. L., Pickles, A., Simonoff, E. et al. (2001). Parental concordance and comorbidity for psychiatric disorder and associated risks for current psychiatric symptoms and disorders in a community sample of juvenile twins. *Journal of Child Psychology and Psychiatry, 42,* 381–94.

Frick, P. J., Lahey, B. B., Loeber, R., Stouthamer-Loeber, M., Christ, M. A. & Hanson, K. (1992). Familial risk factors to oppositional defiant disorder and conduct disorder: parental psychopathology and maternal parenting. *Journal of Consulting and Clinical Psychology, 60,* 49–55.

Garmezy, N. (1974). Children at risk: the search for the antecedents to schizophrenia. *Schizophrenia Bulletin, 8,* 14–90.

Garmezy, N. (1984). Stress resistant children: the search for protective factors. In *Recent Research into Developmental Psychopathology,* ed. J. Stevenson. Monograph supplement No. 4 to *Journal of Child Psychiatry and Psychology.* Oxford: Pergamon Press.

Garralda, M. E., Bowman, F. M. & Mandalia, S. (1999). Children with psychosomatic disorders who are frequent attenders to primary care. *European Child and Adolescent Psychiatry, 8,* 34–44.

Gerada, C. (1996). *The Drug-addicted Mother: Pregnancy and Lactation.* In *Parental Psychiatric Disorder: Distressed Parents and their Families,* ed. M. Göpfert, J. Webster & M. V. Seeman, pp. 87–95. Cambridge: Cambridge University Press.

Gibson, E. (1975). *Homicide in England and Wales 1967–1971.* Home Office Research Study No. 31. London: HMSO.

Glaser, D. & Prior, V. (1997). Is the term child protection applicable to emotional abuse? *Child Abuse Review, 6,* 315–29.

Goodyer, I. M. (1990). Family relationships, life events and childhood psychopathology. *Journal of Child Psychology and Psychiatry, 31,* 161–92.

Goodyer, I. M., Cooper, P. J., Vize, C. M. & Ashby, L. (1993). Depression in 11–26-year old girls: the role of past parental psychopathology and exposure to recent life events. *Journal of Child Psychology and Psychiatry, 34,* 1103–15.

Goodyer, I. M., Kolvin, I. & Gatzanis, S. (1985). Recent undesirable life events and psychiatric disorder in childhood and adolescence. *British Journal of Psychiatry, 147,* 517–23.

Goodyer, I. M., Wright, C. & Altham, P. M. E. (1988). Maternal adversity and recent stressful life events in anxious and depressed children. *Journal of Child Psychology and Psychiatry, 29,* 651–68.

Greenfield, S. F., Swartz, M. S., Landerman, L. R. & George, L. K. (1993). Long-term psychosocial effects of childhood exposure to parental problem drinking. *American Journal of Psychiatry, 150,* 608–13.

Hall, A. (1996). Anorexia nervosa, bulimia nervosa and other eating disorders. In *Parental Psychiatric Disorder: Distressed Parents and their Families*, ed. M. Göpfert, J. Webster & M. V. Seeman, pp. 251–6. Cambridge: Cambridge University Press.

Hall, A. (2002). Emotional abuse. In *Protecting Children from Abuse and Neglect in Primary Care*, ed. M. J. Bannon & Y. H. Carter. Oxford: Oxford University Press.

Harder, D. W. & Greenwald, D. F. (1992). Parent, family interaction and child predictors of outcome among sons at psychiatric risk. *Journal of Clinical Psychology*, 48, 151–64.

Hare, E. H. & Shaw, G. K. (1965). A study in family health: 11. A comparison of the health of fathers, mothers and children. *British Journal of Psychiatry*, 111, 467–71.

Harnish, J. D., Dodge K. A. & Valente, E. (1995). Mother–child interaction quality as a partial mediator of the roles of maternal depressive symptomatology and socio-economic status in the development of child behaviour problems. *Child Development*, 66, 739–53.

Harris, T., Brown, G. W. & Bifulco, A. (1986). Loss of parent in childhood and adult psychiatric disorder: the role of adequate family care. *Psychological Medicine*, 16, 641–59.

Harris, T., Brown, G. W. & Bifulco, A. (1987). Loss of parent in childhood and adult psychiatric disorder: the role of social class position and premarital pregnancy. *Psychological Medicine*, 17, 163–83.

Hill, J., Harrington, R., Fudge, H., Rutter, M. & Pickles, A. (1989). Adult personality functioning assessment 'APFA': an investigator-based standardised interview. *British Journal of Psychiatry*, 155, 24–35.

Hirshfield, D. R., Biederman, J., Brody, L., Faraone, S. V. & Rosenbaum J. F. (1997). Expressed emotion toward children with behavioural inhibition: association with maternal anxiety disorder. *Journal of the American Academy of Child and Adolescent Psychiatry*, 36, 910–17.

Holter, J. C. & Friedman, S. B. (1968). Principles of management in child abuse cases. *American Journal of Orthopsychiatry*, 38, 127–36.

Howe, D. (1998). Adoption outcome research and practical judgement. *Adoption and Fostering*, 22, 6–15.

Humphries, C. (2000). *Social Work, Domestic Violence and Child Protection: Challenging Practice*. Bristol: Polity Press.

Jones, D. P. H. (1987). The untreatable family. *Child Abuse and Neglect*, 11, 409–20.

Kendler, K. S. & Prescott, C. A. (1999). A population based twin study of lifetime major depression in men and women. *Archives of General Psychiatry*, 56, 29–44.

Kessler, R. C., Davis C. G. & Kendler, K. S. (1997). Childhood adversity and adult psychiatric disorder in the US National Co-morbidity Survey. *Psychological Medicine*, 27, 1101–19.

Klimes-Dougan, B., Free, K., Ronsaville, D., Stilwell, J., Welsh, C. & Radke-Yarrow, M. (1999). Suicidal ideation and attempts: a longitudinal investigation of children of depressed and well mothers. *Journal of the American Academy of Child and Adolescent Psychiatry*, 38, 651–9.

Kuperman, S., Schlosser, S. S., Lidral, J. & Reich, W. (1999). Relationship of child psychopathology to parental alcoholism and antisocial personality disorder. *Journal of the American Academy of Child and Adolescent Psychiatry*, 38, 686–92.

Levine, M., Freeman, J. & Compaan, C. (1994). Maltreatment related fatalities: issues of policy and prevention. *Law and Policy*, 16, 4499–71.

Livingston, R. (1993). Children of people with somatisation disorder. *Journal of the American Academy of Child and Adolescent Psychiatry*, *32*, 536–44.

Lung, C. T. & Daro, D. (1996). *Current Trends in Child Abuse Reporting and Fatalities: The Results of the 1995 Annual Fifty-state Survey*. Chicago: National Committee to Prevent Child Abuse.

Main, M. (1995). Recent studies in attachment: overview with selected implications for clinical work. In *Attachment Theory: Social, Developmental and Clinical Perspectives*, ed. S. Goldberg, R. Muir & J. Kerr, pp. 153–84. New Jersey: The Analytic Press, Inc.

Manassis, K., Bradley, S., Goldberg, S., Hood, J. & Swinson, R. P. (1995). Behavioural inhibition, attachment and anxiety in children of mothers with anxiety disorders. *Canadian Journal of Psychiatry*, *40*, 87–92.

Martin, C., Cabrol, S. Bouvard, M. P., Lepine, J. P. & Mouren-Simeoni, M. (1999). *Journal of the American Academy of Child and Adolescent Psychiatry*, *38*, 916–22.

Masten, A. S., Garmezy, N., Tellegen, A., Pellegrini, D. S., Larkin, K. & Larsen, A. (1988). Competence and stress in school children: the moderating effects of individual and family qualities. *Journal of Child Psychology and Psychiatry*, *29*, 745–64.

Mathew, R. J., Wilson, W. H., Blazer, D. G. & George, L. K. (1993). Psychiatric disorders in adult children of alcoholics: data from the epidemiological catchment area project. *American Journal of Psychiatry*, *150*, 793–800.

McFadyen, A., Woolley, H., Wheatcroft, R. & Stein, A. (1999). The influence of maternal eating disorder on children. *Clinical Care: National Association of Primary Care*, 320–4.

McKay, D. & Pollard, J. (1996). Community support networks in education and care settings. In *Parental Psychiatric Disorder. Distressed Parents and their Families*, ed. M. Göpfert, J. Webster & M. V. Seeman. Cambridge: Cambridge University Press.

Mednick, B. (1973). Breakdown in high risk subjects: familial and early environmental factors. *Journal of Abnormal Psychology*, *82*, 469–75.

Merikangas, K. R., Dierker, L. C. & Szatmari, P. (1998*a*). Psychopathology among offspring of parents with substance abuse and/or anxiety disorders: a high risk study. *Journal of Child Psychology and Psychiatry*, *39*, 711–20.

Merikangas, K. R., Swendsen, J. D., Preisig, M. A. & Chazan, R. Z. (1998*b*). Psychopathology and temperament in parents and offspring: results of a family study. *Journal of Affective Disorders*, *51*, 63–74.

Moss, H. B., Mezzich, A., Yao, J. K., Gavaler, J. & Martin, C. S. (1995). Aggressivity among sons of substance abusing fathers: association with psychiatric disorder in the father and son, paternal personality, pubertal development and socio-economic status. *American Journal of Drug and Alcohol Abuse*, *21*, 195–208.

Murphy, M. J., Jellinek, M., Quinn, D., Smith, G., Poitrast, F. G. & Goshko, M. (1991). Substance abuse and serious child mistreatment: prevalence, risk and outcome in a court sample. *Child Abuse and Neglect*, *15*, 197–211.

Murray, L. (1992). The impact of postnatal depression on infant development. *Journal of Child Psychology and Psychiatry*, *33*, 543–61.

Murray, L., Sinclair, D., Cooper, P., Ducournau, P., Turner, P. & Stein, A. (1999). The socio-emotional development of 5-year old children of postnatally depressed mothers. *Journal of Child Psychology and Psychiatry*, *40*, 1259–71.

Neziroglu, F., Anenome, R. & Yaryura-Tobias, J. A. (1992). Onset of obsessive- compulsive disorder in pregnancy. *American Journal of Psychiatry*, *149*, 947–50.

Norton, K. & Dolan, B. (1996). Personality disorder and parenting. In *Parental Psychiatric Disorder: Distressed Parents and their Families*, ed. M. Göpfert, J. Webster & M. V. Seeman, pp. 219–232. Cambridge: Cambridge University Press.

Nunes, E. V., Weissman, M. M., Goldstein, R. B. et al. (1998). Psychopathology in children of parents with opiate dependence and/or major depression. *Journal of the American Academy of Child and Adolescent Psychiatry*, *37*, 1142–51.

Oates, M. (1997). Patients as parents: the risk to children. *British Journal of Psychiatry*, *170* (Suppl. 32), 22–7.

Parnas, J., Schulsinger, F., Schulsinger, H., Mednick, S. A. & Teasdale, T. W. (1982). Behavioural precursors of schizophrenia. A prospective study. *Archives of General Psychiatry*, *39*, 658–64.

Patterson, G. R. (1982). *Coercive Family Process*. Eugene, OR: Castalia.

Pollock, V. E., Briere, J., Schneider, L., Knop, J., Mednisk, S. A. & Goodwin, D. A. (1990). Childhood antecedents of antisocial behaviour: parental alcoholism and physical abusiveness. *American Journal of Psychiatry*, *147*, 1290–3.

Poole, R. (1996). General adult psychiatrists and their patients' children. In *Parental Psychiatric Disorder: Distressed Parents and their Families*, ed. M. Göpfert, J. Webster & M. V. Seeman, pp. 3–6. Cambridge: Cambridge University Press.

Price, R. A., Kidd, K. K. & Weissman, M. M. (1987). Early onset (under age 30 years) and panic disorder as markers for etiologic homogeneity in major depression. *Archives of General Psychiatry*, *44*, 434–40.

Puckering, C. (1989). Maternal depression. *Journal of Child Psychology and Psychiatry*, *30*, 807–17.

Puig-Antich, J., Goetz, D., Davies, M. et al. (1989). A controlled family history study of prepubertal major depressive disorder. *Archives of General Psychiatry*, *46*, 406–18.

Quinton, D. & Rutter, M. (1984). Parenting behaviour of mothers raised in care. In *Longitudinal Studies in Child Psychology and Psychiatry: Practical Lessons from Research Experience*, ed. A. R. Nicol. Chichester: John Wiley & Sons.

Reder, P. & Duncan, S. (1999). *Lost Innocents: A Follow-up Study of Fatal Child Abuse*. London: Routledge.

Reder, P., McClure, M. & Jolley, A. (2000). *Family Matters: Interfaces between Child and Adult Mental Health*. London: Routledge.

Rende, R., Warner, V., Wickramaratne, P. & Weissman, M. M. (1999). *Psychological Medicine*, *29*, 1291–8.

Rice, F., Harold, G. & Thapar, A. (2002). The genetic aetiology of childhood depression: a review. *Journal of Child Psychology and Psychiatry*, *43*, 65–79.

Richman, N., Stevenson, J. & Graham, P. J. (1982). *Preschool to School: A Behavioural Study*. London: Academic Press.

Rodnick, E. H. & Goldstein, M. J. (1974). Premorbid adjustment and the recovery of mothering function in acute schizophrenic women. *Journal of Abnormal Psychology*, *83*, 623–8.

Royal College of Psychiatrists (2002a). *Domestic Violence*. Council Report CR 102. London: Royal College of Psychiatrists.

Royal College of Psychiatrists (2002*b*). Patients as parents. Council Report CR 105. London: Royal College of Psychiatrists.

Rutter, M. (1972). *Maternal Deprivation Reassessed*. Baltimore, MD: Penguin Books.

Rutter, M. (1979). *Changing Youth in a Changing Society: Patterns of Adolescent Development and Disorder*. London: Nuffield Provincial Hospitals Trust.

Rutter, M. (1981). The city and the child. *American Journal of Orthopsychiatry*, *51*, 610–25.

Rutter, M. (1982). Epidemiological-longitudinal approaches to the study of development. In *The Concept of Development*, ed. W. A. Collins, pp. 105–44. Minnesota Symposia on Child Psychology, Vol. 15. Hillsdale, NJ: Lawrence Erlbaum Associates.

Rutter, M. (1990). Psychosocial resilience and protective mechanisms. In *Risk and Protective Factors in the Development of Psychopathology*, ed. J. E. Rolf & A. S. Masten, pp. 181–214. New York: Cambridge University Press.

Rutter, M. & Quinton, D. (1984). Parental psychiatric disorder: effects on children. *Psychological Medicine*, *14*, 853–80.

Rutter, M., Macdonald, H., Le Couteur, A., Harrington, R., Bolton, P. & Bailey, A. (1990). Genetic factors in child psychiatric disorders – II. Empirical findings. *Journal of Child Psychology and Psychiatry*, *31*, 39–83.

Schreier, H. A. & Libow, J. A. (1993). *Hurting for Love: Munchausen-by-proxy Syndrome*. New York: Guilford.

Seeman, M. V. (1996). The mother with schizophrenia. In *Parental Psychiatric Disorder: Distressed Parents and their Families*, ed. M. Göpfert, J. Webster & M. V. Seeman, pp. 190–200. Cambridge: Cambridge University Press.

Sheppard, M. (1997). Double jeopardy: the link between child abuse and maternal depression in child and family social work. *Child and Family Social Work*, *2*, 91–107.

Simonoff, E., Pickles, A., Meyer, J. M. et al. (1997). The Virginia Twin Study of Adolescent Behavioural Development. *Archives of General Psychiatry*, *54*, 801–8.

Stein, A., Murray, L., Cooper, P. & Fairburn, C. G. (1996). Infant growth in the context of maternal eating disorders and maternal depression: a comparative study. *Psychological Medicine*, *26*, 569–74.

Stewart, D. & Gangbar, R. (1984). Psychiatric assessment of competency to care for a newborn. *Canadian Journal of Psychiatry*, *29*, 583–69.

Stewart, D. E., Raskin, J., Garfinkel, P. E., MacDonald, O. L. & Robinson, G. E. (1987). Anorexia nervosa, bulimia and pregnancy. *American Journal of Obstetrics and Gynaecology*, *157*, 1194–8.

Strober, M., Morell, W., Burroughs, J., Lampert, C., Danforth, H. & Freeman, R. (1988). A family study of bipolar I disorder in adolescence: early onset of symptoms linked to increased familial loading and lithium resistance. *Journal of Affective Disorders*, *15*, 255–68.

Taylor, C. G., Norman, J., Murphy, M. et al. (1991). Diagnosed intellectual and emotional impairment among parents who seriously mistreat their children: prevalence, type and outcome in a court sample. *Child Abuse and Neglect*, *15*, 389–401.

Taylor, E. (1991). Developmental neuropsychiatry. *Journal of Child Psychology and Psychiatry*, *32*, 1–48.

Thomas A. & Chess S. (1982). Temperament and follow-up to adulthood. In *Temperamental Differences in Infants and Young Children*, ed. R. Porter & G. M. Collins, pp. 168–72. London: Pitman.

Thomsen, P. H. (1995). Obsessive-compulsive disorder in children and adolescents: a study of parental psychopathology and precipitating events in 20 consecutive Danish cases. *Psychopathology, 28,* 161–7.

Tienari, P., Wynne, L. C., Moring, J. et al. (1994). The Finnish adoptive family study of schizophrenia: implications for family research. *British Journal of Psychiatry, 164* (Suppl. 23), 20–6.

Tsiantis, J., Kokkevi, A. & Agathonos-Marouli, E. (1981). Parents of abused children in Greece: psychiatric and psychological characteristics. *Child Abuse and Neglect, 5,* 281–5.

US Advisory Board on Child Abuse and Neglect (1995). *A Nation's Shame: Fatal Child Abuse and Neglect in the United States.* Washington: Department of Health and Human Services.

Von Knorring, A. (1991). Children of alcoholics. *Journal of Child Psychology and Psychiatry, 32,* 411–21.

Warner, V., Mufson, L. & Weissman, M. M. (1995). Offspring at high and low risk for depression and anxiety: mechanisms of psychiatric disorder. *Journal of the American Academy of Child and Adolescent Psychiatry, 34,* 786–97.

Watt, N., Anthony, E. J., Wynne, L. C. & Rolf, E. (ed.) (1984). *Children at Risk for Schizophrenia: A Longitudinal Perspective.* Cambridge: Cambridge University Press.

Webster, J. & Huxley, P. (1996). Some social work dilemmas and solutions. In *Parental Psychiatric Disorder: Distressed Parents and their Families,* ed. M. Göpfert, J. Webster & M. V. Seeman, pp. 325–334. Cambridge: Cambridge University Press.

Weissman, M. M. & Paykel, E. S. (1974). *The Depressed Woman.* Chicago: University of Chicago Press.

Weissman, M. M., McAvay, G., Goldstein, R. B., Nunes, E. V. et al. (1999*a*). Risk/protective factors among addicted mothers' offspring: a replication study. *American Journal of Drug and Alcohol Abuse, 25,* 661–79.

Weissman, M. M., Warner, V., Wickramaratne, P. J. & Kandel, D. B. (1999*b*). Maternal smoking during pregnancy and psychopathology in offspring followed to adult. *Journal of the American Academy of Child and Adolescent Psychiatry, 38,* 892–9.

Whitman, B. Y., Graves, B. & Accardo, P. J. (1987). The mentally retarded patient in the community: identification method and needs assessment survey. *American Journal of Mental Deficiency, 91,* 636–8.

Wilczynski, A. (1994). The incidence of child homicide: how accurate are the official statistics? *Journal of Clinical Forensic Medicine, 1,* 61–6.

Wilczynski, A. (1995). Risk factors for parental child homicide: results of an English study. *Current Issues in Criminal Justice, 7,* 241–53.

Wilczynski, A. (1997). *Child Homicide.* London: Greenwich Medical Media.

Woodside, D. & Shekter-Wolfson, L. (1990). Parenting by patients with anorexia nervosa and bulimia nervosa. *International Journal of Eating Disorders, 9,* 303–9.

Zeitlin, H. (1986). *The Natural History of Disorder in Childhood.* Institute of Psychiatry/Maudsley Monograph No. 29. Oxford: Oxford University Press.

4

Parental psychiatric disorder and the attachment relationship

Jonathan Hill

Royal Liverpool Children's Hospital, Liverpool, UK

Introduction

In contrast to the attachment of children to their parents and other important adults, the attachment of parents to their children has received little attention. Indeed it is not clear that the term 'attachment' should be used in the same way when referring to parents. However, consideration of the attachment of children to parents will lead to some indicators of the parental contribution to the attachment relationship, and to ways in which this might be threatened by parental mental illness, and what might be protective processes in the face of such threats.

Attachment – background

Bowlby's attachment theory (Bowlby, 1969) proposed that the child's early relationships with parents are internalized as 'working models' for later relationships. These early attachment relationships are characterized by attachment (proximity seeking) behaviour by the infant when there is a perceived threat or stressor such as the presence of a stranger, unfamiliar circumstances, tiredness or illness; and exploration from the 'secure base' of the parent, in general when the level of perceived threat is low. Although children's parents and other important caregivers are often referred to as attachment figures, it should be borne in mind that many other kinds of interaction take place between parents and children. These include ensuring safety and providing structure and discipline, and participating in joint activities such as play, games or conversation about each others' lives. This means that parent–child relationships, and indeed all family relationships, entail not only responding to each others' expressions of attachment needs, but also managing the dynamic equilibrium between attachment and other processes (Hill *et al.*, 2003).

The measurement of the quality of early attachment relationships was established principally through the work of Mary Ainsworth (Ainsworth *et al.*, 1978), who developed the Strange Situation Test, in which infants experience separation from, and reunion with, a parent. Typically, 'secure' infants explore when they are not threatened, they are clearly affected by separation, and seek effectively and confidently for comfort on reunion. 'Insecure avoidant' infants do not acknowledge the separation and ignore their parent on reunion. 'Insecure ambivalent' infants are usually distressed on separation but their reunions are fussy, angry, prolonged and unsatisfying. These two insecure groupings are common in the general population (approximately 40%), but by contrast a third 'disorganized' group is present in only around 10%. Disorganization is however found quite commonly among infants from families with histories of child maltreatment or parental psychiatric disorder (Lyons-Ruth & Jacobvitz, 1999; Main & Hesse, 1990). These infants show a wide range of behaviours on separation and reunion that do not cohere into one particular pattern. For example the infant approaches the parent then walks past her, or brings one part of the body close whilst also turning away. Often the infant seems to be frightened or dazed.

There has been rather inconsistent support for Bowlby's theory that early attachment relationships become internalized and provide the basis for later relationships. Attachment assessments repeated over infancy and young childhood show only modest stability (Vondra *et al.*, 2001), and the few studies that have assessed the continuity of attachment status from infancy to adult life have not found the predicted associations (Weinfeld *et al.*, 2000). On the other hand, many studies have shown continuities from security of attachment in infancy to a range of aspects of child functioning up to around 10 years of age (Sroufe *et al.*, 1990), and intergenerational links between parental and infant attachments (Fonagy *et al.*, 1991). Reformulations of attachment theory are likely to seek to explain development over shorter periods of time, making more explicit reference to the joint role of attachment and other processes, and viewing attachment status as one of a number of sources of vulnerability or resilience.

Attachment — the parent's contribution

Clearly attachment refers both to the individual child and to the relationship. Further consideration of the relationship will lead us to the parent's attachment to the child. Perhaps the most striking aspect of the child's attachment is its adhesiveness. It seems that children are predisposed to hold on to relationships with particular adults, and to do this even in the face of considerable adversity. In turn, most parents will be aware of the very strong feelings of commitment aroused by their children, and this appears often to be the case even where parents are also openly hostile or even abusive towards their children. The concept of commitment has not had a place in the analysis of parenting, however it summarizes the way in which parents give priority to, and generally refuse to give up on, their children. It probably remains present throughout life, however it is subject to developmental change, lessening in intensity as the child grows. Commitment is also, at least in the first years, accompanied by a preoccupation with the child. This was characterized by Winnicott (1956) as 'primary maternal preoccupation', and although there is no reason to suppose it is exclusively a function of being the mother, the phrase summarizes effectively its intensity. The behaviours, the needs, the moods, the intentions and the whereabouts of the infant fill the mind of the mother, and she strives to respond appropriately.

It is likely that the quality of the attachment relationship over years is based at least in part on the participants' previous experiences of parent–child interactions, and therefore refers also to an expectation of the way things will continue to be. Even the young infant appears to have a theory about his parent's behaviour, which in time will become a theory about the parent as a person (Stern, 1985). This is likely to be facilitated where parental behaviours, and reasons for those behaviours have significant consistency over time, and these are more likely to be present where the parent's sense of self also has continuity over time. The developmental sequence in the mind of the child might start in the first weeks in the recognition of consistency, warmth and pleasure in the parent's behaviours, going on to an experience of a reliable sensitive person at around 1 year, and later to an awareness at 3 or 4 years of a person with his own wishes and emotions (Stern, 1985). From the perspective of the parent this implies an experience of the continuity of the self as a person, of the self as parent, and an awareness of the child's experience of the parent over time. Memory is likely to be important to the process. The child's experience of the continuity of the parent is at the same time also an experience of the way events are remembered and their importance understood by the parent. For example, if a child has a frightening experience, the specific memory of the child being frightened has to be integrated by a parent into the relationship, and for the child, the continuity of their particular relationship with that parent is evidenced in the fact that the parent takes account of it over time.

Being an attachment figure entails judgement of intent and meaning in interactions. In particular it requires an ability to recognize when a child has attachment needs, and to respond in relation to them. This may not be straightforward. A child's crying may indicate frustration at not having his or her own way, in which case there is a need to respond in a disciplinary mode, or it may be about fear or worry, in which case understanding and comfort are appropriate (Hill *et al.*, 2003). With older children the parent may have to discriminate between a child's need for comfort, and for a shared exploration of an issue. For example, a child comes home from school and tells a parent that some children are being bullied. He or she may then talk about reasons for bullying and what should be done about it, without reference to the attachment needs of the child. The parent may correctly make the judgement that this conversation does not refer to the child's anxieties about bullying. Equally it may then become apparent that the child is also being bullied, and may need the parent to respond to his or her attachment needs. Thus in all interactions a parent has to generate his or her own hypotheses and expectations regarding the state of mind of the child, whilst remaining sensitive to the actual cues of the infant or child. By analogy with perceptual processes in general there is hypothesis generation of the form 'perhaps my child feels sad or thinks I'm being unfair', and then there is testing of the form 'does his behaviour fit my theory?'. In practice this is worked out through actions between parents and young children. For instance, a 1-year-old momentarily gets lost in the supermarket and cries, the parent rushes to pick him up and cuddle him saying 'It's alright, I'm here' with rhythmic soothing tones, and the child quietens. The parent has identified the key issue for the child, acted upon it, and then has received confirmation of the correctness of his assumption. This requires a fluidity of mental life in the parent so that he or she can generate expectations of sufficient variety, and thus identify the central concerns of the child in relation to context.

The parent's judgement as to the child's needs has implications for action. Two rather different kinds of response can be identified (Hill *et al.*, 2003). In some instances, such as a young child crying, there is a need for the parent to take action that deals with the problem. The nature of the action depends on the judgement as to whether the issue concerns attachment, discipline or safety. In each case the task of the parent is to provide a solution. In other instances the requirements are quite different. Where a child wants to play, or ask questions, or to talk about an issue such as bullying, the role of the parent is to be a partner in joint exploration. There is no implication of a need for the parent to take charge and provide a solution. Within the overall hierarchical relationship of a child with a parent, there can be a more equal, symmetrical, exchange. Indeed, under these circumstances the parent who attempts to solve the issue for the child may inhibit his or her capacity for problem solving. Thus the task of parents is to manage a dynamic equilibrium between the provision of clear, hierarchically organized actions to anticipate and solve problems, and interested, symmetrical responses that promote exploration.

Finally, differences in parent–child attachment also reflect differences in affect regulation. The avoidant infant appears to keep the affective intensity of exchanges to a minimum whilst the ambivalent child is intensely emotional. We are referring here both to the intensity of affect and its variability in relation to attachment-related events such as illness, separation or loss. The extent of association between parental and child attachment status suggests that often the child may be matching his parents' style of affective regulation.

It seems then that the attachment of the parent to the child may be characterized by commitment and preoccupation, continuity of the self as person and parent, awareness of the child's mental life and its relationship to experience, the ability to take appropriate action at the right time and affect regulation.

Mental illness, parenting and attachment

In considering the relationship of psychiatric disturbance, parenting and attachment we need to take account of the context of the parental disorder. First, the factors that have contributed to the risk of parental psychiatric disorder may also directly impinge on the parent–child relationship, and hence on attachment processes. Second, the parental psychiatric disorder together with associated risks may undermine aspects of parent–child attachment. Third, the disorder itself, independently of other factors, may adversely affect attachment. Finally, and crucially, the parent's capacity to preserve the sensitive and effective responses outlined in the previous section may be protective in the face of their psychiatric disorder.

The risks for psychiatric disorder also affect the parent–child relationship

There is considerable evidence that vulnerability to psychiatric disorder, and especially depression, in women, is associated with pathways from childhood to adult life that lead to increased adversities and lack of support (see Puckering, Chapter 12). Children with behaviour problems in childhood have, as adults, an increased rate of severely negative life events of the type that have been shown to be associated with onset of psychiatric disorder (Champion *et al.*, 1995). Girls with behaviour problems and those who have been in care are more likely to have an early unplanned pregnancy, to have cohabiting relationships with men with psychosocial problems, and to have unstable adult relationships with discord and partner violence (Moffitt & Caspi, 1998; Quinton *et al.*, 1993). All of these are associated with an increased risk for depression (Harris *et al.*, 1990; Hill *et al.*, 2001). They are also likely to impact directly on parenting. Marital discord is likely to create dysregulation of affect in the parent–child relationship (Cummings & Davies, 2002), and is associated with critical parenting and low emotional responsivity to children (Webster-Stratton & Hammond, 1999).

A further threat may arise from longstanding attachment problems. Recent studies have provided support for the role of unresolved loss or trauma as a risk for adult psychiatric disorder, especially personality disorder (Fonagy *et al.*, 1996; Patrick *et al.*, 1994), *and* as a threat to the parent–child attachment relationship (Lyons-Ruth & Jacobvitz, 1999). Main & Hesse (1990) proposed that parental unresolved loss or trauma is likely to be associated with frightened or frightening behaviour towards the infant, which in turn contributes to disorganized attachment. These parental behaviours are expected to activate the child's attachment system but without the prospect of relief, because the attachment figure is also the source of the alarm. There has been some, although not entirely consistent, evidence in support of this proposal (Lyons-Ruth & Jacobvitz, 1999). It may not only be frightened or frightening behaviours that contribute to disorganization. Lyons-Ruth and colleagues have also identified parental misattunement to the specific content of an infant's attachment-related communications, and the display of competing caregiving strategies as contributing to risk of disorganized attachment (Lyons-Ruth *et al.*, 1999). These findings support the role of difficulties in identifying accurately whether a child has attachment needs, and in responding to those needs with clear hierarchically organized protection or comfort, in undermining the attachment relationship.

Reference was made earlier to the role of memory in building the relationship between parent and child. It may be that this could be disrupted by factors that predispose parents to psychiatric disorder. A very large body of evidence links child sexual abuse to adult psychiatric disorders, notably adult depression (Bifulco *et al.*, 1991; Hill *et al.*, 2001). The nature of this association has not been established, however, one promising line of enquiry concerns the organization of personal memories Individuals who have suffered episodes of depression have greater difficulties retrieving specific autobiographical memories than controls and are more likely to provide general memories (Brittlebank *et al.*, 1993). It may be that suppression of specific memories arises in childhood as a way of attempting to control memories of abuse and their associated painful emotions (Kuyken & Brewin 1995; Williams 1996). It is thought that a limited capacity to update general memories with specifics, may make it harder for individuals to modify dysfunctional attitudes, and this may render them vulnerable to depression. From the perspective of the child's experience of a parent, failure to remember specifics of that relationship may reduce the child's sense of being kept in mind, and of the continuity of that relationship.

Much of the attachment research has focused on the relationship between episodic and semantic memories (Crittenden, 1992). Semantic memory comprises an overarching integrative framework in which many instances are included. In it memory and personal meaning are fused. Episodic memories are specific instances that linger in the mind. The concept of secure attachment in adult life supposes an integration of semantic and episodic memory and the adult attachment interview is designed to probe the extent of that integration. In the insecure, and especially the 'unresolved with respect to loss or trauma' attachment representation, specific memories have not been integrated and are therefore relatively uncontrollable and intrusive. Thus the adult's own mind is likely to be unpredictable, and so might be her parent. Her experience of herself as having continuity over time may be undermined, and she may be vulnerable to overwhelming and uncontrollable affective states or urges such as seen in episodic disorders.

The combination of pre-existing risks and the disorder affect the parent–child relationship

In the previous section we considered ways in which pre-existing factors may limit a parent's capacity to judge and reflect on the needs of the child, to provide a setting for effective affect regulation, to create a sense of continuity in the relationship. Depressed mood may further reduce these capabilities. Murray (1992) showed a very specific effect of depression on mothers' abilities to focus on the minds of their babies. She found that mother–infant interactions are different among women who had a recurrence of depression following childbirth and those for whom postnatal depression was their first episode. The second group were less likely to talk in an infant-centred way and to ascribe intentions to their 8-week-old infants. These mothers appeared to focus on certain aspects of the behaviour of their child, notably their demands, without a sense of the feelings and intentions and mental life of the infant. Here the depression may well have been a consequence of very specific thoughts and feelings about becoming a mother, such as feelings of inadequacy or helplessness, and the combination of the depression and these ways of thinking and feeling may then have led to an attachment relationship in which the mother's awareness of the emotional life of the child and her own emotional range were limited. In this study two interventions were compared, one which focused on problem solving and the other on the mother–infant relationship. They were found to be equally effective in improving depressive symptoms, however, the relationship-orientated therapy was associated with a greater likelihood of infant security of attachment at 1 year.

Psychiatric disorder alone may affect the parent–child relationship

In considering the impact of psychiatric disorder on parental functioning, it is important to bear in mind that the extent of disruption may not be simply a function of the severity of symptoms. In reviewing the long-term functioning of patients with psychotic disorders, Strauss (1991) contrasted those patients whose psychotic symptoms remitted but whose social and interpersonal functioning remained poor, and others with persistent delusions who otherwise lived effective and fulfilled lives. Similarly, a parent with psychotic symptoms may preserve the parental capacities that we reviewed earlier, and remission of symptoms can not be assumed to be associated with effective parenting.

There will nevertheless be those cases where it is clear that most of what we have described as the parent's contribution to the attachment relationship is disorganized as a consequence of the symptoms of mental illness. For instance, where a parent's mind is filled with delusions and his/her interpretation of events is dominated by such abnormal beliefs, the judgement of the intent and meaning of a child's actions and the ability to respond effectively may be severely limited.

A cardinal feature of schizophrenia is the sufferer's difficulty in interacting appropriately within the social milieu (Doody *et al.*, 1998). Possible causes of these difficulties include problems with understanding context and in judging the intentions of others. Gray *et al.* (1991) have argued that schizophrenic patients have difficulties processing information about context and in particular do not make use of previous experiences to determine what is familiar and what is novel. It is hypothesized that they therefore do not screen out irrelevant aspects of situations and have difficulty focusing on the most important issues. Frith and colleagues have shown that individuals with schizophrenia do poorly on tests of their ability to understand other people's intentions (Doody *et al.*, 1998). As we have seen, it is probable that a central contribution to a secure attachment relationship is a parent's ability to focus on what matters to the child especially when he or she is stressed. Distinguishing between emotionally charged situations that concern attachment issues and therefore call for comfort, and those that relate to opposition or annoyance and call for firm handling, may be more difficult for the parent who has limitations in their ability to judge context or understand another's intentions. Limitations in understanding others' intentions and mental states might also lead to the kind of misattunement to an infant's attachment-related communications described by Lyons-Ruth *et al.* (1999). Frith has also proposed that schizophrenia is associated with a failure of self-monitoring (Johns *et al.*, 2001). This is thought to lead to mistakes as to the origins of speech and actions. Then inner speech may be experienced as coming from outside the head, and a person's own actions may be interpreted as controlled externally. We do not know how such difficulties in self-monitoring may affect the parent–child relationship. However, it is possible that when a parent attributes control of actions to others, that could include the child, and lead to the kind of frightened behaviours observed in the parents of disorganized infants.

Similarly, affect regulation in relation to the needs of the child may be impaired. Crucially in the attachment relationship, affect is related to circumstances and has variability. The attachment is adversely affected where a parent's affective responses are not closely linked to those of the child, or where a parent's mood is dominated by one particular affect, for example depression.

Factors that might be associated with preservation of secure attachment in the face of parental psychiatric disorder

Hall (1996) (see Hall, Chapter 3) and Gorrel Barnes (1996) discuss general protective factors for children in the face of adversity (see Seeman & Göpfert, Chapter 2). Here we are concerned specifically with the ways in which interruptions to the processes reviewed earlier might be limited. In some instances a parent may be able to preserve key parental functions in the face of substantial disruption of their thoughts, emotions and behaviours. The examples quoted by Strauss underline the way in which the intensity of the psychotic symptoms will not necessarily provide the evidence regarding disruption of personal and interpersonal functioning.

Where the parent has difficulty in preserving responsiveness and appropriate actions in relation to a child's attachment needs the child's understanding and interpretation of the parent's behaviour is likely to be crucial. It may be that a psychotic or severe depressive episode is understood by the child as an illness, and therefore not really part of the relationship. Conversely, it may be experienced by the child as part of the identity of the parent, and hence pose a challenge to the continuity of a child's experience of the parent and their relationship. Either way the child has to make sense of very dramatic changes in the mental state of the parent. This means that the quality of the relationship between parent and child outside of the episodes of disturbance is likely to be crucial. The extent to which the attachment relationship is disrupted may be related to the parent's understanding, and particularly his or her reflective capacity in relation to attachment processes when well, and likewise the child's understanding and reflective capacity. Thus the task for the parent becomes one of considering not only accurate reflection on, and action in relation to the child's attachment needs at the time, but also thinking back to a period of disturbance. For example, during a period of disturbance the parent may have frightened, or appeared to have been frightened by, their child. Especially in relation to infants and young children, this might be expected to contribute to disorganized attachment or its equivalents. However a parent reflecting back on such behaviour, and its potential impact on the child, may be able to respond to the child's subsequent attachment needs in relation to the experience. For example, following an acute psychiatric episode, the parent who is aware of the potential impact on the child's attachment security, may have a heightened preparedness to interpret oppositional behaviours as needing a comforting response, or may say something like 'Maybe you got frightened when mummy wasn't very well'. This might be expected to help a child to integrate an experience of a parent as an unresponsive or threatening attachment figure, into the framework of a secure attachment representation. Many other factors in the child, including age and developmental capacities, and affect regulatory capabilities, are likely to make a difference. Other caregivers, such as the well parent, grandparents and other close relatives and family friends may be crucial not only to providing support, but also a framework of continuity and understanding. It may be that under these circumstances, the child is able to maintain an image of the attachment relationship with the ill parent, that bridges the periods of disruption.

Consideration of a brief case history will illustrate the issues. Mrs X was in her mid 30s and had a daughter Jenny, aged 9. The parents were divorced and Jenny had not had recent contact with her father. Mrs X had had symptoms of schizophrenia for 4 years when she was referred to a psychiatrist with a clinical interest in children.

Mrs X and her daughter were seen together. The psychiatrist noted that Mrs X was emotionally flat and unresponsive. Jenny made it absolutely clear that she did not want to live with her mother. The psychiatrist commented on Mrs X's apparent lack of concern about the potential loss of her daughter. Mrs X replied that she felt that she should be upset, and that she could not understand why she was not more upset about the fact that she had not been looking after her daughter better. Here it seemed Mrs X's illness limited her responsiveness to her daughter's attachment needs. She lacked a strong maternal preoccupation with her daughter, she had a limited affective range, and did not respond to the moment to moment cues from her daughter. Perhaps also she struggled to preserve a sense of herself as the mother of her child, and to maintain an awareness of the mental life of her daughter, and of her place in it. However she provided some structure to her daughter's life through the provision of basics such as regular meals and clean clothes.

Some months following the consultation Mr X resumed contact and Jenny went to live with him. Mrs X was sectioned and treated with depot medication. She became less symptomatic and more responsive to her daughter, and participated in joint parenting together with Mr X. Here it seemed that treatment had led to a restoration of some preoccupation and responsiveness to the attachment needs of her daughter. This phase was however relatively shortlived, as Mrs X then defaulted on her medication and became acutely psychotic. The assessment focused both on the extent to which Mrs X understood the need to take regular medication in relation to her role as a parent, on her responsiveness to her daughter's attachment needs within and outside psychotic episodes, and whether when well she understood the potential impact of her illness on Jenny's sense of being understood and cared for by her mother. For example, did she have a sense of her importance and identity as her daughter's mother? Did she have a sense of the mental life of her daughter, and therefore an understanding of the implications for her daughter of the contrast between having an ill mother and a well mother? Did Mrs X at any time read her daughter's behaviours and moods accurately? It would be tempting to assume that because she did not keep to her medication she had deficits in at least a number of these areas. However, equally, the factors contributing to the default of medication for the breakdown might have been quite independent of the quality of the parent–child attachment relationship.

REFERENCES

Ainsworth, M., Blehar, M., Waters, E. & Wall, S. (1978). *Patterns of Attachment.* Hillsdale, NJ: Lawrence Erlbaum Associates.

Bifulco, A., Brown, G. W. & Adler, Z. (1991). Early sexual abuse and clinical depression in adult life. *British Journal of Psychiatry, 159,* 115–22.

Bowlby, J. (1969). *Attachment and Loss: Attachment.* New York: Basic Books.

Brittlebank, A. D., Scott, J., Williams, J. M. G. & Ferrier, I. N. (1993). Autobiographical memory in depression: state or trait marker? *British Journal of Psychiatry, 162,* 118–21.

Champion L. A., Goodall, G. & Rutter, M. (1995). Behaviour problems in childhood and stressors in early adult life. I. A 20 year follow-up of London school children. *Psychological Medicine, 25,* 231–46.

Crittenden, T. M. (1992). Quality of attachment in pre-school years. *Development and Psychopathology, 4,* 209–42.

Cummings, E. M. & Davies, P. T. (2002). Effects of marital conflict on children: recent advances and emerging themes in process-orientated research. *Journal of Child Psychology and Psychiatry, 43,* 31–64.

Doody, G. O., Gotz, M., Johnstone, E. C., Frith, C. D. & Owens, D. G. (1998). Theory of mind and psychoses. *Psychological Medicine, 28,* 397–405.

Fonagy, P., Steele, H. & Steele, M. (1991). Maternal representations of attachment during pregnancy predict the organisation of infant–mother attachment at age one. *Child Development, 62,* 891–905.

Fonagy, P. E., Leigh, T., Steele, M. et al. (1996). The relation of attachment status, psychiatric classification and response to psychotherapy. *Journal of Consulting and Clinical Psychology, 64,* 22–31.

Gorrel Barnes, G. (1996). The mentally ill parent and the family system. In *Parental Psychiatric Disorder: Distressed Parents and their Families,* ed. M. Göpfert, J. Webster & M. V. Seeman, pp. 42–59. Cambridge: Cambridge University Press.

Gray, V. A., Feldon, J., Rawlins, J. M. P., Hensley, D. R. & Smith, A. D. (1991). The neuropsychology of schizophrenia. *Behavioural and Brain Sciences, 14,* 1–84.

Hall, A. (1996). Parental psychiatric disorder and the developing child. In *Parental Psychiatric Disorder: Distressed Parents and their Families,* ed. M. Göpfert, J. Webster & M. V. Seeman, pp. 17–41. Cambridge: Cambridge University Press.

Harris, T., Brown, G. W. & Bifulco, A. (1990). Loss of parent in childhood and adult psychiatric disorder: a tentative overall model. *Development and Psychopathology, 2,* 311–27.

Hill, J., Pickles, A., Burnside, E. et al. (2001). Child sexual abuse, poor parental care and adult depression: evidence for different mechanisms. *British Journal of Psychiatry, 179,* 104–9.

Hill, J., Fonagy, P., Safier, E. & Sargent, J. (2003). The ecology of attachment in the family. *Family Process, 42,* 205–21.

Johns, L. C., Rossell, S., Frith, C. et al. (2001). Verbal self-monitoring and auditory verbal hallucinations in patients with schizophrenia. *Psychological Medicine, 31,* 705–15.

Kuyken, W. & Brewin, C. R. (1995). Autobiographical memory functioning in depression and reports of early abuse. *Journal of Abnormal Psychology, 104,* 585–91.

Lyons-Ruth, K. & Jacobvitz, D. (1999). Attachment disorganisation: unresolved loss, relational violence, and lapses in behavioural and attentional strategies. In *Handbook of Attachment: Theory, Research, and Clinical Application,* ed. J. Cassidy & P. R. Shaver. New York: Guilford Press.

Lyons-Ruth, K., Bronfman, E. & Parsons, E. (1999). Atypical attachment in infancy and early childhood among children at developmental risk. IV. Maternal frightened, frightening, or atypical behavior and disorganized infant attachment patterns. In *Atypical Patterns of Infant Attachment: Theory, Research and Current Directions*, ed. J. Vondra & D. Barnett, Vol. 64, pp. 67–96. Monographs of the Society for Research in Child Development.

Main, M. & Goldwyn, R. (1984). *Adult attachment scoring and classification system.* Unpublished manuscript, University of California at Berkley.

Main, M. & Hesse, E. (1990). Adult lack of resolution of attachment-related trauma related to infant disorganized/disorientated behaviour in the Ainsworth Strange Situation: linking parental states of mind to infant behaviour in a stressful situation. In *Attachment in the Pre-school Years: Theory, Research and Intervention*, ed. M. T. Greenberg, D. Cicchetti & M. Cummings pp. 339–426. Chicago: University of Chicago Press.

Moffitt, T. E. & Caspi, A. (1998). Annotation: implications of violence between intimate partners for child psychologists and psychiatrists. *Journal of Child Psychology and Psychiatry, 39,* 137–44.

Murray, L. (1992). The impact of post-natal depression on infant development. *Journal of Child Psychology and Psychiatry, 33,* 543–61.

Patrick, M., Hobson, R. T., Castle, D., Howard, R. & Maughan, B. (1994). Personality disorder and the mental representation of early social experience. *Development and Psychopathology, 6,* 375–88.

Quinton, D., Pickles, A., Maughan, B. & Rutter, M. (1993). Partners, peers, and pathways: assortative pairing and continuities in conduct disorder. *Development and Psychopathology, 5,* 763–83.

Sroufe, L. A., Egeland, B. & Kreutzer, T. (1990). The fate of early experience following developmental change: longitudinal approaches to individual adaptation in childhood. *Child Development, 61,* 1363–73.

Stern, D. (1985). *The Interpersonal World of the Infant.* New York: Basic Books.

Strauss, J. S. (1991). The person with delusions. *British Journal of Psychiatry, 159* (Suppl. 14), 57–61.

Vondra, J. I., Shaw, D. S., Swearingen, L., Cohen, M. & Owens, E. B. (2001). Attachment stability and emotional and behavioural regulation from infancy to pre-school age. *Development and Psychopathology, 13,* 13–34.

Webster-Stratton, C. & Hammond, M. (1999). Marital conflict management skills, parenting style, and early-onset conduct problems: processes and pathways. *Journal of Child Psychology and Psychiatry, 40,* 917–28.

Weinfeld, N. S., Sroufe, L. A. & Egeland, B. (2000). Attachment from infancy to early adulthood in a high risk sample: continuity, discontinuity, and their correlates. *Child Development, 71,* 695–702.

Williams, J. M. G. (1996). Autobiographical memory in depression. In *Remembering our Past: Studies in Autobiographical Memory*, ed. D. Rubin. Cambridge: Cambridge University Press.

Winnicott, D. (1956). Primary maternal preoccupation. In *Through Paediatrics to Psychoanalyses.* (Reprinted 1992.) Carnac Books.

5

The construction of parenting and its context

Michael Göpfert[1], Jeni Webster[2] and Julia Nelki[3]

[1]Webb House, Crewe, UK; [2]Warrington, UK; and [3]Oxton, Prenton, UK

Introduction

This chapter aims to clarify the term 'parenting' as a social role within a culturally determined social construction. It will provide tools for the formulation of parenting and for the understanding of the complex interface between psychiatric disorder and parenting in the context of mental health services and of family/community. This will establish the ground against which the gestalt of the professional task of performing a parenting assessment is considered (see Göpfert *et al.*, Chapter 7) and against which some of the effects of parental psychiatric disorder on children can be understood.

The chapter will use the role-relationship paradigm (Horowitz *et al.*, 1995; Muran, 2002; Nye, 1976; Nye & Berardo, 1981; Ryle & Kerr, 2002) as a framework for understanding parenting across the spectrum of care. The role-relationship model facilitates an understanding of both the internal/personal and the social aspects of the parenting role, their interface with one another and with the role of the helping professional. Early role experiences are internalized and form the backbone of personality development. This construct overlaps with the concept of internal working models that comes from attachment theory (see Adshead *et al.*, Chapter 15). Roles and role relationships are useful for understanding the interface between a social role, such as parenting, and the personality of the person enacting the role. Services are not currently designed to deal with such complexity and tend to provide a service that either addresses parenting problems or mental illness problems. They too often adhere rigidly to one or the other task and are systemically resistant to the integrative task of providing a service to mentally ill parents.

'Parenting' as a construct

Definition

The word 'parent' derives from Latin and describes a person who has or begets a child. Originally, it referred to the notion of biological parentage, though the more recent verb 'to parent' and the term 'parenting' now encompass the raising of children (The Shorter Oxford English Dictionary, 1986). Parenting is an interpersonal and social construct referring to the actions of one person within a two-person relationship. These actions are reciprocal in nature and determined by the participating individuals, but also by family and social norms.

The relative value of parents and children

Children nowadays appear to be valued more highly than in the past, partly through being in short supply because of declining birth rates, partly through shifts in child-rearing patterns (Rogoff *et al.*, 1991). Paradoxically, increasing numbers of children are currently growing up in relative poverty (Tomison & Wise, 1999). The two may be connected. There is evidence that the decline of birth rates is a social phenomenon associated with the increasing relative cost of children, changes in the role of women and also of improved health-care (Becker, 1991). There is some social value attached to being a parent and having the responsibility of looking after children. On the other hand, being a parent may interfere with self-realization values. Each person has to balance the value of being a parent against the value of self-enhancement (Kashiwagi & Nagahisa, 1999).

Social value norms for children are reflected in statute and legislation. There is growing consensus that parents have responsibilities whereas children have rights (e.g. the UK Children Act, 1989). This has not always been so and – despite the long-venerated icon of Madonna and child – most of the history of European culture has been dominated by the assumption that parents have rights. By implication, children have duties (Cicero 44 BC/1991). Cicero's views are still prevalent in our culture, and concur with much religious teaching and the law in many countries (see Brunt, Chapter 18). This also applies to other cultures outside Europe. This is illustrated in Fig. 5.1, showing a Chinese woodcut by Kuniyoshi where the daughter looks on while her mother breast-feeds her toothless mother-in-law, otherwise unable to feed herself. The traditional moral (no longer true in today's China): you have many children but only one mother-in-law.

This picture can be interpreted as an illustration of parentification, a concept that describes role reversal between parent and child, where the child takes on the role of parenting the parent and sacrificing her own dependency needs (see below). This is a normal expectation in most cultures when the child is grown up and the parent becomes frail. Here it involves grandmother, mother and child, with the clear expectation that the child step aside so that the needs of the grandmother can be met: parentification across three generations (totally unacceptable by most handbooks of child protection agencies in western industrialized countries today). It illustrates how many of the dominant expectations of parenting that inform our professional literature are culturally biased and culturally determined. The world

Figure 5.1   Woodcut by Kuniyoshi (1848) 'Story of To Fu-Jin and her mother-in-law Choson Fu-Jin from the 24 Chinese Paradigms of Filial Piety'.

of parenting by necessity is a world full of beliefs, assumptions and expectations within which children are raised and without which children cannot be raised (Byng-Hall, 1995; Stierlin, 1977) and which reflect cultural diversity (Bornstein, 1991; Bornstein *et al.*, 1998; Brazelton, 1991).

Parenting, mental disorder and its context – a role perspective

The role-relationship paradigm

Being a parent describes a role relationship. Human identity is largely expressed in role enactments and role relationships (Flavell, 1963; Horrocks & Jackson, 1972; Muran, 2002; Nye, 1976; Nye & Berardo, 1981; Touliatos *et al.*, 2001), one of several ways of conceptualizing who we are – i.e. we are what we do with others. Parenting is one such role identity, with its corresponding reciprocal role, the child role (the first social role in life). 'Child' is a term that implies a relationship with a carer and it, too, can be defined as a social role. Role enactments, or the behaviours that accompany and exemplify a specific interpersonal role, represent the internalization of that role. Children's play, for instance, reflects their internalized social roles, their relationship experiences (Oliviera, 1997). 'Parent vs. child' represents the first and most fundamental role enactment that contributes to the formation of human identity.

The understanding of this early role relationship and its formative impact on development elucidates the processes of projective identification and explains why parenting difficulties recreate themselves across generations (Caspi & Elder, 1988). It also reflects cultural difference and identity early on (Brazelton, 1991; Rogoff *et al.*, 1991). Moreover, these role-relationship patterns are re-enacted in helping relationships with health service professionals and can significantly influence the outcome of professional intervention (Norton & Smith, 1994).

Parenting as a role

A number of authors have attempted to define 'parent' or 'parenting' (Hoghughi & Speight, 1998; Reder & Duncan, 1999; Reder & Lucey, 1995). Similarly, courts have variously attempted to define parenting for the purposes of appropriate legal process with children and families (Jones, 2001) (see Brunt, Chapter 18). However, it may not be possible to provide an exact or universal definition, as this varies with culture, circumstance and, not least, the mind set of the person doing the defining. Understanding parenting as a role enactment provides a different perspective, namely one of actors and enactments, a paradigm borrowed from other domains of therapeutic thinking (Minuchin, 1974). The script is clear: children need to grow up and, in the interim, need to be looked after by a carer. This creates a reciprocal role relationship. Each actor in such a role relationship will attempt his or her own individual and unique interpretation of the script. The entire script can only be enacted with a wider cast, which includes not only the child and a parental character but also a network of other actors whose presence is necessary in order for children to grow up in reasonable mental health.

The role of parent can be seen as a composite of many different role enactments (by one and the same person) involving elements of commitment, hierarchy, and the capacity to accurately interpret the child's actions (Hill, 1996). The role may encompass policing and containment, teaching and learning, warmth and being valued, supporting and exploring, feeding and feeling needy. But role enactments of abuser–victim or controlling–helpless should not be part of the script.

Parent role and mental disorder

Becoming a psychiatric patient is also a role enactment, often the end point of a process of social exclusion (Reed, 1999; Scott & Starr, 1981). The patient role has relevance to health (Gunderman, 2000; Parsons, 1957, 1964, 1967, 1978; St John, 1999), mental health (Hunter & Maunder, 2001; Main, 1946/1989; Skogstad, 2001) and to the social construction of health and psychiatric services by their users (Bradshaw, personal communication). While the role of patient might be similar for psychiatric and medical patients in certain circumstances, it is also fundamentally different, especially with respect to stigma (Göpfert *et al.*, 1999) which is further magnified, at least in western society, when the mentally ill patient belongs to disadvantaged black or ethnic minorities (Fernando, 1988; Littlewood & Lipsedge, 1989; Torkington, 1991). Thus, the role of psychiatric patient, intimately linked to one's sense of identity (Flavell, 1963; Horrocks & Jackson, 1972), is one of relative dependency, regression and stigmatization. It is reciprocal to the professional role.

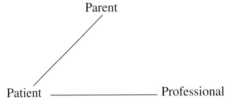

Figure 5.2   Role-relationship constellation arising when the patient is a parent.

The parent as patient and the helping relationship

Particular role-relationship constellations arise when the patient is a parent. These can be construed as a near-triangular relationship as shown in Fig. 5.2.

This incomplete triangle is in keeping with our evidence from a survey of mental health service users who were parents (Göpfert *et al.*, 1999). A recurring theme was the inability of psychiatric services to relate to them as parents (i.e. responsible in their parental role despite their dependency in the patient role).

The professional role is similar to that of parent and the child role to that of patient. Figure 5.3 helps to clarify a systemic dimension of the role relationship

Child–parent dyad	Patient–professional dyad
Parent	*Professional*
Responsible Caring Containing Dependable Knowledgeable	Responsible Caring Containing Dependable Expert
At times: Helpless Needy Inexperienced Dependent	Helpless Needy Does not know what is wrong Dependent
Child	*Patient*

Figure 5.3   The role-relationship between professionals and patients who are parents.

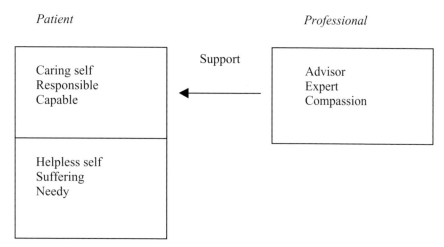

Figure 5.4   An alternative service model, in which the professional supports the self-caring capacity of the patient.

between professionals and patients who are parents: professionals need to be able to combine relating to their patients in a dependent role, as well as in the competent and responsible role of parent. This creates a complexity of relationship for which health services are not always equipped.

Alternative service models circumvent the dependent model of care provision by emphasizing that the responsibility for (self-)care ultimately lies with the patient (Fig. 5.4).

In Fig. 5.4, the parent/patient is metaphorically divided into a caring parental part, and a needy, suffering child part. In this model, the professional supports the self-caring capacity of the patient.

Professional role in relation to patient

The role difference between a child-focused and an adult-focused mental health worker appears subtle, yet is substantial. An understanding of that difference will add to an understanding of the 'split' between adult- and child-based services. In Fig. 5.4 a health professional empowers an adult client and helps her to help herself. When a child is the identified patient, a triangular, inherently more complex, pattern develops involving the child, the parent and the professional charged with helping the child (Fig. 5.5).

In children's services, the patient (child) and the person with ultimate responsibility for the child (parent) are two different people and this gives rise to relationship complexities unique to that situation.

Let us now add a further complication as is not uncommonly the case in child mental health services: If the parent has a mental health problem, that parent is

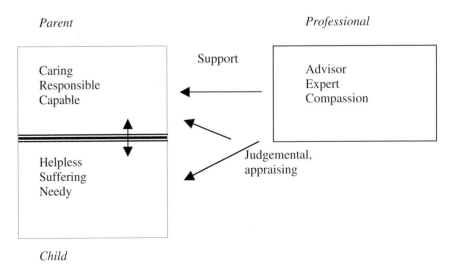

Figure 5.5   A triangular pattern which can develop when a child is the identified patient.

commonly not seen as competent to care for a child, her decision-making with respect to the child is perceived as potentially damaging and parental authority is not always supported by the professional. More generally, a potential for conflict between professionals and parents seems to be built into children's services (Pottick & Davis, 2001).

Parental role and mental illness

There is agreement that the major impact of parental psychiatric disorder on the children may derive not from illness per se (Hill, 1996; Rutter & Quinton 1984) (see Hall, Chapter 3) but from marital conflict (Rutter & Quinton, 1984) or from social and interactional deficits of the parent (Mufson *et al.*, 1994; Riordan *et al.*, 1999).

However, it is useful to attend to the specifics of the parental disorder because the role difficulties of a parent with a personality disorder may be very different from those of a parent with depression or schizophrenia (Pearlmutter, 1996; Reder *et al.*, 2000; Riordan *et al.*, 1999). Symptomatic behaviour and symptomatic behavioural deficits are important in understanding how to support someone with a particular condition, as well as in understanding how the condition may impact on parenting. For instance, paranoid ideation in a sample of mentally ill mothers was strongly associated with those mothers rating their children as having problems (Cunningham, 2001). Such a constellation can lead to vicious cycles of escalating relationship dysfunction where the child is seen by the mother as a problem, which reinforces her paranoid thinking, which in turn reinforces the child's problems, making the mother's paranoia into a self-fulfilling prophecy.

Hill (1996) (see Hill, Chapter 4) has described the parental contribution to the attachment system between parent and child, that is, the commitment, the hierarchical position and the capacity to accurately interpret the child's actions. This capacity to be mindful of the child enables appropriate parental responsiveness. Mental disorder can create preoccupations such as delusional or hallucinatory belief systems which interfere with the parental capacity for keeping the child foremost in mind.

However, there are also other, more complex issues that determine the parent–child relationship if the parent suffers from a mental illness. In families who are struggling with mental health issues, the task of looking after infants and children becomes very challenging. Communication between parents can be faulty, problem solving is impaired, goals are not agreed on, and roles may be unclear, in particular the parent role. Frequently enough, the results are a disorganized household that has detrimental effects on children. As the child grows older and looks to his parents for guidance, these parents are often not up to the task.

At the same time, and this is important to remember, the children of parents who suffer from specific psychiatric disorders may themselves have inherited characteristics of these same disorders. Sixty-one per cent of children whose parents suffer from a major depressive disorder will develop a psychiatric disorder during childhood or adolescence. Problems include general difficulties in functioning, signs of increased guilt, interpersonal difficulties and problems with attachment (Beardslee *et al.*, 1998). This can be put together with the finding that adopted-away children who are at genetic risk for antisocial behaviour are consistently more likely to receive negative parenting than children not at such risk. One would expect that the parenting task in such a situation could be additionally complex because of the genetic disposition of the child, which is also their biological parent's disposition (O'Connor *et al.*, 1998).

Parental role and personality disorder

It is important to understand the interface of parenting and personality disorder. Courts increasingly consider such a diagnosis in their custody proceedings (see Brunt, Chapter 18). Often, people with personality disorder received parental care which fell short of expected minimum standards (Norton & Dolan, 1996) and they may have also experienced abuse. These early experiences are then internalized and form the person's role repertoire. Independently from one another, Benjamin (1998) and Ryle (1998) have made detailed theoretical proposals about linking early experiences, type of personality disorder and patterns of relationship difficulties within an interpersonal framework.

The role-relationship pattern of parents with a personality disorder can make it difficult for professional and parent to form a therapeutic alliance. A possible role

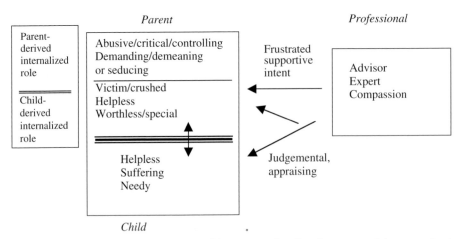

Figure 5.6   The role-relationship pattern of parents with a personality disorder can result in a perceived pattern of victimization and abuse between professional and parent.

pattern of victimization and abuse is shown in Fig. 5.6 in an attempt to illustrate this difficulty. The professional may be experienced as judgemental and critical by the parent because of an internalized victim role derived from childhood experience. Such a state of mind, in turn, may trigger abusive behaviour from the parent toward the professional. When such a parent is in a helpless state of mind, the only available source of personal power within their personal make-up may be that which is derived from the early experience of, and identification with, an abuser.

In this instance, the parent may experience any attempt at help as being controlling and abusive, and any attempt at understanding as being helpless and weak, worthy of contempt. There might not be any capacity in the parent to respond to well-meaning, supportive action unless that parent has a degree of awareness and some reflective capacity (see Asen & Schuff, Chapter 10).

The same person might experience a variety of states of mind reflecting other role patterns, each posing different issues for helping relationships with professionals. For instance, a parent with a narcissistic personality disorder may swing from feeling utterly contemptible of herself, to being totally contemptuous of everyone else, reflecting a childhood history of severe criticism/abuse and compensatory grandiose fantasies. A child's experience of such a parent might be similar to that of a manic-depressive parent. Each mood state represents a different pattern of being a parent and being a patient, which can be reflected in separate diagrammatic formulations.

Spouse/partner

Psychiatric patients sometimes engage in eccentric relationships that meet their own needs for companionship but may pose problems when children arrive. Sometimes people end up with partners who resemble the most undesirable qualities of their parent when they were a child. This may happen through some mechanism of assortative mating as proposed by Hafner (1986). It tends to involve two people initially resonating with each other through the shared experience of deprivation or trauma, but later resulting in problematic relationship patterns, a re-enactment of the early experience of deprivation. These maladaptive patterns are often triggered by the arrival of a child.

Marital conflict

Divorce is common in families with a mentally ill or disturbed parent and can bring social isolation and an increased risk of children going into care (Webster, 1990). There is some evidence, however (Quinton *et al.*, 1990), that serious personality problems in a parent have their most adverse effect on child development if the parent is living with a partner. This is probably related to the high levels of diagnosable disturbance that tend to be found in the spouses, and the cumulative effect it may have between the parents. Parental conflict, abuse or violence between partners, and the triangulation of the child into patterns of parental conflict are very damaging for children (Browne, 1994; Johnston & Campbell, 1993; Kelly, 1993; O'Leary & Jouriles, 1994; Royal College of Psychiatrists, 2002).

Parentification: the effects on the child of role reversal; becoming a young carer

Caring for a parent (termed 'young carer', see Aldridge & Becker, 1993) is the normal attempt of a child to deal with the parent's difficulty in coping. This can be an adaptive response, although it will have consequences for the child's psychological adjustment. Some children cope with these situations by developing task-oriented competencies which can be a strength in their lives (Arias & Pape, 1994; Bleuler, 1974; Breznitz, 1985; Galdstone, 1965; Lystad, 1975; Pound, 1996; Schreier & Libow, 1993; Steinhauer, 1991). Others cannot learn such competencies because their families are rigid in their role structures (Ryckoff *et al.*, 1991). Young carers need professional support and this may not be sufficiently recognized (see Billsborough, Chapter 1).

Parentification refers to a child feeling compelled to enact a parental role and to shoulder inappropriate responsibility (Byng-Hall, 2002; Earley & Cushway, 2002; Jurkovic, 1997; Mika *et al.*, 1987; Sessions, 1986; Valleau *et al.*, 1995). This may be because a parent is enacting a needy and dependent role or because a parent is incapable of parenting.

The effects of parentification on an older sibling who takes on the parental role can be profound. This is particularly so if younger siblings treat a parentified sibling like a parent (with the resentment that goes with the territory) (Jurkovic, 1997; see also Holley & Holley, 1998). In role terms, parentification is a case of role reversal.

Winnicott (1964) observed that the child of a depressed mother can only live *reactively*. Life is suspended here and now, in the hope that a real relationship with the parent will become possible in the future. Occasionally the child may achieve what is hoped for. For many children this never happens, turning the suspension of oneself into an internalized relationship pattern of caring for the parent. Most are left forever longing (sometimes desperately) for the parental care they never received.

Role of siblings

Sibling relationships are probably the longest-lasting relationship anyone has in life. In a family with a mentally ill parent, fragmentation may reinforce competition and conflict between siblings. On the other hand, siblings can compensate for parental shortcomings and act as a buffer against the negative effects of parental psychiatric disorder (with the attendant risk, for the older siblings, of parentification). The parent clearly has a mediating function in conflicts between siblings. When a parent can engage the older sibling as partner in the role of interpreting and managing the needs of the newly arrived baby, sibling relationships are more likely to be positive (Kendrick & Dunn, 1982) but the ability to do this may be lacking in mentally ill parents.

Sibling relationships can also be a risk factor in their own right (Garcia *et al.*, 2000). Conflict between siblings can become an interlocked system of self-reinforcing role enactments, fuelled by the experience of competition with peers in the school setting. Professionals do not always know how to help with such situations though good self-help materials are available (Faber & Mazlish, 1998). The significance of sibling factors is not always appropriately taken into account in family assessments yet there is a considerable body of evidence underlining its importance (Toman, 1988) as well as cultural variability of the sibling role (Rogoff *et al.*, 1991).

The role of extended family and community in relation to the task of parenting

There is reasonable evidence to suggest that children's outcomes depend on the quality of the rearing environment (Levy & Orlans, 1998; Werner & Smith, 1992). Similarly, the quality of family and social relationships predict most reliably the outcome of serious mental illness (Leff, 2001). Communities and the wider family can extend themselves to make up for difficulties a family may experience in bringing up children and looking after mentally ill parents. The role of grandparents is particularly important. Many grandparents play a role in looking after preschool grandchildren while the parents work (Richards & Light, 1990) as well as caring for grandchildren when the parent is unavailable (Smith & Drew, 2002). In a recent sample of 52 mothers who were inpatients in an acute psychiatric service, the overwhelming majority of children were looked after within the family while the mother was in hospital (Cunningham, 2001). Friends, neighbours and church members can also play a supportive role.

Like a family, a community can serve a number of functions. It constitutes the back-up when other systems fail; it serves as insurance, market place, social security service, mating pool and social control institution; it offers a communal place of worship and a shared identity. In terms of parenting, the community can (but may not) serve as substitute for the extended family. Of course, networks and communities can also be a source of stress and adversity (Brassard 1982, quoted after Jack, 2001; Gibbons, 1990; Smale *et al.*, 1994). It has even been postulated that the lack of reparative kinship or community relationships is linked to the aetiology of personality disorder (Corwin, 1996). Additionally, the responsibility of a parent and the role of 'parenting' can be very differently constructed between cultures and communities with differing emphasis on communal responsibilities and the responsibilities of a child's peer group (Rogoff *et al.*, 1991). The variability in developmental pathways of psychopathology according to cultural patterns is not well understood yet.

The social evolution of the past century has led to the warehousing of people in tenement blocks and matchbox housing estates, with an increasing loss of the differentiated and complementary social roles available in villages. The mobility of the labour market in industrialized societies has meant that the social cohesion derived from long-term relationships has disappeared in favour of the dominant values of self-fulfilment, autonomy and personal achievement (see also Leff, 2001). This leaves a significant loss of social role and community. State-run or voluntary support systems such as children's nurseries, play groups or after-school clubs, as well as designing mainstream services so that they are inclusive and empowering, make a significant difference in the lives of families (Ball, 1996, 1998; Donnison, 1998; Sergiovanni, 1994; Spencer, 1996). This social capital needs to be carefully nurtured and reinforced, sometimes in opposition to other economic forces (Cahn, 2000).

One key parental task is the protection of children. A community can contribute to the management and prevention of risk in many different ways: sharing the school run, facilitating children's activities in a safe way, looking out for each other's houses/flats (neighbourhood watch schemes), identifying intruders or strangers and challenging them. Communities sometimes have the capacity to contain and neutralize violence and deviance. Communities have cultures. Such cultures can be supportive, but they can also be potentially abusive, such as in a neighbourhood where dealing and taking of drugs is considered the norm.

Communities may have leaders who organize and facilitate, or conversely, stifle any positive development. For the mental health professional, community leaders are important people to work with (Boyd-Franklin & Bry, 2000).

Families hold an important bridging position between the developing child and the community. They form a dynamic relationship with the cultural environment (Comunian & Mosconi, 1999). One of the tasks of development is to internalize a map of the social and cultural environment one belongs in and to understand its basic values. Two major early influences are (1) what parents do and (2) what they say, the explanations they give. Children identify more with what their parents do (modelling) than with what they say (Steinhauer, 1991). It is important for parents to be available to their children in relation to cultural expectations, to help integrate and bridge experiences within the family and within their community by example and reinforcement (McCord, 1990; McGuire & Earls, 1998; Seeman, 1996; Steinhauer, 1991). Mentally ill parents may have difficulty in fulfilling that aspect of their role because of the effects of their illness.

In summary, the qualities of a community or social network and of the person's identity within it are an important dimension in assessment of parenting capacity and an important part of a parenting formulation (see Cowling Chapter 6).

Poverty as an issue of individual parents and of communities

The relevance of the wider social, economic and political context to parenting is well established (Hughes *et al.*, 1960; Jack, 2001; Rose, 2001; Taylor *et al.*, 2000). There are numerous correlations between socioeconomic status and the quality of parenting and child development outcomes (Bornstein *et al.*, 2003). Deprivation, social exclusion and disenfranchisement need to be addressed and counterbalanced, especially for families with young children (Platt & Noble, 1999; Steinhauer, 1998) and those with mental illness (Göpfert *et al.*, 1999; Göpfert & Mahoney, 2000). Mental health services are limited in their capacity to directly address issues of poverty (Knapp & Harris, 1998).

Clinical implications of the role-relationship model

Role formulations can seem to be overly simple. Sometimes, apparently oversimplistic formulations are helpful because they enable action and movement, similarly to a parent who has to translate the world in simple enough terms for a child to be able to understand and act on the understanding (Vygotsky, 1986/1934; Winnicott, 1964). In our experience, role formulations can also very quickly facilitate quite sophisticated and complex understanding of relationship patterns, in a way that other, less structured models cannot. Role formulations transcend the boundary between the conscious and unconscious, in a similar way to attachment theory (see Adshead *et al.*, Chapter 15), and also transcend the boundary between the internal and social (Balswick & Balkwell, 1977) which increases the capacity for formulating complexity while keeping the formulation simple.

Service dilemmas and the role of organizations

Implications for services of the role-relationship model

The role of mental health services is assumed to be the care of the mentally ill in their role as patients (Parsons, 1978). However, in reality, the role and task of a service is determined by funding structures and power relationships within the organizational context.

In the UK, the needs of children are generally not considered an adult mental health service provider's concern or the task of a social service providing for adult clients.

Patients tell us that achieving any degree of recognition of their role as parent by adult mental health services is difficult (Göpfert *et al.*, 1999) (see Cowling, Chapter 6; Mahoney, Chapter 23; Falkov, Chapter 27). Professionals have commented on this as well (Göpfert *et al.*, 1996; Falkov, 1998; Reder & Duncan, 1999).

Children's services often present the reverse scenario. There may be insufficient understanding of the psychological or psychiatric difficulties of the parent and the task and responsibility of understanding them is disowned (Reder & Duncan, 1999). The dilemma is a systemic one, powerfully reinforced by the way services in most developed countries are increasingly subject to monetary scrutiny. The system seems to conspire against working with the family as a whole (Coffey *et al.*, 2001; Patterson & Lusterman, 1997).

The definition of the service task is usually not in the hands of those using the services but in the hands of someone else who has power, i.e. a political institution, insurance company or private funding organization whose interests may fragment rather than support the family.

Swings and roundabouts of policy between statute and therapeutic support

An assessment of parenting is meant to be an assessment of risk. However, the work that goes into the assessment and management of risk is not always compatible with effective clinical engagement and therapeutic work within a professional relationship context. There is some evidence that a focus on risk may exclude – at least in current practice – engagement with the person and, consequently, effective therapeutic and preventive intervention (Hetherington *et al.*, 2002). Historically, policies in industrialized countries have always swung back and forth on a continuum between risk assessment with a focus on statutory responsibilities, and supportive/preventive intervention with a focus on engagement as the main means of managing risk (Tomison 1996). This may reflect the fact that the responsibility for risk management does not belong to the people at risk or representing a risk, but to the professionals given that responsibility. Depending on the particular structure of service provision, risk is managed according to external considerations, such as financial liability, and party political opinion poll ratings. As a consequence, clinical requirements, such as the need for differentiated service provision for parents disabled by psychosis or other severe mental illness, and for those suffering from more severe personality disorders, are usually given very low priority or not considered at all.

The limits of rationalism

Legal logic prevails directly or indirectly in the presentation of issues to do with public/political risk management. This can be incomprehensible or counterintuitive to the ordinary person. It devalues our essentially and profoundly irrational self as human beings, potentially replacing human relationships and thoughtful decision making with bureaucratic formality. The intent is to contain fear and uncertainty (Woodhouse & Pengelly, 1991). However, the use of policies and regulations as a means of creating certainty usually indicates that the organizational learning necessary for the implementation of such policies is not likely taking place. Policies then can become pseudo-solutions, leaving service users and professionals alike disillusioned, more disempowered and helpless, often in contradiction to the overt content and purpose of such a policy.

The contribution of service culture to outcome

The activity of risk assessment puts the emphasis on the negative. This especially applies to parenting assessment (Milner & O'Byrne, 1998). Paradoxically, many parents who use adult mental health services can accept that their child may be better off being looked after by someone else. Yet they need commitment and compassion (Göpfert *et al.*, 1999) (see Mahoney, Chapter 23). In short, they need such an assessment to be carried out in the context of a therapeutic relationship with a commitment beyond the actual decision about the fate of the child. Even parents who cannot adequately look after their children need realistic hope in order to work toward an improvement of their situation.

The immediate clinical relevance of this is associated with what has been dubbed a culture of therapeutic optimism versus a culture of therapeutic pessimism (Hetherington *et al.*, 2002). A recent follow-up study from Sweden of mentally ill mothers and their children after birth until the end of their school-age period evaluated their physical development, academic achievements and their family situation. The authors found no differences to a control population, a finding at variance with much of the English-language literature. The authors wondered whether this could be a direct result of the higher level of social support available in their country for high-risk families (Ruppert & Bågedahl-Strindlund, 2001). There is other evidence which can be interpreted similarly (Kawachi *et al.*, 1997; Leon *et al.*, 1992;

Vagero & Lundberg, 1989). This is linked to the question of resources and their availability, in itself culturally determined. The structure, design and the advantages and shortcomings of service systems very clearly reflect aspects of the dominant culture.

The dominant culture in UK mental health services is one of individualism. This may be similar in some other countries. For relationships, including relationships between parents and between parents and children, to be served well, services need to develop a broader view that encompasses these relationships (see Hetherington & Baistow Chapter 26). For this we need enhanced service objectives which aim at dealing with relationship outcomes and better bridges between child and adult services if they remain separately organized. This may enable more integrated service provision with a true family orientation. An example of how this can be done is provided in Appendix 1 to Chapter 7 on assessment.

Conclusion

We hope to have illustrated the usefulness of a single paradigm to formulate issues of mental health across a range of domains, beginning with the inner world of the person, to the interface of services and parents with specific mental health problems. The role-relationship paradigm is

- useful intuitively;
- has a comparatively strong evidence base, and validity confirmed by its emergence from more than one professional discipline (sociology, developmental psychology, psychotherapy and medicine), and from several sources and diverse locations;
- can be easily integrated with other frameworks of understanding human behaviour, spanning the conscious and unconscious realms, and interpersonal/ systemic dimensions;
- can be shared with, contributed to and understood by patients;
- provides an explanatory framework which allows the understanding and formulation of the whole range of human relationship qualities from love to abuse and murder;
- is based on a developmental perspective especially suited to formulating parent–child relationships;
- allows the formulation of complex mental health issues with a clear focus on the understanding of the interface between parenting and mental health.

The role-relationship paradigm has been focused on in this chapter because of its usefulness. However, other frameworks of psychological understanding provide other, important contributions to a formulation of the parent–child relationship, and parenting difficulties. Any framework can only ever provide a limited view, and cannot provide the 'truth'. A combination of contributions may be able to provide a pragmatic approximation of a truly helpful clinical formulation that does justice to the practical needs of child and parent in a given situation.

Being a parent is a culturally determined social role, which must be understood against the background of the social context of 'community'. Socio-economic factors are a significant ingredient of this social context, yet they can only be addressed marginally by mental health services, despite their importance.

The task of assessing parenting capacity requires a holistic view. Prescriptive and linear assessment procedures and risk management policies can be inherently limited and disempowering to both professionals and their patients in the mental health field. The authors hope to have provided some of the tools necessary for an appropriate understanding and assessment of parenting.

Acknowledgements

Apart from the helpful editing by Mary V. Seeman, the following have contributed significantly to the writing of this chapter: Antony Ryle, Kate Hellin, Deborah Hodes, Tara Weeramanthri, the many parents and children we have worked with over the years, and our colleagues who helped us grow and develop in our joint clinical and research efforts.

REFERENCES

Aldridge, J. & Becker, S. (1993). *Children who Care: Inside the World of Young Carers*. Loughborough: Loughborough University.

Arias, I. & Pape, K. T. (1994). Physical abuse. In *Handbook of Developmental Family Psychology and Psychopathology*, ed. L. L'Abate, pp. 284–308. Chichester: John Wiley & Sons.

Ball, M. (1996). Round and Round the Circle: Support for families through the Department of Health's childcare circles initiative. London: Department of Health. Quoted after Jack, G. (2000). Ecological influences on parenting and child development. *British Journal of Social Work*, 30, 703–20.

Ball, M. (1998). *School Inclusion: The School, the Family and the Community*. Findings (1998, June). York: Joseph Rowntree Foundation.

Balswick, J. O. & Balkwell, J. W. (1977). Self-disclosure to same- and opposite-sex parents: an empirical test of insights from role theory. *Sociometry*, 40, 282–6.

Beardslee, W. R., Versage, E. & Gladstone, T. (1998). Children of affectively ill parents: a review of the past 10 years. *Journal of the American Academy of Child and Adolescent Psychiatry*, 37, 1134–41.

Becker, G. S. (1991). *A Treatise on the Family – Enlarged Edition*. Cambridge, MA: Harvard University Press.

Benjamin, L. S. (1998). *The Interpersonal Diagnosis and Treatment of Personality Disorders*. New York: Guilford Press.

Bleuler, M. (1974). The offspring of schizophrenics. *Schizophrenia Bulletin, 1*, 93–109.

Bornstein, M. H. (ed.) (1991). *Cultural Approaches to Parenting*. Hillsdale NJ: Lawrence Erlbaum Associates.

Bornstein, H., Haynes, O. M., Azuma, H. et al. (1998). A cross-national study of self-evaluations and attributions in parenting: Argentina, Belgium, France, Israel, Italy, Japan, and the United States. *Developmental Psychology, 34*, 662–76.

Bornstein, M. H., Bradley, R. H. & von Eye, A. (ed.) (2003). *Socioeconomic Status, Parenting, and Child Development*. Mahwah NJ: Lawrence Erlbaum Associates.

Boyd-Franklin, N. & Bry, H. B. (2000). *Reaching out in Family Therapy: Home-based, School and Community Interventions*. New York: Guilford Press.

Brasssard, J. (1982). Beyond family structure: Mother-child interaction and personal social networks. Unpublished doctoral dissertation, Ithaca, New York, Cornell University. Quoted after Jack, G. (2000). Ecological influences on parenting and child development. *British Journal of Social Work, 30*, 703–20.

Brazelton, T. B. (1991). Discussion: cultural attitudes and actions. In *Cultural Approaches to Parenting*, ed. M. H. Bornstein, pp. 144–22. Hillsdale, NJ: Lawrence Erlbaum Associates.

Breznitz, S. (1985). Chores as a buffer against risky interaction. *Schizophrenia Bulletin, 11*, 357–60.

Browne, C. (1994). The impact of divorce on families: the Australian experience. *Family and Conciliation Courts Review, 32*, 149–67.

Byng-Hall, J. (1995). *Re-writing Family Scripts: Improvisation and Systems Change*. New York: Guilford Press.

Byng-Hall, J. (2002). Relieving parentified children's burdens in families with insecure attachment patterns. *Family Process, 41*, 375–88.

Cahn, E. S. (2000). *No more Throw-away People – The Co-production Imperative*. Washington, DC: Essential Books.

Caspi, A. & Elder, G. H. (1988). Emergent family patterns: the intergenerational construction of problem behaviour and relationships. In *Relationships Within Families: Mutual Influences*, ed. R. A. Hinde & J. Stevenson-Hinde, pp. 218–40. Oxford: Clarendon Press.

Cicero, M. T. (44 BC/1991). On Duties (De Officiis). In *Cicero: On Duties*, ed. M. T. Griffin & E. M. Atkins. Cambridge: Cambridge University Press.

Coffey, E. P., Olson, M. E. & Sessions, P. (2001). The heart of the matter: an essay about the effects of managed care on family therapy with children. *Family Process, 40*, 385–400.

Comunian, A. L. & Mosconi, A. (1999). Individual, family and culture. Interactive reality construction: What family therapy application? *Human Systems, 10*, 49–66.

Corwin, M. deO. (1996). Beyond the nuclear family: cultural dissolution and borderline personality disorder. *Smith College Studies in Social Work, 66*, 147–61.

Cunningham, J. (2001). *Children of Mothers with Mental Health Problems*. Ph. D. Dissertation, University of Birmingham, Birmingham.

Donnison, D. (1998). *Policies for a Just Society*. Basingstoke: Macmillan.

Earley, L. & Cushway, D. (2002). The parentified child. *Clinical Child Psychology and Psychiatry, 7*, 163–78.

Faber, A. & Mazlish, E. (1998). *Siblings without Rivalry: helping your Children Live Together so you can Live Too*. New York: Norton/London: Piccadilly Press.

Falkov, A. (ed.) (1998). *Crossing Bridges: Training Resources for Working with Mentally Ill Parents and their Children. An Evidence Based Reader.* Brighton: Pavilion Publishing.

Fernando, S. (1988). *Race and Culture in Psychiatry.* London: Croom Helm.

Flavell, J. H. (1963). *The Developmental Psychology of Jean Piaget.* Princeton: van Nostrand.

Galdstone, R. (1965). Observations on children who have been physically abused and their parents. *American Journal of Psychiatry, 122,* 440–3.

Garcia, M. M., Shaw, D. S., Winslow, E. B. & Yaggi, K. E. (2000). Destructive sibling conflict and the development of conduct problems in young boys. *Developmental Psychology, 36,* 44–53.

Gibbons, J. (1990). *Family Support and Prevention: Studies in Local Areas.* London, HMSO.

Göpfert, M. & Mahoney, C. (2000). Participative research with users of mental health services who are parents. *Clinical Psychology Forum, 140,* 11–15.

Göpfert, M., Webster, J., Pollard, J. & Nelki, J. S. (1996). The assessment and prediction of parenting capacity: a community-oriented approach. In *Parental Psychiatric Disorder: Distressed Parents and their Families,* ed. M. Göpfert, J. Webster & M. V. Seeman, pp. 271–309. Cambridge: Cambridge University Press.

Göpfert, M., Harrison, P. & Mahoney, C. (1999). *Keeping the Family in Mind: Participative Research into Mental Ill-health and how it Affects the whole Family.* Liverpool: Save the Children, Barnardos, Imagine and North Mersey Community Trust.

Gunderman, R. (2000). Illness as failure. Blaming the patients. *Hastings Center Report, 30,* 7–11.

Hafner, R. J. (1986). *Marriage and Mental Illness: A Sex Role Perspective.* New York: Guilford Press.

Hetherington, R., Baistow, K., Katz, I., Mesie, J. & Trowell, J. (2002). *The Welfare of Children with Mentally ill Parents: Learning from Inter-country Comparisons.* Chichester: John Wiley & Sons.

Hill, J. (1996). Parental psychiatric disorder and the attachment relationship. In *Parental Psychiatric Disorder: Distressed Parents and their Families,* ed. M. Göpfert, J. Webster & M. V. Seeman, pp. 7–16. Cambridge: Cambridge University Press.

Hoghughi, M. & Speight, A. N. P. (1998). Good enough parenting – a strategy for a healthier society. *Archives of Disease in Childhood, 78,* 293–6.

Holley, T. E. & Holley, J. (1998). *My Mother's Keeper: A Daughter's Memoir of Growing Up in the Shadow of Schizophrenia.* New York: Morrow.

Horowitz, M. J., Eells, T., Singer, J. & Salovey, P. (1995). Role-relationship models for case formulation. *Archives of General Psychiatry, 52,* 625–32.

Horrocks, J. E. & Jackson, D. W. (1972). *Self and Role: a Theory of Self-process and Role Behaviour.* Boston: Houghton Mifflin Company.

Hughes, C. C, Tremblay, M. -A., Rapoport, R. N. & Leighton, A. H. (1960). *People of Cove and Woodlot. Communities from the Viewpoint of Social Psychiatry. Volume II: The Stirling County Study of Psychiatric Disorder and Sociocultural Environment.* New York: Basic Books.

Hunter, J. J. & Maunder, R. G. (2001). Using attachment theory to understand illness behavior. *General Hospital Psychiatry, 23,* 177–82.

Jack, G. (2001). Ecological perspectives in assessing children and families. In *The Child's World: Assessing Children in Need,* ed. J. Horwath, pp. 53–74. London: Jessica Kingsley.

Johnston, J. R. & Campbell, L. E. G. (1993). Parent–child relationships in domestic violence families disputing custody. *Family Conciliation and Courts Review, 31,* 282–98.

Jones, D. (2001). The assessment of parenting capacity. In *The Child's World: Assessing Children in Need*, ed. J. Horwath. London: Jessica Kingsley.

Jurkovic, G. H. (1997). *Lost Childhoods: The Plight of the Parentified Child*. New York: Brunner & Mazel.

Kashiwagi, K. & Nagahisa, H. (1999). Value of a child for women: Why have a child now? *Japanese Journal of Educational Psychology*, *47*, 170–9.

Kawachi, I., Kennedy, B. P., Lochner, K. & Prothrow-Stith, D. (1997). Social capital, income inequality and morality. *American Journal of Public Health*, *87*, 1491–8.

Kelly, J. B. (1993). Current research on children's post-divorce adjustment: no simple answer. *Family Conciliation and Courts Review*, *31*, 29–49.

Kendrick, C. & Dunn, Judy (1982). Protest or pleasure? The response of first-born children to interactions between their mothers and infant siblings. *Journal of Child Psychology and Psychiatry*, *23*, 117–29.

Knapp, E. K. & Harris, E. S. (1998). Consultation-Liaison in Child Psychiatry – A review of the past 10 years. Part II: Research on treatment approaches and outcomes. *American Academy of Child and Adolescent Psychiatry*, *37*, 139–46.

Leff, J. (2001). *The Unbalanced Mind*. London: Weidenfeld and Nicholson.

Leon, D. A., Vagero, D. & Otterblad Olausson, P. (1992). Social class differences in infant mortality in Sweden: a comparison with England and Wales. *British Medical Journal*, *305*, 687–91.

Levy, T. M. & Orlans, M. (1998). *Attachment, Trauma and Healing: Understanding and Treating Attachment Disorder in Children and Families*. Washington, DC: Child Welfare League of America.

Littlewood, R. & Lipsedge, M. (1989). *Aliens and Alienists: Ethnic Minorities and Psychiatry*. London: Unwin Hyman.

Lystad, M. H. (1975). Violence at home: a review of the literature. *American Journal of Orthopsychiatry*, *45*, 328–45.

Main, T. F. (1946/1989). The hospital as a therapeutic institution. Reprinted in Johns, J. (ed.) (1989). *The Ailment and other Psychoanalytic Essays*. London: Free Associations.

McCord, J. (1990). Long-term perspective on parental absence. In *Straight and Devious Pathways from Childhood to Adulthood*, ed. L. Robins & M. Rutter, pp. 113–34. Cambridge: Cambridge University Press.

McGuire, J. & Earls, F. (1998). Coercive family process and delinquency: some methodological considerations. In *Coercion and Punishment in Long-term Perspectives*, ed. J. McCord, pp. 348–61. Cambridge: Cambridge University Press.

Mika, P., Bergner, R. M. & Baum, M. C. (1987). The development of a scale for the assessment of parentification. *Family Therapy*, *14*, 229–35.

Milner, J. & O'Byrne, P. (1998). *Assessment in Social Work*. Basingstoke: Palgrave.

Minuchin, S. (1974). *Families and Family Therapy*. London: Tavistock Publications.

Mufson, L., Aidala, A. & Warner, V. (1994). Social dysfunction and psychiatric disorder in mothers and their children. *Journal of the American Academy of Child and Adolescent Psychiatry*, *33*, 1256–64.

Muran, J. C. (2002). A relational approach to understanding change: plurality and contextualism in a psychotherapy research program. *Psychotherapy Research*, *12*, 113–38.

Norton, K. & Dolan, B. (1996). Personality dsorder and parenting. In *Parental Psychiatric Disorder: Distressed Parents and their Families*, ed. M. Göpfert, J. Webster & M. V. Seeman, pp. 219–32. Cambridge: Cambridge University Press.

Norton, K. & Smith, S. (1994). *Problems with Patients*. Cambridge: Cambridge University Press.

Nye, F. I. (1976). *Role Structure and Analysis of the Family*. Beverly Hills: Sage.

Nye, F. I. & Berardo, F. M. (1981). *Emerging Conceptual Frameworks in Family Analysis*. Westport: Praeger.

O'Connor, T. G., Deater-Deckard, K., Fulker, D., Rutter, M. & Plomin, R. (1998). Genotype-environment correlations in late childhood and early adolescence: antisocial behavioural problems and coercive parenting. *Developmental Psychology, 34*, 970–81.

O'Leary, K. D. & Jouriles, E. N. (1994). Psychological abuse between adult partners. In *Handbook of Developmental Family Psychology and Psychopathology*, ed. L. L'Abate, pp. 330–49. Wiley, Chichester: John Wiley & Sons.

Oliviera, Z. M. R. (1997). The concept of role and the discussion of the internalisation process. In *Sociogenetic Perspectives on Internalization*, ed. B. D. Cox & C. Lightfoot. Mahwah, NJ: Lawrence Erlbaum Associates.

Parsons, T. (1957). *The Social System*. New York: Free Press.

Parsons, T. (1964). *Social Structure and Personality*. New York: Free Press.

Parsons, T. (1967). *Sociological Theory and Modern Society*. New York: Free Press.

Parsons, T. (1978). *Action Theory and the Human Condition*. New York: Free Press.

Patterson, T. E. & Lusterman, D.-D. (1997). The relational reimbursement dilemma. In *Handbook of Relational Diagnosis and Dysfunctional Family Patterns*, ed. F. W. Kaslow. Chichester: John Wiley & Sons.

Pearlmutter, R. A. (1996). *A Family Approach to Psychiatric Disorders*. Washington, DC: American Psychiatric Press.

Platt, L. & Noble, M. (1999). *Race, Place and poverty: Ethnic Groups and Low Income Distributions*. 'Findings' (1999, February). York: Joseph Rowntree Foundation.

Pottick, K. J. & Davis, D. M. (2001). Attributions of responsibility for children's mental health problems: parents and professionals at odds. *American Journal of Orthopsychiatry, 71*, 426–35.

Pound, A. (1996). Parental affective disorder and childhood disturbance. In *Parental Psychiatric Disorder: Distressed Parents and their Families*, ed. M. Göpfert, J. Webster & M. V. Seeman, pp. 201–18. Cambridge: Cambridge University Press.

Quinton, D., Rutter, M. & Gulliver, L. (1990). Continuities in psychiatric disorder from childhood to adulthood in the children of psychiatric patients. In *Straight and Devious Pathways to Adulthood*, ed. L. Robins & M. Rutter, pp. 259–78. Cambridge: Cambridge University Press.

Reder, P. & Duncan, S. (1999). *Lost Innocents: A Follow-up Study of Fatal Child Abuse*. London: Routledge.

Reder, P. & Lucey, C. (ed.) (1995). *Assessment of Parenting: Psychiatric and Psychological Contributions*. London: Routledge.

Reder, P., McClure, M. & Jolley, A. (2000). *Family Matters: Interfaces between Child and Adult Mental Health*. London: Routledge.

Reed, A. (1999). Psychiatric hospital admission and interpersonal 'closure': network Meetings as a means of countering closure. *Human Systems, 10*, 35–48.

Richards, M. & Light, P. (ed.) (1990). *Children of Social Worlds: Development in a Social Context*. Cambridge, MA: Harvard University Press.

Riordan, D., Appleby, L. & Faragher, B. (1999). Mother–infant interaction in post-partum women with schizophrenia and affective disorders. *Psychological Medicine, 29*, 991–5.

Rogoff, B., Mistry, J., Göncü, A. & Mosier, C. (1991). Cultural variation in the role relations of toddlers and their families. In *Cultural Approaches to Parenting*, ed. M. H. Bornstein, pp. 173–83. Hillsdale, NJ: Lawrence Erlbaum Associates.

Rose, W. (2001). Assessing children in need and their families: an overview of the framework. In *The Child's World: Assessing Children in Need*, ed. J. Horwath, 35–56. London: Jessica Kingsley.

Royal College of Psychiatrists (2002). *Domestic Violence*. Council Report CR 102. London: Royal College of Psychiatrists.

Ruppert, S. & Bågedahl-Strindlund, M. (2001). Children of parapartum mentally ill mothers: a follow-up study. *Psychopathology, 34*, 174–8.

Rutter, M. & Quinton, D. (1984). Parental psychiatric disorder: effects on children. *Psychological Medicine, 14*, 853–80.

Ryckoff, I., Day, J. & Wynne, L. C. (1991). Maintenance of stereotyped roles in the families of schizophrenics. In *Foundations of Object Relations Family Therapy*, ed. J . S. Scharff. Northvale, NJ: Jason Aronson.

Ryle, A. (1998). *Cognitive-analytic Therapy and Borderline Personality Disorder*. Chichester: John Wiley & Sons.

Ryle, A. & Kerr, I. (2002). *Introducing Cognitive-analytic Therapy: Principles and Practice*. Chichester: John Wiley & Sons.

Schreier, H. A. & Libow, J. A. (1993). *Hurting for Love: Munchausen-by-Proxy Syndrome*. New York: Guilford Press.

Scott, R. D. & Starr, I. (1981). A 24-hour family orientated psychiatric and crisis service. *Journal of Family Therapy, 3*, 177–86.

Seeman, M. V. (1996). The mother with schizophrenia. In *Parental Psychiatric Disorder: Distressed Parents and their Families*, ed. M. Göpfert, J. Webster, & M. V. Seeman, pp. 190–200. Cambridge: Cambridge University Press.

Sergiovanni, T. J. (1994). *Building Community in Schools*. San Francisco: Jossey Bass.

Sessions, M. (1986). Influence of parentification on professional role choice and interpersonal style. *Dissertation Abstracts International, 47*, 5066 (University Microfilms No. 87-06815).

Skogstad, W. (2001). Internal and external reality: enquiring into their interplay in an inpatient setting. In *Reflective Enquiry into Therapeutic Institutions*, ed. L. Day & P. Pringle, pp. 45–66. London: Karnac.

Smale, G., Tuson, G., Ahmed, B., Darvill, G., Domoney, L. & Sainsbury, E. (1994). *Negotiating Care in the Community*. London: HMSO.

Smith, P. K. & Drew, L. M. (2002). Grandparenthood. In *Handbook of Parenting: Vol. 3: Being and Becoming a Parent*, 2nd edn, ed. M. H. Bornstein, pp. 141–72. Mahwah, Lawrence Erlbaum Associates.

Spencer, N. (1996). Reducing child health inequalities. In *Working for Equality in Health*, ed. P. Bywaters & E. McLead, pp. 143–60. London: Routlege.

St John, W. (1999). Beyond the sick role: situating community health nursing practice. *Collegian*, 6, 30–5.

Steinhauer, P. D. (1998). *The Least Detrimental Alternative: A Systematic Guide to Case Planning and Decision Making for Children in Care.* Toronto: University of Toronto Press.

Stierlin, H. (1977). *Psychoanalysis and Family Therapy.* New York: Jason Aronson.

Taylor, J. Spencer, N. & Baldwin, N. (2000). Social, economic and political context of parenting. *Archives of Disease in Childhood, 82*, 113–17.

The Shorter Oxford English Dictionary on Historical Principles (1973/1986). Oxford: Clarendon Press.

Toman, W. (1988). Basics of family structure and sibling position. In *Siblings in Therapy: Life Span and Clinical Issues*, ed. M. D. Kahn & K. G. Lewis, pp. 46–65. New York: W. W. Norton.

Tomison, A. M. (1996). *Child Maltreatment and Mental Disorder.* Discussion paper 3. Melbourne: National Child Protection Clearinghouse.

Tomison, A. M. & Wise, S. (1999). *Community-based Approaches in Preventing Child Maltreatment. Issues in Child Abuse Prevention, 11.* Melbourne: National Child Protection Clearinghouse.

Torkington, N. P. K. (1991). *Black Health: A Political Issue.* Liverpool: Catholic Association for Racial Justice and Liverpool Institute of Higher Education.

Touliatos, J., Perlmutter, B. F. & Strauss, M. A. (2001). *Handbook of Family Measurement Techniques.* Thousand Oaks: Sage.

Vagero, D. & Lundberg, O. (1989). Health inequalities in Britain and Sweden. *Lancet, 11*, 35–6.

Valleau, M. P., Bergner, R. M. & Horton, C. B. (1995). Parentification and caretaker syndrome: An empirical investigation. *Family Therapy, 22*, 157–64.

Vygotsky, L. (1986/1934). *Thought and Language.* Cambridge, MA: MIT Press.

Webster, J. (1990). Parenting for children with schizophrenic mothers. *Adoption and Fostering, 14*, 37–43.

Werner, E. & Smith, R. (1992). *Overcoming the Odds: High-risk Children from Birth to Adulthood.* New York: Cornell.

Winnicott, D. W. (1964). The relationship of a mother to her baby at the beginning. In *The Family and Individual Development*, ed. D. W. Winnicott, pp. 17–18. London: Tavistock.

Woodhouse, D. & Pengelly, P. (1991). *Anxiety and the Dynamics of Collaboration.* Aberdeen: Aberdeen University Press.

Part II

Comprehensive assessment and treatment

6

'The same as they treat everybody else'

Vicki Cowling

Maroondah Hospital CAMHS, Victoria, Australia

With: Getting There Together Group, Upper Fern Tree Gully, Victoria, Australia
Parent Support Group, Women's Clinic, Centre for Addiction and Mental Health, Toronto, Canada
Getting There Group, Croydon, Victoria, Australia
Parent Support Group, Employment Options Inc., Marlboro, Massachusetts, USA

Parents want professionals to treat them 'the same as everybody else'. They want professionals to see them as *parents* before they see them as patients, and for services to acknowledge their family relationships and responsibilities, and credit them with the capacity to act in their children's best interests. They want to be treated with dignity.

The 19 parents who contributed to this chapter come from four parent groups in Australia, Canada and the USA. They were approached through the coordinators of the parent groups listed above, and asked to respond to the questions: 'How do you want services to respond to your needs as parent? How do you want them to respond to the issues that affect your families and children?'

This chapter coordinates their responses, often reproduced verbatim. Having agreed to participate, each group met for 1.5 hours, and their responses are summarized by the main author of this chapter (VC). Their comments highlight the impact of legislation, access to public housing, service provision for the mentally ill and the ways that states intervene in the welfare of children. They also reflect very different experiences of interventions, often painful, such as having their children removed from their care.

Parents have written personal accounts about their experiences of mental illness previously as consumers of mental health services and as parents (Aridas & 'Christine', 1999; Kelly, 1999). There is little evidence that parents' voices are included in user groups which increasingly inform ideas about service delivery.

Being a parent should come before being a person with a mental illness

Professionals should understand that parents receiving treatment are parents *first* and should demonstrate that understanding by providing treatment accordingly.

Parents feel supported when the needs of their children are met

Children need to have their parent's mental illness explained to them. Parents may need help to do this. Camps and peer support groups for children help them realize that they are not alone. Adolescents need information about their parent's illness, and may need support to understand how the illness affects their parent.

Professionals sometimes assume that a mother does not know about or understand the needs of her child – but parents may know and be sensitively tuned in to the child

A mother's feelings towards her child can only be understood by her. Parents may be able to recognize when they are not meeting their child's emotional needs, and worry about that.

Service providers need to work out the best way to ensure the health and safety of the child without excluding the mother from the decision-making process when other family members are involved

A child may be affected negatively by several members of a family, but the unwell parent may be a scapegoat. Professionals can be 'taken in' by the father of the child or other relatives. A parent's odd behaviour can be used against her, but parents may start to behave oddly when they feel they are being harshly judged. Sometimes parents feel ostracized by members of their own family who can also have negative attitudes towards people with mental illness. Parents are sometimes led to believe that their own opinion does not count.

A parent should have the opportunity to get support that breaks down into manageable pieces the skills and tasks required in being a parent, so that a parent can learn step by step.

Professionals should be more willing to listen to and value a parent's points of view and experience

Listen to us and put more stock in what we have to say, and a grain of salt in what others might say. Sometimes professionals do not listen because they think they know better. They should think about occasions when they can advocate for the parent rather than make decisions on their behalf. Regardless of the symptoms, and the effect of this on a parent's behaviour, a parent should be respected all the time.

In spite of their best efforts at raising their children, parents sometimes feel like failures – it would help if professionals understood this.

Evaluate parental ability before removing children without question. Removing children from parents with mental illness without an apparent reason is unacceptable and unreasonable

Parents need family-based programmes which meet the varying needs of parents with mental illness and their children, such as counselling, support groups, assistance with budgeting and household management. Counselling should be supportive, and help a parent to understand their low motivation and energy. Parents would like people to care for children and give parents and children a break.

Parents needs housing arrangements that are flexible. A parent who has a mental illness may sometimes not occupy the house, may sometimes not have children with them, but will need appropriate accommodation in order to have their children live with them.

When a child makes accusations (about the situation at home) the education system needs to meet with the family and get all the facts before acting on impulse.

Professionals should have smaller case loads so they can give more time to work with the parents and the family.

Professionals should give the parent with mental illness, and the partner, information about the effects of medication, possible side effects and the effects on a person's behaviour

Professionals need to understand how medication may affect a parent and therefore the children. If medication makes parents drowsy and sleepy, they cannot attend fully to the physical needs of their children, such as protecting them from accidents in the home. Nor can they fully attend to their developmental needs such as providing them with mental stimulation. Medication may affect a person's ability to safely drive a car, so they become more isolated at home.

All family members need to understand how and why mental illness affects people and how medication and other treatments help.

Professional support is needed for the partner when a parent is acutely ill, and education to prepare for ongoing treatment, convalescence and recovery

Professionals need to listen to all family members: the parent with the mental illness, the children, the partner and grandparents. Medication treats symptoms of mental illness, but on its own it is not enough. Other aspects of treatment should be considered such as family therapy and individual counselling.

Childbirth may trigger a mental illness with psychotic symptoms. If this is identified and treated as postnatal depression, such a response will not be helpful to the mother and children in the family if it is something else, for example postnatal psychosis, later diagnosed as schizophrenia.

Please respect confidentiality with regard to sharing information with family members

When a parent has a mental illness they may experience many feelings of loss: the most profound one for some parents is the loss of their children if they are taken away

Parents may feel a loss of capacity to do things they did before, such as having a rewarding job and managing their budget. Professionals need to understand this. Support groups for parents give them a place to talk openly about things that worry them, and also to share positive things such as coming off medication, or the achievements of their children.

Parents feel they are negatively judged when their children are taken away. People should understand that the child is taken away because the parent is unwell, not because the parent is bad.

When parents are not able to care for their children themselves, they want to know that their children are being looked after emotionally, not just physically.

No one from the school asked me: what is your contribution to this child?

Schools need to understand more about how mental illness affects people, and in turn how it affects a child who has a parent with mental illness. Instead of suspending a child from school for bad behaviour, the school might explore what is troubling the child. Schools need counsellors for both the children and the parents with mental illness. More understanding across the whole school community might mean that children who do have a parent with a mental illness would not be bullied for this.

Respect a right to privacy

When a woman is admitted to a hospital for a mental illness and placed under observation, to protect her, she should not be expected to change into a hospital gown in front of male staff.

Be sensitive to our culture

Professionals need to be sensitive towards the different attitudes to mental illness held by different cultural groups: it may be denied, it may be a source of shame. Attitudes may also differ from culture to culture. Have respect for a mother's intuition regardless of whether or not she has been taught the skills required for being a parent. She might have learned certain habits from her culture that may not be ideal for parenting.

Educate service providers to network all available services and link parents into the most useful ones for the family

Community education is needed to reduce the stigma which exists towards people who have a mental illness. More openness about mental illness would help parents to be more open with their children about it.

Police need training so they have a humane and respectful approach towards people with a mental illness, especially if they have to go to a parent's home when children are there. There should be education to better understand the police role, because viewing police in uniform is intimidating, and fear can be heightened very quickly.

General practitioners need more training in psychiatry before graduation so they can understand the issues for parents with children and be supportive to the children. The behaviour of some professionals towards people with mental illness is influenced by stereotypes which still exist – community education would change their attitudes.

How do we want to be viewed? We want to be viewed as being persistent and zealous and working to battle prejudice and injustice

We want to have internet links with other parent groups in other parts of the world.

The statements recorded here emerged from groups working independently of each other, so the points indicate key themes, sometimes apparently contradictory. It is possible, with internet access, that a parent charter may develop, but that would be a later development.

Acknowledgements

Thank you to the parents for recording their comments, and to Julie Cosgrove, Upper Fern Gully; David Clodman and Dr Kulwant Buttar, Toronto; Rose Cuff, Croydon; and Jonathan Clayfield and Shannon Hall, Marlboro.

REFERENCES

Aridas, S. & 'Christine' (1999). Two consumer perspectives on the Mothers Support Programme. In *Children of Parents with Mental Illness*, ed. V. Cowling, pp. 120–3. Melbourne: Australian Council for Educational Research.

Kelly, M. (1999). Approaching the last resort: a parent's view. In *Children of Parents with Mental Illness*, ed. V. Cowling, pp. 60–75. Melbourne: Australian Council for Educational Research.

7

Formulation and assessment of parenting

Michael Göpfert[1], Jeni Webster[2] and Julia Nelki[3]

[1]Webb House Democratic Therapeutic Community, Crewe, UK; [2]Warrington, UK; and [3]Liverpool, UK

Introduction

This chapter presents a framework for assessing parents and their families for both forensic and clinical purposes, and is intended to help ensure that children receive the best care available. The chapter will (1) outline principles that contribute to ethical assessment practice; (2) provide dimensions to consider when making a formulation; (3) offer ideas about the preparation of court reports; and (4) describe practical ways of conducting collaborative and therapeutic assessments.

The three authors come from different backgrounds: family therapy/social work (JW), child psychiatry (JN) and adult psychiatry/psychotherapy (MG). Each of us is frequently asked to contribute to parenting assessments and we all three believe that combining perspectives results in the best product.

Depending on resources, philosophy, culture, and service construction, there are wide regional disparities in the conduct of assessments. There are few areas that can provide the thorough comprehensive assessment service pioneered by Jacobsen *et al.* (1997) (see Jacobsen, Chapter 8). In most situations, staff from different disciplines contribute to the overall assessment and child-care social workers have the responsibility of coordinating perspectives from different agencies and, ultimately, ensuring the safety of the child.

Principles of ethical assessment practice

Commitment to the parent

Although most of the literature in the field focuses on the needs of the child, the needs of the parent who cares for the child are of great importance. The separation of child and adult services makes it hard to encompass the needs of both, especially when the expert knowledge regarding parenting resides in the children's service. Service providers may attempt to overcome this division by agreeing on a service protocol for families with a mentally ill parent (see example in Appendix 7.1). This chapter is intended to help adult professionals better understand issues of parenting and for child professionals to appreciate the mental health needs of the parent. A commitment to the parent–child relationship must include a commitment to the welfare of both child and parent, and an in-depth understanding of the potential consequences for a developing child of living with parents who struggle with mental illness or substance misuse (see Hall, Chapter 3; Hans, Chapter 14).

Ensure appropriate assessment of risk

Although a rare event, children *are* killed by mentally ill parents (D'Orban, 1979; Falkov, 1997; Husain & Daniel, 1984) (see Hall, Chapter 3; Jacobsen, Chapter 8). It is imperative that the prime safety requirement for the child is constantly monitored and appropriate action taken swiftly if the child is not deemed safe. It is also important to keep in mind that a parent's psychiatric assessment can *not* establish whether a child is at risk from that parent nor can a child protection assessment rule out risk from a parent's psychiatric disorder. Neglect, or physical, sexual or emotional abuse is more common in families with mental illness/substance misuse than in the general population (see Hall, Chapter 3). Serious concerns about risks to children can serve as grounds for compulsory admission to hospital (Webster *et al.*, 1999).

Timing

It is important to address differing time frames as part of the assessment process. This is because so many parties are legitimate stakeholders in the assessment and decision-making process, that it becomes crucial to openly include a consideration of each party's framework of time and need, and their potential conflict. The developmental needs of a young child will demand a very different framework of time to be adhered to compared with the needs of a chronically mentally ill parent, or the bureaucratic needs of a court.

Therefore, assessment needs to weigh the developmental needs of the child against the probable time it takes for a parent to recover sufficiently to be able to cope with parenting. Whenever possible, assessments need to be done when the parent is well enough to address the tasks inherent in the evaluation, being observed, for instance, when interacting with the child. Even a seriously ill parent may be able to provide 'good enough parenting' when in recovery, so assessments may need to focus on early identification of relapse and consider novel solutions to such problems as 'intermittent parenting' (Anthony & McGinnis, 1978). This requires an ongoing support/monitoring/intervention system, a commodity in increasingly short supply within the current context of 'targeted' and 'focused' service provision and high staff turnover.

Ensure assessment can address needs of both child and parents

Any assessment which is likely to result in loss of custody needs to ensure – as an integral part of the assessment process – that an adult mental health professional is available to help the parent cope with the aftermath of such a decision. The assessment process in itself is a stressful one and the resultant distress may deprive the vulnerable parent of all spare capacity to address shortcomings in parenting function. When this culminates in custody loss, the parent will need intensive support. The commonly encountered tension between child and adult workers over whose needs take priority can be lessened if the parent's feelings are understood and addressed. This is important in order to preserve any future relationship between parent and child.

There is no avoiding the basic interpersonal construction of a parental capacity assessment: the parent is being judged and the assessor is judging. Many parents, especially those with a background of abuse and deprivation, will find it difficult to relate constructively to an 'assessment' without re-experiencing past abusive patterns (see Göpfert *et al.*, Chapter 5, Fig. 5.6) where, once again, a person in a position of power does them harm. Many guides on 'parenting assessment' or on 'assessing children in need' emphasize the need for a collaborative relationship throughout the process of assessment (e.g. the United Kingdom Children Act, 1989) (Department of Health, 2000). However, not surprisingly, many parents who have been subjected to such assessment have not experienced this 'collaboration' (Göpfert *et al.*, 1996, 1999; Department of Health, 2001) (see Cowling *et al.*, Chapter 6). The children's situation is similar (see Bilsborough, Chapter 1). For an assessment to be experienced as collaborative, the parent and the person(s) carrying out the assessment need to have established a joint agenda within a working alliance. If this is not possible, other ways of assessment should be given consideration. The family need to be clear about how any assessment is going to be conducted, which questions need to be answered and what decisions are going to be made as a result.

Take time to clarify the reason for the assessment

A clear distinction needs to be made between the day-to-day clinical work which may include risk assessment/management and formal assessments, for example for the purposes of court proceedings. Sometimes the agenda is not clear to the person of whom the request for evaluation is being made. A professionals' meeting helps to establish the level of concern on the part of the various parties and the likelihood of progression to court proceedings. Professionals also need to have realistic expectations of each other's capabilities. Some issues may require specialized skills. The aims of the assessment need to be clearly stated in concrete simple terms so that family and professionals can understand and agree on the tasks. This also helps in the feedback stage and will contribute to better parent–professional understanding.

Winnicott's phrase 'good enough mother' (Bettelheim, 1987; Winnicott, 1965) has long been standard in the parenting literature. Yet, when it comes to parenting capacity/competency, there is no definition or clarity about what constitutes 'good enough' (Azar & Benjet, 1994; Budd & Holdsworth, 1996; Budd *et al.*, 2001; Melton *et al.*, 1997) and what 'good enough' might mean at different child ages (Winnicott, 1964*a, b*). Parenting models are based on theories of optimal rather than minimal parenting (Azar *et al.*, 1998; Budd *et al.*, 2001; Greene & Kilili, 1998; Mahoney & Mackechnie, 2001). There are no legal definitions of 'good enough parenting' because it is not possible to create universal definitions of parenting that are sufficiently concrete for the purposes of legal process. The requirement is for a sufficient fit between child and parent within a particular context of culture, extended family, community and developmental need; in short: a good enough relationship within a particular environment (Brodzinsky, 1993; Heilbrun, 1992). The minimal requirements of parenting capacity have to be established in each instance. Broadly, they focus either on what needs to be in place for a child to develop appropriately, or for the parent–child relationship to be able to sustain the developmental needs of a particular child.

Coordination of professional contributions

It is important to ensure that the person(s) doing the assessment are qualified to answer the questions asked of them. A multiprofessional approach is usually needed. One person, usually the social worker, then draws the different perspectives together. Social workers in the UK expect a comprehensive assessment to be comprised of 10–20 weekly sessions of parent–child observations under different circumstances and in different situations.

It is important for the different professionals who contribute to the assessment to clearly state their areas of expertise, and to limit their opinions to these. As examples of the different competencies required, a mother who is a former substance abuser in trouble with the law will need as assessors a social worker with child protection responsibility, perhaps a probation officer, perhaps a debt counsellor. The children will need a child mental health worker or child psychiatrist, and perhaps a school counsellor. All of these individuals would have a contribution to make toward an assessment of the mother's current parenting capacity and risk assessment of the children's safety.

Public policy and clinical literature increasingly recognize the need for multiple perspectives (Department of Health, 2000; Sturge, 2001). There is some evidence that the demand for multidisciplinary assessment is increasing (Budd, 2001; Budd *et al.*, 1998/2000, 2001) but practitioners do not always meet appropriate standards

(Budd *et al.*, 2001). Budd and her colleagues state that assessments should be tailored to the question(s) that need to be answered and need not cover all possible parenting dimensions. Each professional contribution should clarify the question addressed, and all evidence should address both strengths and weaknesses in parenting, enabling balanced conclusions.

Consent

Valid consent is required from all parties involved. Before consenting, the parent needs to understand the stresses involved and the potential for a negative outcome (see Asen & Schuff, Chapter 10). Although the consent options may be very limited for the parent, especially if the assessment is required by a court, the professional carrying out the assessment should negotiate each step of the process with the participants concerned. It is best to be very clear about what needs to be done in order to fulfil the court requirements and to plan how professionals and family members can achieve this together.

Formulation of parenting

Table 7.1 gives an overview of the dimensions that may need to be explored when conducting an assessment. The reader who wishes more detail is referred to other recent writing on assessment (Department of Health, 2000; Jacobsen *et al.*, 1997; Wall & Hamilton, 2000) (see Jacobsen, Chapter 8). Each parenting dimension will be illustrated with a brief case example. This is taken from a clinical case where the mother, Jean, is the identified patient in treatment. This situation is not a formal parenting assessment for the purposes of child protection but the principles of formulation are the same.

Focus on role of parent

Jean looked after her two children well most of the time, and they stayed with her parents when she was in hospital (i.e. *intermittent parenting*; Anthony & McGinnis, 1978). She believed that she kept her depression and her paranoid thoughts to herself, but her older child was well able to describe her symptoms of sadness and worry (*she was, therefore, not able to guide her children on issues of her mental illness*). When her second husband hurt her older child in a frenzy of anger, she immediately left the home in her nightclothes with the two children, to go to her parents (*she therefore demonstrated a capacity to protect*). When she eventually found a new home for herself and the two children, the children were well cared for and they enjoyed living together (*this was a child-centred family*). However, Jean encouraged the older child to stay home from school to keep her company when she felt low (*role reversal*). She felt unsafe alone, especially when one of the children was not well

Table 7.1. Dimensions of parenting formulation

Focus on role of parent

Capacity to attend to child's physical, intellectual, social and emotional needs

Capacity to provide a stable and nurturing environment (secure base)

Capacity to protect child

Age-appropriate understanding and expectations of child including the capacity to talk with child about parent's mental illness

Capacity to initiate or follow, and enjoy child-centred activity (play)

Evidence for role reversal including physical, sexual or emotional abuse

Focus on role of child

Capacity for self-protection

Developmental progress

Child's attachment status (including fear of parent)

Relationships outside the nuclear family, including extended family, peers and school

Unusual behaviours and characteristics (non-child-like)

Relationships outside the nuclear family, including extended family, peers and school

Involvement in parent's symptoms or substance misuse

Parentification

Focus on the impact of mental illness on role of parent

Sense of responsibility for self, child and family

Capacity to acknowledge risks to child

Level of disturbance, instability and violent tendencies (impulse control)

Behaviour and psychiatric symptoms directly affecting parenting capacity, including alcohol/drug addiction

Level of commitment to child

Level of paranoia/capacity to form trusting relationships

Use of help/clinical interventions/potential plus motivation for change including relevant past history

Capacity to reflect

Attitude to social norms/relationship to society

Attitude to professionals; use of help and clinical interventions

Focus on role of 'well'/other parent (if relevant)

Commitment to maintaining the family or commitment to relationship with the child

Capacity to be available/intervene on child's behalf if and when necessary

Relationship to child

Attitude to illness of partner

Health/emotional resources

Focus on role of spouse/partner (if relevant)

History of violence/spouse abuse

Capacity to work together as parents

Patterns, style and intensity of marital conflict

Ability to communicate

(cont.)

Table 7.1. (*cont.*)

Focus on context and extended family
    Access to relationship with an adult who is committed to providing support and care for
        child and/or parent
    Degree and patterns of support from extended family, directly to children as well as to parent
    Parents' relationship to own parents
    Quality of nonfamily network
    Financial/housing status
    Environmental stress/life events/current stressors

(*role reversal*). She saw the younger child's overactivity as age-appropriate (*lack of understanding*). It was not clear whether she considered the impact on her children of her continued relationship with her second husband (*lack of capacity to attend to the children's needs*).

Focus on role of child

The two children had very different needs. The older child became very afraid of going out after the assault by the stepfather. School attendance deteriorated as the child often stayed at home, complaining of feeling sick. Mirroring semed to be occurring between the symptoms of mother and child (*child opting for sick role as an attempt to get maternal care and, in this way, opting out of his parentified role in family*). He was a loner at school and never brought friends home (*showing a limitation of peer relationships*). The younger child was overactive, difficult to contain, and falling behind at school (*insufficient developmental progress*).

Focus on mental illness and the interface of role of parent and role of patient

When Jean was psychotically depressed, she went into hospital voluntarily, although her parents sometimes initiated the admission (*adopted role of patient*). She had valued her relationships with the psychiatrist and mental health worker, but lost these when she moved house. She did not want referral to a particular mental health service where she had been an inpatient. There was, therefore, a delay in finding an appropriate service (*she was not sufficiently contained in role of patient*), during which time she became more preoccupied and worried by her thoughts (*showing preoccupation with level of symptoms; paranoia interfering with trust*). She continued to look after her children to whom she was devoted and committed; nevertheless they both developed symptoms of anxiety (*psychiatric symptoms directly affecting parenting capacity, i.e. capacity to attend to children's emotional needs*). Both children regularly spent time with close relatives, but there were indications that Jean lacked judgement about one of the people to whom they were entrusted, for example sleeping in an adult male relative's bed (*psychiatric symptoms directly affecting parenting, i.e. capacity to protect*).

Focus on parental role of other parent

The children had different fathers, both of whom had mental health difficulties of their own (*spouse's health and emotional resources*). One of the fathers lived a distance away and was unreliable (*no capacity to be available*). The status of the relationship with the second husband continued to be a source of stress (*no commitment to maintaining family as a unit on his part*). He depended on his parents to care for the younger child during visits (*no commitment to relationship with child*). Since the physical assault, the tensions between the elder son and stepfather deteriorated to the extent that the son would not be in the house with the father, and was even afraid to be in the father's proximity (*breakdown of relationship with child*).

Focus on role of spouse/partner

Although physically separated, the couple had not decided whether this was to be permanent and consequently could not sort out issues of parental responsibility (*lack of capacity to work together as parents*). Jean felt 'trapped' between her relationship with her husband and her son (*no capacity to work together as parents*). This had led to numerous arguments before the assault on the oldest child (*intensity of marital conflict*) and these were usually left to 'simmer down' rather than attempting to resolve underlying issues (*lack of ability to communicate*).

Focus on role of context/extended family

The mother's parents had an important role in the routine care of one of the children, although they would have preferred to look after both of them (*access to relationship with adult who is committed to providing support*). The relationship between the mother and her parents became tense when they disapproved of her behaviour and her second husband (*mother's relationship to own parents is somewhat difficult*). Both the fathers of the children were part of the mother's community, and therefore her contact with them was likely to continue (*resulting in environmental stress*). There was very little contact with other people. Jean did not have any friends or social life. However, her sister was willing to get involved; and two school friends with families of their own and living nearby offered to help (*quality of non-family network*).

It is clear from this description that the family's situation is a precarious one with regard to ensuring adequate care of the children. Yet it is by no means certain that taking the children away from their mother would necessarily provide them with better care in a publicly managed care system (Department of Health, 2001). There are untapped resources in the extended family system and community, which could improve the situation. However, no one single professional is likely to have sufficient training and skill to address the family in context. A team is needed to move the whole situation to one where everyone is better connected, relationships are clarified, and the needs of both children and adults are better met. As long as there is adequate parental concern, it is usually possible to arrive at a formulation which addresses both the child's and the parent's needs as being complementary to one another.

Preparation of court reports

It is not possible to cover this topic comprehensively here and the reader may wish to refer to specific literature on child protection (Barker & Hodes, 2002) and to the literature on assessments and writing reports (Budd *et al.*, 2001; Department of Health, 2000). The professional who undertakes an assessment for forensic purposes invariably takes on a different perspective than that of clinician. It has been argued that the two tasks (clinical and forensic) should not normally be combined (Iverson, 2000). However, separation of the two roles is not always realistic. A professional may always be asked to provide information for the court. Such information will be of a different status to that of an independent third party expert for court purposes but, for clinical purposes, it may further ongoing work and help in exploring possibilities for change. If a parent wishes to collaborate with an assessment process, a clinical report need not jeopardize the clinical relationship. Reports may even be written conjointly with the parent, and even signed by both.

Indications for formal assessments

A formal assessment of parenting capacity should only be carried out if there are formal reasons to be concerned for the well-being of children. Where possible, the person making the parent–child assessment should represent neither the child nor the parent but take the referral from the courts and be neutral. Whatever the source of the request, the professional in most jurisdictions has a duty to be independent and focus on the best interests of the child. There needs to be a clear question formulated by the court that sets the terms of reference for the expert assessment. The task of the assessor is to advise the judge about the particular circumstances of the family and their implications. Decisions are left to the judge. An expert advisor should only act within her area of expertise. For instance, an adult psychiatrist is not an expert in parenting. Her expertise is in the delineation and prognosis of psychiatric disorder and this should limit any official opinions.

Standards

An assessment should include observations and information from more than one setting and from several sources (Budd *et al.*, 2001; Department of Health, 2000). The focus of the assessment has to be the parent–child relationship or parent–child fit. Accepting that parenting assessment needs to be carried out within a complex and multidimensional framework, the following methodological components should be considered.

Sequence

(1) Clarify referral question; ensure it is specific enough and falls within the professional expertise of the assessor; review all available background information; formulate a hypothesis about why this issue has arisen now and what it might be about; develop a plan for the assessment; request other people with complementary expertise to be involved if appropriate.

(2) Set up interviews with the parent(s) and child(ren). If possible, seek third party information and parent–child observation, and possibly administer tests or questionnaires.

(3) Review all information collected; write a report that answers the original question and stays within the limits of the author's professional expertise.

Content

(4) An assessment for court purposes usually will have to make a prediction about the future. The most accurate predictor of the future is the past. Hence, a thorough history of the parent's personal, family and psychiatric history is essential, including reviews of past records, third-party history as well as a direct interview with the parent.

(5) A thorough psychiatric, family and parenting assessment should be informed by interviews with all family members and parent–child observation, and may be complemented by paper-and-pencil tests or standardized interviews. Any instruments used must be valid and reliable, and its application must be within the competence of the assessor. Information from tests or other measurement instruments should only be used in conjunction with clinical information and, for maximum validity, any such test information should be interpreted in triangulation with interview and observational information. Observation of relationships should be specific for each dyad in the family where appropriate and possible, and all dyadic relationship constellations may be briefly considered in the way they form part of the overall interactional pattern of the family as a whole. Observation must include an evaluation of the home setting and of the child in a child-care or school setting if at all possible.

(6) Assumptions/beliefs of the assessor should be clearly stated, and scientific evidence should only be quoted where relevant. Within an adversarial legal system cross-examination may focus on the expert's beliefs rather than on their expertise because this is what can be more easily questioned in a court.

(7) Specific risk factors relating to a parent's mental health issues should be addressed (Jacobsen *et al.*, 1997) (see Jacobsen, Chapter 8).

Recommendations for writing court reports

The report needs to be written so that a lay person can understand it. All technical terms should be explained. If reference is made to research, the status of the particular research evidence should be outlined. Research evidence does not necessarily increase the credibility of the report. The recommendations for the format of reports vary slightly from country to country (Budd, 2001; The Expert Witness Group, 1997; Tufnell *et al.*, 1996) and may depend on the instruction given. The report may form the basis for cross-examination of the expert witness in court. Lawyers prepare for this by looking at the assumptions in the report as a relatively easy target for cross-examination. Assumptions, if relevant, should be stated explicitly as such and carefully considered.

Our strong recommendation is not to prescribe any particular intervention unless it is known to be available and acceptable to the parties concerned. Outcomes cannot be guaranteed but can be described as objectives.

Giving evidence in court hearings

Many professionals do not like giving evidence in court, because they feel intimidated, do not understand the nature of the proceedings, and feel helpless. It is important to establish a good enough working relationship with the lawyer handling the case. It may be helpful to go over the written report carefully to prepare for cross-examination. It is advisable to enquire about any new evidence that has come to light since writing the report. Above all, it is important to keep in mind that the court hearing is for the benefit of the family and children. If expert evidence submitted to the court is contradictory, it is common practice in many jurisdictions to convene discussions to clarify and resolve such differences. Ideological battles based on differing professional assumptions are usually unhelpful.

Methods of assessment/intervention

As outlined above, it is not always recommended that the same person who works clinically with a parent also conduct an assessment for forensic purposes (Iverson, 2000). The main reasons for this are that:

The agenda of a family court or child-care assessment is very different from a clinical assessment in terms of its purpose, even though the content may be similar.

The court report needs to be neutral and neutrality enhances the power differential between the person assessed, and the person assessing.

For the parent concerned, and often for the children or the whole family, neutrality can mean nonengagement and betrayal of trust. Court or child welfare proceedings may translate into perceived disempowerment and loss of control. Below we briefly outline some approaches that bridge the gap between clinical engagement and formal assessment.

Parent–child game

The Parent–child game is a short-term focused behavioural intervention for parents with strongwilled young children (Forehand & Long, 1996; Forehand & McMahon, 1981; Jenner, 1999). It can be used as a means of assisting parenting assessment as well as a therapeutic intervention, by providing a baseline measure, a circumscribed short piece of work and a repeat measure that indicates whether change is possible. Working with a family over a period of weeks enables an accurate assessment of the capacity to change. Other ways of working therapeutically, such as solution-focused interventions (Berg, 1991; Lethem, 1994) or network meetings (see Göpfert *et al.*, 1996; Reed, 1999; Rueveni, 1979) (see Asen & Schuff, Chapter 10), similarly can provide an assessment of the capacity to change which cannot be achieved without a trial of therapeutic work.

Family group conferences

The New Zealand Children, Young Persons and Their Families Act (1989) introduced the idea of the family group conference as the country's main statutory process. This is an attempt to integrate indigenous and western cultures in a way that safeguards children's needs for care and protection. It has since been adopted in many other countries such as Australia, USA, UK and Sweden (Marsh & Crow, 1998; Merkel-Holguin, 1996) in order to address a number of issues:

(1) An escalating number of children, with a substantive minority representation, are looked after out-of-home.
(2) Time in care is unacceptably long for many children.
(3) Many children experience multiple series of care placements.
(4) Child care services often are not optimally culture-sensitive.
(5) Family group conferences have also been used in juvenile justice settings and with children in need of supervision as a result of delinquent behaviour (Cunha, 1999; Kogan, 2001).

A family group conference is a discussion, facilitated by service providers, between members of the extended family with the purpose of arriving at a common standpoint that subsequently informs the action plan. It gives the extended family increased responsibility and utilises their resources and networks to find solutions. A suitable coordinator/facilitator from the statutory agency is assigned and convenes a meeting of the extended family. This will involve individual contacts to start with and is a skilled activity. The aim is to empower the family and build support around weaknesses.

Conclusion

The craft of parenting assessment has developed since the last edition of this book. However, it is still necessary to improve access to parenting assessments further and develop more accessible clinical interventions for families at the margins. Any assessment by a child mental health team will only ever be able to provide a small part of the overall picture but done in a therapeutic context can lay the foundation for future therapeutic work. Family group conferences (see above) illustrate one successful principle of working with risk in child protection contexts, namely to give the task of risk management back to the people rather than keeping it in the professional domain. A partnership approach emphasizing the joint responsibility between staff and patients works well in the therapeutic community model of treatment for personality-disordered people (Jones, 1976; Lees *et al.*, 1999). There are elements of this in the work of Schuff & Asen (1996) (see Asen & Schuff, Chapter 10) and the Mellow Parenting approach (see Puckering, Chapter 12). These are tasks for the future which may yet provide us with better and more preventive ways of engaging with and working in support of marginal families.

Acknowledgements

The following have provided valuable assistance in compiling this chapter: Karen Budd, Kate Hellin, Deborah Hodes, Nora McClelland and Tara Weeramanthri.

Appendix 7.1

We gratefully acknowledge the permission to reprint the following excerpt of a practice protocol. This was jointly developed by Dorian Cole, Eddie Wilde and Sue Lewis from Lambeth Social Services Department and South London & Maudsley NHS Trust.

Assessment of the needs of mentally ill parents and their children

Joint Protocol between Lambeth Social Services Children's Division and Lambeth Adult Mental Health Services of the South London and Maudsley NHS Trust
(1)   Principles
• Children's needs are paramount.
• Children's needs are best met when parents are supported.
• Parents with mental illness have the right to be supported in fulfilling their parental roles and responsibilities.

- Children have the right to be protected from harm and to receive services when their health or development is at risk.
- A multi-agency approach to assessment and service provision is in the best interests of parents and children.
- Risk is reduced when information is shared effectively across agencies.
- Risk to children is reduced through effective multi-agency and multidisciplinary working.
- Services should be needs-led.
- Resources may influence the services that can be provided to meet identified need.
- While many parents with mental health and/or substance problems safeguard their children well, children's life chances may be limited as a result of those factors, and health professionals need to consider this possibility for all patients with children.

(2)   Practice standards

- Mentally ill parents' needs should be defined as including those occasioned by parenting, as well as by the adults' own personal needs, e.g. personal care of the child; preparation of meals and drinks; attending to the child's health needs; parental involvement in indoor and outdoor play; support in education.
- Parenting needs should also be seen as tasks that do not directly involve the parent, but support their parenting choices, e.g. providing child-care while a parent rests.
- When a referral to Children and Family Social Services is made to consider an assessment of a child's needs, parents and children (where appropriate) need to be informed of the referral and their consent obtained to contact other agencies. If a referral is made where there is likely or actual risk of harm to a child, consent is not required.
- Parents and children (where appropriate) should receive copies of assessments in formats accessible to each individual.
- Assessments and care plans should always be interagency in their approach.
- Care plans must ensure a clear focus on the welfare of the child.
- Adults and children (where appropriate) should always be advised as to how to make representations or complaints about any part of the assessment and care planning process and be supported should they wish to do so.

(3)   Referrals to social service child-care teams

- Child-care teams should routinely record whether a parent has a mental health problem at the initial assessment.
- A decision should be made about whether the child is potentially a child in need within the terms of Lambeth's threshold criteria, within 24 hours of a referral.
- If a child is not identified as 'in need', and a parent has a mental health disorder, consideration should first be given to referring any concerns to the patient's GP.

Where the problem is significant or acute and the person is previously known to Adult Mental Health Services, then referral to a Lambeth Community Mental Health Team (CMHT) would be appropriate.

- If a child is potentially 'in need' as well as a parent experiencing a mental health disorder, a referral should be made to CMHT, and arrangements made for a joint initial assessment. This should be led by CMHT staff, who should take responsibility for contacting the family.

(4)   Referrals to Community Mental Health Teams

- CMHTs should routinely record whether there is a child in the family.
- At the first visit, if the child is considered to be in need, or if there are any concerns, they should be referred to the child and family services. Questions about whether a child is in need should be made within the terms of Lambeth's threshold criteria (Appendix 11).
- If the children are not 'in need', CMHTs should carry on with their usual assessment and care planning process. *This should always include frequent and active consideration of whether the child's needs are being met.*
- If the children are potentially 'in need', or in need of protection, a referral should be made to the Referral and Assessment Team, Children's Services in Lambeth Social Services and arrangements made for a joint initial assessment. Where a child has emotional difficulties, consideration should also be given to referring to Child and Adolescent Mental Health Services (CAMHS) in Lambeth (Appendix V).
- If there are concerns about possible significant harm to a child, an immediate telephone referral is required to the relevant District Referral and Assessment team, North or South of the Borough, followed by written referral record within 24 hours.

(5)   Young carers

When a young person is undertaking any caring role within the family the first consideration should be whether or not the adult is receiving the necessary services. Referrals to Children's Services in relation to young carers should therefore automatically be referred to CMHTs and a joint assessment carried out, *led by CMHTs.*

(6)   The referral and information point

The Referral and Assessment service of Children and Families Social Services Department will determine whether an initial assessment will occur within 24 hours of receiving the inter-agency referral record. This record will include questions as to whether the consent of the service user has been sought and that they are aware of the referral.

Explicit and recorded conversation should take place at this point between relevant Team Leaders/Practice Managers or persons acting in their absence (not the Service Manager) on who will lead on the case.

When it concerns Child Protection, however, Children's Services will automatically take the lead.

(7)   The initial assessment

The initial assessment should be completed within 7 working days of referral to Children's Services, who will take responsibility for coordinating the process. The childcare social worker is expected to see the child and complete the DoH assessment framework documentation. The CMHT worker should complete their assessment forms.

The initial assessment should:

- Identify the core needs of the mentally ill parent.
- Explore the degree of permanency of the parent's mental illness.
- Identify the child's developmental needs, and the parents' capacity to meet those needs within the context of their environment.
- Take account of known variations in the need for assistance, such as additional support during school holidays, at weekends, etc.
- Agree a joint action plan with the parent(s) and child (if appropriate) which identifies the care package to be provided, responsibility for provision and timetable for review. Clear links between child-care procedures and mental health procedures (i.e. Care Programme Approach) should be apparent.
- This plan should include contingencies such as fluctuating medical conditions, hospitalization of parent or child, and partner's absence, so that should any of these eventualities occur a reassessment is not required, and prior authorization of services has been obtained.
- Decide whether a full/core assessment is required.

(8)   Criteria for a full/core assessment

A full/core assessment should be carried out when:

- The needs of the parent are complex.
- There is a risk of significant harm to a child in the family.
- The adult's impairment or illness is stable, but the child's/children's needs are complex.
- The absence of a full/core assessment is likely to lead to a re-referral.
- Three or more initial assessments have been carried out within the last 12 months.

(9)   The full/core assessment

This assessment is an in-depth assessment of need, which should be carefully planned and involve all relevant agencies. It should be completed within 42 working days of the original referral.

At the start of a full/core assessment, a planning meeting should take place between a member of staff from each service, the family and relevant professionals from other agencies who might be asked to contribute to the assessment process. At this meeting, a recommendation should be made as to the most appropriate service to take the lead and a written agreement completed with the family.

A full assessment should be led by CMHTs when:

- The parent has a significant, acute, and enduring need complex, and requires a package of care to support them in their parenting role.

A core assessment should be carried out in line with the assessment framework for children in need, and will be led by Children's Services when:

- There is a risk of significant harm to a child in the family.
- The adult's impairment or illness is stable, but the child's/children's needs are complex.

At the end of a full/core assessment, a care plan should be jointly agreed between Children's Service and the CMHT. This should be recorded within Children's Division and on the CPA care plan. Both Team Managers should approve this care plan and agree the allocation of resources to support a care package before presentation to the Adults Joint Funding Panel.

(10)   Review

Timescales for review will be identified at the point that a joint action plan or joint care plan is agreed.

The review process should take account of the fact that the needs of people with mental health problems constantly change in both foreseen and unforeseen ways. A timescale should therefore be set in response to

- the particular circumstances surrounding the adult service user's needs (through clinical and funding reviews),
- the changing needs of the child, and
- the complexity and size of the package being provided.

There should always be the flexibility for a case to be re-reviewed at any time or re-opened speedily if they have been closed.

Should the priority for review differ between the two services then a shorter timescale will be adopted.

REFERENCES

Anthony, E. J. & McGinnis, M. (1978). Counseling very disturbed parents. In *Helping Parents Help Their Children*, ed. L. E. Arnold, New York: Brunner/Mazel.

Azar, S. T. & Benjet, C. L. (1994). A cognitive perspective on ethnicity, race and termination of parental rights. *Law and Human Behavior*, *18*, 249–68.

Azar, S. T., Lauretti, A. E. & Loding, B. V. (1998). The evaluation of parental fitness in termination of parental rights cases: a functional-contextual perspective. *Clinical Child and Family Psychology Review*, *1*, 77–100.

Barker, J. & Hodes, D. (2002). *The Child in Mind: A Child Protection Handbook*. London: City and Hackney Primary Care Trust.

Berg, I. K. (1991). *Family Preservation: a Brief Therapy Workbook*. London: BT Press.

Bettelheim, B. (1987). *A Good Enough Parent*. London: Thames and Hudson.

Brodzinsky, D. M. (1993). On the use and misuse of psychological testing in child custody evaluations. *Professional Psychology, Research and Practice, 24*, 213–19.

Budd, K. S. (2001). Assessing parenting competence in child protection cases: a clinical practice model. *Clinical Child and Family Psychology, 4*, 1–18.

Budd, K. S. & Holdsworth, M. J. (1996). Issues in clinical assessment of minimal parenting competence. *Journal of Clinical Child Psychology, 25*, 1–14.

Budd, K. S., Felix, E. & Poindexter, L. (1998, revised 2000). Clinical assessment code book: Parent evaluations. Chicago: Clinical Evaluation and Services Initiative, Cook County Juvenile Court.

Budd, K. S., Poindexter, L. M., Felix, E. D. & Naik-Polan, A. T. (2001). Clinical assessment of parents in child protection cases: an empirical analysis. *Law and Human Behavior, 25*, 93–108.

Cunha, J. M. (1999). Family group conferences: healing the wounds of juvenile property crime in New Zealand and the United States. *Emory International Law Review, 13*, 283–92.

Daro, D. (1990). *Confronting Child Abuse: Research for Effective Program Design.* New York: Free Press.

D'Orban, P. T. (1979). Women who kill their children. *British Journal of Psychiatry, 134*, 560–71.

Department of Health (2000). *Framework for the Assessment of Children in Need and their Families.* London: The Stationery Office.

Department of Health (2001). *The Children Act now: Messages from Research.* London: The Stationery Office.

Falkov, A. (1997). Adult psychiatry – a missing link in child protection. *Child Abuse Review, 6*, 41–5.

Forehand, R. & Long, N. (1996). *Parenting the Strongwilled Child: The Clinically Proven Five-week Program for Parents of two- to six-year olds.* Chicago: Contemporary Books.

Forehand, R. & McMahon, R. (1981). *Helping the Non-compliant Child: A Clinician's Guide to Parent training.* New York: Guilford Press.

Göpfert, M., Webster, J., Pollard, J. & Nelki, J. S. (1996). The assessment and prediction of parenting capacity: a community-oriented approach. In *Parental Psychiatric disorder: Distressed Parents and their Families*, ed. M. Göpfert, J. Webster & M. V. Seeman, pp. 271–309. Cambridge: Cambridge University Press.

Göpfert, M., Harrison, P. & Mahoney, C. (1999). *Keeping the Family in Mind: Participative Research into Mental Ill-health and how it Affects the Whole Family.* Liverpool: Save the Children, Barnados, Imagine and North Mersey Community Trust.

Greene, B. F. & Kilili, S. (1998). How good does a parent have to be? Issues and examples associated with empirical assessments of parenting adequacy in cases of child abuse and neglect. In *Handbook of Child Abuse Research and Treatment*, ed. J. R. Lutzker, pp. 53–72. New York: Plenum.

Heilbrun, K. (1992). The role of psychological testing in forensic assessment. *Law and Human Behavior, 16*, 257–72.

Husain, A. & Daniel, A. (1984). A comparative study of filicidal and abusive mothers. *Canadian Journal of Psychiatry, 29*, 596–8.

Iverson, G. L. (2000). Dual relationships in psycho-legal evaluations: treating psychologists serving as expert witnesses. *American Journal of Forensic Psychology, 18*, 79–87.

Jacobsen, T., Miller, L. J. & Kirkwood, K. (1997). Assessing parenting competency in mentally ill individuals: a comprehensive service. *Journal of Mental Health Administration, 24,* 189–99.

Jenner, S. (1999). *The Parent/Child Game.* New York: Bloomsbury.

Jones, M. (1976). *Maturation of the Therapeutic Community – an Organic Approach to Health and Mental Health.* New York: Human Sciences Press.

Kogan, M. (2001). The problems and benefits of adopting family group conferencing for PINS (CHINS) children. *Family Court Review, 39,* 207–22.

Lees, J., Manning, N. & Rawlings, B. (1999). *Therapeutic Community Effectiveness.* NHS Centre Reviews and Dissemination Report, No. 17. York: University of York.

Lethem, J. (1994). *Moved to Tears, Moved to Action. Solution-focussed Brief Therapy with Women and Children.* London: BT Press.

Mahoney, C. & Mackechnie, S. (2001). *In a Different World: Parental Drug and Alcohol use. A Consultation into its Effects on Children and Families in Liverpool.* Liverpool: Liverpool Health Authority.

Marsh, P. & Crow, G. (1998). *Family Group Conferences in Child Welfare.* Oxford: Blackwells.

Melton, G. B., Petrila, J., Pouythress, N. G. & Slobogia, C. (1997). *Psychological Evaluations for the Courts,* 2nd edn. New York: Guilford Press.

Merkel-Holguin, L. (1996). Putting families back into the child protection partnership: Family Group Decision Making. *Protecting Children, 12,* (3). Online: http://www. ahafgdm.org/what_is. htm

Reed, A. (1999). Psychiatric hospital admission and interpersonal 'closure': network meetings as a means of countering closure. *Human Systems, 10,* 35–48.

Rueveni, U. (1979). *Networking Families in Crisis.* New York: Human Sciences Press.

Schuff, H. & Asen, E. (1996). The disturbed parent and the disturbed family. In *Parental Psychiatric Disorder: Distressed Parents and their Families,* ed. M. Göpfert, J. Webster & M. V. Seeman, pp. 135–51. Cambridge: Cambridge University Press.

Sturge, C. (2001). A multi-agency approach to assessment. *Child Psychology and Psychiatry Review, 6,* 16–20.

The Expert Witness Group (1997). *The Expert Witness Pack.* Bristol: Family Law.

Tufnell, G., Cottrell, D. & Georgiades, D. (1996). 'Good Practice' for expert witnesses. *Clinical Child Psychology and Psychiatry, 1,* 365–83.

Wall, N. & Hamilton, I. (2000). *Expert Witnesses in Children Act Cases.* Bristol: Family Law.

Webster, J., Hatfield, B. & Mohamad, H. (1999). Assessment of parents by approved social workers under the Mental Health Act 1983. *Practice, 11,* 5–18.

Winnnicott, D. W. (1964a). *The Child, the Family and the Outside World.* Harmondsworth: Penguin.

Winnicott, D. W. (19964b). *The Family and Individual Development.* London: Tavistock.

Winnicott, D. W. (1965). *The Maturational Processes and the Facilitating Environment: Studies in the Theory of Emotional Development.* London: The Hogarth Press and the Institute of Psychoanalysis.

8

Mentally ill mothers in the parenting role: clinical management and treatment

Teresa Jacobsen

University of Illinois at Chicago, Illinois, USA

Introduction

When a woman with a major psychiatric disorder becomes a parent, the path that lies ahead for her and her child can be very uncertain. While some mothers are able, despite their illness, to raise their children successfully, as many as 60% of mothers with major mental disorders relinquish or lose custody of their children (Coverdale & Aruffo, 1989; Miller & Finnerty, 1996). Some mothers in this situation provide intermittent parenting or coparenting (Caton *et al.*, 1998) during the years of infancy, childhood and adolescence. Even when mother and child lose contact, each may continue to exert a profound emotional influence over the life of the other (Holley & Holley, 1997).

Intervening to alleviate parenting problems in mothers with major psychiatric disorders is recognized as a challenge to mental health providers (Nicholson & Blanch, 1994). This chapter provides an overview of clinical services and treatments that address serious parenting problems in mothers with major mental illness.

Approach to treatment

Components of a comprehensive evaluation

A comprehensive parenting evaluation is the cornerstone of treatment. It directly examines a mother's ability to read her child's cues, her ability to empathize with and understand the child as an individual, her cognitive understanding of development and childrearing, her ways of coping with stress, her ability to meet basic parenting tasks such as providing food, housing, and safety, and her skill in adjusting her behaviour to meet the changing needs of children as they grow (Jacobsen *et al.*, 1997). A good evaluation of parenting also assesses the context of the mother-child interaction:

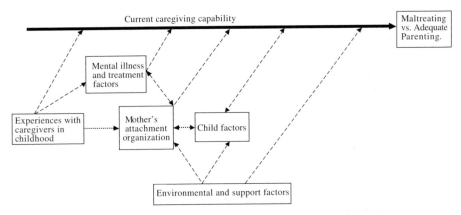

Figure 8.1   Determinants of caregiving capability in mothers with chronic mental disorders.

Mental illness and treatment factors

Important aspects of mental illness that need examination include the type and nature of a mother's symptoms, the severity of her illness and its prognosis, the insight a mother has into her illness, the presence of suicidal and homicidal ideation or substance addiction, and the mother's compliance and responsiveness to past and current treatment regimens (Jacobsen & Miller, 1998).

Environmental and demographic factors

A mother's economic resources and housing are key factors influencing successful parenting. The extent to which a mother is supported in the parenting role is critical (Crittenden, 1985). Family relationships can work as a buffer against stress, while also providing concrete help to the mother. Family relationships can have adverse effects on parenting as well, especially if there is family violence, or when relatives reinforce the sick role by failing to consult a mother in her child-care decisions (Nicholson et al., 1998).

Maternal attachment

A mother's current parenting capabilities can be strongly influenced by past experiences with her own attachment figures during the years of infancy, childhood and adolescence. If a mother experienced abuse, gross neglect or loss in childhood, she is more likely to have difficulties in caring for her own children. For instance, if a mother continues to be retraumatized by past experiences, then her own attachment needs may take priority over appropriate parenting (Bowlby, 1988) (see Hill, Chapter 4).

Child factors

The nature and quality of children's relationship with their mother and the children's own special needs are also important components of a parenting evaluation (see Göpfert *et al.*, Chapter 7; Seneviratne & Conroy, Chapter 9). The relation between a mother's caregiving capabilities and a child's vulnerabilities must be weighed against the projected time frame of favourable change in both mother and child. The crucial question is: will the mother's symptoms respond to treatment and allow her to respond appropriately to the special needs of her child while the mother–child bond is still emotionally significant?

Components of a comprehensive approach to parenting rehabilitation

Necessary components of a comprehensive approach to parenting rehabilitation include interventions that directly address a mother's specific parenting needs and deficits, psychiatric treatment and close liaison with other services, such as gynaecology, paediatrics and child psychiatry. Coordination among services enhances a mother's acceptance of care and ensures continuity in treatment recommendations.

Sensitivity to gender issues in mental illness and to a family's cultural, ethnic and religious background are part and parcel of a sound treatment approach (Lieberman, 1989) (see Göpfert *et al.*, Chapter 5). Interventions that are sensitive to children's developmental and attachment needs are also essential.

Treatment is likely to be most successful if it is undertaken with no negative labels or blame attached to mental illness, and no preconceptions about the relationship between mental illness and parenting capability. Being empathetic with the mother does not, of course, mean being blind to risks for the child. Nonetheless, interventions will be more effective if they focus on a parent's strengths and if they involve a collaborative process.

Services for pregnant mothers

Working with a pregnant psychotic mother can pose specific risks with regard to care of the fetus and future parenting. Inpatient treatment is necessary if a mother threatens violence towards her unborn infant, if there is serious neglect of the fetus due to delusional beliefs or there is a risk of precipitous delivery (Spielvogel & Wile, 1986) (see Seneviratne & Conroy, Chapter 9). Inpatient treatment allows for careful behaviour management of symptoms by a team also able to address the medical, social service and legal interventions that may ensue.

Several successful inpatient programmes have been implemented for pregnant women who cannot be safely managed with outpatient treatment (Miller, 1990;

Seeman & Cohen, 1998; Spielvogel & Wile, 1986). Women are typically admitted in their third trimester of pregnancy or in times of acute crisis. Integration of psychiatric and obstetric care is a crucial part of the treatment. Focus is given to helping women maintain adequate nutrition, rest and activity, while providing a safe environment. In addition to treating a mother's psychiatric disorder, the following treatments may be offered: psychoeducational groups, electroconvulsive therapy, individual and/or family therapy, parenting skills training, family planning and practical assistance with child-care, and other available social programmes (Miller, 1992). A woman is also encouraged to become involved in the therapeutic milieu, with focus given to helping her remain in contact with reality.

On an inpatient unit, medication effects can be monitored and doses altered as needed. Since psychotropic drugs pass through the placental barrier, decisions about use of medication during pregnancy involve weighing the risks and benefits to the mother and fetus (see Seeman & Seeman, Chapter 16).

Given that some women may not note impending signs of labour, staff members need to be careful at all times to note both physical markers and behavioural changes signifying the onset of labour. Forcier (1990) described one patient who, 24 hours prior to going into labour, placed an assortment of linens on the floor that resembled a nest. Her behaviour provided a powerful signal of the upcoming birth. In emergency situations, the staff become the patient's labour coach.

Psychotic denial of pregnancy

Psychotic denial of pregnancy is rare, but constitutes a clinical emergency, especially since it prevents prenatal care and adequate nutrition, and jeopardizes safe and planned deliveries (Spielvogel & Hohener, 1995). If psychotic denial is prolonged, comprehensive psychiatric and obstetric care and hospitalization may be required. Ultrasound examinations can be effective in helping some psychotic mothers see the baby and accept their pregnancy (Look & Howe, 1984). Antipsychotic medication can be useful in reducing agitation, disorganization, delusional ideas about pregnancy, hallucinations and violent or self-destructive behaviour (Miller, 1991). This needs to be coupled with supportive psychotherapy and psychosocial interventions geared at preparing the mother for delivery, and managing the anticipated loss of the infant to Children's Social Services after delivery. Since the incidence of psychotic denial of pregnancy is higher in mothers who have lost custody of prior children (Miller, 1990), it is critical to address ongoing processes of past mourning during treatment. Mothers who have lost custody of a child, may grieve for several years, even though the child only existed for them in hopes and fantasy (Rynearson, 1982).

The mother's parenting skills should be evaluated prior to delivery to assess whether she can safely care for her newborn. Such an evaluation can determine how the mother feels about her unborn baby, examine her past caregiving history, her ability to learn from instruction, her support network and her adaptive living skills. If it is determined that the baby is at high longer-term risk, arrangements about guardianship need to be made.

Intervening in the postpartum period

Mothers who become severely depressed or psychotic after childbirth may experience a loss of love for their infants, or hold bizarre beliefs about the baby and the birth process (Sneddon *et al.*, 1981). They may have highly negative attitudes about parenting or feel that the baby hates them. Many express feelings of guilt about their parenting capabilities (Kissane & Ball, 1988). In extreme cases, there may be risk of infanticide or suicide, requiring admission to a psychiatric unit. Hospitalization in the postpartum period disrupts the developing mother–infant attachment bond, and may undermine a mother's confidence in her ability to care for her infant.

If available, inpatient psychiatric units that allow mothers and infants to visit or stay with each other can facilitate continuity in the developing mother–child relationship. During hospitalization, staff can also help a mother to recognize and manage aspects of projection or identification, which may interfere with her ability to relate to the infant. Educational information on childrearing and development is useful. Mothers are encouraged to assume responsibility for the care of their infant as quickly as possible.

While on the unit, a parenting skills assessment can be undertaken. Important areas to evaluate include psychiatric and psychological functioning, daily living skills, quality of mother–infant interaction and relationship, and a developmental evaluation of the infant (Ramsay *et al.*, 1998) (see Seneviratne & Conroy, Chapter 9). Planning postdischarge child-care arrangements is critical, as is continuity in treatment and outreach services for the mother.

If a mother does not require hospitalization in the postpartum period, outpatient therapy to address her symptoms may be coupled with regular home visits that focus on helping her improve her caregiving skills.

Crittenden & Snell (1983) have utilized a behaviourally based intervention, which involves teaching high-risk mothers to hold the baby face-to-face. This intervention led to significant improvement in how mothers interacted with their infants. Their infants also showed improvement in their linguistic and cognitive skills when pre- and postintervention scores were compared. Such techniques are likely to be most effective when they are one component of a comprehensive treatment protocol.

Cooper & Murray (1997) studied a large group of mothers who were diagnosed with postpartum depression (n = 207). The women were assigned to four groups. The control group received routine primary care. Women in the intervention groups received either (a) nondirective counselling which focused on their current concerns and feelings; (b) cognitive-behavioural therapy, which emphasized helping a mother examine her patterns of thinking about her infant and modelling aspects of her parenting interaction style; and (c) dynamic psychotherapy, which focused on understanding her relationship with her infant by exploring her own attachment history. Mothers in the intervention group were also visited weekly in the home from 8 to 18 weeks postpartum.

Mothers in all four groups showed a reduction in their depressive symptoms, but the percentage varied dramatically across the four groups. After the intervention, 75% of the women in the psychodynamic group, 59% of the women in the cognitive-behavioural and 52% of women in the non-directive counselling group no longer qualified for Major Depressive Disorder. The rates of women who were in remission were significantly lower (40%) in the control group. Following the intervention, mother–infant relationship problems showed significant improvement in the three treatment groups, but not in the control group. Infants of mothers who received treatment had less difficulties in play, fewer separation problems and were less demanding of their mothers' attention than infants in the control group. Improved relationships were also linked to early remission of depressive symptoms.

There were no effects of treatment or illness remission on infant attachment quality (insecure/secure) at age 18 months. This suggests that while short-term interventions can reduce a mother's mental illness symptoms and facilitate some change in infant outcomes, long-term changes in maternal behaviour and in the quality of the mother–infant attachment bond may require more intensive and longer-term interventions (see Puckering, Chapter 12).

Parent coaching, skills training and parenting groups

Parenting coaching and skills training can be helpful interventions, especially for those mothers who did not experience effective role models in childhood, or those who lack knowledge about specific parenting behaviours. Parenting coaching provides feedback about parenting skills within the confines of a safe relationship. Often it targets a mother's ability to read her child's cues, and focuses on techniques of holding and talking to a child. Parenting skills training is similar, but emphasizes direct teaching methods and education.

Waldo *et al.* (1987) developed a comprehensive programme for mothers with schizophrenia who had preschool children. Mothers participating in the programme received regular psychiatric services in the clinic and were taught concrete parenting skills. Staff members also provided close monitoring of the developmental progress of the children. In addition, mothers were visited regularly at home and met with a child development specialist. Meetings in a small group setting provided mothers with didactic information about childrearing and an opportunity for role modelling and coaching. Mothers remained in the programme as long as they felt it was helpful. On pre- and postintervention measures, the programme reportedly contributed to a drop in the number of children mothers had in foster care, to improved mother–child interactions and to a reduction in the number of maternal hospitalizations.

Lyons-Ruth and her colleagues (1990) designed a comprehensive intervention programme to improve maternal sensitivity and mother–infant attachment. Mothers in the study had been referred for clinical services and were judged to be at high risk due to the combined effects of poverty, maternal depression and caretaking inadequacy. Services included home-based interventions and began when infants were between the ages of 0–9 months and continued until they reached 18 months. The interventions included weekly home visits by a lay visitor or by a professional home visitor. The goals of the home visits were to establish a secure relationship with mothers, to increase their competency in obtaining necessary resources, to model positive interaction behaviour with their infants, and to increase social support. In addition, women in the intervention group participated in weekly group meetings, and received services to aid with their social service and health needs. The intervention group was compared with two groups of mothers who received no interventions. One control group included women and infants who were referred through the same referral process as the intervention group. However, they had not yet received any services. The second control group were a matched comparison group of mothers and infants from the same neighbourhoods who had never sought or received services directed at improving their parenting.

The intervention had a significant effect on infant attachment quality. Untreated depressed mothers were twice as likely to have infants with an insecure-disorganized attachment pattern than treated mothers. This type of pattern is associated with high levels of insecurity in the mother–child attachment bond, and with later behavioural problems in the child (Lyons-Ruth, 1996).

Mothers with chronic mental illness who participate in therapeutic nurseries receive intensive parenting skills training 5 days a week, along with psychosocial rehabilitation and substance abuse treatment. Housing is provided for some women with their infants and young children. Mothers also participate in daily group sessions and work in the centre. Supportive relationships amongst programme participants are fostered (Grunebaum *et al.*, 1982).

The parent's clinic at the University of Illinois

Parenting groups provide a mother with help in learning better parenting skills. The Parent's Clinic at the University of Illinois specializes in mothers with chronic mental illnesses. Mothers who attend the group all have young children and receive medication management and individual psychotherapy in the clinic. The clinic focuses on issues that are of concern to mothers, including experiences of childhood trauma or loss, partner problems, fears of custody loss, pregnancy, family planning and mental illness crises. Helping mothers to recognize role reversal in their children and to learn when and what to tell children about their mental illness are also addressed. While mothers are in the group, a psychologist works with the children. The children later join their mothers, while the therapists provide hands-on parenting coaching and modelling of specific parenting behaviours. Children who have special needs receive individual or play therapy, or are seen with their mothers together in individual sessions that utilize parenting coaching.

If a mother lacks skill or experience in interacting with her child, this can often be corrected through parenting coaching, modelling or through use of videotape feedback. If a mother is judged not emotionally available, however, brief behavioural interventions are not indicated as they require addressing unresolved issues from a mother's childhood that block her ability to empathize with her child (Egeland *et al.*, 2000).

Mother–infant psychotherapy

Selma Fraiberg (1980) coined the term 'parent–infant psychotherapy' to describe the treatment of disturbances in the infant–parent relationship in the first 3 years of life. This approach is based on the notion that parents may re-enact with their young child conflicts with their own attachment figures that remain unresolved. Re-enactments of unresolved conflicts from a parent's own childhood contribute to attachment disturbances in children, probably because they do not, under those circumstances, experience the parent as emotionally available or as a reliable protector against internal or external distress (Lieberman *et al.*, 1997). According to Fraiberg (1980), it is necessary for a parent to recognize, remember and confront the underlying emotional pain associated with childhood experiences in order to favourably change the parent–infant relationship.

Therapy typically includes the mother and infant together either in the home or clinic setting. The role of the therapist is to observe the parent and child together. The therapist focuses on spontaneous feelings that the pair enact when they are together. The therapist uses the immediacy of the moment to explore these feelings, and relate them to a parent's childhood experiences. The primary goal of therapy is to free the infant or young child from the engulfment in the mother's distortions and displaced affects. The therapeutic process involves moving back and forth between the current difficulties in the parent–child relationship and the mother's memories of emotional experiences from childhood relationships. As the mother gains insight into past experiences and empathy for her own feelings, she is better able to empathize with her infant's needs and feelings.

Emotional support and understanding from the therapist is crucial for establishing a relationship with the mother and for exploring past childhood experiences in relation to actual parenting. Fraiberg emphasizes the importance of a therapist being nonjudgemental and sympathetic to a mother's subjective perceptions of her infant, no matter how disturbing these perceptions may seem. In essence, the therapist provides the mother with a 'corrective attachment experience' by functioning as a secure base (Bowlby, 1988).

Conclusion

In an era of limited resources for mothers with mental illness, providing adequate interventions to address the parenting needs of women and their children can be a highly challenging task (Miller, 1992). This chapter has outlined the necessary components to deliver comprehensive parenting services to mothers with psychiatric disorders and has emphasized the close relationship between assessment and treatment. Organized collaboration between existing agencies is critical, especially since it is unlikely that all components of the service can be offered by one agency (Seeman & Cohen, 1998).

Common sense guidelines in implementing effective treatment include intervening as early as possible in order to optimize change, providing intensive interventions of long duration whenever possible to ensure more enduring effects, and providing services that are flexible in meeting the special needs of each individual family (Egeland *et al.*, 2000). To be effective in the long run, treatment must help families develop sustaining relationships with others, as these relationships are likely to continue long after therapeutic interventions end (DePanfilis, 1999).

REFERENCES

Bowlby, J. (1988). *A Secure Base: Clinical Applications of Attachment Theory*. London: Routledge.

Caton, C. L. M., Cournos, F., Felix, A. et al. (1998). Childhood experiences and current adjustment of offspring of indigent patients with schizophrenia. *Psychiatric Services, 49*, 86–90.

Cooper, P. J. & Murray, L. (1997). The impact of psychological treatments of postpartum depression on maternal mood and infant development. In *Postpartum Depression and Child Development*, ed. L. Murray & P. J. Cooper, pp. 201–20. New York: Guilford Press.

Coverdale, J. H. & Aruffo, J. F. (1989). Family needs of female chronic psychiatric outpatients. *American Journal of Psychiatry, 146*, 1489–91.

Crittenden, P. M. (1985). Social networks, quality of child rearing, and child development. *Child Development, 56*, 1299–1313.

Crittenden, P. M. & Snell, M. E. (1983). Intervention to improve mother–infant interaction and infant development. *Infant Mental Health Journal, 4*, 23–41.

DePanfilis, D. (1999). Intervening with families when children are neglected. In *Neglected Children: Research, Practice, and Policy*, ed. H. Dubowitz, pp. 211–36. Beverley Hills, CA: Sage.

Egeland, B., Weinfield, N. S., Bosquet, M. & Cheng, V. K. (2000). Remembering, repeating, and working through lessons from attachment-based interventions. In *Infant Mental Health in Groups at High Risk*, Vol. 4, ed. J. D. Osofsky & H. E. Fitzgerald, pp. 35–89. *WAIMH Handbook of Infant Mental Health*. New York: John Wiley & Sons.

Forcier, K. (1990). Management and care of the mentally disturbed pregnant patient. *Journal of Psychosocial Nursing*, *28*, 11–16.

Fraiberg, S. (1980). *Clinical Studies in Infant Mental Health*. New York: Basic Books.

Grunebaum, H., Weiss, J. L., Cohler, B. J. et al. (1982). *Mentally Ill Mothers and their Children*. Chicago: University of Chicago Press.

Holley, T. E. & Holley, J. (1997). *My Mother's Keeper: A Daughter's Memoir of Growing Up in the Shadow of Schizophrenia*. New York: Morrow.

Jacobsen, T. & Miller, L. J. (1998). Mentally ill mothers who have killed: three cases addressing the issue of future parenting capability. *Psychiatric Services*, *49*, 650–7.

Jacobsen, T., Miller, L. J. & Kirkwood, K. (1997). Assessing parenting competency in mentally ill individuals: a comprehensive service. *Journal of Mental Health Administration*, *24*, 189–99.

Keller, M., Beardslee, W., Dorer, D. et al. (1986). Impact of severity and chronicity of parental affective illness on adaptive functioning and psychopathology in children. *Archives of General Psychiatry*, *43*, 930–7.

Kissane, D. & Ball, J. R. B. (1988). Postnatal depression and psychosis – a mother and baby unit in a general hospital. *Australian and New Zealand Journal of Obstetrics and Gynaecology*, *28*, 208–12.

Lieberman, A. F. (1989). What is culturally sensitive intervention? *Early Child Development and Care*, *50*, 197–204.

Lieberman, A. F., Van Horn, P., Grandison, C. M. et al. (1997). Mental health assessment of infants, toddlers, and preschoolers in a service program and a treatment outcome research program. *Infant Mental Health Journal*, *18*, 158–70.

Look, P. E. & Howe, B. (1984). Unusual use of ultrasound in a paranoid patient. *Canadian Medical Association Journal*, *131*, 539.

Lyons-Ruth, K. (1996). Attachment relationships among children with aggressive behavior problems: the role of disorganized early attachment patterns. *Journal of Consulting and Clinical Psychology*, *64*, 64–73.

Lyons-Ruth, K., Connell, D. B. & Grunebaum, H. U. (1990). Infants at risk: maternal depression and family support services as mediators of infant development and security of attachment. *Child Development*, *61*, 85–98.

Miller, L. J. (1990). Psychotic denial of pregnancy: phenomenology and clinical management. *Hospital and Community Psychiatry*, *41*, 1233–7.

Miller, L. J. (1991). Clinical strategies for the use of psychotropic drugs during pregnancy. *Psychiatric Medicine*, *9*, 275–98.

Miller, L. J. (1992). Comprehensive care of pregnant mentally ill women. *Journal of Mental Health Administration*, *19*, 170–7.

Miller, L. J. & Finnerty, M. (1996). Sexuality, pregnancy, and childrearing among women with schizophrenia-spectrum disorders. *Psychiatric Services, 47*, 502–6.

Nicholson, J. & Blanch, A. (1994). Rehabilitation for parenting roles for people with serious mental illness. *Psychosocial Rehabilitation Journal, 1*, 109–19.

Nicholson, J., Sweeney, E. M. & Geller, J. L. (1998). Mothers with mental illness: II. Family relationships and the context of parenting. *Psychiatric Services, 49*, 643–9.

Ramsay, R., Howard, L. & Kumar, C. (1998). Schizophrenia and safety of parenting of infants: a report from a UK mother and baby service. *International Journal of Social Psychiatry, 44*, 127–34.

Rynearson, E. K. (1982). Relinquishment and its maternal complications: a preliminary study. *American Journal of Psychiatry, 139*, 338–40.

Seeman, M. V. & Cohen, R. (1998). A service for women with schizophrenia. *Psychiatric Services, 49*, 674–7.

Sneddon, J., Kerry, B. J. & Bant, W. P. (1981). The psychiatric mother and baby unit: a 3-year study. *Practitioner, 225*, 1295–300.

Spielvogel, A. & Hohener, H. (1995). Denial of pregnancy: a review and case reports. *Birth, 22*, 220–6.

Spielvogel, A. & Wile, J. (1986). Treatment of the psychotic pregnant patient. *Psychosomatics, 26*, 487–92.

Waldo, M.C., Roath, M., Levine, W. et al. (1987). *Hospital and Community Psychiatry, 48*, 1110–12.

9

Perinatal mental illness: nature/nurture

Gertrude Seneviratne and Sue Conroy

Institute of Psychiatry, University of London, London, UK

Not only do pregnancy and childbirth exert important psychological and physiological effects on a woman's life but a mother's pregnancy and postnatal difficulties impact indelibly on her child and, reciprocally, the temperament health and behaviour of the child impact on the mother's well-being. The psychological fit between the two, in the context of the larger family, carries significant implications for both (Oates, 1996, 2001). Childbearing is associated with a marked increase in the incidence and prevalence of psychiatric disorder although exact causal mechanisms (such as hormonal changes) remain unclear. Postnatal depression is extremely common, being consistently found in 10–15% of mothers (O'Hara & Swain, 1996). Acute postpartum affective or schizoaffective psychosis is less common, affecting about 1–2 in every 1000 deliveries. Though rare, these illnesses are severe and usually require hospitalization with consequent mother–child separation, unless mother and baby units are accessible. In addition, about 2% of pregnant women suffer from chronic severe mental health problems which are exacerbated postpartum (Kumar & O'Dowd, 2000).

This chapter explores how childbirth can contribute to the onset or exacerbation of psychiatric disorder and discusses the relative contributions of aetiological factors, including biological, environmental and psychosocial factors. The potentially serious effects of perinatal mental health problems require specialist clinical services (see Asen & Schuff, Chapter 10; Seeman, Chapter 11; Puckering, Chapter 12), including specialist inpatient facilities for joint admission of mother and baby. Women with mental health problems, unless supports are in place, will have difficulties in caring for their babies. These difficulties may result directly from the mother's illness, from secondary mother–child separations owing to early and recurrent hospitalizations, or from marital problems. Gaps in the support network of the mother may be the major contributory factor. Characteristics of the children themselves, perhaps inherited, can increase the difficulties of parenting (O'Connor *et al.*, 1998), exacerbating the effects of the illness on the mother's capacity to parent. The effect of illness on the child, the effects of the child on the illness, and the repercussions on the wider family and social system always need to be borne in mind (see Göpfert *et al.*, Chapter 5).

Postpartum psychiatric illness

Psychiatric disorders associated with childbirth are traditionally divided into three categories, reflecting severity: maternity blues, postnatal depression and postpartum psychosis. 'Maternity blues' is not a disorder, but is included to distinguish the condition from the more important and clinically significant disorders of postnatal depression and postpartum psychosis. Current classification systems, such as DSM-IV (American Psychiatric Association, 1994) and ICD–10 (World Health Organization, 1993) contain no clear definitions of the nosological status of the disorders (such as onset post delivery), reflecting the overall lack of consensus on whether they are aetiologically related to childbirth.

The 'maternity blues' (minor transitory mood disturbance)

The 'blues' is considered to be a normal phenomenon in terms of both its mildness and its transience. It is very common, with a prevalence of 50–75% of women experiencing a dysphoric reaction in the first week following delivery. As women may experience mild 'highs' as well as depressive episodes (Glover *et al.*, 1994; Hannah *et al.*, 1993), the term 'minor transitory mood disturbance' may be more accurate. The cause of the 'blues' remains unknown, with the literature inconsistent on associated aetiological factors such as hormonal changes (Harris *et al.*, 1994; Okano & Nomura, 1992). Although the condition may cause considerable distress to the mother and relatives, optimal management usually involves little more than reassurance and explanation. Rarely, symptoms of tearfulness, irritability, depression and emotional lability are extreme or prolonged and need to be differentiated from the prodromal features of a puerperal psychosis, which often begins at a similar time. Similarly, if symptoms persist for over 2 weeks, a diagnosis of depression should be considered. Mood instability at this time is expected and requires sufficient social supports for the mother to minimize the impact of symptoms on her care of the child. It is not clear whether characteristics of the infant during the first week (disappointment over the sex of the child, resemblance of the child to a specific family member, appearance or prematurity or health of the child) affect the prevalence or severity of maternity blues.

Postnatal depression (PND)

Postnatal depression refers to a nonpsychotic depressive episode beginning or extending into the postpartum period. The clinical picture is similar to other types of depression, but in addition, the woman may experience difficulty with parenting, feel guilty that she is not coping or be excessively concerned about the baby's health. Despite the increase in psychiatric morbidity in the puerperium, the suicide rate in the first year postpartum has been reported as lower than at other times, ranging from as low as one-sixth to one-half the rate of an age and sex-matched non-pregnant population (Appleby, 1991). This needs to be kept in mind because suicide (usually accompanied by infanticide) during the postpartum period receives wide media coverage, making it appear more common than it really is.

Recent studies have demonstrated adverse effects of postnatal depression on the mother–infant relationship (Martins & Gaffan, 2000), children's (particularly boys) later cognitive and social development, attachments and emotional regulation (Essex *et al.*, 2001; Murray & Cooper, 1996; Sharp *et al.*, 1995) which may persist until the age of 11 (Hay *et al.*, 2001). These effects highlight the need for early detection and interventions that work. Pitt's (1968) study, which was the first to describe the onset of depression occurring in the first 6 weeks following delivery, showed a prevalence of 10% in women who were not depressed antenatally. A more recent meta-analysis of nearly 60 studies (O'Hara & Swain, 1996) placed the prevalence at 13%.

The concept of postnatal depression as a specific clinical entity has been challenged. Cox *et al.* (1982) showed that the relative risk of depression is about three times greater in childbearing women than in a group of approximately matched controls, but only in the first month postpartum (Cox, 1993). Some studies have reported rates of depression in childbearing women to be no greater than the rates in nonchildbearing control women, or in the general population (Cooper *et al.*, 1988; O'Hara *et al.*, 1990). A history of depressive illness heightens the risk of postnatal depression (Marks *et al.*, 1992) which may be an expression of depressive illness following a stressor, in this case childbirth. Both severe 'blues' and a past history of depression were independent predictors of postnatal depression, each raising the risk by almost 3. It is not clear yet whether there are depressions specific to the postnatal period.

Aetiology falls into two main areas: psychosocial factors and neuroendocrine factors (Kumar & O'Dowd, 2000). Epidemiological studies have shown the major aetiological factors to be psychosocial ones in combination with a pre-existing vulnerability to depression. A history of depression is the most powerful predictor, and stressful life events, unemployment, marital conflict and the absence of social support have all consistently been found to add to the risk.

Earlier onset depression may in part have an endocrine cause. Childbirth is a time of massive endocrine changes with the sudden loss of the placenta, the effects of lactation (Wieck, 1996) and the re-establishment of the ovarian cycle. Oestrogen may have mood-elevating properties in postnatal depression (Gregoire *et al.*, 1996) and in menopause (Sherwin, 1994). The mechanism remains unclear. Other hormonal investigations, which have been even less consistent, include the role of progesterone insufficiency (Harris *et al.*, 1994) and cortisol dysregulation (Checkley, 1992). Depressions that occur after the first postnatal month, in contrast, seem to have an aetiological profile that resembles any other depression (Brown & Harris, 1978; Paykel *et al.*, 1980) i.e. a combination of social adversity, life stress and vulnerability factors.

In the UK, diagnosis and management of postnatal depression occur mainly in primary care, with the midwife, health visitor and GP in an ideal position to assess and diagnose, although up to 50% of cases may remain undetected (Sharp, 1992). Only small percentages (2–3%) of severe or treatment-resistant cases are referred to psychiatrists. Both antidepressants and psychological treatments are effective. Treatment needs to be tailored to the individual, depending on suspected causal mechanisms. For example, early-onset depression may respond better to certain therapeutic interventions such as hormones and medication (Gregoire *et al.*, 1996; Harris *et al.*, 1994) than to psychological treatments (Holden *et al.*, 1989). Antidepressants should be prescribed with caution, with due consideration to a woman's desire to breastfeed, and while monitoring the baby (Burt *et al.*, 2001; Yoshida *et al.*, 1999) (see Seeman & Seeman Chapter 16). Reassurance and supportive counselling may be provided by trained nonmedical professionals, such as health visitors (Holden, 1996; Prettyman & Friedman, 1991). There is supportive evidence for cognitive–behavioural counselling (Appleby *et al.*, 1997) or interpersonal psychotherapy (O'Hara *et al.*, 2000). Self-help and support groups can encourage mutual support and advice concerning mothering and child-care, as well as more specific issues related to depression. For severe, psychotic depression, neuroleptics or electroconvulsive therapy (ECT) may be indicated. The aim of treatment in postnatal depression is the preservation of the mother–child bond, reinforcement of the mother's developing confidence in caring appropriately for her child and the child's healthy development.

Postpartum psychosis

There is much evidence to suggest that childbirth can precipitate a bipolar affective or schizoaffective psychosis. The clinical profile may vary, but there is typically an initial 'lucid interval' lasting a few days following delivery. Prodromal features of the illness may coincide with the onset of the 'blues'. As mothers are now discharged early from maternity wards or deliver at home, initial symptoms may be observed by family members who notice difficulty in sleeping, confusion and odd behaviour. Patchy perplexity is common and the clinical presentation may be that of a manic illness or of an agitated depression. The mother may be preoccupied by rigid routines for the baby and minor health problems may become overwhelming. Sometimes, the picture is of a labile affect; in other cases, there may be persecutory delusions or ideas of reference, such as special messages or hallucinations.

Epidemiological studies (Kendell *et al.*, 1987; Terp & Mortensen, 1998) have shown that there is a greatly increased risk of admission to psychiatric hospital in the first few months after delivery. For all mothers, the risk is increased sevenfold in the month after delivery, for first-time mothers and admissions for a psychotic illness only, this relative risk rises even further by a factor of 35 (Kendell *et al.*, 1987). A recent study linking the Danish birth and psychiatric register (Terp & Mortensen, 1998) reported a relative risk of 6.82 for a first-episode bipolar manic-depressive psychosis occurring between 2 to 28 days following delivery. This is a high relative risk, although considerably lower than Kendell's figure. In contrast, the same study gave a relative risk for the onset of an episode of schizophrenia as less than one. Comparisons of rates across cultures and over time have shown a remarkable consistency at about 1–2 episodes of postpartum psychosis per 1000 births (Kumar, 1994).

There has been speculation that the mechanism by which childbirth precipitates a psychosis is related to the sudden falling levels of sex steroids following labour, but studies remain inconclusive. One suggestion, that dopaminergic functioning is affected by postpartum oestrogen withdrawal (Cookson, 1985; Wieck, 1996), led to examining the use of both oestrogen and progesterone to prevent the condition (Wieck, 1996). Administration of sex steroids is not part of routine clinical practice (since it may have potent effects on general health and lactation in particular) but merits further investigation.

A history of bipolar affective disorder, irrespective of whether the previous episode was puerperal or not, confers an extremely high risk of relapse following childbirth. The rate rises from the general population prevalence of 0.1–0.2% to between 25 and 50%, i.e. up to a 500-fold increase in risk (Marks *et al.*, 1992). It is therefore essential to enquire systematically about previous psychiatric history at the antenatal clinic. There is no other medical complication of childbearing with a comparable relative risk of recurrence. The potential risk, to both mother and baby, of relapse and untreated illness requires proactive management. Women who have experienced an episode of puerperal psychosis remain at high risk of developing further affective episodes (Davidson & Robertson, 1985; Robling *et al.*, 2000) and puerperal episodes of illness follow 20–30% of births to women with a history of bipolar disorder or affective psychosis (Brockington *et al.*, 1981).

There are no reliable differences in symptomatology between puerperal and nonpuerperal psychoses (Dean & Kendell, 1981). Family studies and follow-up investigations (Platz & Kendell, 1988) lead to the conclusion that puerperal psychoses are the same as affective psychoses at other times, but perhaps with an added genetic predisposition to occur and recur after childbirth. A recent genetics study showed that episodes of puerperal psychosis clustered in families, with episodes occurring in 74% of 27 women with bipolar disorder who had a history of puerperal psychosis in a first-degree relative (Jones & Craddock 2001). The authors concluded that familial factors are implicated in susceptibility to triggering of puerperal episodes in women with bipolar disorder and that heredity (rather than environmental factors) provide the most plausible mechanism for this familiality. Molecular genetic studies have addressed this issue with a recent study reporting a variation at the serotonin transporter gene as associated with the susceptibility to bipolar affective puerperal psychosis (Coyle *et al.*, 2000). These findings have implications for future research and will be of use clinically in the advice given to women with bipolar disorder who are considering pregnancy. The main challenge remains, which is to discover how childbirth provokes an acute affective psychosis in some women but not in others, and thus to develop specific preventive interventions. Postpartum psychosis impairs the mother–child bond through (1) symptoms of the illness; (2) the mother's hospitalization away from her child; and (3) therapeutic medication which may preclude breastfeeding and may sedate the mother so much as to prevent effective parenting.

Generally, if a woman develops a postpartum psychosis, she will require admission to hospital, preferably to a mother and baby unit, where she and the baby may be cared for together. Since there are few of these units, she may be admitted to a general psychiatric ward with a provision for the baby, and failing that, she may be admitted alone. A community-based service to manage severe postnatal illness at home has been described (Oates, 1988, 1996). On a mother and baby unit, all contact between the mother and baby is initially constantly supervised by the nursing and nursery nurse staff, with supervision levels gradually decreasing as the woman's mental state improves. Pharmacological treatment depends on the clinical picture and conventional treatments including antidepressants, antipsychotics and mood stabilizers, such as lithium or carbamazepine/valproate, may be used, with due consideration to breastfeeding (Yoshida *et al.*, 1999). Electroconvulsive therapy has been reported to be particularly useful in extreme cases (Reed *et al.*, 1999), especially if there are symptoms of confusion and perplexity, but is usually reserved until after other treatments have failed. The short- to medium-term prognosis is good, with most patients responding well to treatment and making a complete recovery and being able to resume usual activities. The effect of even a short illness, however, during this critical time may have long-term effects on children. Illness relapse is well-recognized and the risk of relapse following a subsequent pregnancy remains high, ranging from 20–50% (Marks *et al.*, 1992).

This has prompted the suggestion of prophylaxis, and one report suggested starting lithium immediately after delivery to protect against relapse (Steward *et al.*, 1991).

Chronic mental illness

Psychosis

For women with chronic severe psychiatric illness overall, there is a slight but significant reduction in rates of contact with psychiatric services and admissions during pregnancy, compared with periods before and after childbirth (Kendell *et al.*, 1981, 1987). For bipolar manic-depressive illness, pregnancy is usually a time of remission (Marks *et al.*, 1992.). Pregnancy does not seem to result in a flare-up of pre-existing schizophrenia (Davies *et al.*, 1995; McNeil 1986).

A study of childbearing schizophrenic women (Davies *et al.*, 1995) showed that women with chronic illnesses of the disorganized type, or with residual symptoms (DSM-IV) showed little variation in their symptomatology, whereas those with a paranoid psychosis with shorter illnesses, or periods of remission following treatment, were at high risk (40%) of recurrence or exacerbation of their illnesses. Postnatal management depends on type of illness, with a better outcome for women with 'positive' symptoms of schizophrenia, both in terms of response to treatment and in their ability to care for their babies. For women with marked negative symptoms, it is advisable to take a proactive approach in planning during pregnancy. If it is considered that a woman is unlikely to be able to care for the baby and if there is no alternative carer, then the process of identifying alternative carers should start early.

Nonpsychotic disorder

Studies are inconclusive about the exacerbation of pre-existing affective disturbance during pregnancy. Some have suggested an increase in rates, especially in the early stages of pregnancy (Kitamura *et al.*, 1993; Kumar & Robson, 1984), but a comparison study with nonpregnant women found no such association (O'Hara *et al.*, 1990). Reviewing the available controlled studies, Kitamura *et al.* (1996) concluded that the incidence of antepartum depression lay between 4 and 29%, the latter estimate being significantly higher than in nonpregnant women. Data from a large longitudinal cohort study of pregnant women (Evans *et al.*, 2001) demonstrated that symptoms of depression were no more common or severe after childbirth than during pregnancy and that research and clinical efforts needed to be directed more towards antenatal depression. Depression may be twice as likely to occur in pregnant adolescents than in pregnant adults (Miller, 1998). Children born to teenage mothers are already at risk; depression increases that risk.

Pregnancy may trigger the onset of obsessive-compulsive disorder (Neziroglu *et al.*, 1992) or may cause it to worsen (Shear & Mammen, 1995), possibly through the effects of steroids on the serotonergic system (Stein *et al.*, 1993). There are limited data on the effects on other anxiety disorders. Pregnancy only rarely precipitates the onset of an eating disorder, but it is a difficult time for sufferers, particularly those with anorexia nervosa (Fahy & O'Donoghue, 1991). In severe cases of anorexia, there may be cessation of ovulation and menstruation (Brinch *et al.*, 1988) with fertility impaired initially, but normalization on recovery. Fertility is less likely to be affected in bulimia nervosa, as the women are more likely to be of normal weight and to be more sexually active (McNicholas, 1996). Obsessive-compulsive disorders, anxiety and phobic states and eating disorders may continue unchanged following delivery or they may worsen.

Treatment considerations of chronic conditions

In general, it is advisable to manage all kinds of nonpsychotic illness during pregnancy by psychotherapeutic and supportive measures. Psychotropic drugs should only be prescribed when absolutely necessary, using the lowest possible dose and following consultation with a psychiatrist. However, management of psychotic disorders such as schizophrenia may involve the continuation of maintenance neuroleptic medication and the decision should be based on knowledge of the illness and the likelihood of relapse on cessation of pharmacotherapy. Fortunately, most bipolar manic-depressive illnesses remain in remission during pregnancy and the time of maximum risk of relapse is during the first few weeks after delivery. Thus medication with mood stabilizing or antipsychotic drugs is likely to be an issue only in the most vulnerable cases, who relapse rapidly if their drugs are discontinued. In such cases it is often necessary to maintain the medication and to monitor the fetus for possible malformations. In all cases, close collaboration between professionals is essential.

Maternal psychiatric disorder and parenting of babies

Many women with a mental illness are competent and caring parents, and others can cope with appropriate support. In some, the nature of their illness may impair their ability to care for infants and growing children. In others, it is the developmental delays and temperamental difficulties of their children (who may have inherited mental health problems which show themselves in subtle ways even during infancy) that cause difficulty. Difficult children make parenting difficult and may lead to the mother's self-perception of herself as an incompetent parent. This is a domain where psychological interventions, general support and respite can be crucial. Where there is concern about risks to the safety and welfare of the baby, a formal assessment of parenting should be conducted, to assist the courts and social services in planning the short- and long-term placement of the child (Budd & Holdsworth, 1996; Cleaver *et al.*, 1999; Henry & Kumar, 1999). The assessment may be conducted by professionals working in the community, or in a range of specialist facilities, including inpatient facilities, such as a psychiatric mother and baby unit (see below). The methods for evaluation of risk to infants, in the presence of maternal mental illness, are less well established (Louis *et al.*, 1997).

Specialized clinical services for mentally ill mothers and their babies

A survey of services for mentally ill mothers and their infants in the UK (Royal College of Psychiatrists, 1992; updated by Oates, 2001) concluded that there were 'few comprehensive services with specialist knowledge of the impact of mental illness on the baby and older siblings, as well as on the infant's father'. The following recommendations were made:

- Every health authority should have a perinatal mental health strategy that aims to ensure that the knowledge, skills and resources necessary for detection and prompt and effective treatment are in place at all levels of health-care provision.
- Every health authority should identify a consultant with a special interest in perinatal psychiatry. This consultant should take a lead role in promoting these aims and in establishing a specialist multidisciplinary team.
- All women with perinatal psychiatric disorder who require specialist psychiatric care should, irrespective of their place of residence, have access to a consultant and other mental health professionals with a special interest in their condition.
- Mother and baby units to serve the needs of a number of health authorities should be established.

Women are in contact with a range of professionals throughout pregnancy, delivery and the postpartum period, giving rise to opportunities for screening, detection and early intervention where problems are identified. Unfortunately, opportunities for identifying women in pregnancy are rarely taken up (Oates, 1996).

Men may also experience mental health problems in relation to childbirth and there have been reports of mild depressive episodes and anxiety (Ballard *et al.*, 1994) as well as relapse of a bipolar illness (Davenport & Adland, 1982). One study showed that around 50% of partners of women admitted with severe postpartum mental illness suffered psychiatric illness themselves (Lovestone & Kumar, 1993). The role of fathers or partners within the context of maternal postnatal illness is important (Marks & Lovestone, 1995) and warrants greater consideration in service development.

Inpatient mother and baby services

The aim of a mother and baby unit is to try to preserve and to facilitate the relationship between mother and baby, often despite the presence of severe maternal
psychopathology. In the UK, babies are usually admitted with their mothers into
general adult psychiatric wards in which one or more rooms may flexibly be used
as nurseries or bedrooms. There exist, in addition, a few specialized mother and
baby units with facilities and staff entirely devoted to the care of severely mentally
ill mothers together with their babies. Such units can offer specialist therapeutic
activities such as mother–infant interaction guidance and baby massage, as well as
serving an important role in taking on difficult secondary or tertiary referrals, in
carrying out research, and in education. As yet, there is no specific evidence in support of the effectiveness of mother and baby units, or comparing the effectiveness
of community support versus joint admission. The British experience seems to be
that mother and baby units and their ancillary facilities serve an important client
group, that they are generally safe and are desired by the majority of those who use
them (Margison & Brockington, 1982).

The following case example illustrates a number of aspects of a perinatal
service.

Case example A

A was a woman with a history of recurrent depressive disorder, including one previous postnatal depression. She was working, had a supportive partner and this was her third pregnancy. In the antenatal clinic, the midwife had noted her past psychiatric history and current
low mood. She was referred to the liaison perinatal team during the second trimester. The
current episode of low mood seemed to be triggered by ambivalent feelings towards the
current pregnancy and by worries about how the family would cope financially with three
children. As the pregnancy progressed she stopped working earlier than planned, stating that
she was feeling suicidal and no longer wanted the baby. Her mental state was monitored
closely by the liaison perinatal team (including home visits) but A's mood deteriorated further, with accompanying anhedonia, lack of energy, disturbed sleep and continuing suicidal
ideation. In the consultation clinic several options were discussed including the possibility
of starting medication and admission to hospital but A declined both suggestions. She was
therefore cared for by close collaboration between the obstetric team, mental health team,
general practitioner and her family.

The team felt that A would benefit from a joint admission with her baby to the mother
and baby unit, when the baby was born. She agreed to visit the unit and following the birth,
the two were transferred there. A continued to have symptoms of major depression, and
felt she could not bond with her baby, although she was able to provide adequate physical
care for the child. While on the mother and baby unit, she had a range of treatments including antidepressants, psychological interventions, such as cognitive-behavioural therapy and
family therapy, and was also referred to the perinatal psychotherapy service for long-term
psychodynamic work. A was discharged after almost 3 months.

Parenting assessments on a mother and baby unit

Details of assessment are covered elsewhere in the book (see Chapters 5, 7, 8 and 10). Aspects of parenting assessment include evaluations of:

(1) Practical parenting tasks (including feeding, washing, changing nappies, etc.), establishing a routine, which is organized and aware of safety.

(2) Provision of adequate emotional care, including ability to stimulate the infant age-appropriately.

(3) Ability to adapt to the infant's changing developmental needs.

(4) Ability to prioritize the infant's needs.

(5) Risk assessment including a mother's ability to protect and safeguard the infant's welfare.

(6) Developmental assessment of the infant, including paediatric review.

(7) Medical and psychiatric assessment of the parent with appropriate investigations, including the impact of the mental illness on ability to parent adequately.

(8) Psychological investigations, including psychometric testing.

(9) The mother's psychological and social functioning, including assessment of her own experience of being parented and the impact on her own parenting.

(10) Social work assessment.

(11) Relationship with partner, family and wider support networks.

(12) Occupational therapy review of daily living skills, and management of stress and coping mechanisms.

A recent study of 61 consecutive parenting assessments on the mother and baby unit showed that fewer than half (44%) of the mothers were discharged together with their babies at the end of the assessment period, and at follow-up, less than a third (29%) were still caring for their children. In the majority of these cases, social services decision-making appeared to have been guided by the recommendations of the mother and baby unit (Seneviratne *et al.*, 2001).

The future

The effects of maternal mental health problems are varied with profound potential effects on the maternal–child unit and the subsequent development of the child. Clearly, closer collaboration between obstetric, paediatric and mental health teams, as well as between health and social services, is crucial.

Acknowledgements

We wish to acknowledge helpful comments from Maureen Marks.

REFERENCES

American Psychiatric Association (1994). *Diagnostic and Statistical Manual of Mental Disorders*, 4th edn. New York: APA.

Appleby, L. (1991). Suicide in pregnancy and in the first postnatal year. *British Medical Journal*, *302*, 137–40.

Appleby, L., Warner, R., Whitton, A. & Faragher, B. (1997). A controlled study of fluoxetine and cognitive-behavioural counselling in the treatment of postnatal depression. *British Medical Journal*, *314*, 932–6.

Ballard, C. G., Davis, R., Cullen P. C., Mohan, R. N. & Dean, C. (1994). Prevalence of postnatal psychiatric morbidity in mothers and fathers. *British Journal of Psychiatry*, *164*, 782–8.

Brinch, M., Isager, T. & Tolstrup, K. (1988). Anorexia nervosa and motherhood: reproductional pattern and mothering behaviour of 50 women. *Acta Psychiatrica Scandinavica*, *77*, 98–104.

Brockington, I. F., Cernick, K. F., Schofield, E. M., Downing, A. R., Francis, A. F. & Keelan, C. (1981). Puerperal psychosis: phenomena and diagnosis. *Archives of General Psychiatry*, *38*, 829–33.

Brown, G. W. & Harris, T. (1978). *Social Origins of Depression*. London: Tavistock.

Budd, K. S. & Holdsworth, M. J. (1996). Issues in clinical assessment of minimal parenting competence. *Journal of Clinical Child Psychology*, *25*, 2–14.

Burt, V., Suri, R., Altshuler, L., Stowe, Z., Hendrick, V. & Muntean, E. (2001). Use of psychotropic medication during breast feeding. *American Journal of Psychiatry*, *158*, 1001–9.

Checkley, S. (1992). Neuroendocrine mechanisms and the precipitation of depression by life events. *British Journal of Psychiatry*, *160*, 7–17.

Cleaver, H., Unell, I. & Aldgate, J. (1999). *Children's Needs – Parenting Capacity: The Impact of Parental Mental Illness, Problem Alcohol and Drug Use, and Domestic Violence on Children's Development*. London: The Stationery Office.

Cookson, J. C. (1985). The neuroendocrinology of mania. *Journal of Affective Disorders*, *8*, 233–41.

Cooper, P. J., Campbell, E. A., Day, A. et al. (1988). Non-psychotic disorder after childbirth: a prospective study of prevalence, incidence, course and nature. *British Journal of Psychiatry*, *152*, 799–806.

Cox, J. (1993). Psychiatric disorders of childbirth. In *Companion to Psychiatric Studies*, 5th edn, ed. R. Kendell & A. Zeally, pp. 577–87. Edinburgh: Churchill Livingstone.

Cox, J. L., Connor, Y. & Kendell, R. E. (1982). Prospective study of the psychiatric disorders of childbirth. *British Journal of Psychiatry*, *140*, 111–17.

Coyle, N., Jones, I., Robertson, E., Lendon, C. & Craddock, N. (2000). Variation at the serotonin transporter gene influences susceptibility to bipolar affective puerperal psychosis. *Lancet*, *356*, 1490–1.

Davenport, Y. B. & Adland, M. L. (1982). Postpartum psychoses in female and male bipolar manic depressive patients. *American Journal of Orthopsychiatry*, *52*, 288–97.

Davidson, J. & Robertson, E. L. (1985). A follow-up study of postpartum illness, 1946–1978. *Acta Psychiatrica Scandinavica*, *71*, 451–7.

Davies, A., McIvor R. & Kumar, R. (1995). Impact of childbirth on a series of schizophrenic mothers; possible influence of oestrogen on schizophrenia. *Schizophrenia Research, 16,* 25–31.

Dean, C. & Kendell, R. E. (1981). The symptomatology of puerperal illness. *British Journal of Psychiatry, 139,* 128–33.

Essex, M. J., Klein, M. H., Miech, R. & Smider, N. A. (2001). Timing of initial exposure to maternal major depression and children's mental health symptoms in kindergarten. *British Journal of Psychiatry, 179,* 151–6.

Evans, J., Heron, J., Francomb, H., Oke, S. & Golding, J. (2001). Cohort study of depressed mood during pregnancy and after childbirth. *British Medical Journal, 323,* 257–60.

Fahy, T. A. & O'Donoghue, G. (1991). Eating disorders in pregnancy [editorial]. *Psychological Medicine, 21,* 577–80.

Glover, V., Liddle, P., Taylor, A. et al. (1994). Mild hypomania (the highs) can be a feature of the first postpartum week. Association with later depression. *British Journal of Psychiatry, 164,* 517–21.

Gregoire, A. J. P., Kumar, R., Everritt, B. et al. (1996). Transdermal oestrogen for severe postnatal depression. *Lancet, 347,* 930–3.

Hannah, P., Cody, D., Glover, V. et al. (1993). The tyramine test is not a marker for postnatal depression: early postpartum euphoria may be. *Journal of Psychosomatic Obstetrics and Gynaecology, 14,* 295–304.

Harris, B., Lovett, L., Newcombe, R. et al. (1994). Cardiff mood and hormone study. Paper 2: Maternity blues and major endocrine changes – the progesterone factor. *British Medical Journal, 308,* 949–53.

Hay, D. F., Pawlby, S., Sharp, D., Asten, P., Mills, A. & Kumar, R. (2001). Intellectual problems shown by 11-year-old children whose mothers had postnatal depression. *Journal of Child Psychology and Psychiatry, 42,* 871–90.

Henry, L. & Kumar, R. (1999). Risk assessments of infants born to parents with a mental health problem or a learning disability. In *Child Protection and Adult Mental Health. Conflict of Interest,* ed. A. Weir & A. Douglas, pp. 49–62. Oxford: Butterworth-Heinemann.

Holden, J. (1996). The role of health visitors in postnatal depression. *International Review of Psychiatry, 8,* 79–86.

Holden, J. M., Sagovsky, R. & Cox, J. L. (1989). Counselling in the general practice setting: controlled health visitor intervention in treatment of postnatal depression. *British Medical Journal, 298,* 223–6.

Jones, I. & Craddock, N. (2001). Familiality of the puerperal trigger in bipolar disorder: results of a family study. *American Journal of Psychiatry, 158,* 913–17.

Kendell, R. E., Rennie, D., Clarke, J. A. & Dean, C. (1981). The social and obstetric correlates of psychiatric admission in the puerperium. *Psychological Medicine, 11,* 341–50.

Kendell, R. E., Chalmers, J. C. & Platz, C. (1987). Epidemiology of puerperal psychosis. *British Journal Psychiatry, 150,* 662–73.

Kitamura, T., Shima, S., Sugawara, M. & Toda, M. A. (1993). Psychological and social correlates of the onset of affective disorders among pregnant women. *Psychological Medicine, 23,* 967–75.

Kitamura, T., Shima, S., Sugawara, M. & Toda, M. A. (1996). Clinical and psychosocial correlates of antenatal depression: a review. *Psychotherapy and Psychosomatics, 65,* 117–23.

Kumar, R. (1994). Postnatal mental illness; a transcultural perspective. *Social Psychiatry and Psychiatric Epidemiology, 29*, 250–64.

Kumar, R. & O'Dowd, L. (2000). Psychiatric problems in childbearing women. In *Medical Disorders during Pregnancy*, 3rd edn, ed. M. D. Lindheimer & W. M. Barrow, pp. 611–34. St. Louis: Mosby.

Kumar, R. & Robson, K. M. (1984). A prospective study of emotional disorders in childbearing women. *British Journal of Psychiatry, 144*, 35–47.

Louis, A., Condon, J., Shute, R. & Elzinga, R. (1997). The development of the Louis MACRO (Mother and child risk observation) forms: assessing parent–infant–child risk in the presence of maternal mental illness. *Child Abuse and Neglect, 21*, 589–606.

Lovestone, S. & Kumar, R. (1993). Postnatal mental illness. The impact on spouses. *British Journal of Psychiatry, 163*, 210–16.

Margison, F. & Brockington, I. F. (1982). Psychiatric mother and baby units. In *Motherhood and Mental Illness*, ed. I. F. Brockington & R. Kumar, pp. 223–38. London: Academic Press.

Marks, M. & Lovestone, S. (1995). The role of the father in parental postnatal mental health. *British Journal of Medical Psychology, 68*, 157–68.

Marks, M. N., Wieck, A., Checkly, S. A. & Kumar, R. (1992). Contribution of psychological and social factors to psychiatric and non psychiatric relapse after childbirth in women with previous histories of affective disorder. *Journal of Affective Disorders, 29*, 253–64.

Martins, C. & Gaffan, E. A. (2000). Effects of early maternal depression on patterns of infant–mother attachment: a meta-analytic investigation. *Journal of Child Psychology and Psychiatry and Allied Disciplines, 41*, 737–46.

McNeil, T. F. (1986). A prospective study of postpartum psychosis in a high risk group. *Acta Psychiatrica Scandinavica, 74*, 204–16.

McNicholas, F. (1996). Eating psychopathology and its effect on pregnancy, infant growth and development. *Irish Journal of Psychological Medicine, 13*, 67–9.

Miller, L. (1998). Depression among pregnant adolescents. *Psychiatric Services, 49*, 970.

Murray, L. & Cooper, P. J. (1996). Impact of postpartum depression on child development. *International Review of Psychiatry, 8*, 55–63.

Neziroglu, F., Anemone, R. & Yaryura-Tobias, J. A. (1992). Onset of obsessive-compulsive disorder in pregnancy. *American Journal of Psychiatry. 149*, 947–50.

Oates, M. (1988). The development of an integrated community-oriented community service for severe postnatal mental illness. In *Motherhood and Mental Illness: Causes and Consequences*, ed. R. Kumar & I. F. Brockington, pp. 133–58. London: Wright.

Oates, M. (1996). Postnatal mental illness: its importance and management. In *Parental Psychiatric Disorder: Distressed Parents and their Families*, ed. M. Göpfert, J. Webster & M. V. Seeman, pp. 63–80. Cambridge: Cambridge University Press.

Oates, M. (2001). *Perinatal Mental Health Services. Recommendations for Provision of Services for Childbearing Women. Council Report.* London: Royal College of Psychiatrists.

O'Connor, T. G., Deater-Deckard, K., Fulker, D., Rutter, M. & Plomin, R. (1998). Genotype-environment correlations in late childhood and early adolescence: antisocial behavioural problems and coercive parenting. *Developmental Psychology, 34*, 970–81.

O'Hara, M. & Swain, A. (1996). Rates and risk of postpartum depression – a meta-analysis. *International Review of Psychiatry, 8,* 37–54.

O'Hara, M., Zekoski, E. M., Phillips, L. H. & Wright, E. J. (1990). Controlled prospective study of mood disorders: comparison of childbearing and non childbearing women. *Journal of Abnormal Psychology, 99,* 3–15.

O'Hara, M. W., Stuart, S., Gorman, L. L. & Wenzel, A. (2000). Efficacy of interpersonal psychotherapy for postpartum depression. *Archives of General Psychiatry, 57,* 1039–45.

Okano, T. & Nomura, J. (1992). Endocrine study of the maternity blues. *Progress in Neuro-psychopharmacology and Biological Psychiatry, 16,* 921–32.

Paykel, E. S., Emms, E. M., Fletcher, J. & Rassaby, E. S. (1980). Life events and social support in puerperal depression. *British Journal of Psychiatry, 136,* 339–46.

Pitt, B. (1968). Atypical depression following childbirth. *British Journal of Psychiatry, 136,* 339–46.

Platz, C. & Kendell, R. E. (1988). A matched control study and family study of puerperal psychosis. *British Journal of Psychiatry, 153,* 90–4.

Prettyman, R. J. & Friedman, T. (1991). Care of women with puerperal psychiatric disorders in England and Wales. *British Medical Journal, 302,* 1245–6.

Reed, P., Sermin, N., Appleby, L. & Faragher, B. (1999). A comparison of clinical response to electroconvulsive therapy in puerperal and non-puerperal psychoses. *Journal of Affective Disorders, 54,* 255–60.

Robling, S. A., Paykel, E. S., Dunn, V. J., Abbott, R. & Katona, C. (2000). Long-term outcome of severe puerperal psychiatric illness: a 23 year follow-up study. *Psychological Medicine, 30,* 1263–71.

Royal College of Psychiatrists (1992). *Working Party Report on Postnatal Mental Illness. Council Report CR 28.* London: RC Psych.

Seneviratne, G., Conroy, S. & Marks, M. (2001). Parenting assessment in a psychiatric mother and baby unit. *British Journal of Social Work, 33,* 535–55.

Sharp, D. (1992). *A Prospective Longitudinal Study of Childbirth Related Emotional Disorders in Primary Care.* Ph.D. thesis, London University.

Sharp, D., Hay, D., Pawlby, S., Schmucker, G., Allen, H. & Kumar, R. (1995). The impact of postnatal depression on boys' intellectual development. *Journal of Child Psychology and Psychiatry, 36,* 1315–36.

Shear, M. K. & Mammen, O. (1995). Anxiety disorders in pregnancy and postpartum women. *Psychopharmacology Bulletin, 31,* 693–703.

Sherwin, B. B. (1994). Impact of the changing hormonal milieu on psychological functioning. In *Treatment of Postmenopausal Women: Basic and Clinical Aspects,* ed. Lobo. New York: Raven Press.

Stein, D. J., Hollander, E., Simeon, et al. (1993). Pregnancy and obsessive compulsive disorder. *American Journal of Psychiatry, 150,* 1131–2.

Steward, De., Klompenhower, J. L., Kendell, R. E. & Van Hulst, A. M. (1991). Prophylactic lithium in puerperal psychosis. The experience of three centres. *British Journal of Psychiatry, 158,* 393–7.

Terp, I. M. & Mortensen, P. B. (1998). Post-partum psychoses: clinical diagnoses and relative risk of admission after parturition. *British Journal of Psychiatry, 172,* 521–6.

Wieck, A. (1996). Ovarian hormones, mood and neurotransmitters. *International Review of Psychiatry*, *8*, 17–25.

World Health Organization (1993). *The International Classification of Mental and Behavioural Disorders, Diagnostic Criteria for Research*, 10th edn. Geneva: WHO.

Yoshida, K., Smith, B. & Kumar, R. (1999). Psychotropic drugs in mothers' milk: a comprehensive review of assay methods, pharmacokinetics and safety of breastfeeding. *Journal of Psychopharmacology*, *139*, 64–80.

Yoshida, K., Marks, M. N., Craggs, B., Smith, B. & Kumar, R. (1999). The sensorimotor and cognitive development of infants of schizophrenic mothers. *British Journal of Psychiatry*, *175*, 380–7.

10

Assessment and treatment issues when parents have personality disorders

Eia Asen and Heiner Schuff

Marlborough Family Service, London, UK

Many disturbed parents referred for parenting assessments do not present with acute mental illness, but with severe, emotionally unstable, borderline personality disorders. Here we usually find a persistent identity disturbance; self-damaging impulsivity; marked reactivity of mood; a pattern of unstable and intense interpersonal relationships; frequent displays of anger; chronic feelings of emptiness; transient paranoid ideation and dissociative symptoms. In our view the major underlying problem of this unfortunate condition is one of *disconnectedness*. We see this as profound difficulties of establishing and maintaining connecting relationships of mutuality (see Adshead *et al.*, Chapter 15). These difficulties present both internally, that is, between parts of the self, and externally, in relation to partners, children and others – including therapists. Whilst there is usually plenty of observable powerful interacting – or 'acting out' – going on, this does not lead to a mutually connecting way of relating. Such individuals show levels of extreme emotional sensitivity and fluctuating affective states. These can provoke at times overinvolved or profound distancing behaviours. The primary concern is not about relating and negotiating with others, but about how to regulate and control one's own feeling states. There is a considerable preoccupation with the experience of others – including children – being able to trigger powerful and problematic feelings. To cope with this the parent often uses angry defences against being emotionally vulnerable. This can take the form of self-hate or attack on child, partner or helper. There are high expectations of the child to repair parental problems or remove them altogether. At the same time there may be a wish to protect the child from one's own fate and to give the child a better life than the parent had. This results in rapid changes: either the child is 'good' and the self 'bad', or the self is 'good' and the child is 'bad'. Similar extreme oscillations can be observed in relation to partners to both compensate for and mirror one's own difficulties, with pseudorelationships that lack mutuality. The result is continuous emotionally charged control battles, in an effort to maintain structure for both the self and its environment. In such a frame of mind the issue of 'winning' or 'losing' becomes all-important in often very concrete ways, and particularly so in the context of being assessed for a court case.

There are a number of other implications of this type of personality organization when it comes to carrying out assessments. The profound difficulties of relating and connecting with others make it difficult if not impossible to establish traditional therapeutic relationships in which goals are mutually negotiated (see Göpfert et al., Chapter 5). Therefore the assessment process needs to be specifically tailored to the needs of this client group. The parent is invited to explore her patterns of feelings and interactions within a framework that can identify the workings of disconnected and split parts of the self. To do this, the clinician develops with the client a model which distinguishes between differentiated and nondifferentiated parts of the self. Differentiated parts (DP) are seen as showing ordinary, mature and capable ways of coping, parts which can observe, reflect, understand and act accordingly. Undifferentiated parts (UDP) show themselves in immature, disorganized and disorganizing, emotionally driven and rather concrete ways of coping, which lack reflection and act with hardly any consideration for consequences, both for the whole of self and of others. Descriptions of feelings and interactions put forward by the client are examined together. A map is created which shows how disconnected parts of the self are and how this leads to battles between them for survival and control. The map is a first step of seeing the disconnection between the differentiated and undifferentiated parts of the self. It also demonstrates the usually existing dominance of the UDP over the DP and the attempt to get rid of the latter. In practice, the clinician continuously reminds the client of the existence of DP and the DP's 'option' to speak up for itself and the 'whole self' – with an understanding of UDP's plight. For example, a parent might quite regularly become physically violent in an attempt to remove unpalatable feelings (UDP) whilst at the same time knowing (DP) the inappropriateness and negative consequences of such behaviour for both self and others. The clinician will invite the DP to acknowledge UDP's aim of 'solving' a particular problem, without having to resort to the usual strategy of then violently attacking UDP for being so 'bad' – or to allow UDP to eliminate DP's stance. The clinician continues to emphasize to the client that the main problems (generated by UDP) are only one part of their self, which can or could be understood and dealt with differently by DP.

Case example 1

The family consists of 28-year-old Jill, mother of Paul (4) and Ann (1). Both children have different fathers who have no contact with them. Ron is Jill's new partner – he aggressively backs Jill's fight against social services whilst at the same time beating her up intermittently. Ann is described by her mother as a 'little angel'. Paul is a bright, overactive and angry boy who has been caught stealing from shops several times. He received as yet unexplained bruises which resulted in him and Ann being taken into care. Jill has a long history of episodic drinking and use of illegal drugs. She intermittently under- and overeats, she self-harms by cutting and overdosing, but less so since the birth of her daughter. At the request of her social workers Jill had for some time erratically attended substance misuse, eating disorder and general psychiatric services, with brief admissions and self-discharges. Under the social services' department threat of taking her child(ren) into care, Jill has attended several family support agencies/day services in succession over the last 3 years. A whole range of different professionals has been involved. Their numbers have fluctuated with Jill's oscillations between 'almost' good enough parenting and 'borderline' neglect of the children, always related to yet another personal crisis. Little changes were made, with Jill feeling wrongly accused of having caused Paul's bruises. She had speculated that Paul had got his bruises from falling down the stairs. At another time she had wondered whether one of Paul's bruises might have been the unintended result of 'holding him down' during a temper tantrum, a technique 'they taught me in the family centre'.

In the first, individual assessment session Jill said she was puzzled as to why this meeting had been arranged – despite having asked for 'counselling' herself. She then launched into a coherent, well-reasoned series of accusations about the failings and lack of understanding of social workers. When the clinician questioned how often Jill allowed a part of her that might feel awful and cornered, to push away what she knew, she replied: 'I don't know what you are talking about, I'm not schizophrenic, split mind!' The clinician showed respect for her ability to reason in this way, having a part of mind which can observe and reason ('at least as well as I'). He told her that he knew a part of himself which also tries to push his knowing away every morning when waking up. He said: 'That part just follows what I feel, wants to stay comfortable and not deal with anything difficult, turn around and sleep again, with not a thought about the consequences for me as a whole person. If I had not activated my grown-up part of mind, that knows better and wants a full life, I would still be in bed now, would have failed you and what I believe in'…(Jill laughs)…'so you know that part in you too…mind you, I also promised this part of me that he will get his way a bit next Sunday when he can have a lie-in'. Jill replied: 'Like my Paul, he never wants to get up'. Then she started talking about the seemingly endless battles in her life and now the one over the children. She said that she could not cope with not having them, that she thought things had got better…'until 'that' happened…I want to be dead, kill myself, seriously, believe me, I'm going to do it!'. By tracing the information given, clinician and client gradually came to some agreement that her battles were battles for life. Even the part that screams 'I want to kill myself' wants to get rid of unbearable feelings in order to have a life (without a problem that threatens to kill) rather than be dead altogether. Clinician: 'What, if you allowed one part of you to do it, and find out, when the other part wakes up, that both of you are really dead?'…(Jill laughs, then coughs)…'Wouldn't it be tragic if you, that part of you which understands the dilemma, would just stand by or even agree with the solution of a desperate part of you, that could destroy everything you battled for, without even wanting to do that really?' Jill became tearful and then cried intensely and freely. After a while she said: 'Shit…I don't know what to do!' The clinician then challenged her to think (DP) of what she could say to and do with that part of her which gets desperate (UDP): 'How could you (DP) show her (UDP) that you understand some of her feelings (UDP) and accept her, but that you (DP) do not condone her (immature) behaviour, her ways of trying to solve the problem of desperation?' Jill moved from another 'I don't know' to 'maybe she wants a hug?...Ann always wants hugs...Paul can't stand it, he pushes me away...I get so angry when that happens'.

With this, as yet rudimentary map of DP and UDP, clinician and client continued to explore the next dilemma of DP trying to get rid of the problem (UDP) by 'calling herself stupid' and 'hating herself', UDP's response of accusing DP 'not to care' (like Jill's parents) and concluding that 'nobody cares'. Over the next two sessions, the clinician consistently challenged Jill (DP) whenever she (UDP) disqualified herself (DP), whenever she allowed her thinking (DP) to be coerced into serving as the (UDP) 'propaganda spokesperson', whenever she (DP) showed no understanding of UDP. Whenever Jill tried to turn the clinician into her DP (or her UDP's desired, magical transformer) and thus tried to get rid of her own DP (or make the clinician eliminate her troubled UDP and replace it with an ideal one), the clinician would explain – and at times concretely enact – the above framework. This could take the form of: 'I don't think it would help you (DP and UDP) to grow, if I helped you (UDP) to fool yourself. As you (DP and UDP) know from bitter experience, painful disillusionment would be guaranteed and add to what is already so difficult to bear. Remember what you told me about all those helpers who were never good enough. You (DP) know, that they could not switch off your awful feelings. They are part of your life experience. Do you (DP) really want me to make things worse? Do you want me to give a drink to an alcoholic and believe her (UDP) that it will help to solve problems ('just for now, it will make me feel better')? Even if you (UDP) begged or tried to bully me into giving such 'help', I would not, because I respect you and care about your dilemma'.

Within this framework, clinician and client traced her constant shifts of positions, both in terms of intentions and of effects. More and more links were made between comparable splits, shifts in UDP alliances and wars between parts in her family of origin and in her present family. Particularly poignant were the similarities, which emerged between Jill's and Paul's internal parts, how they were mirrored in 'wars' between them and replicated with Ron. Given that family and multifamily work was done in parallel, enactments of similar problems and rehearsals of similar, new, understanding ways of connecting inside and outside, started to happen in multiple contexts. After a few further sessions Jill shared the true cause of Paul's bruising: it was the result of a destructive escalation of Jill's, Ron's and Paul's desperate and forceful UDP interactions, which involved both adults beating and chasing Paul who fell down a staircase whilst trying to escape from them. Jill separated from Ron and continued to work on herself and with the children. The court hearing, 3 months later, was painful and disturbing, but no longer the centre stage in a battle over winning and losing. Only Ron continued the battle.

The assessment process

Assessment is a dynamic and interactional process looking at the family's responses to interventions which aim to bring about change. This allows to predict the various family members' potential for change. In order to do this, the family and its individual members have to be seen in a whole variety of different contexts. These include the home, school and nursery, clinical settings, hospital wards and day units, playgrounds, supermarkets and any other contexts that may be relevant to the family, be that their mosque, church, temple or synagogue. The latter permits to look at the supports the family has through its religious or cultural affiliations. Both assessment and therapeutic intervention address different levels of the system – individual, parental couple, family, social, cultural and professional network.

Individual level: parent

This is not a solitary task, carried out in isolation – in an integrated child and adult service it is possible to feed back and forward observations from interaction between children and their parents. This includes the impact of individual work on the parenting behaviours, as well as the impact of family work on the state of mind of the individual parent, and it can be observed directly and documented jointly. Special confidentiality for individual psychotherapy sessions is not granted, not only because of the court context, but also because secrecy so often becomes a dangerous elimination from the mind in these cases.

It is usually possible to form quite quickly preliminary opinions during a few individual assessment sessions as to the likelihood of connecting UDP and DP in a parent presenting with a borderline personality disorder. For example, in a first session the client may be able to make some tangible connections, by enacting in the session how DP could connect in an understanding way to UDP. The clinician could find out from the parent what UDP would say and what actions would follow and whether this could lead to creating a relationship rather than result in maintaining an ongoing elimination battle.

This model of work takes into account the profound relationship problems as well as the need of the client to be in control. It concretely accepts these dynamics. Rather than focusing on the emerging relationship between client and therapist, the focus is on challenging DP to form an understanding and caring relationship with UDP. Whilst this is a major aim of many therapeutic approaches, it is particularly important here: there is no pretence of forming a traditional psychotherapeutic working relationship. Instead it is a direct challenge to forming pseudorelationships with therapists and to the inadvertent giving in to the patient's massive wish for concrete dependency. This runs in parallel with the task of finding out whether a parent is prepared to understand the child's predicament, to connect to it and to take care of the child's needs in a mature parent-like manner. The steps that are taken by the parent's DP to deal with their own UDP are similar to those parents' need to deal with their children's as yet not fully differentiated parts of self. This would apply as much to parents setting boundaries for their children – as well as to their own UDP. It also applies to playing imaginatively with their children – and their UDP – without massive fears of things getting out of control. Possibly the most promising way of fostering good enough parenting is the fostering of a loving relationship between DP and UDP, manifesting itself in an evolving loving, mutually connecting relationship between parent and child.

Individual level: child

Part of any parenting assessment and family intervention is the assessment of the child. Temperamental characteristics, disabilities, past experiences and many other factors all shape the interaction between parents and their children. Understanding the child's specific needs clearly affects any recommendations regarding their parents' capacity and both assessment and treatment of children of disturbed parents must be specifically addressed (see Bilsborough, Chapter 1; Seeman & Göpfert, Chapter 2; Hall, Chapter 3; Göpfert *et al.*, Chapter 7; Jacobsen, Chapter 8; Seneviratne & Conroy, Chapter 9; Cooklin, Chapter 21; Cooklin & Gorrel Barnes, Chapter 22; Falkov, Chapter 27) but are not described here.

Parental couple level

The relationship between the parents is often a major area of assessment and also focused therapeutic intervention. With many single parents there is an absent father, or a present partner or other carer. The relationship between primary carer and absent parent, between the primary carer and a new partner, or between the primary carer and another significant parental figure are all important areas of assessment (see Göpfert *et al.*, Chapter 7). Some of this work has to be done without the child present as it can be inhibiting or indeed inappropriate, as children may need to be protected from being centrally involved in what are essentially adult issues. Parenting issues can be discussed by the adults alone and one way of doing this is to invoke hypothetical family scenarios and to explore likely parental responses. The parents are encouraged to pinpoint a typically difficult situation and then to consider a whole range of possible strategies of dealing with it. This allows parents to identify specific parenting issues which can be concretely discussed and analysed in the relative calm of the consulting room.

Family level

Talking about problematic parenting in the absence of children is one thing, observing it 'in vivo' is another. Particularly for families containing preschool children it is helpful to elicit live samples of issues. The technique of 'enactment'

(Minuchin, 1974) can be adapted to therapeutic work with parenting issues. Here the therapist encourages all family members to 'show' some interactions that they themselves have identified as being problematic. There are various ways in which this can be done. Assuming that child and parent are not already displaying the very problems that have prompted the referral overtly, the clinician can say: 'Your child is behaving very well now. What is it that you would have to say or do now for your son to produce the type of behaviours that makes it so difficult for you to cope with him?'. Interestingly, almost all parents know how to trigger problematic responses in their offspring – they know, like their children, what button to push to get things going. Once in motion, entrenched interaction patterns unfold automatically, no matter whether a therapist is present or a camera recording it or not. Studying 'in vivo' such sequences involving all players allows the therapist to get a clear idea of how problem behaviours evolve and escalate. If video-recorded it also allows subsequent joint reflections and analysis with parents – and children if required.

Children who feel pressured to side with the parent who is defined as the competent one, frequently join into dismissing the troubled parent as 'mad' and then feel afraid of acknowledging what is disturbing to them. One of the fears, often unspoken, is that they themselves might end up like their 'mad' parent. If the family system is already overloaded with stress then there may be a mutual unspoken agreement not to bring out into the open any more problems. This has to be at the expense of the children: they have to keep secret their worries – a time bomb that is likely to go off in the not too distant future.

Social level assessments and interventions

The social context families live in often reflects and reinforces the parenting difficulties they encounter. Social deprivation and financial hardship, poor housing, discrimination and racism, cultural alienation are just a few factors contributing to these. Protective factors include friendships, religious and cultural ties, local facilities within the community, schools and nurseries, voluntary organizations and other resources. Intervening at the social level means addressing negative influences as well as mobilizing positive resources (see Göpfert *et al.*, Chapter 5). Mapping with families the social contexts they live in is a first step to designing appropriate interventions.

One useful technique is to draw neighbourhood maps which concretely depict the very context the family lives in. Parent(s) draw their flat or house on a large piece of paper. The clinician inquires who lives next door on either side, who lives above or below, a few houses on etc. Bit by bit, with the help of the clinician, a picture emerges with roads and shops, safe and unsafe places. The clinician draws this map together with the parent(s) and asks, for example, where 'good' and 'bad' people live. This can help parents to identify potentially positive contacts and relationships, particularly in those families which are socially isolated.

One of the reasons for creating day units for families, where up to six or eight families attend together for the most part of the day, is to address their social isolation. Here parents can experiment with making contact with others, with testing how to learn to trust others and how to make friendships. Families can rehearse in the safe environment of the day unit how to connect with one another and then be encouraged to consider how to export their ideas to their home setting. The presence of other families also allows the possibility of joint outings. Places where traditionally crises or difficulties arise can be visited, with some rehearsal prior to doing so, anticipating the difficulties they are likely to encounter. For many families visits to the supermarket or zoo, going on the underground or bus, are nightmare scenarios. They have had ample experience of not managing their children in public settings. Seeking out precisely those feared situations, with three families at a time, allows 'in vivo' exposure in the presence of experienced clinicians and, often more importantly, fellow sufferers. Families do comment on, observe and support one another. For example, if a seemingly uncontrollable toddler behaves dangerously in a public place, then other families can comment and act. This is experienced as less persecutory coming from other parents, particularly from those who are having to cope with similar behaviours of their own children, than coming from staff. Filming such outings and then reviewing them afterwards with a group of families elicits help from other parents.

Any intensive therapeutic intervention does not need to be confined to the nuclear or extended family. Relevant others may include friends, a person from the religious community (priest, rabbi, mullah), lawyers or other advocates whom the family experiences as helpful. It is the combination of interventions at a number of levels simultaneously, including the social level, which leads to change in these families.

Cultural level assessments

Another major area requiring assessment is that of culture and ethnicity. How does one assess family structures that do not conform to North American or Western European norms? How is one to decide whether certain childrearing practices are culture-determined or not? Lau (1991) attempts to answer some of these questions and outlines some guidelines which can be summarized as follows:

(1) Assessment of the belief systems which influence role expectations and define the limits of acceptable behaviour.

(2) Assessment of the structures relevant to authority and decision making in the family.

(3) Assessment of the traditional solutions which the family uses to resolve conflict.

(4) Assessment of the traditional networks and rituals of the family.

(5) Assessment of the significant stresses and losses which arise from the family's own experience in their country of origin and from their adaption to the host culture.

Immigration to a new culture and the loss of significant networks can contribute to a family's sense of everincreasing helplessness and disturbance. Parents whose marriage has been arranged and who come from a hierarchical extended family background may in the host culture not have the protection of such extended family networks around them. This increases their vulnerability and may be reflected in what appears to be 'disturbed behaviour'. The assessment of parenting capacity must be sensitive to cultural and ethnic issues and take into account the meaning of symptomatic behaviours.

Professional network assessments and interventions

Families with longstanding mental health problems often tend to be multi-agency families. The seemingly ever-increasing number of helpers joining the system runs the risk that the parents' already dented self-esteem might be further undermined. Such 'help' can enhance the parents' sense of failure – thus requiring more help which, in turn, leads to an even more helpless posture of the parents. Their children remain at risk despite – and at times because of – multiple inputs. Not infrequently the degree of anxiety among the professionals is greater than that of the family itself. In order to address these complex issues, network meetings need to be convened which are attended not only by all the professionals who are actively involved, but also by the parents and their own personal network.

Characteristically the degree of anxiety among the professionals is often far greater than that of the family itself, with mutually dependent relationships developing between family members and professionals. Child abuse and neglect are a way of fostering such relationships, resulting in 'dangerous professionals' (Dale *et al.*, 1986) who unwittingly maintain or enhance the abusive behaviours. It is not rare to encounter families who have no less than 20 different professionals attached to themselves, raising the question whether there is in fact any parenting left for the parents to do! The assessment of the professional network is essential in the work with multi-agency families, prior to making a detailed assessment of the family itself (Schuff & Asen, 1996). This allows those concerned to:

• map all professionals involved in the life of the family, including their specific concerns, tasks and positions;

• ensure that the parents can define what their own concerns and needs are;

• jointly agree on the areas of work, timescale issues and consequences.

The parents in particular need to understand what it is that they need to do to decrease the justified or unjustified anxieties of the various professionals. Usually a considerable amount of information is already well documented in heavy court bundles, but new 'process' information might come to light during the course of the network meeting. This can include the following: verbal and nonverbal signs of conflict between professionals into which a parent may get triangulated; vagueness about minimum criteria or timetable of rehabilitation; reluctance on the part of specific professionals to commit themselves to any particular course of action etc. Such dynamics give vital clues to the family's predicament and how professional responses may feed into this and create further disturbance.

Bringing together so many different views and perspectives reduces the risk that parental disturbance is overlooked. 'Child centred' views of the problem(s) see the child as the 'victim' of adult psychopathology or mental illness. This usually contrasts with the parents' perceptions that it is the child which is the main 'site' requiring treatment. Many parents with psychological disturbance are likely to focus on the child if only to manage their own distress. Furthermore, it is not uncommon that the partner of a disturbed parent colludes by making the child the prime concern and thereby the 'patient' who requires treatment. Such action, possibly self-protective or protective of the ill partner, of course amounts to emotional abuse of the child.

The patterns of how various agencies are engaged with disturbed parents and their families can give valuable clues to the covert parental dynamics. For example, agencies frequently get called in with parents who appear helpless. This may well be a request of a parent to be parented, particularly when there is no available coparent or grandparent(s). Chronic relationships with helping professionals develop, who – unable to satisfy the many needs of the parents and other family members – may ask other helpers to join the system. In general, it has been our experience that the more severe the overt or imagined pathology of the parent(s), the greater the number of professionals. Helpers get drawn in because of the drama surrounding a person labelled as 'severely disturbed'.

There are also situations where the apparent sanity of an individual (or family) is maintained by projecting different aspects of the problem into different agencies who each hold on to different fragments. The policy of having a joint agency/family meeting therefore brings all these diverse bits into one room and allows family and professionals to get into a participant observer position of an otherwise disjointed process. In such meetings it is not infrequent that professionals, becoming aware of how many colleagues are involved, realize that this is a 'mad situation' and then ask the question as to how such madness came into being (Schuff & Asen, 1996).

Case example 2

Mrs K, a single mother in her 40s, was referred for an assessment of her parenting capacity. Her three boys were aged 13, 9 and 5. Mrs K's parents had died years ago and the children had no contact with their father. A network meeting revealed that she had had a number of admissions to a psychiatric hospital over the previous 3 years where a diagnosis of bipolar manic-depressive illness had been made. Twenty-six professionals were involved at the point of referral of whom 18 attended the network meeting. Mrs K alone had no less than three different psychiatrists treating her (medication and support), she also attended a weekly group, a social skills workshop, art therapy, poetry therapy (!) and had recently started cognitive therapy. Two GPs attended the network meeting stating how much anxiety she caused their group practice. Each of her children had weekly individual psychotherapy with different child psychiatrists. They also attended a children's group, had social workers, health visitors, paediatricians and so on…When Mrs K was asked what she believed each of the professionals was doing for her family she was not surprisingly totally at a loss. She said that sometimes she wondered whether she was 'allowed' to discuss certain issues with her children or whether these would be better discussed with their psychotherapists. In fact, she described how she sometimes had to think hard which particular 'specialist' should deal with which particular aspect of her or her children's life and she said that at times she got it wrong and had contacted the 'wrong' professional. It seemed that with all these helpers there was very little that was left for her to do as a mother. To assess her parenting capacity one would have to turn her into a 'full-time' mother. This would of course involve 'firing' the helpers, at least for a limited time, whilst the family was attending the Resource Centre. This suggestion provoked an enormous amount of anxiety in a number of professionals who believed that she would be unable to cope. Their reluctance to having to leave the field temporarily caused a stalemate: how could mother's parenting capacity be tested realistically if so many professional coparents stood by? The poetry therapist turned out to be most resistant to the idea of Mrs K ceasing to attend her poetry therapy group: she argued that this group would collapse as Mrs K had been its most valuable member for years. In the event the Resource Centre staff stated that they would only consider undertaking an assessment if the majority of helpers were prepared to disengage for an initial period of 10 weeks with only a minimum of professional input maintained (medication and some social work input). This precipitated a crisis as there was a lot of anxiety about the children's welfare and their future placement. In a further network meeting 2 weeks later a decision was made to go ahead with the proposed course of action.

This rather extreme case demonstrates how the needs of professionals may be counter-therapeutic. Addressing such ambiguity, confusion and indecision can be a successful intervention in its own right. If confusion is acknowledged and the network asks for help then a temporary handover of the family can take place. Interventions at the professional network level have to continue throughout the work with disturbed parents and their families. This is in part to guard against the dangers of poor or distorted communications between the professionals as well as to counteract some families' temptation to split the professionals into 'good' and 'bad'. Regular review meetings need to be built in from the outset and they should always include the family. Professionals should generally not meet without parents present as this avoids getting involved in 'confidential' or secret communications that on the whole rarely benefit the family.

Outreach work

Following the network meeting, a contract is made with the parent(s) and referrer(s) to specify in some detail everyone's expectations, outlining the consequences of change or no change. Almost always there is a request for a formal report on assessing parenting capacity with a view to making a recommendation regarding rehabilitation or permanent separation plans. It is made clear that staff are going to discuss all their findings and observations, positive and negative, on a daily basis with the families concerned. Certain structures are built into the programme to ensure that this happens. In this way families and referrers are aware that open communication about positive or negative findings is the norm rather than the exception. If at all possible, a home visit is arranged so that the family can be seen in its natural environment, understanding concretely their day-to-day difficulties and how these reflect parental and family disturbance. Seeing people in vivo helps to map out their concrete connections with their environment: the space, state and location of the accommodation, the immediate neighbourhood and the family's various connections with their environment – or lack thereof. The drawing up of neighbourhood maps with existing or potential contacts with others is a pointer to possible changes. Getting parents to think about how to reach out, how to make use of their neighbours, local shops and helpers can be a first step to questioning social isolation: 'what would happen if you connected with that person? How could you do it? What would be the first step you would have to take?' These are questions to get parents to think about different ways of relating to their social environment, having both diagnostic as well as therapeutic value. Certain parental disturbances seriously affect the socialization process of their offspring and an inability to change carries a poor prognosis for these children's ability to relate to others.

Outreach work connects the clinician with the daily reality of their clients. Unemployment, racism, overcrowding, economic hardship or downright poverty are all factors that affect parenting in highly significant ways. To hear about them is one thing. It is something else for clinicians to expose themselves to these factors by visiting families in their homes. Walking through a dilapidated housing estate, blinded by racist graffiti, scared of being mugged in the lift, interviewing the family in a cold damp flat with the electricity cut off and water pouring through the ceiling – all this can be highly informative – even though it may be quite disturbing to those professionals who are only used to seeing their clients in the relative comfort of a clinic or area office.

Intensive phase

In this section we describe the specific work carried out in a multiple family day setting. The work of the Marlborough Family Day Unit has been described in some detail elsewhere and undergone a number of changes over the past decade (Asen, 2000; Asen *et al.*, 1982, 1989; Cooklin *et al.*, 1983). However, the main ingredients of the programme have remained the same. It currently operates a 12-week programme for the assessment and treatment of multiproblem families. In many of these at least one of the parents arrives with a diagnosis of acute or chronic mental illness (schizophrenia, manic-depressive psychosis) or severe personality problems (most commonly borderline personality disorder). This programme takes place once every 3–4 months and around six families attend at the same time. Not all families start and finish at the same time, as some may require less intensive work than others. Families can enter half-way through each scheduled programme and the work is tailored to each family's specific needs. This is quite different from how the unit was run some years ago. At present families attend for an initial day, from 8.45 a.m. to 3.15 p.m. The following week families attend for 5 days, and during the 2 subsequent weeks for 1 or 2 days per week. Following this there will be another whole week's attendance, followed again by 2 weeks of 1 or 2 days' attendance each. This pattern is repeated again twice so that in effect a family could attend the programme for 4 whole weeks and 8 to 12 separate days in between. The reason for having such an intermittent pattern is to find an appropriate balance between an institutionalized setting and the home environment. It allows families to 'export' experiences from the day unit to the home environment and to experiment with these in their homes. These experiences are then fed back during the day unit attendance.

The concept of a day unit for families is in line with the idea of connecting socially isolated parents and their families with one another. The Marlborough Family Day Unit is a multiple family environment which seeks to diminish the stigma which many of the families experience (Asen *et al.*, 2001). It is a context in which parents and families can contribute constructively to the welfare of other families and support each other during the stressful periods when they are attempting to achieve changes. It is a context where families bring in another observational vantage point which is not a professional one. Families receive feedback about their own problematic or disturbed behaviours from other families in the unit – and all families will themselves be, in multifamily activities, at the receiving end of problematic or disturbed behaviours which may not be dissimilar from their own. Whilst it is likely for defensive collusion between families to emerge in order to divert attention away from their specific problems, being affected by one another also challenges such pathological alliances. Furthermore it provides an opportunity for families to give constructive advice to one another and thereby feel validated in a helper- rather than patient-role. It is not an uncommon observation that parents will both formulate and implement more desirable behaviours with individual members of other families – be that children, grandparents or perhaps another father or mother.

As this is a day setting where families attend whole days, a level of emotional intensity can be achieved which is not usually possible in nonresidential settings. This 'hot-house effect' tends to bring out the problems in relationships experienced within any given family in a dramatic fashion, but under relatively controlled and therefore safe conditions. As a result specific barriers to change, which constrain many of these families, are broken. This multifamily group therapy has as its focus the sharing of common experiences and difficulties and encourages families to learn from one another and give help to each other. Each family also receives (family) therapy by themselves and there is also individual input to specific family members. A tightly constructed programme involves family members in interactional events of a great variety, e.g. as a couple, a family, as mothers with children, children by themselves, as individual adults and so on. Different contexts such as outings, shopping trips, the joint preparation and eating of meals, supervision of children in playgrounds, all make heavy demands on parents. It not only requires them to demonstrate their competence but also makes overt how parental disturbance may or may not interfere with childrearing ability.

Working in such a pressurized environment faces the staff with dilemmas: parental or family disturbance is likely to become more 'public' and this can clash with the often desired aim of providing symptomatic relief. However, studying conflict-ridden family interactions and having problematic behaviours enacted 'live' makes it possible to understand how sequences arise. The potential for change can then be tested in vivo. The intensity of this programme implies a gradual challenge to, if not exposure of, the protective structure of parents who may superficially appear to be 'together'. It may be particularly effective with borderline patients with 'normal' facades where referring agencies have the strong suspicion but no hard evidence that something is amiss. Sticking to concrete tasks and challenging rigid behaviours reduces the possibility of covering up and often leads to a much clearer manifestation of disturbance.

Case example 3

Mr and Mrs L attended the centre because of developmental delays and failure to thrive of their 2- and 4-year-old children. Mr L had initially hoped that his wife could be helped to be taught some parenting skills. He was certain that the problem was located in her and convinced that he himself was 'perfectly normal'. The referring agency had no hard evidence that the children were neglected whilst at the same time being extremely concerned about their welfare. Whenever allegations of emotional abuse and neglect were investigated father would accuse social services that they were seeing problems where there were none. He stated repeatedly that this was simply not helping his wife to get on with the job of being a better mother. When father was put in the position of having direct playful contact with the children during specific activities in the Family Day Unit, for instance in situations where other fathers were also playing with their children, it became obvious that Mr L could not leave his rational posture of being 'perfectly normal'. He lectured other fathers on how to play with their children whilst being totally incapable of connecting physically and emotionally with his own children. Some parents commented on this and encouraged him to kneel on the floor and relate to his children in age-appropriate ways. He resisted these suggestions continuously. On one occasion, however, he gave in, burst into tears and ran out of the room. He then spoke to a member of staff and said that he had always found it unbearable to be at the same eye level as his children as it faced him with all the hurt he himself had been exposed to when he was that age. He felt ashamed about this and added that he was afraid that he was going to 'break down if I am made to behave like a child'. He then started talking about his fear of 'cracking up' if he was unable to keep up his 'perfectly normal' facade. Seeing this family over time it became clear that the children made very little emotional contact with either parent, attaching themselves instead to other parents and staff.

Connecting with past traumatic experiences, or in our terminology, connecting UDP and DP, fostering a loving relationship between DP and UDP, can help to create a loving, mutually connecting relationship between parent and child. Interestingly, in a peer culture such as the Family Day Unit, parents with borderline disorders may seem a lot of the time relatively normal when interacting with other parents or children. However, it is often through play or interfamily games that parts of a person get touched that other more cognitive interventions do not reach.

In another scenario it may be the 'disturbed' parent's spouse who will locate the problem or illness in the children, making it thereby more difficult to see his or her own disturbed behaviour. The allegedly 'sane' spouse may adopt this position, thereby not allowing clinicians to observe the degree of disturbance in the other parent. Again, in the multifamily context of the Family Day Unit it is through the continuous challenging of other parents that some of these underlying dynamics get revealed. For instance, one might observe a sudden upsurge of symptoms which appear to have been produced by the allegedly 'therapeutic' setting, with the 'sane' then blaming the institution for the ostensible deterioration in the disturbed parent's mental state. If the expectation of a cure of the disturbed person is not met, the service will come under pressure from relatives who unite with the ill person. Exposure to other families in multifamily and multicouple settings make the interactional aspects of problem maintenance more apparent. In addition, the often-found intrinsic belief in severely disturbed patients that nothing could be possibly improved, is more likely to be challenged by peers who may be in a similar situation.

Feedback is an important isssue. Most families attend on a semivoluntary basis and await court cases which are likely to result in the making of major decisions regarding their future. They are aware that their daily performance is being observed if not judged and are, not surprisingly, extremely keen to know what the staff's observations and recommendations are. Experience has shown that the best policy is to be as open as possible about all observations, positive and negative. This avoids disappointment later on. Moreover, it curbs problematic collusions with clients who are addicted to secret-keeping. The fact that there are video cameras in every room (which may or may not be switched on) is a constant reminder to patients and staff alike that everything is open to discussion. At the end of each day a review meeting is held when staff share their observations with all families. At the end of each week there is a more formal meeting when staff discuss in some detail their weekly impressions about each family. This staff discussion is videotaped and then replayed to the families who can reflect on the staff's 'reflections'. This feedback process, chaired by a systemically trained psychiatrist, is very popular and allows families to put themselves in an observer position – commenting on the staff's observations of themselves. It thus allows new perspectives, not only of themselves, but the institution, staff, other families and so on.

Assessment and intervention in a residential mother and baby unit

Parenting assessments can also be carried out in residential settings, allowing the opportunity for assessment and intervention around the clock. Clearly such intensity of work is only indicated with high-risk parents and families. The work in the residential mother and baby unit at the Maudsley and Bethlem Royal Hospital takes place in a 12-bed setting (see Seneviratne & Conroy, Chapter 9). There is space for 10 acutely disturbed women and their babies and two places (once called 'beds') for disturbed parents and their infants or young children. Over the years this unit has made a successful shift from working with mothers and their infants only, to admitting whole families – including fathers and siblings. Parents and their babies stay in the unit on average for a period of 6 weeks, at a time when the index parent is thought to be at their optimal level of functioning. If the mother is in an acute psychotic episode, it is regarded as not being 'fair' for her parenting to be evaluated as this is inevitably affected. The admission will be postponed until the mental state is improved. The focus of the work is initially on direct observations and evaluation of mother–baby interactions and their relationship and the parent's provision of routine physical and emotional care for the baby. This includes feeding, bathing, changing nappies and other routines, their organization and the parent's awareness of safety issues. The intensity and degree of observation and supervision during the family's first week in the unit is considerable, reflecting the often huge anxieties of professionals regarding the baby's safety. A large proportion of the babies admitted have suffered horrendous brain injuries; in quite a number of cases the parent may have had children previously who have been killed by a parent; or in other cases complex presentations of Munchausen's by proxy and dangerous parental behaviours require intensive monitoring. It is common that after the first week the levels of supervision are decreased and the focus of the work shifts to looking at the provision of adequate emotional care, including the parent's ability to stimulate the infant age-appropriately; to adapt to the infant's changing developmental needs and to the parent's ability to prioritize the infant's needs in all sorts of different contexts. There is an ongoing medical and psychiatric assessment of the parent with appropriate investigations, including psychometric testing. The presence of a social worker and occupational therapist make it possible for there to be detailed work in relation to child protection issues, as well as assessing the daily living skills, and the management of stress and coping mechanisms in a whole range of situations, such as cooking, budgeting, shopping etc. Baby massage is another popular activity which is offered by the occupational therapist, enabling parents and babies to experience one another through touch and generating feedback loops that mediate emotional connections.

When considering the team's recommendations and examining the outcome data – more than half of the babies not being rehabilitated with their parents – one needs to keep in mind the very severe spectrum of cases referred to the mother and baby unit. This type of parenting assessment consists of 24-hour work and involves a skilled multidisciplinary team – it is therefore expensive and local authorities will tend to only refer their most 'dangerous' and hopeless cases to the unit. The team is multidisciplinary and consists of nurses, nursery nurses, psychologist, psychiatrists, occupational therapist and social worker. Most professionals are well acquainted with or have had formal training in systemic therapy. Paediatric neurodevelopmental assessment of babies is also an essential ingredient in order to identify significant health problems which may add to potential parenting difficulties and possible risk.

This residential setting is very different from the Marlborough Family Day Unit. Above all, it does not use a multiple family approach in an active way. One of the major reasons for this is the presence of often five or six acutely psychotic mothers who cannot care for their own children. In their acute phases they are not capable of reflecting on other families – preoccupied as they are with often intensely persecutory inner voices and scenarios.

Follow-up phase

The intensity of multifamily day settings or residential units acts like a hot-house in which growth spurts may happen. However, a time of consolidation needs to follow when the organism will have to adapt to a more natural environment. Follow-up of families in their home settings is most important to allow monitoring of how certain experiences and new skills are imported to their own homes. A series of home visits centre around a re-examination of the various eco-maps. Frequently families are heartened by the experience of having spent a lot of time with other families. They may have made friends and invite one another to their flats. They may talk to another mother on their estate and discover that she is in need of help. Many parents use their newly learned skills and are eager to pass them on to others and give advice. It is often a difficult transition and some families may require follow-up for months if not years. During follow-up the network needs to be reconvened so that decisions regarding further work can be made. In addition, requests for reports are made, requiring the staff to comment on the quality of a family's parenting capacity.

Outlook

Assessments which test how the family and its individual members respond to change-inducing interventions permit informed decision making. If significant changes are observed during a 6–12-week intensive period of work, or if, alternatively, there are no such changes, then predictions can be made about timescale and permanency issues. If no changes take place, then permanent removal of the child from his parents may be one of the recommended outcomes.

The approach put forward in this chapter is 'systemic' in the sense that it views children and parents in context: that of the nuclear and extended family, within their social settings, in relation to the professional network as well as the changing cultural and societally sanctioned patterns of childrearing. The assessment process itself is not a simple one-off 'photograph' of parenting capacity at the time of interview, but could be described as the assembly of a five-dimensional picture, consisting of:

(1) A 'snapshot' of the current child–parent(s) relationship.
(2) A 'photo-album' of the parent's own history.
(3) An 'aerial shot' of the family's eco-map.
(4) A 'video recording' of current family interactions.
(5) A 'film script' for possible future scenarios.

The assessment of parenting capacity consists of putting together a whole variety of pieces of information gained from different levels of the larger system. Only then does it do justice to the complexity of family relationships and the individual characteristics of parents. Basing recommendations regarding children's rehabilitation with, or their permanent separation from, their parents, merely on a few factors, has serious limitations. In fact it can resemble the picture some borderline parents present: that of fragmentation and disconnectedness.

REFERENCES

Asen, E. (2000). Working with families where there is parenting breakdown. In *Family Matters*, ed. P. Reder, M. McClure & A. Jolley, pp. 227–36. London: Routledge.

Asen, K. E., Stein, R., Stevens, A. et al. (1982). A day unit for families. *Journal of Family Therapy*, *4*, 345–58.

Asen, K. E., George, E., Piper, R. & Stevens, A. (1989). A systems approach to child abuse: management and treatment issues. *Child Abuse and Neglect, 13*, 45–7.

Asen, E., Dawson, N. & McHugh, B. (2001). *Multiple Family Therapy – the Marlborough Model and its Wider Applications*. New York: Karnac.

Cooklin, A., Miller, A. & McHugh, B. (1983). An institution for change: developing a family day care unit. *Family Processes, 22*, 453–68.

Dale, P., Davies, M., Morrison, T. & Waters, J. (1986). *Dangerous Families*. London: Tavistock.

Lau, A. (1991). Cultural and ethnic perspectives on significant harm: its assessment and treatment. In *Significant Harm: Its Management and Outcome*, ed. M. Adcock, R. White & A. Hollows, Croydon: Significant Publishers.

Minuchin, S. (1974). *Families and Family Therapy*. London: Tavistock.

Schuff, G. H. & Asen, K. E. (1996). The disturbed parent and the disturbed family. In *Parental Psychiatric Disorder: Distressed Parents and their Families*, ed. M. Göpfert, J. Webster & M. V. Seeman, pp. 135–51. Cambridge University Press.

Part III

Specific disorders: the impact on parent–child relationships

11

Schizophrenia and motherhood

Mary V. Seeman

Centre for Addiction and Mental Health, University of Toronto, Toronto, Canada

In the first edition of this book, I used case examples to illustrate how women with schizophrenia, because of illness, have difficulty with tasks of parenting such as nurturing independence, establishing intimacy, enhancing growth through stimulation, modelling appropriate social habits and communicating effectively (Seeman, 1996). Since then, much new research has emerged and broader questions can now be addressed:

(1) How many women with schizophrenia become parents? How many actually bring up their children? In other words, what are the dimensions of the potential problems that the conjunction of motherhood and schizophrenia poses?

(2) What is the subjective experience of these mothers? How important is the parenting role to them as individuals and how do they perceive the assistance they receive in fulfilling that role?

(3) What determines parenting capacity and how and when should assessments be done?

(4) What are the mental health outcomes in children of mothers with schizophrenia, whether reared with or reared away from their mothers?

(5) What is the subjective experience of these children?

(6) Does schizophrenia impact differently at different stages of a child's life and/or at different phases of the mother's illness?

(7) How can psychiatric services best assist mothers with schizophrenia?

Scope

Van Bussel undertook a survey of the total population of a community inner city programme for schizophrenia in Toronto, Canada (Van Bussel, pers. comm.). Fifty-one women attended the programme. Seventeen were interviewed and information about the others was obtained from their case managers. Twenty-seven of the women (53%) had had at least one full-term birth. Together, they had produced 65 children (the median per mother was two children; one woman had given birth to seven children). Seventeen of the 27 women interviewed (63%) reported at least some contact with their children during their growing-up years. Two of the 27 had sole custody, three had shared custody and, in the case of 12 mothers, the children had been reared by a family member. The rest were either fostered via Children's Aid or adopted. At the time of the survey, two of the women lived with a child and, in all, 14 of the 27 maintained regular contact.

Several recent studies have reported rates of parenting in women with schizophrenia which are very similar to ours. Ritsher *et al.* (1997) asked case managers to fill out a questionnaire on 419 women, the whole population of a schizophrenia outpatient clinic. Half had had children and half of those had retained custody of at least one child. Of these, 44% lived alone with their child and 29% required no assistance with child-care (Ritsher *et al.*, 1997). Caton *et al.* (1999) reported that, out of 400 patients with schizophrenia, 47 men and 111 women were parents. On average, each of the children had lived in three different settings from birth to age 18 (i.e. with family members or foster parents). Most often, the surrogate parent was a family member (Caton *et al.*, 1998). Joseph *et al.* (1999) administered a questionnaire to 32 women with schizophrenia. Sixty-one per cent were mothers. Twenty per cent of the mothers had full custody but only 12% were the primary care-givers. Less than one quarter of the mothers had seen their children in the week preceding the survey. Hearle *et al.* (1999) report that 59% of the 110 women in their clinic for schizophrenia were parents and, in 9%, the partner also suffered from a serious mental illness. There were 198 live births and 42% of these children lived with their parents (see McLean *et al.*, Chapter 24).

Investigators from Chicago controlled for socioeconomic background and substance abuse. They found that significantly more mothers with schizophrenia had children in foster care (49 vs. 2%) and significantly more mothers with schizophrenia, despite having custody, had relegated the care of their children to their own mothers (36 vs. 9%) (Miller & Finnerty, 1996).

Despite different populations and different circumstances, the overall findings indicate that over 50% of women with schizophrenia recruited from treatment facilities become parents, a rate that is comparable with the general population. Of those who are parents, approximately half retain some custody of their children, although the children may actually be brought up by others, usually grandmothers. Apart from the potential impact of the mother's illness on the child, there are several other consequences to mothers, children and grandparents: because of frequent loss of custody, the mothers suffer bereavement; children left in the mother's care are usually fatherless (over 90% of marital relationships in this population are severed); the children's care-taking arrangements are frequently unstable and fragmented (Caton *et al.*, 1999); the grandmother bears an extra burden of stress (Gamache *et al.*, 1995; Miller & Finnerty, 1996).

The dimensions of these potential problems are substantial and becoming more so. The number of women suffering from schizophrenia who become mothers will undoubtedly increase in the future since the newer antipsychotic drugs do not interfere with fertility to the same extent as the older medications did (Currier & Simpson, 1998). This forecast may, however, be tempered by effective family planning on the part of women with schizophrenia. The percentage who retain custody will depend on a number of factors: effectiveness of treatment and access to mental health services, available supports, and reduction of the stigma of mental illness within society at large and within child protection agencies in particular. Is a shift toward keeping children with their mothers to be welcomed?

Mothers' experience

As emphasized in a comprehensive review (Mowbray et al., 1995b), the subjective experience of mothers is not well captured in statistics. Clinical notes and client reports speak to the pride of looking after a child, the motivation that responsibility for another's life can bring, and the ability of a child to mobilize extended family support. A study by Sands (1995) voices the concerns of mothers with respect to child discipline and the impact of stress and role strain in their lives. Reports of the impact of illness may be minimized, she estimates, because of the fear of loss of custody. Mowbray et al. (1995a) report on interviews with 24 mothers with serious mental illness. In their study, half of the women acknowledged feeling bad about their illness. Parenthood was described as stressful, but also growth-promoting. Disciplining the children was the number one problem for fully one quarter of the mothers.

In focus groups conducted separately with 42 seriously mentally ill (mainly affective disorders rather than schizophrenia) mothers and with their case managers, stigma about mental illness ranked high on the list of concerns (Nicholson et al., 1998a). These mothers felt they had to prove themselves. They (and their case managers) felt that mental illness was wrongly equated with child abuse and that, whatever their children's problems, they would be held accountable. Managing illness in addition to the stress of parenting was experienced as a difficult burden, and personal needs were often neglected. Role strain was accompanied by guilt. Mothers found it hard to distinguish between the effects of stress and the effects of illness. Their child-care standards were frequently higher than those of other mothers and they tended to look too much for tell-tale signs of mental illness in their children. Discipline was a problem for many, especially when the child had special needs. Some mothers reported purposely missing their medication doses in order to stay alert and focused on their child. When they got ill, they put off seeking help because there was no alternative caregiver for the child. They feared losing custody should they voluntarily place their child in care during times of increased symptoms. In their minds, worrying about the potential loss of custody contributed to decompensation. When their children were in care, some mothers reported losing motivation to get better. The grief of permanent custody loss was reported to last a lifetime (Nicholson *et al.*, 1998*a*).

In the Hearle *et al.* (1999) study, mothers acknowledged that they needed support but were unable to find it. In the Nicholson *et al.* (1998*b*) study, mothers reported that family members varied considerably in their ability to provide support. Some relatives made matters worse by reinforcing the mother's sick role and failing to consult her in child-care decisions. Some 'well' husbands or partners were described as abusive. This put mothers in an insoluble bind, staying with a violent partner or leaving him and losing the children because the 'well' parent was no longer at home (Nicholson *et al.*, 1998*b*).

A Canadian study, using focus groups with 28 woman participants diagnosed with schizophrenia and schizoaffective disorder, also found that women were faced with choices 'constrained by contradiction' (Chernomas *et al.*, 2000). The women felt isolated, yet they did not initiate relationships because of fear of rejection and fear of falling prey to undesirable men. They were conscious of the problems of taking antipsychotic drugs, especially during pregnancy, but feared the alternative. They reported the benefits of motherhood (love, purpose, identity, support) but these were offset by stress, exhaustion, poverty, fear of losing the children and fear of the children developing schizophrenia. They spoke of a persistent sense of grief and anger following the loss of children to foster care or adoption. They expressed needs for support, information and therapeutic programmes that include social activities, exercise classes, substance abuse counselling, relationship and assertiveness groups, family planning and antipoverty strategies. They felt that professional awareness of women's reproductive health issues was suboptimal (Chernomas *et al.*, 2000).

Clearly, women with schizophrenia, as a group, are aware of the pros and cons of raising children. They want to be mothers, but acknowledge the need for professional help in fulfilling this very important responsibility. About half of the children of women with schizophrenia are born prior to the diagnosis being made, approximately 9 years prior (Barkla *et al.*, 2000). About half of the pregnancies are unplanned, but that figure is similar to the US average for unplanned pregnancy (Barkla *et al.*, 2000). A quarter of the unplanned pregnancies are terminated, which speaks to the extreme seriousness with which this group of women take their parenting role.

Parenting assessments

There is a great variety of opinion among assessors as to what is crucial to parenting capacity and what assessment tools to use. Assessors use questionnaires and self-report scales, direct observation methods, developmental tests administered to the children and clinical interviews. These are well described in Jacobsen *et al.* (1997) (see Jacobsen, Chapter 8) and various shortcomings of these tools are addressed. Crucial to mothers with schizophrenia are issues of parenting assessment procedures not validated for this population and not adjusted for cultural or socioeconomic norms. Jacobsen *et al.* present two case histories where dramatically different conclusions were possible, depending on the type of assessment used. They underscore interactive risk factors for child maltreatment in this population: active psychotic symptoms, history of violent behaviour, denial of illness or need for treatment, verbal threats toward the child, denial of parenting problems, drug addiction, personal history of abuse in childhood, social isolation, unrealistic expectation of the child, difficulty in responding to the child's cues, high levels of stress and a hazardous home environment. On the basis of their experience, these authors suggest not only specific assessment strategies which include at-home observation of parent–child interaction, but also remedial interventions such as parenting classes, support groups, respite care and therapeutic nurseries (Jacobsen *et al.*, 1997).

It is important that mothers suffering from schizophrenia be aware of the comprehensive criteria by which their parenting capacity is being evaluated. They need to be assured that parenting decisions are not made solely on a diagnosis of schizophrenia; otherwise they will deny their illness and refuse treatment.

Having said that diagnosis should not be the main criterion by which to judge safety of parenting, several recent studies have indicated that, of all psychiatric diagnoses, schizophrenia is most associated with low mother–infant interaction scores on assessment scales that are designed to predict a healthy development in neonates (Hipwell & Kumar, 1996). Using the Global Rating Scales of Mother–Infant Interaction applied to videotaped interactions of mother and 4-month-old infant, Riordan *et al.* (1999) found that mothers with schizophrenia were more remote, silent, verbally and behaviourally intrusive, self-absorbed, flaccid, insensitive and unresponsive than mothers in the affective disorders group. They were less demanding of their infant. Their infants were more avoidant and the interaction was less mutually satisfying, less excited and more serious. Engagement was reduced (Riordan *et al.*, 1999). Mothers with schizophrenia in this study present a picture of detachment and insensitivity, though the authors do acknowledge that many factors, including drug treatments, could be contributory. Another relatively recent study stressed the impact of the negative symptoms of schizophrenia on mother–infant interaction (Snellen *et al.*, 1999).

It is important to note that maternal schizophrenia is very frequently exacerbated postpartum and that assessments done at that time, especially when used to determine final custody status, put birth mothers at a disadvantage. This is also true for mothers with depression (see Seneviratne & Conroy, Chapter 9), but treatments used for schizophrenia are more likely than are antidepressants to contribute to apathy and withdrawal.

Outcomes in children

An early study where infants were assessed at birth, 4 months, 12 months, 30 months and 4 years had suggested that the specific diagnosis of schizophrenia has less impact on the child's development than does social status and severity/chronicity of mother's illness. In this study, children of mothers suffering from depression were found to be more impaired than those with mothers diagnosed with schizophrenia (Sameroff *et al.*, 1987). A concurrent 3-year study testing children under age 5 of black, low income, single mothers, came to a somewhat different conclusion. Mothers were diagnosed with either schizophrenia, depression or no mental illness. The children of the mothers with schizophrenia had the most problems although, in some areas, children of depressed mothers scored lower. The child-rearing environment of the children of mothers with schizophrenia was characterized by less play, fewer learning experiences, less emotional and verbal involvement. Mothers of both illness groups were less affectively involved with their children than were well mothers. The following protective factors were identified: less severe illness, older age of mothers, higher education and IQ, a history of work experience and the presence of another adult in the house (Goodman, 1987). In a later report on this study, the authors stated that parenting practices, not mother's diagnosis, were the key to healthy child development (Goodman *et al.*, 1990).

In a more recent study, Yoshida *et al.* (1999) found that infants of mothers with schizophrenia had more motor and cognitive impairments at 2 and 7 months than infants of mothers with other diagnoses, but that this could be explained by the infant's initial birth weight and the mother's social class. Custody decisions based on infant impairment must take into account the fact that developmental delay is not necessarily attributable to poor parenting; it may be the partial expression of genetically transmitted schizophrenia (see Seneviratne & Conroy, Chapter 9).

Perhaps the more important question is what happens to these children once they are adults. An Israeli 25-year follow-up of 50 such children found that, compared with controls, the high-risk children developed more schizophrenia spectrum disorders, as was to be expected, but also more mood disorders (Mirsky *et al.*, 1995). Contrary to what might be predicted from a social support perspective, the children who grew up in a kibbutz had more Axis I disorders than those who were raised in nuclear families. The results of the Copenhagen high-risk study (207 children of schizophrenic mothers and 104 control children followed since 1962) are that 16.2% of the high-risk children developed schizophrenia and another 4.6% developed other nonaffective, nonorganic psychosis. Twenty-one per cent developed cluster A personality disorders. The corresponding figures for the control group were 1.9%, 0.9% and 5% for the respective diagnoses (Parnas *et al.*, 1993). The rate of mood disorder was the same in the two groups.

Fifty of the Copenhagen children of mothers with schizophrenia (25 reared with their mothers and 25 reared apart) were evaluated with a 3-hour structured interview. More psychopathology was found in those reared *away* from their mothers. Although the explanation may lie in the fact that more severely ill mothers were more likely to have lost custody, so that the reared-apart children inherited more severe psychopathology, this finding underscores the fact that rearing by a mother with schizophrenia does not necessarily lead to greater than expected incidence of psychiatric illness (Higgins *et al.*, 1997).

Subjective experiences of children of psychotic mothers

Dunn obtained information via semistructured interview from nine adults with a psychotic parent who answered a newspaper advertisement (Dunn, 1993). Five themes emerged from the qualitative analysis: (a) abuse and neglect; (b) isolation; (c) guilt and loyalty; (d) grievances with mental health services; and (e) supports. The abuse and neglect from the ill mother was poignantly described, but these children were also neglected by the father. Three of the fathers simply left after the mother became ill. The children spoke of being isolated from their peers, their extended families and their communities. They were also isolated from information – the mothers' behaviour, hospitalizations and treatments were never explained to them. The participants described not wanting friends to visit because of their mothers' bizarre behaviour. Most continued to be very loyal to their mothers and to want to look after them. They expressed guilt, thinking their birth had somehow precipitated their mothers' illnesses. They also felt guilt if they had 'abandoned' their mother by being placed in foster care or in the custody of the other parent. They contrasted their own successes to the ill health of their mothers. All but one study participant described negative contacts with mental health services. Visits in hospital were recalled as terrifying. No one explained anything; they felt their mothers were mistreated in hospitals and felt guilty for facilitating the admissions. They felt that mental health professionals never took the trouble to understand their situations (see Bilsborough, Chapter 1). All nine identified specific people who had been helpful and supportive to them during their childhood and who made big differences in their lives. Although they all described painful connections with their mothers, five of the nine also recalled a special, loving mother–child relationship (Dunn, 1993).

Caton *et al.* (1998) interviewed 39 adolescent and adult offspring of psychotic parents. These participants reported residential instability growing up and frequent corporal punishment. The worst problem was their parents' occasionally embarrassing or frightening behaviour. They noted the parents' inability to support the family, 'sitting around and doing nothing all day'. The level of knowledge of the participants varied greatly. One in four believed their parents would recover. A substantial minority were playing an active care-taking role with their parent, sometimes sacrificing school or work. Eight per cent had to care for their siblings. Their relationship with the well parent was flawed and sometimes nonexistent, but there was usually a surrogate parent in their lives who was important to them.

It is clear from these reports that children who speak out about their experiences of growing up with a mother with schizophrenia have many unhappy stories to tell. What is not clear is how representative these stories are nor how they compare with accounts of children growing up under analogous conditions of poverty, single parenthood and ill health.

Stages and phases in children and in mothers

Parent characteristics considered important to effective parenting such as warmth, protectiveness and authoritarianism as measured by the Parental Bonding Instrument (PBI) (Parker, 1989), can be conceptualized as wielding more or less influence depending on the stage of a child's life. In fact, a factor such as mother's protectiveness, for instance, can easily be conceived of as positive in the early life of a child and negative in later life. How do maternal traits associated with schizophrenia (lack of emotional responsivity, unpredictable behaviour, avoidance, indecision) affect children at different ages? Stromwall & Robinson (1998) have tried to situate schizophrenia difficulties within a life-cycle model. Understanding the tasks needed for effective parenting at different developmental stages helps to design rehabilitative strategies for mothers with schizophrenia and helps with child placement decisions. Not only do children at different ages require differently nuanced parenting but schizophrenia itself, like any illness, fluctuates and evolves over time. In men with schizophrenia, the first decade of illness is the most difficult; symptoms become more manageable with time. The course of illness in women tends to be mild in the first two decades (except for postpartum periods); menopause subsequently ushers in more severe symptoms (Seeman, 1998). Child protection decisions which put weight on the nature of the parental illness need to be based on the anticipated course of illness in women (which in itself is not uniform).

How to help

Psychiatric services can best serve mothers with schizophrenia and their children by instituting comprehensive programmes such as those described in Barkla *et al.*

(2000), Dincin & Zeitz (1993) and Seeman & Cohen (1998). Services need to be in place prior to the birth of the baby. For instance, women with schizophrenia frequently do not avail themselves of prenatal care (Kelly *et al.*, 1999). Their risk for premature delivery and low birth weight infants is 50% over that of the general population (Bennesden *et al.*, 1999; Sacker *et al.*, 1996). Adequate prenatal care, if in place, can potentially reduce the incidence of familial schizophrenia in these children (Warner, 2001). A comprehensive service needs to include diagnostic and treatment components, emergency, inpatient and outpatient services and outreach to parents and children, linkages with schools, camps, extended families, child protection and legal services and obstetric and paediatric facilities. Among the required resources there should be case management outreach teams, neuropsychological assessors, parenting capacity assessors, group leaders, child, adult and family therapists and pharmacotherapists. Interventions should include symptom management, parenting classes, addiction treatments, family planning education, therapeutic nurseries, support and information groups, occupational and vocational help, homemakers and respite care. Income supplementation and safe housing needs to be provided. Because of turf wars and opposing loyalties, seamless integration of required services has not been easy, but exemplary progress has been made since the first edition of this book was written.

REFERENCES

Barkla, J., Byrne, L., Hearle, J., Plant, K., Jenner, L. & McGrath, J. (2000). Pregnancy in women with psychotic disorders. *Archives of Women's Mental Health*, *3*, 1–4.

Bennesden, B. E., Mortensen, P. B., Olesen, A. V. & Henriksen, T. B. (1999). Preterm birth and intra-uterine growth retardation among children of women with schizophrenia. *British Journal of Psychiatry*, *175*, 239–45.

Caton, C. L. M., Cournos, F., Felix, A. & Wyatt, R. J. (1998). Childhood experiences and current adjustment of offspring of indigent patients with schizophrenia. *Psychiatric Services*, *49*, 86–90.

Caton, C. L., Cournos, F. & Dominguez, B. (1999). Parenting and adjustment in schizophrenia. *Psychiatric Services*, *50*, 239–43.

Chernomas, W. M., Clarke, D. E. & Chisholm, F. (2000). Living with schizophrenia: the perspectives of women. *Psychiatric Services*, *51*, 1517–21.

Currier, G. W. & Simpson, G. M. (1998). Antipsychotic medications and fertility. *Psychiatric Services*, *49*, 175–6.

Dincin, J. & Zeitz, M. (1993). Helping mentally ill mothers. *Hospital and Community Psychiatry*, *44*, 1106–7.

Dunn, B. (1993). Growing up with a psychotic mother: a retrospective study. *American Journal of Orthopsychiatry*, *63*, 177–89.

Gamache, G., Tessler, R. C. & Nicholson, J. (1995). Child care as a neglected dimension of family burden. *Research in Community and Mental Health*, *8*, 63–90.

Goodman, S. H. (1987). Emory University project on children of disturbed parents. *Schizophrenia Bulletin*, *13*, 411–23.

Goodman, S. H. & Brumley, H. E. (1990). Schizophrenic and depressed mothers: relational deficits in parenting. *Developmental Psychology*, *26*, 31–9.

Hearle, J., Plant, K., Jenner, L., Barkla, J. & McGrath, J. (1999). A survey of contact with offspring and assistance with child care among parents with psychotic disorders. *Psychiatric Services*, *50*, 1354–6.

Higgins, J., Gore, R., Gutkind, D. et al. (1997). Effects of child-rearing by schizophrenic mothers: a 25-year follow-up. *Acta Psychiatrica Scandinavica*, *96*, 402–4.

Hipwell, A. E. & Kumar, R. (1996). Maternal psychopathology and prediction of outcome based on mother-infant interaction ratings (BMIS). *British Journal of Psychiatry*, *169*, 655–61.

Jacobsen, T., Miller, L. J. & Kirkwood, K. P. (1997). Assessing parenting competency in individuals with severe mental illness: a comprehensive service. *Journal of Mental Health Administration*, *24*, 189–99.

Joseph, J. G., Joshi, S. V., Lewin, A. B. & Abrams, M. (1999). Characteristics and perceived needs of mothers with serious mental illness. *Psychiatric Services*, *50*, 1357–9.

Kelly, R. H., Danielsen, B. H., Golding, J. M., Anders, T. F., Gilbert, W. M. & Zatzick, D. F. (1999). Adequacy of prenatal care among women with psychiatric diagnoses giving birth in California in 1994 and 1995. *Psychiatric Services*, *50*, 1584–90.

Miller, L. J. & Finnerty, M. (1996). Sexuality, pregnancy, and childbearing among women with schizophrenia-spectrum disorders. *Psychiatric Services*, *47*, 502–5.

Mirsky, A. F., Kugelmann, S., Ingraham, I. J., Frenkel, E. & Nathan, M. (1995). Overview and summary: twenty-five-year follow-up of high-risk children. *Schizophrenia Bulletin*, *21*, 227–39.

Mowbray, C. T., Oyserman, D. & Ross, S. (1995*a*). Parenting and the significance of children for women with a serious mental illness. *Journal of Mental Health Administration*, *22*, 189–200.

Mowbray, C. T., Oyserman, D., Zemencuk, J. K. & Ross, S. R. (1995*b*). Motherhood for women with serious mental illness: pregnancy, childbirth, and the postpartum period. *American Journal of Orthopsychiatry*, *65*, 21–38.

Nicholson, J., Sweeney, E. M. & Geller, J. L. (1998*a*). Mothers with mental illness: I. The competing demands of parenting and living with mental illness. *Psychiatric Services*, *49*, 635–42.

Nicholson, J., Sweeney, E. M. & Geller, J. L. (1998*b*). Mothers with mental illness: II. Family relationships and the context of parenting. *Psychiatric Services*, *49*, 643–9.

Parker, G. (1989). The Parental Bonding Instrument: psychometric properties reviewed. *Psychiatric Developments*, *4*, 317–36.

Parnas, J., Cannon, T. D., Jacobsen, B., Schulsinger, H., Schulsinger, F. & Mednick, S. A. (1993). Lifetime DSM–III–R diagnostic outcomes in the offspring of schizophrenic mothers. Results from the Copenhagen High-Risk Study. *Archives of General Psychiatry*, *50*, 707–14.

Riordan, D., Appleby, L. & Faragher, B. (1999). Mother–infant interaction in post-partum women with schizophrenia and affective disorders. *Psychological Medicine*, *29*, 991–5.

Ritsher, J. E. B., Coursey, R. D. & Farrell, E. W. (1997). A survey on issues in the lives of women with severe mental illness, *Psychiatric Services*, *48*, 1273–82.

Sacker, A., Done, D. J. & Crow, T. J. (1996). Obstetric complications in children born to parents with schizophrenia: a meta-analysis of case-control studies. *Psychological Medicine*, *26*, 279–87.

Sameroff, A., Seifer, R., Zax, M. & Barocas, R. (1987). Early indicators of developmental risk: Rochester longitudinal study. *Schizophrenia Bulletin, 13,* 383–94.

Sands, R. G. (1995). The parenting experience of low-income single women with serious mental disorders. *Journal of Contemporary Human Services, 76,* 86–96.

Seeman, M. V. (1996). The mother with schizophrenia. In *Parental Psychiatric Disorder: Distressed Parents and their Families,* ed. M. Göpfert, J. Webster & M. V. Seeman, pp. 190–200. Cambridge: Cambridge University Press.

Seeman, M. V. (1998). Narratives of twenty to thirty years of schizophrenia outcome. *Psychiatry, 61,* 249–61.

Seeman, M. V. & Cohen, R. (1998). A service for women with schizophrenia. *Psychiatric Services, 49,* 674–7.

Snellen, M., Mack, K. & Trauer, T. (1999). Schizophrenia, mental state, and mother–infant interaction: examining the relationship. *Australian and New Zealand Journal of Psychiatry, 33,* 902–11.

Stromwall, L. K. & Robinson, E. A. R. (1998). When a family member has a schizophrenic disorder: practice issues across the family life cycle. *American Journal of Orthopsychiatry, 68,* 580–9.

Warner, R. (2001). The prevention of schizophrenia: What interventions are safe and effective? *Schizophrenia Bulletin, 27,* 551–62.

Yoshida, K., Marks, M. N., Craggs, M., Smith, B. & Kumar, R. (1999). Sensorimotor and cognitive development of infants of mothers with schizophrenia. *British Journal of Psychiatry, 175,* 380–7.

12

When a parent suffers from an affective disorder: effect on the child

Christine Puckering

Royal Hospital for Sick Children, Glasgow, UK

Aetiology, prevalence and risk factors for depression in parents

By the year 2020, the World Health Organization estimates that clinical depression will be the second most common cause of morbidity (Murray & Lopez, 1996). Depression is widespread throughout adult life and, therefore, affects men and women who are parents. The negative effects of depression on children of all ages is well documented, but variations in timing, chronicity and the adverse social circumstances that often surround depression make the disaggregation of effects difficult. Some of the evidence that parental depression has adverse effects on children comes from studies where one or sometimes both parents have bipolar disorders, which is a vastly different picture from a more typical postnatal depression, treated, or as often not treated, in the community. In the more severe case, children can be affected by separation from parents because of parental hospitalization, and disruption to the children's daily lives as well as parental depression as such. Quick assessment and treatment, and special focus on children would seem advantageous, but in reality few controlled trials of the effectiveness of treatment for the children have been made. There is some evidence that even treatments which successfully relieve the maternal depression may not automatically improve the parent–child relationship. Much attention is given to postnatal depression, although the rate of depressed mood in pregnancy is already high, higher in fact than postpartum (Evans *et al.*, 2001).

One to two women in every 10 will suffer a depressive disorder after childbirth. One in a thousand will suffer a puerperal psychosis, a more extreme form of psychological disorder often taking the form of a schizoaffective or bipolar disorder (Kendell *et al.*, 1987; O'Hara & Swain, 1996) (see Seneviratne & Conroy, Chapter 9). What gives postnatal depression a special status is the dependency of the young infant in a situation where the mother's functioning is impaired. Studies are almost equally divided in reporting postnatal depression as more or less severe than at other times, but there is little evidence that the pattern of symptoms is different, or de facto that postnatal depression is a separate diagnostic entity (Augusto *et al.*, 1996; Cooper & Murray, 1995; Hendrick *et al.*, 2000; Murray *et al.*, 1995; Whiffen & Gotlib, 1993; Wisner *et al.*, 1999).

Unpicking the effects of parental depression on children is complicated by the fluctuating nature of depression. Whenever the first onset of depression, and regardless of the temporal proximity of the episode to the birth of a child, it is likely that the parent will suffer further fluctuations in their psychological well-being, and the child may be subject not only to parental depression in the early days, but chronic dysphoria and episodes of depression of variable severity and length. The heterogeneity of depression and its timing and length interact with the developmental tasks of the child. There are also differences associated with the current status of the mother at the time of assessment. Some patterns of interaction or disorder may be associated only with current depression, while others reflect a more chronic influence. There is some evidence that even after a mother's recovery from depression, adverse patterns of interaction with her child can continue (Cox *et al.*, 1987*a*).

Risk factors for depression, whether or not it starts postnatally, are indistinguishable. These include a past history of depression, low social support, a poor marital relationship and recent life events (Beck, 1996; O'Hara & Swain, 1996; Wilson *et al.*, 1996). Weaker associations with a history of abuse, low family income and lower occupational status have been demonstrated (Nielson Forman *et al.*, 2000).

Some factors specific to the experience of childbirth are specifically implicated in the risk of postnatal depression including depression in pregnancy, a weak association with obstetric complications and the experience of the 'Baby blues', the common experience of a period of marked emotional lability in the first few days after delivery which is usually self-limiting and benign. Social factors, including poor perceived parental care in childhood, unplanned pregnancy, unemployment, depression in the partner and having two or more children, all contribute to a bleak picture (Areias et al, 1996; Augusto *et al.*, 1996; Gotlib *et al.*, 1991; Warner *et al.*, 1996).

The mother's mental health may also be affected by the health of her baby. Maternal depression has shown an association with neonatal risk, stillbirth, neonatal or sudden infant death syndrome and very low birth weight babies (Bennet & Slade, 1991; Boyle *et al.*, 1996; O'Brien *et al.*, 1999; Singer *et al.*, 1999). Understandably, both worries about the baby's health, and guilt and anxiety about not being able to produce a healthy baby, undermine a parent's feeling of efficacy and self-worth.

Identification

Since the majority of pregnant women attend for antenatal care, this would seem to be an ideal time to screen for a history of depression, and depression in pregnancy as predictors of later depression. The Edinburgh Post Natal Depression Scale (EPDS) (Cox *et al.*, 1987*b*) has been used in this context as well as postnatally but accurate evaluation of sensitivity and specificity has not been completed. Postnatally a cutoff score of 9 has been taken to indicate possible depression and 12 or more as an indicator of probable depression. Both the EPDS and other screening instruments used outside the perinatal period suffer the same weaknesses. They are not diagnostic tools, and clinical evaluation is always necessary.

Help seeking

Many sufferers from depression may not recognize their own distress as depression and many do not seek help. This is particularly compounded when the sufferer is caring for young children. Brown & Moran (1997) illustrate the particular difficulties for a new mother seeking help and having her distress recognized. She may be very reluctant to reveal her feeling of inadequacy, particularly if she fears that she may be considered unfit to look after her child. Equally, her intense distress may be brushed aside as only what is expected when looking after a new baby, suffering sleepless nights and extra demands. Affonso *et al.* (1990) described the difficulty in differentiating depressive symptoms in the postnatal period from the normal emotional changes contingent on childbirth. These issues provide a barrier to recognition of the seriousness of the problem and the delivery of effective treatment.

Effects on partner

There is some slight evidence that women who are depressed also have depressed partners. There is no doubt that the company of a depressed person is depressing. Gotlib & Robinson (1982) described how in interaction with a depressed individual, conversation becomes difficult. Fathers are more likely to experience depression and physical ill health when their partners are depressed (Ballard *et al.*, 1994). If both partners are depressed they are not available to offer support to each other, and the risk to children increases, with neither parent available to compensate for the difficulties of the other.

Effects on children

Although the children of depressed mothers are at increased risk of depression (Radke-Yarrow *et al.*, 1992) the links are not straightforward, as they are also at increased risk of a wide range of other emotional and behavioural problems, particularly when depression is chronic and affects more than one member of the family.

A recent review (Rice *et al.*, 2002) suggested that major depressive disorder in adulthood has familial and genetic heritability. However, the risk for children is rather more complex. Children who have an early onset of depression are thought to be more vulnerable to genetic risk, but twin and adoption studies suggest that the rater and the measurement instrument made a marked difference to the apparent risk. Self-reported symptoms were less common than parent-reported symptoms. If the state of the child was viewed through the lens of a depressed parent, or even a parent who is on the lookout for depression because of a familial tendency to depression, then the meaning of the child's behaviour may be misinterpreted.

Possible mechanisms of the transmission of difficulties between generations include both genetic and interactional forces, but the frequent co-occurrence of depression with a whole range of other social adversity and the association of depression with poor marital partnerships suggests that at least some of the mechanisms reflect difficulties in sustaining good relationships. Depressed young mothers in a community sample in south London described a pattern starting with poor relationships with their own mothers, and lack of engagement in school. Early cohabiting and childbearing initially seemed to offer an escape route from an unhappy home but proved demanding and difficult and when their partners proved to be equally unskilled in engaging in an intimate relationship, having grown up in a similarly depriving emotional environment, the scene was set both for depression and another cycle of deprived parenting (Cox *et al.*, 1987*a*).

Jaenicke *et al.* (1987) further examined the pathways of transmission of depression from parent to child. Children's negative cognition, demonstrated by child self-criticism, was more directly related to maternal criticism of the child than to maternal self-criticism. That is, the child comes to internalize or accept the parent's critical view of him or herself rather than learn self-criticism as modelled by the parent.

Attachment

One possible mechanism by which early depression may have long-term effects is via the attachment relationship between the mother and the child (see Hill, Chapter 4). Lyons-Ruth *et al.* (1990) reported higher rates of disorganized attachment in a small sample of depressed women. The group however was a particularly high-risk single parent group. Where samples are chosen that are subject to multiple social and economic problems it is less easy to attribute the effects unequivocally to maternal depression. The self-same factors that predisposed the mother to depression may have an entirely separate adverse effect on the child.

Early findings of insecure attachment in toddlers whose mothers suffered depression were later shown to be demonstrated only in the bipolar subgroup (DeMulder

& Radke-Yarrow, 1991; Radke-Yarrow *et al.*, 1985) and Sameroff *et al.* (1982) found no systematic influences on attachment of any psychiatric diagnosis, no matter what its chronicity or severity.

Campbell & Cohn (1996) reported no increase in insecure attachment when the child was aged 12 months when the mother had been depressed through the child's first 6 months. A similar pattern at 1 year, and 18 months of age, for mothers who continued to be depressed, confirmed that maternal depression in the first 6 months of the child's life did not lead to an excess of children with insecure attachments to their mother. Campbell & Cohn speculated what might buffer the children against the effects of the mother's depression, and concluded that good relationships with caretakers other than the mother, including of course the father, may offer the necessary support even when the mother remains depressed. In studies including families where both parents are depressed this buffering may not be available. Micro-analysis of the interaction between infants and mothers however showed that insecure attachment was related to observed mother negative interaction at 2 months and decreased positive interaction at 6 and 12 months. It is therefore the quality of interaction that predicts attachment rather than depression, which is notably heterogeneous.

Specific effects of postnatal depression

What gives maternal postnatal depression its special status and impact is the involvement of a second party, the infant, who is dependent and acutely tuned to the emotional environment in which he or she arrives. Radke-Yarrow *et al.* (1992) capture this situation:

The (depressed) parent is the primary environment of the young child.

The particular vulnerability of the human infant is predicated on the immaturity and dependence of the baby at birth with his or her restricted range of capacities tuned specifically to participation in the social world. For example, the baby has a fixed visual range, which is just the distance from the baby's eyes to an adult face when the baby is cradled in an adult's arms. Early work by Fantz (1963) showed that the infant had a preference for face-like visual stimuli. By 2 months, infants showed a preference for a stimulus with a pattern resembling two eyes.

When an infant was face to face with his or her mother, the infant's gaze was not constant, but was a cycle of engagement and disengagement. The cycle matched the mother's cycle of activity and 'listening' with partners taking turns, in a pattern, which, if smooth, is compared to a dance (Stern, 1974). In normal dyads, from 1 month of age, if this pattern of alternating action and listening was disrupted by the mother making her face still, the infant became disengaged from the interaction

(Tronick *et al.*, 1978). If the mother had had a period of postnatal depression, however, the infant did not react adversely to the still-face situation (Field, 1984). This suggested that the infant had already accommodated to a muted level of interaction. More worrying still, the infant was also less active in a face-to-face interaction with a lively and nondepressed stranger, showing that the pattern of interaction developed with the depressed mother had the capacity to influence the baby's other relationships (Field *et al.*, 1988).

While developmental psychologists have become reluctant to invoke ideas of sensitive periods, it does seem that the specific developmental agenda of the infant and his or her particular priming for the development of social behaviour may set in train a series of expectations which serve to form later relationships.

The cognitive outcome for children of postnatally depressed mothers is impaired in the long term. Coghill *et al.* (1986) reported on the outcome at 4 years of children whose mothers had been postnatally depressed. The authors reported that, in this rather upwardly socio-economically skewed population, the children's performance was reduced by about 10 IQ points on the McCarthy scales if their mother was depressed in the first year of the child's life. This effect was evident even in the first 3 months. No equivalent drop was seen with mother's antenatal depression or for concurrent maternal depression at age 4.

Redressing the social class bias, a second sample was later studied in south London, recruited during the pregnancy at two general practices (Sharp *et al.*, 1995). Mothers' history of depression antenatally did not influence IQ scores, but depression in the first year of the child's life was associated with a 6-point deficit in the index group, pointing to a very specific vulnerability to the effects of maternal depression in the first year of the child's life. Finer grained analysis revealed that the decrement was only reliable for boys, with a discrepancy of about 17 IQ points.

Murray (1992) studied a prospective sample of 113 primiparous women in the Cambridge area. At 18 months, the infants of mothers who had a period of postnatal depression were significantly less likely to succeed at Object Concept tasks, regardless of the mother's previous experience of depression antenatally. Murray *et al.* (1993), describing in more detail a subsample of this study, indicated that the quality of the maternal communication with the infant, and particularly infant-focused speech measured between 8 and 11 weeks postpartum, mediated the association between depression and infant cognitive development. Murray *et al.* (1999) also identify social and emotional deficits in these children in their first year at school. While it is difficult to give credence to the long-term effects of the content of maternal speech at such an early age, while the baby is preverbal, infant-focused speech may act as a marker of the pre-occupation of the mother with her own experience and her lack of engagement in the child's world, which might persist and have longer-term effects. If we propose that depressed women have difficulty in investing in mutually satisfying relationships, this pattern may be seen both in poor marriages, which are so commonly associated with depression, and poor parent–child relationships.

In contrast, Kurstjens & Wolke (2001) attributed the majority of the difference between the IQs of the children of postnatally depressed women to the adverse social and economic situations commonly associated with depression. They reported that when these factors were partialled out statistically, the apparent disadvantage suffered by the children of depressed women disappeared.

Case example

Janice illustrates fully the external pressures and internal pain leading to depression and poor parenting. She entered the parenting programme at her local family centre in Glasgow at the urging of her social worker and family aide. When interviewed for the group she showed a clear determination to undertake this piece of work and an openness to change, partly as a result of their careful preparation.

She had three children. The oldest, Stewart, was in voluntary foster care with her mother, following an incident in which Janice had hit him, resulting in his placement on the child protection register. He returned to the family home three evenings a week, to eat tea with his mother and younger half-siblings. His younger sister, Caitlin, aged 4, was about to start school and was also on the child protection register. His younger brother, Mark, was aged 10 months.

Janice was raised by her parents until they separated when she was aged 11. Her memory of their marriage and separation was of constant conflict. At times, her father was physically violent to her mother when he was drunk. When her parents separated, Janice lived with her mother and was forbidden to see her father, but she sneaked out every week to see him. Two years later her parents got back together, but split up again. Her mother left, taking with her Janice's younger brother. Janice was then in the care of her father, but because of his excessive drinking, she spent much of the time with her grandparents. Janice described both her parents as strict. She was afraid of her father, and could remember little positive interaction with him. If as little as 5 minutes late in returning home, she would be hit with a leather belt. Janice had no contact with him at the time of the group, or with the stepmother whom he had married a year after Stewart's birth.

Her mother never had much time for Janice, and used her as a skivvy while favouring her brother. Although she was physically well cared for, Janice described her mother as cruel, expecting Janice as the oldest child to do all the chores, and not hesitating to give her a 'clout around the ear' if she did not do as her mother wished. At the time of the group Janice had no face-to-face contact with her mother or father, with whom she had had an argument when she found she was pregnant with Mark.

Janice left school at 16 without passing any exams. She liked school, as it was a chance to get out of the house, but truanted regularly from lessons she did not like. She has no confidence in her own abilities, and no view of the path to the future.

Janice did not experience depression until the birth of Stewart, when she had severe postnatal depression. This deepened when her partner, with whom she had lived for 2 years, died when the baby was 6 weeks old. With the birth of each child she experienced a further postnatal depression, but remained troubled between these episodes, anxious at night about intruders, worrying about her children, her partner and her parents and feeling she had wasted her life. She did not live with her new partner, father of Caitlin and Mark, but he was her chief confidante and played a large part in the lives of the children except when he was drinking. His drinking was episodic, with heavy intake every 3 weeks or so, with abstinence between. Janice worried about him, especially in view of his also having chronic heart disease. There was a clear dependency on him as well as exasperation and concern about him.

Janice took part in the Mellow Parenting Project in 1995, and made good use of the opportunity to reflect on her own childhood and parenting and what she needed to develop a life of her own and be the parent she wished to be. The group offered Janice support and personal exploration as well as asking her to confront the difficulties in her parenting. This came to a head when she had to participate in the decision-making about Stewart's future. She felt that she was not able to offer him the consistency and support he needed to address his developing behavioural and attentional problems. Painfully aware of the damaging effects of her upbringing on her confidence and emotional containment, she was torn then about entrusting her son to her own mother's care, the solution advocated by the social work department.

A year after participating in the group she reported no depressive symptoms and felt that it had changed her life. Finding that she was not the only parent who found the task difficult, but that she could share her experiences and learn from others' experiences was a painful but rewarding journey. She found herself more confident and able to plan ahead, and took pleasure in her new ability to talk and understand people better, and in particular the opportunity to help others to help themselves.

Three years after the group, she was following a full-time computer-training course and was chair of a local resident group who had applied successfully for funding to establish a Safer Cities project, to support local residents in improving their physical and social environment. She no longer had contact with her previous partner. Her new partner was employed and after the birth of a new baby she had not experienced any depression.

Some 5 years later, she still had no depressive symptoms, and had coped well with the revelation that her new partner had sexually abused her daughter. She had immediately ejected him from the family and she and the children were thriving. She described her understanding that though she might go 'up and down' she now knew there was a ladder, and even when she went down she knew she could climb up again one rung at a time.

Before entering the Mellow Parenting programme Janice had a life-long experience of poor relationships with her own parents, lack of personal success and self-esteem and loss and disappointment in her partners. After the programme she showed a clear change in her evaluation of herself and her capacity to be of value to her children and the community. Sadly, she had not been able to mend her relationship with her oldest child. This appears to confirm the model previously suggested, that is, recovery from depression does not automatically improve the relationship between parent and child unless this is actually addressed. Since Stewart was already in foster care when Janice entered the programme, he did not participate directly, and perhaps missed out on the therapeutic input which enabled Janice to change the nature of her relationships with her subsequent children.

Intervention

If parental depression and/or the adverse constellation of social and relationship factors that predict and surround it impairs parent–child relationships, and if simply relieving the depression does not automatically repair the relationship, then therapeutic intervention needs to address the parental depression acting as a barrier to changing parenting along with the parent–child relationship.

The Mellow Parenting Project was designed for parents and children with relationship problems, and not specifically for depressed parents. However, in a research study (Puckering *et al.*, 2000), the majority of women entering the programme were depressed, with many of them reporting the onset of depression in the context of being a new mother. Almost 70% of the women reported that they had no friends or family in whom they could confide. Almost by definition, lack of trust and confiding and being depressed must go together. Not being good at relationships extends to relationships with children. Some women 'kept themselves to themselves', others put their hopes in the latest of a string of men friends who were often as deprived and emotionally disabled as themselves, and each of whom failed to meet the woman's need for intimacy and support, either becoming distant and unavailable or violent and controlling. The intensity of their wish for support led many women into patterns of making rapid and intense sexual or other relationships that quickly broke down as the intimacy became too demanding. Yet another loss compounded the need to seek another relationship.

For many, the group provided a safe forum for the first time to reflect on their own situation, to make links between the past and the present and to make changes in their parenting. The programme combined psychotherapeutic support for the parents in a personal group, and in vivo and video-recorded work on parenting, in a 14-week course lasting a full day for both parents and children. Throughout the programme, links were made between past experiences of relationships, particularly the parenting the mothers received, and the ways in which that shaped their own parenting, for good or evil. The programme has been shown to make a marked impact not only on the well-being of the mothers, but also on their interaction with their children and their children's development (Puckering *et al.*, 1994, 2000).

It is helpful to try to deconstruct the processes by which change came about. Parents giving anonymous feedback particularly noted the value of being listened to, and not being judged. The group also intervened directly in parenting, but took a very deliberate stance of not solving parenting problems, but enabling parents to generate their own solutions to the problems that they themselves identified. The staff in the groups, psychologist, social worker and nursery nurse had to learn not to problem-solve on behalf of parents but to create a space where the women could safely reveal and modify their feelings and behaviour.

Conclusions

There is little doubt that depression in parents is associated with long-term adverse effects on children, in cognitive, emotional and behavioural domains. By contrast, there is considerable controversy over the mechanisms that might account for the effects. Familial clustering is evident, with genetics, adverse parenting and the social disruption caused by parental mental disorder playing a role, separately and in combination. There is rather little information on depressed fathers, and rather a lot on postnatal depression, perhaps because it occurs in a period when mother and baby are most visible to service providers, and when there is most concern about the vulnerability of the baby. Careful analysis suggests that it is the quality of the parent–child interaction rather than depression per se that impinges on the child's development. Poor interaction and maternal depression are not coterminous although they do overlap to a degree.

Intervention needs to be multimodal and integrated (see Seeman & Göpfert, Chapter 2; Göpfert *et al.*, Chapter 5; Mahoney, Chapter 23; Baistow & Hetherington, Chapter 26; Falkov, Chapter 27). Addressing just the depression may fail to have an impact on the parent–child relationship. Conversely, being depressed may impair the ability to engage in a parenting programme. There is also an issue about service delivery, with adult mental health services, unaware of the impact of depression in parents on their children, and probably considering this outside their remit. Child mental health services, however, rarely see children until after the early months when the damage may already have been done. Treatment for postnatal depression is effective, but the needs of the child require special attention and only in rare cases are infant mental health services developed. Effective intervention for parents and children will require the co-ordination of primary and secondary care services across the age range, in combinations that may lie outside the usual multidisciplinary boundaries.

REFERENCES

Affonso, D. D., Lovett, S., Paul, S. M. & Shetpak, S. (1990). A standardised interview that differentiates pregnancy and postpartum symptoms from perinatal clinical depression. *Birth*, *17*, 121–30.

Areias, M. E., Kumar, R., Barros, H. & Figueiredo, E. (1996). Correlates of postnatal depression in mothers and fathers. *British Journal of Psychiatry*, *169*, 36–41.

Augusto, A., Kumar, R., Calheiros, J. M., Matos, E. & Figueredo, E. (1996). Post natal depression in an urban area of Portugal: comparison of childbearing women and matched controls. *Psychological Medicine, 26*, 135–41.

Ballard, C. G., Davis, R., Cullen, P. C. Mohan, R. N. & Dean, C. (1994). Prevalence of postnatal psychiatric morbidity in mothers and fathers. *British Journal of Psychiatry, 164*, 782–8.

Beck, C. T. (1996). A meta-analysis of predictors of postpartum depression. *Nursing Research, 45*, 297–303.

Bennet, D. E. & Slade, P. (1991). Infants born at risk: consequences for maternal post partum adjustment. *British Medical Journal, 64*, 159–72.

Boyle, F. M., Vance, J. C., Najman, J. M. & Thearle, M. J. (1996). The mental health impact of stillbirth, neonatal death, or SIDS: prevalence and patterns of distress among mothers. *Social Science in Medicine, 43*, 1273–82.

Brown, G. W. & Moran, P. M. (1997). Single mothers, poverty and depression. *Psychological Medicine, 27*, 21–33.

Campbell, S. B. & Cohn, J. F. (1996). The timing and chronicity of post partum depression: implications for Infant Development. In *Postpartum Depression and Child Development*, ed. L. Murray & P. J. Cooper, pp. 165–94. New York: Guilford Press.

Coghill, S., Caplan, C., Alexandra, H., Robson, K. & Kumar, R. (1986). Impact of postnatal depression on cognitive development in young children. *British Medical Journal, 292*, 1165–7.

Cooper, P. J. & Murray, L. (1995). Course and recurrence of postnatal depression. Evidence for the specificity of the diagnostic concept. *British Journal of Psychiatry, 166*, 191–5.

Cox, A. D., Puckering, C., Pound, A. & Mills, M. (1987*a*). The impact of maternal depression on young children. *Journal of Child Psychology and Psychiatry, 28*, 917–28.

Cox, J. L., Holden, J. M. & Sagovsky, R. (1987*b*). Detection of post natal depression: development of the 10 item Edinburgh Postnatal Depression Scale. *British Journal of Psychiatry, 150*, 782–6.

DeMulder, E. K. & Radke Yarrow, M. (1991). Attachment with affectively ill and well mothers. Concurrent behavioural correlates. *Development and Psychopathology, 3*, 227–42.

Evans, J., Heron, J., Francomb, H., Oke, S. & Golding, J. (2001). Cohort study of depressed mood during pregnancy and after child birth. *British Medical Journal, 323*, 257–60.

Fantz, R. L. (1963). Pattern vision in new-born infants. *Science, 140*, 296–7.

Field, T. (1984). Early interactions between infants and their post-partum depressed mothers. *Infant Behaviour and Development, 7*, 517–22.

Field, T., Healy, B., Goldstein, S. et al. (1988). Infants of depressed mothers show "depressed" behaviour even when with non-depressed adults. *Child Development, 59*, 1569–79.

Gotlib, I. H. & Robinson, L. A. (1982). Responses to depressed individuals: discrepancies between self-report and observer-rated behaviour. *Journal of Abnormal Psychology, 91*, 231–40.

Gotlib, I. H., Whiffen, V. E., Wallace, P. M. & Mount, J. H. (1991). Prospective investigation of postpartum depression: factors involved in onset and recovery. *Journal of Abnormal Psychology, 100*, 122–32.

Hendrick, V., Altshuler, L., Strouse, T. & Grosser, S. (2000). Post partum and non post partum depression: differences in presentation and response to pharmacological treatment. *Depression and Anxiety, 11*, 66–72.

Jaenicke, C., Hammon, C., Zupan, B. et al. (1987). *Journal of Abnormal Child Psychology*, *15*, 559–72.

Kendell, R. E, Chalmers, J. C. & Platz, C. (1987). Epidemiology of puerperal psychoses. *British Journal of Psychiatry*, *150*, 662–73.

Kurstjens, S. & Wolke, D. (2001). Effects of maternal depression on cognitive development of children over the first 7 years of life. *Journal of Child Psychology and Psychiatry*, *42*, 623–36.

Lyons-Ruth, K., Connell, D. B., Grunebaum, H. U. & Botein, S. (1990). Infants at social risk: maternal depression and family support services as mediators of infant development and security of attachment. *Child Development*, *61*, 85–98.

Murray, C. J. & Lopez, A. D. (1996). Evidence based health policy – lessons from the Global Burden of Disease Study. *Science*, *274*, 740–3.

Murray, D., Cox, J. L., Chapman, G. & Jones, P. (1995). Childbirth: life event or the start of a long term difficulty? Further data from the Stoke on Trent controlled study of post natal depression. *British Journal of Psychiatry*, *166*, 595–600.

Murray, L. (1992). The impact of post-natal depression on infant development. *Journal of Child Psychology and Psychiatry*, *33*, 543–61.

Murray, L., Kempton, C., Woolgar, M. & Hooper, R. (1993). Depressed mothers'speech to their infants and its relation to infant gender and cognitive development. *Journal of Child Psychology and Psychiatry*, *34*, 109–19.

Murray, L., Sinclair, D., Cooper, P., Ducournau, P., Turner, P. & Stein, A. (1999). The socioemotional development of 5-year-old children of postnatally depressed mothers. *Journal of Child Psychology and Psychiatry*, *39*, 1259–71.

Nielson Forman, D., Videbach, P., Hedegaard, M., Dalby Salvig, J. & Secher, N. J. (2000). Postpartum depression: identification of women at risk. *British Journal of Obstetrics and Gynaecology*, *107*, 1210–17.

O'Brien, M., Heron Asay, J. & McCluskey-Fawcett, K. (1999). Family functioning and maternal depression following premature birth. *Journal of Reproductive and Infant Psychology*, *17*, 178–88.

O'Hara, M. W. & Swain, A. M. (1996). Rates and risks of postnatal depression: a meta-analysis. *International Review of Psychiatry*, *8*, 37–54.

Puckering, C., Rogers, J., Mills, M., Cox, A. D. & Mattsson-Graff, M. (1994). Process and evaluation of a group intervention for mothers with parenting difficulties. *Child Abuse Review*, *3*, 299–310.

Puckering, C., Mills, M., Cox, A. D., Maddox, H., Evans, J. & Rogers, J. (2000). *Improving the Quality of Family Support: An Intensive Programme: Mellow Parenting*. London: Department of Health.

Radke-Yarrow, M., Cummings, M., Kuczynski, L. & Chapman, M. (1985). Patterns of attachment in two and three year olds in normal families and in families with parental depression. *Child Development*, *56*, 884–93.

Radke-Yarrow, M., Nottelman, E., Martinez, P., Fox, M. & Belmont, B. (1992). Young children of affectively ill parents. A longitudinal study of psychosocial adjustment. *Journal of the American Academy of Child and Adolescent Psychiatry*, *31*, 68–77.

Rice, F., Harold, G. & Thapar, A. (2002). The genetic aetiology of childhood depression: a review. *Journal of Child Psychology and Psychiatry, 43*, 65–79.

Samaroff, A. J., Seifer, R. & Zax, M. (1982). Early development of children at risk for emotional disorder. *Monographs for the Society for Research in Child Development, 47* (7, Serial No. 199).

Sharp, D., Hay, D., Pawlby, S., Schmucker, G., Allen, H. & Kumar, R. (1995). The impact of postnatal depression on boys' intellectual development. *Journal of Child Psychology and Psychiatry, 36*, 1315–37.

Singer, L. T., Salvator, A., Guo, S., Collin, M., Lilien, L. & Baley, J. (1999). Maternal psychological distress and parenting stress after the birth of a very low birthweight infant. *Journal of the American Medical Association, 281*, 799–805.

Stern, D. (1974). The goal and structure of mother–infant play. *Journal of the American Academy of Child Psychiatry, 13*, 402–21.

Tronick, E. Z., Als, H., Adamson, L., Wise, S. & Brazelton, T. B. (1978). The infant's response to entrapment between contradictory messages in face to face interaction. *Journal of the American Academy of Child Psychiatry, 17*, 1–13.

Warner, R., Appleby, L., Whitton, A. & Farragher, B. (1996). Demographic and obstetric risk factors for post natal psychiatric morbidity. *British Journal of Psychiatry, 168*, 607–11.

Whiffen, V. E. & Gotlib, I. H. (1993). Comparison of postpartum and non postpartum depression: clinical presentation, psychiatric history, and psychosocial functioning. *Journal of Consulting and Clinical Psychology, 61*, 485–94.

Wilson, L. M., Reid, A. J., Midmer, D. K., Biringer, A., Carroll, J. C. & Stewart, D. E. (1996). Antenatal psychosocial risk factors associated with adverse postnatal family outcomes. *Canadian Medical Association Journal, 154*, 785–99.

Wisner, K. L., Peindl, K. S., Gigliotti, T. & Hanusa, B. H. (1999). Obsessions and compulsions in woman with postpartum depression. *Journal of Clinical Psychiatry, 60*, 176–80.

13

Alcohol and drug problems in parents: an overview of the impact on children and implications for practice

Richard Velleman

Mental Health Research and Development Unit, University of Bath, Bath, UK

Alcohol and other drugs are used in socially acceptable ways in many diverse cultures but may, under some conditions, produce problems. Problem drinking/ drug-taking is defined as any drinking or taking of drugs which causes problems to the drinker/drug-taker or to someone else. The majority of problem drinking/ drug-taking is done by people who use alcohol or drugs inappropriately or in an unsafe or hazardous manner, as opposed to people who are seriously dependent or 'addicted'.

How common is problem drink or drug use?

Figures for the year 2000 (Office for National Statistics, 2001) show that in the UK, 26% of adults report hazardous drinking patterns (as measured by the AUDIT questionnaire; Babor *et al.*, 1992), and about 7% show symptoms of dependence on alcohol (as measured by the SADQ; Stockwell *et al.*, 1983). Men are much more likely to report both hazardous drinking behaviour and signs of dependence than women: for hazardous drinking, the rates were 38% of men vs. 15% of women. Although these figures vary with age as well as gender, the prevalence rate for men never falls below 30% until the 60–64 age group, whereas the prevalence rate for women falls from around 30% for both the 16–19 and 20–24 age groups to around 24% in the 25–29 age group, and to below 20% thereafter.

These figures represent a large growth since the previous survey of this type in 1993. At that time, the estimated rate of alcohol dependence was 47 per 1000 population; the 2000 survey estimates it at 74 per 1000 population (119 per 1000 for men, 29 per 1000 for women) (i.e. 7.4% of the entire adult population; almost 12% of the entire adult male population and almost 3% of the entire adult female population). Furthermore, these figures are a low estimate, because of the usual problems of national household surveys with underrepresentation of younger single people, students, those living in institutions and those with no fixed address; all groups with high proportions of heavy drinkers. Nevertheless, because these surveys focus on households, they are of particular relevance to the impact of substance misuse on families.

Obtaining reliable estimates of the numbers of people who use drugs is fraught with even more difficulties, due to the illegality of most drug use. Nevertheless, latest estimates suggest that 13% of men and 8% of women (aged between 16 and 75) reported using illegal drugs in the past year (Office for National Statistics, 2001). These figures are highly linked with both age and gender: for men, 32% of 16–19-year-olds report using drugs in the previous year, 37% of 20–24-year-olds, 34% of 24–29-year-olds, 18% of 30–34-year-olds, and 9% of 35–39-year-olds. For women, the figures for the same age ranges are 22, 29, 15, 9 and 7%. The 20–40 age range for both men and women is when alcohol or drug-induced behaviour is most likely to affect young children (see Hans, Chapter 14 for comparison figures for women who abuse drugs in the USA).

The numbers of problem drug users in the UK are also hard to estimate, but the same survey suggested that the prevalence of drug dependence was 37 per 1000 (i.e. exactly half of the prevalence rate for alcohol dependence). For 20–24-year-olds, however, this prevalence rate rises to 94 per 1000 for women and 199 per 1000 for men (i.e. nearly 10% of all women and nearly 20% of all men in this age group).

These figures equate to almost 4 million people in the 16–65 age group in the UK being dependent on alcohol and/or drugs. Assuming (conservatively) that every substance misuser will negatively affect at least two close family members, this suggests that about 8 million family members (spouse, children, parents, siblings) in the UK are living with the negative consequences of someone else's drug or alcohol misuse. These numbers apply to those dependent on alcohol or illicit drugs and exclude the more than 9 million people who drink at hazardous or risky levels, with the resultant 18 million family members potentially affected by that drinking; and the further numbers of individuals who take drugs at sufficiently risky levels to threaten their family's well-being.

Problems for the family?

The structure and functioning of the family as a system of relationships is affected by alcohol and drug problems.

Rituals

A fairly substantial part of family life consists of rituals in the sense of repeated gatherings and set modes of behaviour which define the occasion or the day as being special, different from other days and occasions, and especially important precisely in the sense of being designed or expected to cement family relationships. One of the prime consequences of alcohol or drug misuse is that it is highly disruptive of family rituals (Bennett & Wolin, 1990; Wolin *et al.*, 1980). The problem is encapsulated by a comment made by one of the children interviewed by Margaret Cork for her book *The Forgotten Children* – 'Dad's spoiled every Christmas I can remember because he smashed the tree' (Cork, 1969, p. 69).

Roles

Alcohol or drug misuse also tends to change the roles played by family members in relation to one another and the outside world (Moos & Billings, 1982; Roosa *et al.*, 1988). As a family member develops a drinking problem, the others take over his or her role. Eventually, one member may be performing all the family roles – finances, disciplining, shopping, cleaning and household management (see Göpfert *et al.*, Chapter 5).

Routines

Another likely consequence of problem drinking or drug taking is that behaviour becomes unpredictable, and this makes it very difficult for the family to plan or commit to routines (Jones & Houts, 1992). Will he be able to collect the child from school? When will she come home, and in what state? Should meals be served or not? This constant uncertainty can be highly disruptive and it helps to explain a commonly found paradox in such families: that while the problem drinker/drug-taker may be doing little in the family, he or she nonetheless appears to dominate life.

Communication

Alcohol or drugs affect communications between family members (Jones & Houts, 1992; Steinglass *et al.*, 1987). The person with the problem may refuse to talk about it. Alternatively, alcohol or drugs may loosen the tongue and things might be said which would otherwise not have been, thereby increasing marital and family conflict. Alcohol or drug misuse not only changes the emotional quality of communication – discussions turning into rows and recriminations – but also may grow to dominate its content.

Social life

Most people find it extraordinarily difficult to explain to friends and neighbours that a family member has a drug or alcohol problem. The social embarrassment, and the unpredictability associated with drinking or drug problems, make it awkward to invite others into the family home, or accept invitations, or attend social gatherings. The family tends to become increasingly socially isolated (Reich *et al.*, 1988; Seilhamer, *et al.*, 1993).

Finances

Financial problems are a further major strain for the family (Reich *et al.*, 1988). Money spent on drink or drugs is not available for other family expenditures and drink or drug problems result in the family's income being greatly diminished. Jobs are lost, the rent is not paid, debts accumulate, accommodation is lost, power is cut off.

As well as problems in family structure and functioning, there are many specific problems for the family related to alcohol and drug misuse; among the most serious of these is violence. It has been estimated that more than 80% of cases of spouse-to-spouse violence are alcohol related (Hamilton & Collins, 1981; Powers, 1986). Physical abuse of children involves 20–30% of parents who are heavy drinkers (Creighton, 1984). Often, the child-abusing parent is under the influence of alcohol at the time the incident occurs (Powers, 1986). The results are the same for the families of problem drug users (Velleman *et al.*, 1993). Alison (2000) also cites domestic violence as a main factor associated with risk to children.

Clearly, all these problems can have dire consequences for family members (Velleman, 2000; Velleman *et al.*, 1993, 1998). And these are worldwide phenomena, essentially similar in various cultures (Mathews & Velleman, 1997; Orford, 1990; Orford *et al.*, 1998*a*, *b*, 1999, 2001*a*, *b*). These families need help, both for themselves and their substance-misusing relative. And they ask for it: between a third and a half of calls to alcohol advice centres in the UK come from partners, families and friends (Brisby *et al.*, 1997).

Specific effects on children

A particularly important area is the impact of drug and alcohol problems on children (Velleman, 2000; Velleman & Orford, 1999). There is a growing realization that their needs are not adequately met within current service provision. The effects on children occur in three stages: during childhood, adolescence and adulthood.

Childhood

A great deal of research shows that many children brought up in families where alcohol or drug problems occur experience negative childhoods, including high levels of violence (Black *et al.*, 1986) and inconsistency from one or both parents (Jarmas & Kazak, 1992; Jones & Houts, 1992; Roosa *et al.*, 1988). Children may also have to adopt responsible or parenting roles at an early age (Cleaver *et al.*, 1999). They subsequently demonstrate high levels of behavioural disturbance, antisocial behaviour (conduct disorder) (Nylander, 1979; Robins, 1966; West & Prinz, 1987), emotional difficulties (Cleaver *et al.*, 1999; Orford & Velleman, 1990), school problems

(Knop *et al.*, 1985), precocious maturity and a difficult transition from childhood through adolescence (Orford & Velleman, 1995; Velleman & Orford, 1999).

Adolescence

During adolescence, the literature reports two common patterns. On one hand, an adolescent may become increasingly introspective and socially isolated. He or she may experience friendship difficulties (e.g. unlikely to visit or invite friends to their own home) (Black *et al.*, 1986; Cork, 1969), anxiety or depression (Velleman & Orford, 1999) (for which they may be prescribed psychoactive medication), or may try to escape from their family home (e.g. leaving home earlier, or entering into long-term relationships) (Velleman & Orford, 1999). On the other hand, an adolescent may develop strong peer relationships but keep these separate from their family of origin (Velleman & Orford, 1999). These relationships may themselves involve early alcohol or drug use (Chassin *et al.*, 1996; Velleman & Orford, 1999), participation in subcultures perceived to be deviant (Nylander & Rydelius, 1982) or antisocial activity (Nylander & Rydelius, 1982).

Adulthood

For some time it has been assumed that children with one or more problem-drinking parents are more likely themselves to develop problematic drinking patterns in their adulthood (Heller *et al.*, 1982; Sher, 1991). Whilst such intergenerational continuities can occur (Pandina & Johnson, 1990; Parker & Harford, 1988; Schuckit & Sweeney, 1987), this assumption may have been exaggerated. A review of the current literature suggests that most adults who had problem-drinking parents do not have worse problems than others, either in terms of substance misuse or other areas of adulthood adjustment (Velleman & Orford, 1999).

The sections above have grouped together the effects of alcohol and drugs. These will now be looked at separately.

Alcohol

For reviews, see Velleman (1993, 1996, 2002) and Velleman & Orford (1999).
- Many children experience very negative childhoods, with high levels of both violence and inconsistency.
- Many children show very negative effects of these experiences, showing high levels of behavioural disturbance and antisocial behaviour, of emotional difficulties, of school problems, and a difficult transition from childhood through adolescence. These effects are frequently worse if both parents have alcohol problems, or if the problem drinking occurs at home.
- For some children, these problems continue into adulthood with well-documented intergenerational continuities, i.e. children developing drinking

patterns in their adulthood. Further, if the family also suffers from high levels of disharmony, the children may grow up depressed and demoralized (Velleman & Orford, 1993*b*).

Drugs

It is unclear to what extent the alcohol findings are mirrored in children of problem drug-users (Alison, 2000; National Children's Bureau, 1998; Velleman & Townsend, 1997) (see Hans, Chapter 14). There are problems with examining the question of the effects of parental drugs as opposed to alcohol. Many published studies use samples made up of 'substance misusers', i.e. they do not discriminate between alcohol or drug problems in the parents. Rising levels of comorbidity between these two groups mean that many drug-misusing parents are also misusing alcohol. Grouping 'drug misuse' into one category obscures the differences among drugs and their effects. Finally, almost all of the available literature stems from the USA, where social problems and responses to such problems differ markedly from the UK.

Nevertheless, it seems that these children are affected in similar ways to children of alcohol misusers. The impact of parental drug problems on a child can result in a wide range of effects:

- Psychological difficulties: lower self-esteem, depression, anxiety, hyperactivity, withdrawal, high psychopathology scores.
- Physical difficulties: more overnight hospitalizations for medical problems, somatic complaints and, for children who experienced withdrawal symptoms at birth, developmental delays, low IQ scores and low heights and weights.
- Social and interpersonal difficulties: impaired social development and poor levels of social competency (as measured by social activities, social abilities and school functioning).
- Academic and school problems: arithmetic and reading problems, repeating a year at school, suspension and expulsion from school.
- Behaviour problems: truancy, discipline problems, trouble with the law, membership of deviant peer groups, involvement in drugs and/or alcohol, aggression. Not surprisingly, these problems tend to correlate.

It must be acknowledged that not all children whose parents misuse drugs are negatively affected. One study reported that 73% of the children of their sample of drug-misusing parents participated in afterschool activities, especially athletics; 72% received academic awards, 33% received athletic achievements and 13% received other awards (Kolar *et al.*, 1994). Much depends on the child's individual needs and the parents' skills and experience. The provision of opportunities, social support and access to and availability of services are also important factors. Various studies emphasize the need for teachers, health visitors and general practitioners to be aware of the potential for disturbance in children from households where adults have alcohol or drug problems. A number of commentators emphasize the need for specialist care workers, especially within the child welfare system: 'It is imperative that child welfare practitioners be equipped with the knowledge and skills necessary to identify and intervene appropriately and successfully in substance abusing families' (Dore *et al.*, 1995, p. 540). Removing the child from the home is not a viable or even a desirable option, except in certain risk-assessed circumstances. There are few residential substance misuse programmes that make provision for child-care, and this can be a major barrier to treatment.

One main focus of research relating to parents' drug misuse is the area of child mistreatment. It has been suggested that the nature of child mistreatment might be dependent on the type of substance being misused by the parent, with cocaine misuse being a particular risk factor for sexual (although not physical) maltreatment, alcohol misuse being significantly related to physical (although not sexual) mistreatment, and opiates not being significantly associated with either type of mistreatment. It is also useful to distinguish between abuse and neglect in children: children of drug-misusing parents seem less likely to be abused than children with alcohol-misusing parents (although still slightly more than controls); but they seem just as likely to be neglected.

There is also evidence to suggest that substance-misusing parents are more likely to come to the attention of child-care professionals and the courts more frequently than others. The issue of the interaction with child protection services is not a simple one, however. One study (Murphy *et al.*, 1991, who examined a sample of over 200 cases) showed that drug-misusing parents were more likely to be rated as high-risk parents, and much more likely to have their children permanently removed from their care (i.e. 90%, compared with 60% for parents who only misused alcohol) than was the case in other child protection cases. This study also showed, however, that these drug-misusing parents were much more likely to reject services than were alcohol-misusing parents. This implies that drug-misusing parents are more likely to be alienated from the court system, and to reject offers of help. There are also major implications here for care services and court procedures, with the point needing to be emphasized that the issue is whether or not parenting ability and actual behaviour is satisfactory, not whether or not one or both parents use or misuse hard drugs.

Why do parental alcohol or drug problems affect children as badly as they do?

There appear to be three linked factors which underlie the process through which parental problem drinking and drug taking affect children. There are large effects on family functioning: serious disruptions in family roles, family rituals, family routines, family communication systems, family social life and family finances. These, in turn, can result in uncertainty and unpredictability (Cork, 1969), and research into the upbringing of children in general suggests that unpredictability and the absence of order and routine are key factors in impairing children's ability to lead successful and healthy childhoods and adulthoods (Bowlby, 1971, 1973, 1980; Rutter, 1980). In problem-drinking and drug-taking families, unpredictability leads to many difficulties including a deteriorating parent–child relationship, self-blame and diminishing feelings of self-esteem (El-Guebaly & Offord, 1977, 1979; West & Prinz, 1987; Wilson, 1980), social isolation and feelings of exclusion (Reich *et al.*, 1988; Seilhamer *et al.*, 1993; Velleman & Orford, 1999). Children in these families may feel that they are 'different' and in some way to blame and responsible for their parents' drinking or drug taking. It is easy to see why self-blame and low self-esteem are very common with these children.

Some of the factors which can exacerbate the situation (Alison, 2000; Velleman & Orford, 1984; Wilson, 1980) include:

- Violence: Even if violence is not directed at the child, it greatly increases the risk of the child experiencing the kind of problems described above (Huesman *et al.*, 1984; Velleman & Orford, 1999).
- Marital conflict: Margaret Cork's classic study (1969), cited earlier, showed that marital arguments disturbed children most.
- Separation, divorce and parent loss: The dissolution of the parental relationship increases the likelihood of severe problems in the children. Although one in five children experience parental divorce before age 16 (Kieman & Wicks, 1990), a particular factor in problem drinking/drug-taking families is that separation and divorce often entails complete parental loss for the child, without any further contact (Black *et al.*, 1986; Nylander, 1960).
- Inconsistency and ambivalence in parenting: Children may experience poor parenting from both the substance-misusing and the non substance-misusing parent (Jarmas & Kazak, 1992; Jones & Houts, 1992; Roosa *et al.*, 1988).
- The problems are worse when both parents have an alcohol or drug problem (Orford & Velleman, 1991; Velleman & Orford, 1990).
- The problems are also worse when problem drinking or drug-taking occurs in the home (Orford, 1990; Orford & Velleman, 1991; Velleman & Orford, 1990).
- Importantly, the literature indicates that family disharmony is a far more important factor underpinning both childhood and adulthood problems than parental substance misuse (Velleman & Orford, 1993*a*, *b*).

Protective factors

The range of detrimental effects outlined above are not *certain* to occur. There are some factors which make them *less* likely to occur. These 'protective factors' are those which make children more resilient, more able to cope with problems (Moos *et al.*, 1990; Velleman & Orford, 1999; Werner, 1986):

- The risks of a negative outcome are reduced if the non substance-misusing parent can provide a stable environment where a child can develop, and can offer the time and attention that children require.
- Research indicates that the quality of the family environment is more important than parental problem drinking. If a cohesive parental relationship is maintained, and they manage to present a united and caring front to the children, the children will be at less risk.
- Even if parents do not retain cohesion within their own relationship, risk will be reduced if family relationships, family affection, and family activities are maintained.
- The ability of children to separate family life from any disruptive behaviour of the problem drinker is also protective. This can be achieved through 'planning', or 'deliberateness' (Rutter, 1985, 1988): the active and deliberate attempt to make one's life more ordered and structured, and less disrupted by the problems in the family. Another aspect is family disengagement or external engagement: the ability of the child to disengage from the disruptive elements of family life and engage with others outside the family (e.g. school-mates) or with stabilizing activities (e.g. a major hobby).
- The literature also confirms the importance of external support systems such as the presence of important others (a nonparental adult, a grandparent, an influential teacher or a neighbour) (Bennett *et al.*, 1987; Cowen & Work, 1988; Garmezy, 1985; Velleman & Orford, 1999).

The factors outlined above can all lead to resilience, as they can help produce feelings of attachment and security, as opposed to unpredictability, insecurity, exclusion and isolation. Protective factors can also continue into adulthood as well (Belsky & Pensky, 1988; Bennett *et al.*, 1987; Velleman & Orford, 1999). These include the selection of a stable partner, formation of a new family and the deliberate attempt to select positive family rituals (e.g. to work out with one's partner which components of the rituals of both families of origin the new family wishes to retain).

Dual disorder: when a parent has both a substance misuse problem and a serious mental health problem

Good prevalence data on dual disorder are rare, but one extensive community-based survey found that nearly half of those who had a diagnosis of schizophrenia and nearly a third of those with a mood disorder, also misused or were dependent upon alcohol or drugs (Regier *et al.*, 1990). A further addition to this literature was provided by Callingham (1999) in a survey of more than 23 000 adults across the

UK. He looked at how many were brought up by a parent with either an alcohol problem, or a mental health one, or the experience of severe trauma (such as death or disablement) affecting the family. He also looked at the co-occurrence of these events, as well as the reported impact on the lives of these adults. His findings suggest that over 16% of people grew up in a home with one of these issues, and that 3.5% grew up in a home with more than one of these. Callingham suggests that there were great similarities in the ways that people brought up in homes with either an alcohol or a mental health problem were affected, both at the time and latterly in adulthood.

The issue of dual disorder has moved up the agenda within the UK, with the recent reports from the Royal College of Psychiatrists (Crawford, 2001) and the Health Advisory Service (Abdulrahim, 2001), and the section on psychiatric comorbidity within the Department of Health's Model of Care for Substance Misuse (Abdulrahim *et al.*, 2001). However, the particular impact that dual disorder has on children and families has received relatively little attention. For example, it is not mentioned at all in either the Department of Health or the Royal College of Psychiatrists documents, and is only mentioned in passing in the HAS Substance Use and Mental Health CoMorbidity Standards document, where Standard 47 (which suggests that users, carers and families are involved in service delivery) states that 'families and other carers have support to care for people with mental illness and substance misuse', and Standard 54 (on parents with comorbidity, which states that 'the care of parents with comorbidity focuses on the needs of the children, assessing the need for support and interventions to prevent harm') suggests that staff should be familiar with the requirements of the Children Act, with issues of child protection, risk assessment and intervention, that staff address child protection issues where appropriate, and that parents are provided with support, practical help, parenting skills, benefits assessments and other relevant support.

Nevertheless, the issue has been rather better addressed from within the child mental health community, where two important publications (Crossing Bridges (Falkov, 1998); Cleaver *et al.*, 1999) both started to address the impact on children of parental mental health problems, and the issues of dual disorder. Both of these publications review the available evidence for any additive effects of comorbidity over and above the impact of the mental health problem itself. Both conclude that mental health problems are likely to be exacerbated by the misuse of alcohol or drugs; that this is likely to lead to a number of further complications (such as a reduced compliance with treatment, more severe mental health problems, greater risks of self-harm and harm to others, greater family discord, greater likelihood of domestic violence, and increased social and financial problems, such as unemployment and criminal activities). Both Falkov (1998) and Cleaver *et al.* (1999) conclude that all of these factors (especially in combination) are likely to lead to greater difficulties for parents in effectively meeting the needs of their children.

What does all this mean? Implications for practice

The research reviewed above indicates that the severity and duration of problems for children are amenable to intervention. Some of the most immediate areas for intervention are listed here.

- Those working with children should be made aware of the signs of parental problem drinking or drug-taking. Currently, such children are not routinely assisted by helping agencies, or underlying problems of parental substance misuse are not recognized. Workers should be made aware of potential signs in children such as behavioural disturbance, antisocial behaviour, emotional difficulties, school problems, precocious maturity and difficult transition from childhood through adolescence.
- Family disharmony is a prime focus for intervention, even if the parental substance misuse itself is not amenable to change.
- A knowledge of 'protective factors' can help guide behaviour change. It is possible that helping agencies can work with parents to 'build-in' or incorporate protective factors into their familial life. For example, work could be conducted with non problem-drinking parents to encourage them to provide a stable environment, or work could focus instead on other adult figures outside of the nuclear family, ensuring that there is at least someone who can provide the necessary stabilizing influence (Velleman, 2001*b*).
- Some interventions do exist and do work in helping family members. These range from brief interventions within primary care (Copello *et al.*, 2000*a*, *b*), through to solution-focused brief interventions (Watts, 2000), to more extensive family-based interventions (reviewed by Velleman & Templeton (2002) and including working within a family systemic approach, unilateral family therapy, cooperative counselling, the use of community reinforcement training and of social networks) to more specific therapeutic work with the children of substance misusing parents (Harbin, 2000).

It is clear that there is much that can be done to help, but the lack of services for the children and other family members of problem drinkers and drug users shows that, to a very large extent, they are the forgotten and ignored victims of alcohol or drug misuse.

What services do exist?

The success of self-help groups specifically for family members (Al-Anon, Al-Ateen, Families Anonymous, and now Adult Children Of Alcoholics) underscores the need; but self-help, especially if linked to one particular framework, and existing primarily for adults and older children, is unlikely to be sufficient to meet the needs of all family members, especially children. There are important implications here for specialist and generic professionals. For example, we know that family members are subject to high levels of stress, often have low self-esteem and lack assertiveness. Therefore, these clients will need specific help with stress-management, assertiveness training and self-esteem improvement.

Alcohol Concern, the national alcohol agency in England, has started a network where people and services interested in developing family-focused services can exchange ideas. But there are very few of these services, and children, who are the most vulnerable, are the least well looked after (Robinson & Hassall, 2000). This recent report by the National Society for the Prevention of Cruelty to Children (NSPCC) and the Alcohol Recovery Project (ARP) described the results of a brief national survey within the UK of services for family members. Only a small number of such services were identified across the UK: two child-focused services, five family-focused services (which tended to be residential) and seven adult-focused services.

Besides these few specialist services, there is a small amount of other help. Al-Ateen, a self-help group based on the Alcoholics Anonymous model, helps the children of problem drinkers but it is not very widespread in the UK, and will only help older children (usually mid-teens or older). Childline offers a helpful telephone lifeline, but it requires access to and ability to use a telephone. Child and Family Counselling services (or Child and Adolescent Mental Health Services) are run by the NHS in most areas, but can only offer help ('treatment') with parental consent. The issue is rarely addressed of how a child who wants help because of the behaviour of one or both parents, can ask for that help, if the agency needs to tell the parents and ask them for consent to 'treat' the child? Youth services, voluntary agencies such as the Children's Society, and a limited amount of in-school counselling services do exist, but access for younger children is limited, and most have to follow the same statutory procedures outlined above which would necessitate informing the parents of the fact that they have been approached by the child.

Even if service provision for children suffering difficulties due to their parents' alcohol- or drug-using behaviour were to improve, one significant barrier to providing help still remains: confidentiality. This is touched upon above, where the point is made that statutory obligations mean that if a child approaches an agency for help, the parents must be notified. In some circumstances, similar statutory obligations mean that child protection procedures might be invoked, even if this was in opposition to the expressed wishes of the child in question, who simply wanted to discuss their situation with an informed and helpful adult.

This necessity to breach confidentiality is linked, in the UK, to the 1989 Children Act (HMSO, 1992). This Act was meant to ensure that the welfare of the child was paramount, and that children's needs and rights would be protected. One of the central ideas of the Act is that of parental responsibility, which leads on to the importance of working in partnership with parents (see Adshead *et al.*, Chapter 15). Unfortunately, for many children who have reason to fear their parents, this is not workable. Hence the essential problem of confidentiality: children need to know that they can access confidential help, without their parents being informed, and without child protection procedures being invoked against their wishes. Such children should be enabled to get help if needed, and this should be kept confidential unless and until the child agrees that informing the parent or invoking child protection procedures are realistic and sensible options.

Practical issues

The need for more designated and confidential services aimed at children is self-evident. Agencies dealing with alcohol or drug problems should be given the resources to make their services available to any family members affected by another's alcohol or drug use. Many agencies working with clients with alcohol or drug problems will see family members, but only as appendages of the user, rather than as legitimate clients in their own right, who need access to counselling to help with the problems caused by alcohol or drug use in the family.

A good first step would be for one or more members of each team working with alcohol or drug users to specialize in work with children. These individuals could set up cross-referral systems, and joint working, with school counselling and child psychology and psychiatry services. They should adopt the role of ensuring that the children of clients using the alcohol or drug service are monitored, assisted and their problems addressed.

The second practical step is to also train workers in generic services dealing with children to clarify whether alcohol played a major role in the problems which led to the child being originally referred. Generic services for children need to be aware that many difficulties presented by children may have parental alcohol or drug problems as an underlying causative factor. Often such parents will resist discussing this, and staff within children's services may need training in raising the topic in an unthreatening manner (Velleman, 2001*a*).

Conclusion

People with drinking or drug problems often claim that it does not affect their families. The research reviewed in this chapter leads to the conclusion that living with a problem drinker or drug user can affect other family members, particularly children, in many negative ways. Families can influence each other positively, as when partners influence each other to moderate their drinking, or children learn about sensible drinking, rather than being given an example of inappropriate use.

When the influence is negative, however, it is very powerful indeed, able dramatically and adversely to affect the lives of all family members, sometimes over quite long periods of their lives. It is imperative to develop services which adequately help these family members.

REFERENCES

Abdulrahim, D. (2001). *Substance Use and Mental Health Co-Morbidity (Dual Diagnosis): Standards for Mental Health Services.* London: Health Advisory Service.

Abdulrahim, D., Annan, J., Cyster, R. et al. (2001). *Developing an Integrated Model of Care for Drug Treatment: Promoting Quality, Efficiency and Effectiveness in Drug Misuse Treatment Services.* The Department of Health Models of Care Project. London: Department of Health.

Alison, L. (2000). What are the risks to children of parental substance misuse? In *Substance Misuse and Child Care*, ed. F. Harbin & M. Murphy, pp. 9–20. Lyme Regis: Russell House.

Babor, T., de la Fuente, J., Saunders, J. & Grant, M. (1992). *AUDIT: The Alcohol Use Disorders Identification Test: Guidelines for use in Primary Health Care.* Geneva: World Health Organization.

Belsky, J. & Pensky, E. (1988). Developmental history, personality and family relationships: toward an emergent family system. In *Relationships within Families*, ed. R. Hinde & J. Stevenson-Hinde, pp. 193–217. Oxford: Clarendon Press.

Bennett, L. & Wolin, S. (1990). Family culture and alcoholism transmission. In *Alcohol and the Family: Research and Clinical Perspectives*, ed. R. Collins, K. Leonard & J. Searles. New York: Guilford Press.

Bennett, L., Wolin, S., Reiss, D. & Teitelbaum, M. (1987). Couples at risk for alcoholism recurrence: protective influences. *Family Process*, *26*, 111–29.

Black, C., Bucky, S. & Wilder-Padilla, S. (1986). The interpersonal and emotional consequences of being an adult child of an alcoholic. *International Journal of the Addictions*, *21*, 213–321.

Bowlby, J. (1971, 1973, 1980). *Attachment and Loss, Volumes 1–3.* London: Penguin.

Brisby, T., Baker, S. & Hedderwick, T. (1997). *Under the Influence: Coping with Parents who Drink too much – a Report on the Needs of the Children of Problem Drinking Parents.* London: Alcohol Concern.

Callingham, M. (1999). The AcoA fact finder. *Addiction Today*, Nov/Dec, 17–19.

Chassin, L., Curran, P., Hussong, A. & Colder, C. (1996). The relation of parent alcoholism to adolescent substance use: a longitudinal follow-up study. *Journal of Abnormal Psychology*, *105*, 70–80.

Cleaver, H., Unell, U. & Aldgate, J. (1999). *Children's Needs – Parenting Capacity: The Impact of Parental Mental Illness, Problem Alcohol and Drug Use and Domestic Violence on Children's Development.* London: Department of Health.

Copello, A., Orford, J., Velleman, R., Templeton, L. & Krishnan, M. (2000*a*). Methods for reducing alcohol and drug related family harm in non-specialist settings. *Journal of Mental Health*, *9*, 329–43.

Copello, A., Templeton, L., Krishnan, M., Orford, J. & Velleman, R. (2000*b*). A treatment package to improve primary care services for the relatives of people with alcohol and drug problems: feasibility and preliminary evaluation. *Addiction Research, 8*, 471–84.

Cork, M. (1969). *The Forgotten Children*. Toronto: Paperjacks.

Cowen, E. & Work, W. (1988). Resilient children, psychosocial wellness and primary prevention. *American Journal of Community Psychology, 16*, 591–607.

Crawford, V. (2001). *Co-existing Problems of Mental Health and Substance Misuse ('Dual Diagnosis'): A Review of Relevant Literature*. London: Royal College of Psychiatrists, College Research Unit.

Creighton, S. (1984). *Trends in Child Abuse*. London: NSPCC.

Dore, M., Doris, J. & Wright, P. (1995). Identifying substance abuse in maltreating families: a child welfare challenge. *Child Abuse and Neglect, 19*, 531–43.

El-Guebaly, N. & Offord, D. (1977). The offspring of alcoholics: a critical review. *American Journal of Psychiatry, 134*, 357–65.

El-Guebaly, N. & Offord, D. (1979). On being the offspring of an alcoholic: an update. *Alcoholism: Clinical and Experimental Research, 3*, 148–57.

Falkov, A. (Ed.) (1998). *Crossing Bridges: Training Resources for Working with Mentally Ill Parents and their Children*. London: Department of Health.

Garmezy, N. (1985). Stress-resistant children: the search for protective factors. In *Recent Research in Developmental Psychopathology*, ed. J. Stevenson, pp. 213–33. A book supplement to the *Journal of Child Psychology and Psychiatry, 4*. Oxford: Pergamon.

Hamilton, C. & Collins, J. (1981). The role of alcohol in wife beating and child abuse: a review of the literature. In *Drinking and Crime*, ed. J. Collins, pp. 253–87. New York: Guilford Press.

Harbin, F. (2000). Therapeutic work with children of substance misusing parents. In *Substance Misuse and Child Care*, ed. F. Harbin & M. Murphy. Lyme Regis: Russell House.

Heller, K., Sher, K. & Benson, C. (1982). Problems associated with risk overprediction in studies of offspring of alcoholics: implications for prevention. *Clinical Psychology Review, 2*, 183–200.

HMSO (1992). *Children Act Report – presented to Parliament by the Secretaries of State for Health and for Wales*. London: HMSO.

Huesman, L., Eron, L., Lefkowitz, M. & Walder, L. (1984). Stability of aggression over time and generations. *Development Psychology, 20*, 1120–34.

Jarmas, A. & Kazak, A. (1992). Young adult children of alcoholic fathers: depressive experiences, coping styles and family systems. *Journal of Consulting and Clinical Psychology, 60*, 244–51.

Jones, D. C. & Houts, R. (1992). Parental drinking, parent-child communication, and social skills in young adults. *Journal of Studies on Alcohol, 53*, 48–56.

Kieman, K. & Wicks, M. (1990). *Family Change and Future Policy*. London: Family Policy Studies Centre.

Knop, J., Teasdale, T., Schulsinger, F. & Goodwin, D. (1985). A prospective study of young men at risk for alcoholism: school behaviour and achievement. *Journal of Studies on Alcohol, 46*, 273–8.

Kolar, A., Brown, B., Haertzen, C. & Michaelson, B. (1994). Children of substance abusers: the life experiences of children of opiate addicts in methadone maintenance. *American Journal of Drug and Alcohol Abuse, 20*, 159–71.

Mathews, Z. & Velleman, R. (1997). New age travellers, urban slum dwellers, Aborigines and drug users: experiences of collecting sensitive data from marginalised communities. *Bulletin de Methodologie Sociologique, 57*, 65–85.

Moos, R. & Billings, A. (1982). Children of alcoholics during the recovery process: alcoholic and matched control families. *Addictive Behaviour, 7*, 155–63.

Moos, R., Finney, J. & Cronkite, R. (1990). *Alcoholism Treatment: Context, Process and Outcome.* New York: Oxford University Press.

Murphy, J. M., Jellinek, M., Quinn, D., Smith, G., Poitrast, F. & Goshko, M. (1991). Substance abuse and serious child mistreatment: prevalence, risk, and outcome in a court sample. *Child Abuse and Neglect, 15*, 197–211.

National Children's Bureau (1998). *Children of Drug-Using Parents. Highlight No. 163.* London: National Children's Bureau.

Nylander, I. (1960). Children of alcoholic fathers. *Acta Paediatrica Scandinavica*, Suppl. 121.

Nylander, I. (1979). A 20-year prospective follow–up study of 2164 cases at the child guidance clinics in Stockholm. *Acta Paediatrica Scandinavica*, Suppl. 276.

Nylander, I. & Rydelius, P. (1982). A comparison between children of alcoholic fathers from excellent versus poor social conditions. *Acta Paedriatrica Scandinavica, 71*, 809–13.

Office for National Statistics (2001). *Psychiatric Morbidity Among Adults Living in Private Households.* London: Office for National Statistics.

Orford, J. (1990). Alcohol and the family: an international review of the literature with implications for research and practice. In *Research Advances in Alcohol and Drug Problems*, Vol. 10, ed. L. Kozlowski, H. Annis, H. Cappell et al. pp. 81–155. New York: Plenum Press.

Orford, J. & Velleman, R. (1990). Offspring of parents with drinking problems: drinking and drug taking as young adults. *British Journal of Addiction, 85*, 779–94.

Orford, J. & Velleman, R. (1991). The environmental intergenerational transmission of alcohol problems: a comparison of two hypotheses. *British Journal of Medical Psychology, 64*, 189–200.

Orford, J. & Velleman, R. (1995). Childhood and adulthood influences on the adjustment of young adults with and without parents with drinking problems. *Addiction Research, 3*, 1–15.

Orford, J., Natera, G., Davies, J. et al. (1998*a*). Stresses and strains for family members living with drinking or drug problems in England and Mexico. *Salud Mental, 21*, 1–13.

Orford, J., Natera, G., Davies, J. et al. (1998*b*). Tolerate, engage or withdraw: a study of the structure of family coping in England and Mexico. *Addiction, 93*, 1799–813.

Orford, J., Natera, G., Davies, J. et al. (1999). Social support in coping with alcohol and drug problems at home: findings from Mexican and English families. *Addiction Research, 6*, 395–420.

Orford, J., Natera, G., Velleman, R. et al. (2001*a*). Ways of coping and the health of relatives facing drug and alcohol problems in Mexico and England. *Addiction, 96*, 761–74.

Orford, J., Templeton, L., Copello, A., Velleman, R. & Bradbury, C. (2001*b*). *Worrying for Drinkers in the Family: An Interview Study with Aboriginal Australians in Urban Areas and Remote Communities in the Northern Territory.* Casuarina, Northern Territory: Living with Alcohol Program, Territory Health Services, Northern Territory.

Pandina, R. & Johnson, V. (1990). Serious alcohol and drug problems among adolescents with a family history of alcoholism. *Journal of Studies on Alcohol, 51*, 278–82.

Parker, D. & Harford, T. (1988). Alcohol-related problems, marital disruption and depressive symptoms among adult children of alcohol abusers in the United States. *Journal of Studies on Alcohol, 49,* 306–13.

Powers, R. (1986). Aggression and violence in the family. In *Violent Transactions,* ed. A. Campbell & J. Gibbs, pp. 27–45. Oxford: Blackwells.

Regier, D. A., Farmer, M. E., Rae, D. S. et al. (1990). Co-morbidity of mental disorders with alcohol and other drug abuse. Results from the Epidemiologic Catchment Area (ECA) Study. *Journal of the American Medical Association, 262,* 2511–18.

Reich, W., Earls, E. & Powell, J. (1988). A comparison of the home and social environments of children of alcoholic parents. *British Journal of Addiction, 83,* 831–9.

Robins, L. (1966). *Deviant Children Grown Up.* Baltimore, MD: Williams & Wilkins.

Robinson, W. & Hassall, J. (2000). *Feasibility Study Report on a Specialist Family Alcohol Service.* London: NSPCC and ARP.

Roosa, M., Sandler, I., Beals, J. & Short, J. (1988). Risk status of adolescent children of problem drinking parents. *American Journal of Community Psychology, 16,* 225–9.

Rutter, M. (1980). *Maternal Deprivation Reassessed, 2nd edn.* London: Penguin.

Rutter, M. (1985). Resistance in the face of adversity: protective factors and resistance to psychiatric disorder. *British Journal of Psychiatry, 147,* 598–611.

Rutter, M. (1988). Longitudinal data in the study of causal processes: some uses and some pitfalls. In *Studies of Psychosocial Risk: the Power of Longitudinal Data,* ed. M. Rutter, pp. 210–44. Cambridge: Cambridge University Press.

Schuckit, M. & Sweeney, S. (1987). Substance use and mental health problems among sons of alcoholics and controls. *Journal of Studies on Alcohol, 48,* 528–34.

Seilhamer, R., Jacob, T. & Dunn, N. (1993). The impact of alcohol consumption on parent–child relationships in families of alcoholics. *Journal of Studies on Alcohol, 54,* 189–98.

Sher, K. (1991). Children of alcoholics: a critical appraisal of theory and research. *Clinical Psychology Reviews, 14,* 87–90.

Steinglass, P., Bennett, L., Wolin, S. & Reiss, D. (1987). *The Alcoholic Family.* New York: Basic Books.

Stockwell, T., Murphy, D. & Hogson, R. (1983). The severity of alcohol dependence questionnaire: its use, reliability and validity. *British Journal of Addiction, 78,* 145–55.

Velleman, R. (1993). *Alcohol and the Family.* London: Institute of Alcohol Studies.

Velleman, R. (1996). Alcohol and drug problems: an overview of the impact on children and the implications for practice. In *Parental Psychiatric Disorder: Distressed Parents and their Families,* ed. M. Göpfert, J. Webster & M. Seeman, pp. 233–43. Cambridge: Cambridge University Press.

Velleman, R. (2000). Alcohol and the family. In *Alcohol Use: The Handbook,* ed. D. Cooper. Abingdon: Radcliffe Medical Press.

Velleman, R. (2001*a*). *Counselling For Alcohol Problems,* 2nd edn. (Counselling in Practice Series). London: Sage.

Velleman, R. (2001*b*). Working with substance misusing parents as part of Court Proceedings. *Representing Children, 14,* 36–48.

Velleman, R. (2002). *The Children of Problem Drinking Parents.* Executive Summary Series. London: Centre for Research on Drugs and Health Behaviour.

Velleman, R. & Orford, J. (1984). Intergenerational transmission of alcohol problems: hypotheses to be tested. In *Alcohol-Related Problems*, ed. N. Krasner, J. S. Madden & R. J. Walker, pp. 97–113. Chichester: John Wiley & Sons.

Velleman, R. & Orford, J. (1990). Young adult offspring of parents with drinking problems: recollections of parents' drinking and its immediate effects. *British Journal of Clinical Psychology*, *29*, 297–317.

Velleman, R. & Orford, J. (1993*a*). The importance of family discord in explaining childhood problems in the children of problem drinkers. *Addiction Research*, *1*, 39–57.

Velleman, R. & Orford, J. (1993*b*). The adulthood adjustment of offspring of parents with drinking problems. *British Journal of Psychiatry*, *162*, 503–16.

Velleman, R. & Orford, J. (1999). *Risk and Resilience: Adults who were the Children of Problem Drinkers*. London: Harwood.

Velleman, R. & Templeton, L. (2002). Family interventions in substance misuse. In *Working with Substance Mis-users: A Guide to Theory and Practice*, ed. A. McBride & T. Peterson, pp. 145–53. London: Routledge.

Velleman, R. & Townsend, L. (1997). The children of drug misusing parents. *Alcohol Update*, *32*, 2–3.

Velleman, R., Bennett, G., Miller, T., Orford, J., Rigby, K. & Tod, A. (1993). The families of problem drug users: the accounts of fifty close relatives. *Addiction*, *88*, 1275–83.

Velleman, R., Copello, A. & Maslin, J. (Ed.) (1998). *Living with Drink: Women who live with Problem Drinkers*. London: Longmans.

Watts, P. (2000). Solution focussed brief therapy used in a substance misuse setting. In *Substance Misuse and Child Care*, ed. F. Harbin & M. Murphy, pp. 95–110. Lyme Regis: Russell House.

Werner, E. (1986). Resilient offspring of alcoholics: a longitudinal study from birth to age 18. *Journal of Studies on Alcohol*, *47*, 34–40.

West, M. & Prinz, R. (1987). Parental alcoholism and childhood psychopathology. *Psychological Bulletin*, *102*, 204–18.

Wilson, C. (1980). The family. In *Women and Alcohol*, ed. Camberwell Council on Alcoholism, pp. 101–32. London: Tavistock Press.

Wolin, S., Bennett, L., Noonan, D. & Teitelbaum, M. (1980). Disrupted family rituals: a factor in the intergenerational transmission of alcoholism. *Journal of Studies on Alcohol*, *41*, 199–214.

14

When mothers abuse drugs

Sydney L. Hans

The University of Chicago, Chicago, USA

Although substance abuse was once considered to be predominantly a problem of men, abuse of drugs has become increasingly common in women. In the United States, 7.9% of women between the ages of 14 and 44 use illicit drugs such as cocaine and heroin (Office of Applied Studies, 1999), and approximately 3 million women use these drugs on a regular basis (National Center on Addiction and Substance Abuse, 1996). Most substance-abusing women serve as custodial parents to their children.

Children whose mothers abuse illicit drugs are at risk for developmental problems. During middle childhood and adolescence, they show high levels of delinquency and other conduct problems as well as internalizing problems such as depression and anxiety (Stanger *et al.*, 1999; Wilens *et al.*, 1995). During infancy and early childhood, they show subtle developmental delays and problems with regulation of attention and affect (Hans, 1998).

A variety of factors may place children of substance abusers at risk. Most public attention has focused on the possible adverse effects of prenatal exposure to drugs on the developing brain. During the early 1990s, grave concerns were raised about the problem of 'crack babies' and predictions were made that such children would be emotionally disturbed and uneducable and would overwhelm the capacities of schools and social service agencies. Although such dire predictions proved unfounded (Mayes *et al.*, 1992), a growing body of research has documented subtle behavioural alterations related to prenatal exposure to drugs that remain of significant public health concern (Lester *et al.*, 1998).

Behaviour problems and developmental delays in children with substance-abusing mothers could also be the result of exposure to environmental risks deriving from the neighborhoods and families in which children are raised. It is widely assumed that women affected by substance abuse provide their children with less than optimal care. Substance abuse is viewed by the public not as a mental illness, but as a voluntary activity and even a moral failure. Use of drugs is particularly strongly stigmatized for women for whom substance abuse is strongly dissonant with cultural ideals of femininity and motherhood (Finkelstein, 1993; Murphy & Rosenbaum, 1999). In the United States, the popular press labels mothers who use drugs as 'junkies' and 'addict mothers'. Television presents vivid images of women selling their babies' formula to fund their drug habits, parents shooting up in front of their children, and children huddling in filthy homes while their mothers are out on the streets seeking a fix or selling their bodies to obtain money to purchase drugs. During the height of the crack cocaine epidemic of the early 1990s, governmental bodies across the USA equated maternal use of illicit drugs with child abuse and passed laws mandating loss of child custody or even incarceration for women using drugs during pregnancy (Humphries, 1999). For no other mental illness have society's penalties to parents been so harsh.

Yet despite such grave concerns, only recently have the social and medical sciences directed their research toward understanding the quality of care substance-abusing mothers provide for their children. The purpose of this paper is to (1) review what is known about the parenting of women who abuse drugs, (2) examine some of the correlates of parental care by women who abuse drugs and (3) discuss the clinical implications of findings.

Does drug abuse affect parenting?

Parenthood is a complex role that involves many responsibilities including providing for children's basic physical needs, protecting children from harm, serving as a stable source of support and guidance over a period of many years, and responding sensitively to children's needs for affection and attention. Although evidence suggests that most chemically dependent parents feel love and concern toward their children (Hinds, 1990) and that many provide adequate care to their children (Finnegan *et al.*, 1981), many women who use drugs do fail to provide environments for their children that are safe and meet their basic needs. Parental substance abuse has long been recognized as a major challenge for the child protection system (Semidei *et al.*, 2001; Young *et al.*, 1998). Accurate data on whether substance-abusing mothers are more likely to abuse or neglect their children than other women are difficult to gather since parents are reluctant to disclose information on substance abuse and child maltreatment to researchers. Official records contain biases deriving from poor institutional record keeping, prejudices concerning drug users, and laws that sometimes do not differentiate between drug abuse during pregnancy and child abuse. Yet when court records of children with clearly documented histories of maltreatment are carefully reviewed, at least one parent has a substance abuse problem in most cases (Besinger *et al.*, 1999; Famularo *et al.*, 1992). When children whose mothers abuse illicit drugs during pregnancy are followed prospectively, there are 3- to 12-fold increases in rates of documented child maltreatment reports compared with children whose mothers have similar demographic backgrounds but did not use drugs (Jaudes *et al.*, 1995; Wasserman & Leventhal, 1993). Types of child maltreatment reported in families with substance-abusing mothers are varied, but most typically involve allegations of child neglect (Black & Mayer, 1980). Child physical and sexual abuse reports are also prevalent, but typically involve perpetrators other than the mothers and often could most accurately be described as mothers' failures to protect children from threats in their environment (Miller *et al.*, 1997).

Although mothers are typically viewed as children's primary caregivers, children whose mothers use illicit drugs are highly likely to experience changes in primary caregivers over time. Prospective studies have documented that, among children who are prenatally exposed to heroin or cocaine, between one quarter and one half experience temporary or permanent disruptions in maternal care during infancy and early childhood (Fiks *et al.*, 1985; Rodning *et al.*, 1991; Wilson, 1989), even when mothers are involved in methadone treatment (Hans *et al.*, 2002). Many reasons explain why women who use drugs are not always able to remain a stable presence in their children's lives over time. When child abuse and neglect are documented, children are often removed from the custody of their substance-abusing mothers; and although plans for eventual reunification are typical, they often fail to be executed. In addition, women who use illicit substances often die at young ages from overdose or violence, may be separated from their children during incarceration, or be unable to care for children when they enter treatment (Hans *et al.*, 2002). Mothers who use drugs often voluntarily relinquish care of their children to relatives or their children's father, and sometimes relatives informally assume custody of children, usually without going through the legal system (Minkler & Roe, 1993). Maternal loss and separation are potentially psychologically damaging to children, particularly if they lead to care by family members or nonrelatives with little interest in the child or who are overburdened with other responsibilities. Sometimes however, changes in caregivers can be positive turning points in children's lives when they result in stable lifestyles with loving parental figures.

Other research has examined characteristics of substance abusers' parenting during interaction with their infants and young children. Typically in such studies, mothers and children are videotaped while engaged in common tasks such as feeding or play. Observers, blind to information about parents' substance-abuse history, code tapes for maternal behaviour reflecting responsiveness to the child's needs, sensitivity to child's interests and warmth toward child. Such techniques are widely used within developmental psychology, and in a large variety of research studies, maternal responsiveness and warmth with infants have been linked to a variety of positive child outcomes at later ages such as social competence, secure attachments and lack of behaviour problems (Shaw *et al.*, 1994; Wakschlag & Hans,

1999). Drug-abusing mothers, compared with other mothers, show less warm, positive behaviour with their infants (Fitzgerald *et al.*, 1990) and preschool children (Bauman & Dougherty, 1983). They are also less responsive to their infants' needs and interests than other mothers (Bernstein & Hans, 1994; Rodning *et al.*, 1991) and more likely to engage in conflictual interactions with their infants (Das Eiden, 2001). Not all studies, however, have found that substance-abusing mothers engage in less responsive or warm parenting when videotaped by researchers (Ukeje *et al.*, 2001).

Considerably less is known about the warmth or responsiveness of parenting behaviour of substance abusers whose children are older, although evidence suggests that substance-abusing mothers may use overly harsh discipline (Miller *et al.*, 1999), but also be less engaged than other parents in monitoring their children and adolescents (Miller *et al.*, 1987; Suchman & Luthar, 2000). A large body of research from developmental psychology, not focused specifically on parental substance abuse, documents that harsh but disengaged parenting is often related to young people's delinquent behaviour and substance abuse (Steinberg *et al.*, 1994).

How does drug abuse affect parenting?

The reasons through which parenting may be compromised in women who use drugs are many. Parenting behaviour is influenced by a complex system of factors that includes a mother's personality, her history of care in her own childhood, stresses in her current life and support from her social network (Johnson *et al.*, 1999). Women who use illicit drugs often struggle with many challenges in their lives that include poverty, single parenthood, large family size, domestic conflict, dangerous neighbourhoods, poor quality schools, poor housing or lack of housing. Several studies have documented that the negative behaviour and attitudes of some drug-using women toward their children are in large part attributable to the accumulation of large numbers of stressors in the mothers' lives (Bernstein & Hans, 1994; Kettinger *et al.*, 2000).

A number of explanations specific to drug abuse have been offered for why parenting may be compromised by substance abuse. When women abuse drugs, their parenting may be directly affected by pharmacological influences of the drug – either drug intoxication or withdrawal (Klee, 1998; Richter & Bammer, 2000). Mothers who are under the influence of a substance may be less motivated or able to provide attentive care and monitoring. Women sometimes report that, when intoxicated, they feel detached from their children or have feelings toward their children that seem ungenuine. Women express concern that when intoxicated by heroin they might 'nod' and be unable to look after their children or that they might harm their children or put them at risk by driving while intoxicated. Mothers who are abstaining may be irritable, hostile or disengaged while they are preoccupied with the physiological and psychological symptoms of withdrawal. Women report that, when going through withdrawal, they were likely to be preoccupied with their discomfort, impatient and irritable, resentful of physical closeness and inattentive to their children's needs.

Parenting may also be affected by aspects of the drug-abusing lifestyle. Mothers using illicit drugs organize their lives around drug-seeking that usually takes them out of the home, distracts them away from childrearing concerns, and exposes their children to undesirable people (Baker & Carson, 1999; Hutchins & DiPietro, 1997; Johnson *et al.*, 1987; Klee, 1998). Procuring drugs and the money to pay for them can be a full-time occupation for users of illicit substances. When women are actively seeking drugs and money to pay for drugs, children may be left alone or left with others to care for them for days at a time. Mothers' needs to purchase drugs may take precedence over children's needs for food, clothing and other necessities, and even tending to children in emergencies or during illness. The lifestyles associated with drug addiction tend to be very unstructured or focused on evening hours, and addicted parents may have trouble providing their children with regular schedules and ensuring that they attend school or other scheduled activities.

Parenting among substance-abusing women may also be compromised by the presence of other mental health problems such as depression or personality disorders (Hans, 1999). The prevalence rate of lifetime clinical depression in women who are dependent on drugs is likely greater than 50%. Maternal depression has been linked to lack of maternal attentiveness in women who use cocaine (Ball *et al.*, 1997) and to disruptions in maternal care among women who use polydrugs (Nair *et al.*, 1997). The prevalence of personality disorders among women who are addicted to drugs may also be as high as 20%, with antisocial personality disorder being the most commonly reported personality disorder (Ross *et al.*, 1988; Rounsaville *et al.*, 1982). Signs of personality disorder (including histrionic, narcissistic, borderline, paranoid personality) have been correlated with insensitive parenting in women who use drugs (Fineman *et al.*, 1997; Howard *et al.*, 1995) and to disorganized attachment in their children (Espinosa *et al.*, 2001). Children whose drug-using mothers have antisocial personality features are especially likely to experience disruptions in maternal care (Hans *et al.*, 1999). In addition, many women who use drugs have experienced physical or sexual victimization and violence in their own early or recent lives (Fullilove *et al.*, 1993; Triffleman *et al.*, 1995) that could impact on the care they provide their own children.

Parenting among women who use illicit substances may also be compromised by characteristics of their children. When children have been prenatally exposed to drugs they may be especially irritable or difficult to arouse as a consequence of prenatal exposure (Jeremy & Hans, 1985; Johnson & Rosen, 1990; Mayes, 1999). They may have abnormal and unpleasant cry patterns (Huntington *et al.*, 1990; Lester *et al.*, 1991). These characteristics may challenge parents' abilities to read infant cues and to remain patient (Beeghly & Tronick, 1994; Bernstein & Hans, 1994; Freier, 1994). The strain on parenting may in turn interfere with infants' efforts to regulate arousal and affect, which would further exacerbate parenting stress and problems. Such back and forth exchanges between parent and child are transactions that could ultimately lead to a variety of child behaviour problems and increasingly punitive parenting.

Clinical implications

The central strategy for improving the parenting of women who are actively abusing drugs must always be to aim for a drug-free lifestyle or other stable lifestyle such as one facilitated by methadone maintenance treatment. Women who are using illicit substances are acutely aware of the risks their drug use poses for their children and experience considerable shame and guilt about their use. Out of concern for their children, chemically dependent women devote considerable effort to altering their drug-use patterns (Baker & Carson, 1999). Women will often employ strategies such as cutting back on use of drugs, using drugs only to relieve withdrawal symptoms rather than to get high, stopping use in the home, changing patterns of substance use so as not to expose children to drug paraphernalia, and using only when children are in school or child-care. The most common reason given by women for entering treatment programmes is concern for their children, including unborn children (Colten, 1982; Rosenbaum & Murphy, 1990).

Drug abuse treatment programmes, however, have often failed to meet the needs of women, particularly those with children (Marsh & Miller, 1985). Programmes serving women need to address the barriers that women face in accessing treatment. Compared with their male counterparts, women needing treatment often meet with greater opposition from friends, families and partners; feel more guilt and shame; and in particular, experience great concerns over having to surrender the care of their children temporarily or even possibly losing custody of their children (Clayson *et al.*, 1995; Davis, 1990). More than three-quarters of women in treatment have young children, and the single most common reason women fail to remain in substance abuse treatment is failure to find suitable child-care (Zankowski, 1987). Compliance with treatment is enhanced when child-care is made available (Finkelstein, 1994).

In the past decade there has been a movement to expand services for women who are drug addicted (Acuff *et al.*, 1991; Mackie-Ramos & Rice, 1988). A number of models now exist for intervention programming for drug-dependent women who are pregnant, including services integrated into general outpatient treatment settings (Kaltenbach, 1992), methadone maintenance facilities (Carroll *et al.*, 1995), paediatric clinics (Kaplan-Sanoff & Leib, 1995) and adolescent pregnancy and parenting programmes (Palinkas *et al.*, 1996). It is generally agreed that programmes that are most effective for women are those that are comprehensive, addressing women's addiction, but also their social needs and especially their needs for mental health services and support in parenting activities (Brindis *et al.*, 1997; Finkelstein, 1993; Uziel-Miller *et al.*, 1998). Comprehensive treatment programmes designed to address the needs of pregnant and parenting addicted women report significant rates of treatment success and changes in parenting.

Important for comprehensive programming is an emphasis on the treatment of female patients' comorbid psychopathology, notably depression and trauma-related disorders (Grella, 1996). Such comorbid disorders, if not directly addressed, complicate substance-abuse treatment and recovery (Evans & Sullivan, 1990; Solomon *et al.*, 1993). Addressing pre-existing risk factors such as traumatic childhood experiences, negative feeling states and ineffective social support networks may be as important as providing substance-abuse treatment in order to alter poor parenting practices among chemically dependent women (Davis, 1997; Hans *et al.*, 1999). Model programmes of treatment and recovery services for dually diagnosed pregnant and parenting women requires changes in all aspects of the programme including treatment philosophy, treatment content, milieu management and attention to staff self-care (Mosley, 1996).

Comprehensive programming must also recognize women's responsibilities to their children. Models have been developed for residential inpatient treatment programmes that admit women with their children (Glider *et al.*, 1996). Although parenting interventions have been shown to be effective in a variety of high-risk populations, such interventions with addicted parents are particularly challenging. Evidence is only beginning to be gathered suggesting that parenting interventions can work even with women who are drug dependent. In one nurse home-visiting programme (Black *et al.*, 1994), drug-using women who were randomly assigned to receive home visitation intervention were more likely to be drug free and compliant with primary-care appointments. Importantly, mothers receiving intervention were more emotionally responsive and provided their infants with more opportunities for stimulation. Pregnant and parenting women participating in the parenting component of two urban residential treatment programmes experienced improved self-esteem and positive changes in parenting attitudes (Camp & Finkelstein, 1997). However, not all short-term parenting interventions have been effective in altering the quality of maternal caregiving among women who use drugs (Howard *et al.*, 1995). Parenting interventions with women in treatment are unlikely to be successful if they are short-term and consist only of traditional, didactic instruction about childrearing practices. Rather, issues of childrearing need to be addressed within a context of supportive, relationship-based experiences for parents such as parenting groups (Greif & Drechsler, 1993; Luthar & Walsh, 1995; Plasse, 1995). Effective intervention addresses how parenting is affected by the parent's substance abuse; adverse experiences in the parent's past; and problems in the parent's immediate relationships with other family members, partners and friends. However, effective intervention does not allow these other difficulties to distract from the focus on parent–child relationships. Model parenting interventions go beyond classes and support groups to include child–parent play groups and videotaping of parent–child interaction to help parents observe, evaluate and understand their own parenting behaviour (Bernstein *et al.*, 1996; VanBremen & Chasnoff, 1994). In conjunction with support for parenting, substance-abuse treatment programmes, particularly those providing day or residential care for children, can also conduct screening for developmental disorders such as attention deficits, monitor for signs of abuse or other emotional problems, and intervene or refer affected children for help (Goldman & Rossland, 1992; Gross & McCaul, 1992; LePantois, 1986; Springer *et al.*, 1992). Although ideas abound for addressing parenting and child development issues in the context of substance abuse programmes, in practice such ideas have rarely been implemented.

Conclusion

Although mothers who use illicit drugs vary in the quality of care they provide their children, many are unable to remain stable primary caregivers in their children's lives over time. Even when they do remain involved as primary caregivers, their children are at risk for harsh or unresponsive parenting that sometimes can be abusive or neglectful. A variety of factors may impede women's capacity to parent while using drugs, including an accumulation of stressful life experiences, changes in mood or alertness related to intoxication or withdrawal, comorbid mental health problems such as depression or antisocial personality and the chaotic lifestyle associated with maintaining an expensive and illicit habit. If women who abuse illicit drugs are to become effective parents to their children, substance-abuse treatment is essential. That treatment, however, must address the special needs of women, including support for parenting and mental health problems.

Acknowledgement

Support during the preparation of this paper was provided by NIDA grants R01-DA09595 and R01-DA11671.

REFERENCES

Acuff, K., Spolarich, A. W., Andrulis, D. P. & Gerstein, S. (1991). *Vulnerable Women and Visionary Programs: Safety Net Programs for Drug-involved Women and their Children.* Washington, DC: The National Public Health and Hospital Institute.

Baker, P. L. & Carson, A. (1999). "I take care of my kids": Mother practices of substance-abusing women. *Gender and Society, 13,* 347–63.

Ball, S. A., Mayes, L. C., DeTeso, J. A. & Schottenfield, R. S. (1997). Maternal attentiveness of cocaine abusers during child-based assessments. *American Journal on Addictions, 6,* 135–43.

Bauman, P. S. & Dougherty, F. E. (1983). Drug-addicted mothers' parenting and their children's development. *International Journal of the Addictions, 18,* 291–302.

Beeghly, M. & Tronick, E. Z. (1994). Effects of prenatal exposure to cocaine in early infancy: toxic effects on the process of mutual regulation. *Infant Mental Health Journal, 15,* 158–75.

Bernstein, V. J. & Hans, S. L. (1994). Predicting the developmental outcome of two-year-old children born exposed to methadone: the impact of social-environmental risk factors. *Journal of Clinical Child Psychology, 23,* 349–59.

Bernstein, V. J., Percansky, C. & Wechsler, N. (1996). Strengthening families through strengthening relationships: the Ounce of Prevention Fund developmental training and support program. In *Model programs in child and family mental health,* ed. M. Roberts, pp. 109–33. Hillsdale, NJ: Lawrence Erlbaum Associates.

Besinger, B. A., Garland, A. F., Litrownik, A. J. & Landsverk, J. A. (1999). Caregiver substance abuse among maltreated children placed in out-of-home care. *Child Welfare, 78,* 221–39.

Black, M. M., Nair, P., Kight, C., Wachtel, R., Roby, P. & Schuler, M. (1994). Parenting and early development among children of drug-abusing women: effects of home intervention. *Pediatrics, 94,* 440–8.

Black, R. & Mayer, J. (1980). Parents with special problems: alcoholism and heroin addiction. *Child Abuse and Neglect, 4,* 45–54.

Brindis, C. D., Berkowitz, G., Clayson, Z. & Lamb, B. (1997). California's approach to perinatal substance abuse: toward a model of comprehensive care. *Journal of Psychoactive Drugs, 29,* 113–22.

Camp, J. M. & Finkelstein, N. (1997). Parenting training for women in residential substance abuse treatment: results of a demonstration project. *Journal of Substance Abuse Treatment, 14,* 411–22.

Carroll, K. M., Chang, G., Behr, H., Clinton, B. & Kosten, T. R. (1995). Improving treatment outcome in pregnant methadone-maintained women. *American Journal on Addictions, 4,* 56–9.

Clayson, Z., Berkowitz, G. & Brindis, C. (1995). Themes and variations among seven comprehensive perinatal drug and alcohol abuse treatment models. *Health and Social Work, 20,* 234–8.

Colten, M. E. (1982). Attitudes, experiences, and self-perceptions of heroin-addicted mothers. *Journal of Social Issues, 38,* 77–92.

Das Eiden, R. D. (2001). Maternal substance use and mother–infant feeding interactions. *Infant Mental Health Journal, 22,* 497–511.

Davis, S. K. (1990). Chemical dependency in women: a description of its effects and outcomes on adequate parenting. *Journal of Substance Abuse Treatment, 7,* 225–32.

Davis, S. K. (1997). Comprehensive interventions for affecting the parenting effectiveness of chemically dependent women. *Journal of Obstetric, Gynecologic and Neonatal Nursing, 26,* 604–10.

Espinosa, M., Beckwith, L., Howard, J., Tyler, R. & Swanson, K. (2001). Maternal psychopathology and attachment in toddlers of heavy cocaine-using mothers. *Infant Mental Health Journal, 22,* 316–33.

Evans, K. & Sullivan, J. M. (1990). *Dual diagnosis: Counseling the Mentally Ill Substance Abuser.* New York: Guilford Press.

Famularo, R., Kinscherff, R. & Fenton, T. (1992). Parental substance abuse and the nature of child maltreatment. *Child Abuse and Neglect, 16,* 475–83.

Fiks, K. B., Johnson, H. L. & Rosen, T. S. (1985). Methadone-maintained mothers: 3-year follow-up of parental functioning. *International Journal of the Addictions, 20,* 651–60.

Fineman, N., Beckwith, L., Howard, J. & Espinosa, M. (1997). Maternal ego development and mother–infant interaction in drug-abusing women. *Journal of Substance Abuse Treatment, 4,* 307–17.

Finkelstein, N. (1993). Treatment programming for alcohol and drug-dependent women. *International Journal of the Addictions, 28,* 1275–309.

Finkelstein, N. (1994). Treatment issues for alcohol and drug-dependent pregnant and parenting women. *Health and Social Work, 1,* 7–15.

Finnegan, L. P., Oehlberg, S. M., Regan, D. O. & Rudrauff, M. E. (1981). Evaluation of parenting, depression, and violence profiles in methadone maintained women. *Child Abuse and Neglect, 5,* 267–73.

Fitzgerald, E., Kaltenbach, K. & Finnegan, L. (1990). Patterns of interaction among drug dependent women and their infants. *Pediatric Research, 10A,* 24.

Freier, K. (1994). In utero drug exposure and maternal–infant interaction: the complexities of the dyad and their environment. *Infant Mental Health Journal, 15,* 176–88.

Fullilove, M. T., Fullilove, R. E. I., Smith, M. et al. (1993). Violence, trauma, and post-traumatic stress disorder among women drug users. *Journal of Traumatic Stress, 6,* 533–43.

Glider, P., Hughes, P., Mullen, R. et al. (1996). Two therapeutic communities for substance abusing women. *National Institute on Drug Abuse Research Monograph, 166,* 32–49.

Goldman, B. M. & Rossland, S. (1992). Young children of alcoholics: a group treatment model. *Social Work in Health Care, 16,* 53–65.

Greif, G. L. & Drechsler, M. (1993). Common issues for parents in a methadone maintenance group. *Journal of Substance Abuse Treatment, 10,* 339–43.

Grella, C. E. (1996). Background and overview of mental health and substance abuse treatment system: meeting the needs of women who are pregnant or parenting. *Journal of Psychoactive Drugs, 28,* 319–43.

Gross, J. & McCaul, M. E. (1992). An evaluation of a psychoeducational and substance abuse risk reduction intervention for children of substance abusers. *Journal of Community Psychology, Special issue,* 75–87.

Hans, S. L. (1998). Developmental outcomes of prenatal exposure to alcohol and other drugs.

In *Principles of Addiction Medicine*, 2nd edn, ed. A. W. Graham & T. K. Schultz, pp. 1223–37. Chevy Chase, MD: American Society of Addiction Medicine.

Hans, S. L. (1999). Demographic and psychosocial characteristics of substance abusing pregnant women. *Clinics in Perinatology*, *26*, 55–74.

Hans, S. L., Bernstein, V. J. & Henson, L. G. (1999). The role of psychopathology in the parenting of drug-dependent women. *Development and Psychopathology*, *11*, 957–77.

Hans, S. L., Bernstein, V. J. & Henson, L. G. (2002). Children born to drug-using mothers: a longitudinal perspective on maternal care and child adjustment. In *Assessing Youth Behavior: Using the Child Behavior Checklist in Family and Children's Services*, ed. N. Le Prohn, K. Wetherbee, E. Lamont, T. Achenbach & P. Pecora, pp. 107–20. Washington, DC: Child Welfare League of America.

Hinds, M. D. (1990). The instincts of parenthood become part of crack's toll. *New York Times*, 17 March 1990, p. 9.

Howard, J., Beckwith, L., Espinosa, M. & Tyler, R. (1995). Development of infants born to cocaine-abusing women: biologic/maternal influences. *Neurotoxicology and Teratology*, *17*, 403–11.

Humphries, D. (1999). *Crack mothers: pregnancy, drugs, and the media*. Columbus, OH: Ohio State University Press.

Huntington, L., Hans, S. L. & Zeskind, P. S. (1990). The relationships among cry characteristics, demographic variables, and developmental test scores in infants prenatally exposed to methadone. *Infant Behavior and Development*, *13*, 533–8.

Hutchins, E. & DiPietro, J. (1997). Psychosocial risk factors associated with cocaine use during pregnancy: a case-control study. *Obstetrics and Gynecology*, *90*, 142–7.

Jaudes, P. K., Ekwo, E. & Voorhis, J. V. (1995). Association of drug abuse and child abuse. *Child Abuse and Neglect*, *19*, 1065–75.

Jeremy, R. J. & Hans, S. L. (1985). Behavior of neonates exposed in utero to methadone as assessed on the Brazelton scale. *Infant Behavior and Development*, *8*, 323–36.

Johnson, H. L. & Rosen, T. S. (1990). Difficult mothers of difficult babies: mother–infant interaction in a multi-risk population. *American Journal of Orthopsychiatry*, *60*, 281–8.

Johnson, H. L., Glassman, M. B., Fiks, K. B. & Rosen, T. (1987). Path analysis of variables affecting 36-month outcome in a population of multi-risk children. *Infant Behavior and Development*, *10*, 451–65.

Johnson, H. L., Nusbaum, B. J., Bejarano, A. & Rosen, T. S. (1999). An ecological approach to development in children with prenatal drug exposure. *American Journal of Orthopsychiatry*, *69*, 448–56.

Kaltenbach, K. A. (1992). Studies of prenatal drug exposure and environmental research issues: the benefits of integrating research within a treatment program. *National Institute on Drug Abuse Research Monograph Series*, *117*, 259–69.

Kaplan-Sanoff, M. & Leib, S. A. (1995). Model intervention programs for mothers and children impacted by substance abuse. *School Psychology Review*, *24*, 186–99.

Kettinger, L. A., Nair, P. & Schuler, M. (2000). Exposure to environmental risk factors and parenting attitudes among substance-abusing women. *American Journal of Drug and Alcohol Abuse*, *26*, 1–11.

Klee, H. (1998). Drug-using parents: analysing the stereotypes. *International Journal of Drug Policy, 9*, 437–48.

LePantois, J. (1986). Group therapy for children of substance abusers. *Social Work With Groups, 9*, 39–51.

Lester, B. M., Corwin, M. J., Sepkoski, C. et al. (1991). Neurobehavioral syndromes in cocaine-exposed newborn infants. *Child Development, 62*, 694–705.

Lester, B. M., LaGasse, L. L. & Seifer, R. (1998). Cocaine exposure and children: the meaning of subtle effects. *Science, 282*, 633–4.

Luthar, S. & Walsh, K. G. (1995). Treatment needs of drug-addicted mothers: integrated parenting psychotherapy interventions. *Journal of Substance Abuse Treatment, 12*, 341–8.

Mackie-Ramos, R. & Rice, J. (1988). Group psychotherapy with methadone maintained pregnant women. *Journal of Substance Abuse Treatment, 5*, 995–1019.

Marsh, J. & Miller, N. (1985). Female clients in substance abuse treatment. *International Journal of the Addictions, 20*, 995–1019.

Mayes, L. C. (1999). Developing brain and in utero cocaine exposure: effects on neural ontogeny. *Development and Psychopathology, 11*, 685–714.

Mayes, L. C., Granger, R. H., Bornstein, M. H. & Zuckerman, B. (1992). The problem of cocaine exposure: a rush to judgment. *Journal of the American Medical Association, 267*, 406–8.

Miller, B. A., Downs, W. R., Gondoli, D. M. & Keil, A. (1987). The role of childhood sexual abuse in the development of alcoholism in women. *Violence and Victims, 2*, 157–72.

Miller, B. A., Maguin, E. & Downs, W. R. (1997). Alcohol, drugs, and violence in children's lives. (Ed.), In *Recent Developments in Alcoholism, Vol. 13, Alcoholism and Violence*, ed. M. Galanter, pp. 357–85. New York: Plenum Press.

Miller, B. A., Smyth, N. J. & Mudar, P. J. (1999). Mothers' alcohol and other drug problems and their punitiveness toward their children. *Journal of Studies on Alcohol, 60*, 632–42.

Minkler, M. & Roe, K. M. (1993). *Grandmothers as caregivers: raising chidlren of the crack cocaine epidemic.* Newbury Park, CA: Sage.

Mosley, T. M. (1996). PROTOTYPES: An urban model program of treatment and recovery services for dually diagnosed perinatal program participants. *Journal of Psychoactive Drugs, 28*, 381–8.

Murphy, S. & Rosenbaum, M. (1999). *Pregnant Women on Drugs: Combating Stereotypes and Stigma.* New Brunswick, NJ: Rutgers University Press.

Nair, P., Black, M. M., Schuler, M., Keane, V., Snow, L. & Rigney, B. A. (1997). Risk factor for disruption in primary caregiving among infants of substance abusing women. *Child Abuse and Neglect, 21*, 1039–51.

National Center on Addiction and Substance Abuse (1996). *Substance Abuse and the American Woman.* New York: Columbia University.

Office of Applied Studies (1999). *Summary of Findings from the 1999 National Household Survey on Drug Abuse.* Washington, DC: Department of Health and Human Services.

Palinkas, L. A., Atkins, C. J., Noel, P. & Miller, C. (1996). Recruitment and retention of adolescent women in drug treatment research. *NIDA Research Monograph, 166*, 87–109.

Plasse, B. R. (1995). Parenting groups for recovering addicts in a day treatment center. *Social Work, 40*, 65–74.

Richter, K. P. & Bammer, G. (2000). A hierarchy of strategies heroin-using mothers employ to reduce harm to their children. *Journal of Substance Abuse Treatment, 19*, 403–13.

Rodning, C., Beckwith, L. & Howard, J. (1991). Quality of attachment and home environments in children prenatally exposed to PCP and cocaine. *Development and Psychopathology, 3*, 351–66.

Rosenbaum, M. & Murphy, S. (1990). Women and addiction: process, treatment, and outcome. *National Institute on Drug Abuse: Research Monograph Series, Mono 98*, 120–127.

Ross, H. E., Glaser, F. B. & Stiasny, S. (1988). Sex differences in the prevalence of psychiatric disorders in patients with alcohol and drug problems. *British Journal of Addiction, 83*, 1179–92.

Rounsaville, B. J., Weissman, M. M., Kleber, H. D. & Wilber, C. H. (1982). The heterogeneity of psychiatric disorders in treated opiate addicts. *Archives of General Psychiatry, 39*, 161–6.

Semidei, J., Radel, L. F. & Nolan, C. (2001). Substance abuse and child welfare: clear linkages and promising responses. *Child Welfare, 80*, 109–28.

Shaw, D. S., Keenan, K. & Vondra, J. I. (1994). Developmental precursors of externalizing behavior: ages 1 to 3. *Developmental Psychology, 30*, 355–64.

Solomon, J., Zimberg, S. & Shollar, E. (1993). *Dual Diagnosis: Evaluation, Treatment, Training, and Program Development.* New York: Plenum Medical Book Company.

Springer, J. F., Phillips, J. L., Phillips, L., Cannady, L. & Kerst-Harris, E. (1992). CODA: a creative therapy program for children in families affected by abuse of alcohol or other drugs. *Journal of Community Psychology, Special Issue*, 55–74.

Stanger, C., Higgins, S. T., Bickel, W. K. et al. (1999). Behavioral and emotional problems among children of cocaine- and opiate dependent parents. *Journal of the American Academy of Child and Adolescent Psychiatry, 38*, 421–8.

Steinberg, L., Lamborn, S., Darling, N., Mounts, N. & Dornbusch, S. (1994). Over-time changes in adjustment and competence among adolescents from authoritative, authoritarian, indulgent, and neglectful families. *Child Development, 65*, 754–70.

Suchman, N. E. & Luthar, S. S. (2000). Maternal addiction, child maladjustment and socio-demographic risks: implications for parenting behaviors. *Addiction, 95*, 1417–28.

Triffleman, E., Marmar C. R., Delucchi, K. L. & Ronfeldt, H. (1995). Childhood trauma and posttraumatic stress disorder in substance abuse inpatients. *Journal of Nervous and Mental Disease, 183*, 172–6.

Ukeje, I., Bendersky, M. & Lewis, M. (2001). Mother–infant interaction at 12 months in prenatally cocaine-exposed children. *American Journal of Drug and Alcohol Abuse, 27*, 203–4.

Uziel-Miller, N. D., Lyons, J. S., Kissiel, C. & Love, S. (1998). Treatment needs and initial outcomes of a residential recovery program for African–American women and their children. *American Journal on Addictions, 7*, 43–50.

VanBremen, J. R. & Chasnoff, I. J. (1994). Policy issues for integrating parenting interventions and addiction treatment for women. *Topics in Early Childhood Special Education, 14*, 254–74.

Wakschlag, L. S. & Hans, S. L. (1999). Relation of maternal responsiveness during infancy to the development of behavior problems in high-risk youths. *Developmental Psychology, 35*, 569–79.

Wasserman, D. R. & Leventhal, J. M. (1993). Maltreatment of children born to cocaine-abusing mothers. *American Journal of Diseases of Children, 147*, 1324–8.

Wilens, T. E., Biederman, J., Kiely, K., Bredin, E. & Spencer, T. J. (1995). Pilot study of behavioral and emotional disturbances in the high-risk children of parents with opioid dependence. *Journal of the American Academy of Child and Adolescent Psychiatry, 34,* 779–85.

Wilson, G. S. (1989). Clinical studies of infants and children exposed prenatally to heroin. In *Prenatal Abuse of Licit and Illicit Drugs,* ed. D. E. Hutchings, pp. 195–207. *Annals of the New York Academy of Sciences, 562.*

Young, N., Gardner, S. & Dennis, K. (1998). *Responding to Alcohol and other Drug Problems in Child Welfare: Weaving Together Policy and Practice.* Washington, DC: CWLA Press.

Zankowski, G. L. (1987). Responsive programming: meeting the needs of chemically dependent women. *Alcoholism Treatment Quarterly, 4,* 53–66.

15

Personality disorder in parents: developmental perspectives and intervention

Gwen Adshead,[1] Adrian Falkov[2] and Michael Göpfert[3]

[1]Broadmoor Hospital, Crowthorne, UK; [2]Children's Hospital Westmead, Australia; [3]Webb House, Crewe, UK

Introduction

Both personality disorder and parental inability to meet children's needs have their origins, at least in part, in the quality of early experiences. Where individuals engaged in the constellation of disruptive behaviours and interpersonal role and relationship difficulties associated with personality disorder also have child-care responsibilities, the implications for the well-being and safety of children will be considerable. For individuals with severe relationship difficulties who are, or become, parents, that key life transition will have profound implications for themselves as individuals, as partners and as parents. Personality disorder itself presents considerable diagnostic, risk management and therapeutic challenges for (mental) health, social care and criminal justice systems because of the diverse and competing needs of parents and children which challenge the existing separateness of the various adult and children's services.

This chapter will use two theoretical frameworks, attachment theory and role relationships, to examine the concept of personality disorder, and how/why personality disorder interferes with 'good enough' parenting. These frameworks will also be used to describe implications for assessment and therapeutic interventions. This includes use of alternative care provision for children within the public sector.

Background issues and definitions

Personality disorder (PD) is defined by DSM–IV (American Psychiatric Association, 1994) as: 'Behaviours or traits that are characteristic of the person's recent and long-term functioning. The behaviours and traits must be sufficient to cause impairment of functioning or subjective distress.' Especially problematic behaviours include self–harm and violence to others; dysfunctional personality traits include impulsivity, poor affect control and the capacity to arouse hostility and rejection from others.

This emphasis on behaviour leaves out any account of the pervasive difficulties that people with PD have in making and sustaining intimate relationships due to dysfunctional self–other representations and unstable affect and arousal regulation. Self-representations and affects may be intense, fearful and labile (as in borderline personality disorder: BPD), or they may be grandiose, unempathic and associated with anger and violence (as in antisocial personality disorder; ASPD).

Personality disorder as a diagnosis generates conceptual debate. Some question whether it is a psychiatric disorder at all (Gergen *et al.*, 1996; Kendell, 2002). It is not clear whether personality generally (and PD specifically) should be seen in terms of category or dimension. A categorical account would suggest that people with PD are statistically different from the norm; whereas a dimensional account would argue that there are degrees of PD, with only moderate and severe PD leading to dysfunction. The more severe the personality disorder is, the more complex its presentation tends to be, with more complications including complex physical health problems. The risks to children's well-being and safety are similarly magnified.

The current diagnostic criteria for 'personality disorder' have little explanatory power, lack validity and offer no increased understanding of interpersonal difficulties (Norton & Dolan, 1996; Westen, 1997) let alone parenting difficulties. Yet the label continues to be used: perhaps in recognition of a group of individuals who struggle with interpersonal relationships, and whose behaviours put them at odds with others (including their dependants) to such a degree that they seem more like the disabled than the simply deviant.

Personality disorder and parenting

Between them, BPD and ASPD are twice as common as any other PD. They more likely occur in younger people of childbearing age, and are more common in men (Samuels *et al.*, 2002). Both BPD and ASPD are the personality disorders most associated with child maltreatment (Dinwiddie & Bucholz, 1993; Famularo *et al.*, 1992; Stanley & Penhale, 1999). Many parents with PD are challenged by the task of parenting in many ways and at many levels. Parenting requires empathy, the capacity to control impulses and delay gratification of one's own needs and to take a long-term view, the capacity to tolerate angry feelings and children's distress, and to have a positive response to the vulnerability and dependency needs of others (Pryce, 1995). It requires consistency and the capacity to respond firmly but sensitively according to the age and development of the child and an ability to set boundaries; all of which are problematic for parents with PD because of their own substantial unmet needs. Most of the behaviours associated with PD, including domestic violence (Royal College of Psychiatrists, 2002*a*), substance misuse and social impairment will lead to difficulties in meeting children's needs, emotional well-being and physical safety.

Parents with PD often have multiple psychological problems. Comorbidity with other psychiatric conditions is common, especially with mood disorders, eating disorders and substance misuse (Radke-Yarrow, 1998; Westen & Harnden-Fischer, 2001). The interactions between a parent's disorder and psychological functioning, the quality of parenting, the parent–child relationship, the individual attributes and needs of a particular child, together with family factors and broader social/community supports all contribute to a child's adjustment. The interplay between individual, family and environmental risk factors and protectors will amplify or ameliorate the emergence of difficulty and disorder. The greater the number of adversities experienced, the greater will be the likelihood that vulnerabilities will emerge along with difficulties in successful adaptation.

People with PD may be refused access to mental health services (Adshead, 2001; Davison, 2002) and often are disliked by professionals (Appleby & Lewis, 1988; Campling, 1997). This rejection may further exaggerate people's sense of stigmatization (Hadden & Haigh, 2001/2002) which affects the whole family. Their diverse needs challenge existing mental health service structures which are geared towards 'single problems', such as depression or schizophrenia, and therefore struggle with social, family and contextual factors. Equally, child-care and social services focus on the needs and safety of children and parenting but struggle to incorporate the mental health needs of parents, especially when there is diagnostic uncertainty.

The issue of PD in the context of parenting therefore challenges various domains of service provision across all agencies, and practitioners are often insufficiently trained or supported to work across key interfaces (adult/child; hospital/community; mental health/social care). When the capacity of parents to meet their children's needs is under scrutiny, professional anxieties may be greatly raised, and there is increased potential for unhelpful polarization of views across different services. This type of 'splitting' of view impairs the potential for collaboration and integrated provision for parents and children. Parents are left insufficiently supported and children remain at significant risk of emotional and physical harm. The importance of early communication, clarity of professionals' roles and responsibilities and the need for collaborative approaches to reduce risk to children is illustrated in Case 1.

Case example 1

Mrs Lewis, a married mother of three children aged 2, 8 and 12 had required six admissions over a 7-year period to her local psychiatric hospital with a variety of diagnoses and dysfunctional behaviours: alcohol misuse, overdosing and self-harm, depression, anxiety, PD and marital discord. Only when she expressed anxiety about harming her children was a referral made to the local children's social services department. Attempts to support Mrs Lewis were unsuccessful. Concerns about safety led to the children's names being put on the child protection register, much against the wishes of Mr Lewis who felt that social workers were 'overreacting' or simply 'protecting their backs'. Lack of progress led to child-care proceedings being initiated and assessments from an adult psychiatrist, a forensic psychiatrist and a child psychiatrist were obtained.

The professionals from adult services emphasized that Mrs Lewis had not harmed her children, while child-oriented professionals emphasized the emotional harm that she was doing to them, and that absence of physical harm was only one component to the assessment. Child professionals also emphasized the need to address the marital relationship, which they perceived as affecting parenting capacity, whereas the adult service professionals took the view that marital therapy was optional. The mother remained passive in her responses to both her children and professionals, and seemed unable to take a view. The father felt that he and the family were being unfairly victimized by the professionals working with children, and thus supported the views of adult service professionals, including the view that marital therapy was optional, not essential.

Where will practitioners encounter people with PD?

Moderate PD is common in primary care (Casey & Tyrer, 1990) and other community settings. More severe PD is found in specialist services. Different diagnostic subgroups are found in different settings (Davison, 2002). Personality disorder patients who are parents will present across the whole range of generic and specialist adult mental health services, in forensic and penal services, and all parts of the child protection system. Those who cause anxiety in others are most likely to be seen in forensic, penal or substance misuse services or may be presenting with complex child protection issues.

There is no precise information about the number of people diagnosable as suffering from a personality disorder who are parents looking after children. Many adult services still do not register whether their patients are parents, and as organizations they therefore may not have any capacity of 'knowing' about parenting issues (Falkov, 1997). This has profound implications for parents, children and professionals as well as service planning. The demographic characteristics of PD parents in adult mental health services may differ from those of other mentally disordered parents by being younger and by gender balance, i.e. more fathers. Finally, given the controversy and stigma of PD, there will be substantial numbers of undiagnosed parents.

Childhood origins of PD: lifespan and generational perspectives

Personality disorder is best understood as a developmental disorder in which childhood difficulties are associated with enduring, lifelong problems in adjustment and relationships including susceptibility to difficulties in the transition to parent-hood. These parenting difficulties form a key component in the transmission of adversity to their children, thereby perpetuating the cycle of adversity into the next generation.

Childhood experiences amongst adults with PD reveal high levels of abuse and neglect (Flynn *et al.*, 2002; Johnson *et al.*, 1999; Modestin *et al.*, 1998; Raczek, 1992; Sabo, 1997; Zanarini *et al.*, 2000). Personality disorder in adulthood may be asso-ciated with conduct disorder and attention-deficit hyperactivity disorder (ADHD) in childhood (Bernstein *et al.*, 1996). These studies highlight the influence of dis-ruption and discontinuities of early child–parent attachments in the development of the personality. Problems in the parental care-giving system and the social milieu of an increasingly entrenched pattern of problematic interpersonal relationships within the family and with peers, increase the risk for maladjustment. Other vari-ables such as genetic loading of the child and relationships with siblings are also important (Livesley *et al.*, 1993; Reiss *et al.*, 2001). Risk factors, such as poverty and social deprivation, are associated with adverse parenting and child maltreat-ment, which in turn may increase the risk of the development of PD in adulthood (Radke-Yarrow, 1998; Taylor *et al.*, 2000).

The concept of resilience is crucial. Some individuals exposed to early trauma and hardship will not develop psychiatric disorders in adulthood (including PD). Equally, many parents with a variety of personality and psychiatric problems will be able to meet their children's emotional and material needs. However, parents with a PD can undoubtedly be dangerous and harmful to their children as the following case example illustrates.

Case example 2

Anita (29), her partner (38) and their children aged 7, 4 and 1 were referred by a health visitor to social services because of suspected failure to thrive of the middle child and school concerns for the oldest child. When the social worker visited, Anita's partner eventually asked her to leave. Anita had threatened to hit the social worker if she continued to 'ask all those poxy questions about the kids – they're my . . . kids, I know what is best for them, no one is going to take them from me'. The social worker was frightened but also had noticed bruises on Anita.

Anita herself was in care for several years because of abuse by her stepfather and generally was regarded as an out-of-control child. As an adult she was known for alcohol problems and had taken three overdoses. Anita was referred for psychiatric assessment. The psychi-atric report stated that Anita had no psychiatric disorder and would be referred to her GP for counselling. Consequently, the social worker closed the case. The family were re-referred 6 weeks later by the emergency department because the 1-year-old child had been brought in with a fractured skull, broken ribs and extensive bruising. The story from Anita was incompatible with the evidence.

One important message for professionals is that a report which states that there is no evidence of psychiatric disorder or mental illness, in the presence of clear difficulties of a psychological nature, will be divisive for professionals and can be positively harmful for parents and children.

Theoretical approaches

Theories of interpersonal function help in the understanding of the development of early and ongoing relationships between child and parent, including the emergence of individual differences in relationships and their persistence across generations. This will include the connection between early relationship patterns and adult personality function.

Concepts such as 'role-relationship' (Horowitz *et al.*, 1995; Kelly, 1955) help to formulate the interplay between social roles (such as parenting), the parent's personality and their attachment relationships in order to enable a more specific understanding of the particular relationship difficulties with which people with personality disorders struggle. Using a 'role-relationship model' assumes that the role repertoire of the adult person is an expression of the internalized experience of both having been a 'child' and 'parent', together with other significant relationships during childhood, reflecting the early experience of dependence-independence (see Göpfert *et al.*, Chapter 5). Others experience these patterns of relationship as the person's 'personality'.

Kelly's work, in combination with object relations theory, led to the development of the concept of 'reciprocal roles', referring to internalized child and parent role patterns that have proved useful for working clinically with PD patients (Ryle, 1998). In patients with PD such reciprocal roles tend to be restrictive, reflecting a degree of role reversal, or 'parentification' proper where the child is pressed into meeting the needs of the parent by taking on a caring role prematurely (Chase, 1999; Earley & Cushway, 2002). Such an approach is particularly useful for understanding relationships with professionals and their limitations. A core dimension is the interpersonal perception of power as part of personality functioning which is reflected in the capacity to use services. The implications for the child who is coerced (intentionally or not) into this developmentally inappropriate role must also be considered. Having to cope alone with difficult, confusing feelings, fears and frustrations has long-term costs (see Bilsborough, Chapter 1).

Benjamin (1993) postulated links between particular labels of PD and childhood relationship patterns. She also emphasized the need to separately address the parenting dimension in clinical work as the relationship patterns of people with PD also affect their relationships with their children.

Attachment theory has proved particularly useful for understanding intergenerational effects of childhood adversity on parenting and child development (see Hill, Chapter 4). The utility, elegance and testability of the theory has provided insights into the nature of attachment and care-giver relationships and a way of understanding long-term outcomes of early adversity within child–parent relationships. In particular, it provides a way of understanding how early rearing patterns can lead to severe personality/interpersonal problems and psychopathology in adolescence and adulthood.

Many parents with personality disorder will find it particularly difficult to make the transition to parenthood, given the likelihood of having a history of dysfunctional attachment in their own childhoods. Further, because of their childhood histories, and their dysfunctional ways of coping with distress, a number of risk factors for child maltreatment may be present in people with personality disorders. These include a parent's own childhood experience of trauma and adversity, including discontinuities in carers and experience of abuse and being 'looked after' (in care); a history of violence (as perpetrator or victim) with unstable, discordant inter-parental relationships; poor compliance with treatment, problematic relationships with professionals, diagnostic uncertainty and a history of overdose and self-harm (prior to and especially since having children), especially more than one such action; poor quality support and social isolation in association with multiple adversities such as discrimination (on grounds of gender, ethnic minority status and mental illness), material deprivation and poverty.

Specifically, the demands of a dependent child can outstrip the capacity of the parent with PD to meet the child's needs safely and effectively; it may even be the case that the perception of the child as dependent increases the risk of maltreatment in adults with PD (Adshead & Bluglass, 2001). This can be understood as an instance of role reversal, where the dependent child may be experienced as demanding and powerful and the parent as helpless and impotent (Bugental & Lewis, 1998).

Attachment theory: secure and insecure care-giving

Attachment theory is particularly useful for understanding parenting difficulties in PD because it presents relationships between parents and children as reciprocal systems of care eliciting and care giving (George & Solomon, 1996). It is a specific behavioural system between one person who is relatively dependent on another (attachment) person which is activated when the dependent person feels threatened. Activation of the attachment system brings the attachment person (parent/carer) and dependent person (child) closer, reducing stress on the dependent person and deactivating the attachment system. The theory postulates that secure attachment occurs as a result of the attachment person providing a secure base for the child to explore the world. Secure attachment facilitates children's development and acquisition of internal psychological representations or 'internal working models', originally a term from rocket science (Byng-Hall, 1995; Craik, 1943). This is a model of the child's own worth and of others' views of the child which form the basis of the child's expectations of carers at times of threat, and their capacity to manage their own responses to threat (Bowlby, 1969).

Carers who have a secure 'working model' of themselves as effective caring parents, and as people who can be cared for, are most likely to provide a secure base for their child's attachment needs. These 'models' are mental representations with both cognitive and affective elements, both conscious and unconscious. These models are especially active in relationships with peers, intimates and dependants, because they include mental aspects of both the cared-for self and the carer; the affects and thoughts that are associated with both roles, and interactions where there is vulnerability. Positive attachment experience is associated with the development of what Kraemer has called a 'caregiver icon' (1992).

Unsuccessful attachment can result in highly dysfunctional social behaviours, including parenting behaviours. In monkeys, insecurely attached adults attacked themselves and their own offspring. It is reasonable to hypothesize that parents with PD, and those parents who maltreat their children, may have insecure internal working models of attachment. It has been argued that the development of both personality and parenting skills are influenced by early childhood attachments (Van Ijzendoorn, 1995). Specifically, the capacity for effective care-giving seems to be related to a parent's own experience of being parented (George & Solomon, 1996). However, parents are not the only predictive factor of a child's attachment pattern. Siblings and family size may be significantly associated with a child's attachment status (Ahnert et al., 2000).

In adults, mental representations of attachment have been studied using a variety of questionnaires and interviews, of which the best known is the Adult Attachment Interview (AAI; George et al., 1994). Insecure attachment is more common in clinical samples, including individuals with personality disorder, especially BPD and ASPD (Fonagy et al., 1996; Sack et al., 1996; Van Ijzendoorn et al., 1997). Insecurity of attachment is also overrepresented in samples of maltreating parents (Crittenden et al., 1991; Delozier, 1982; Mitchell, 1990). The most common pattern of attachment insecurity was dismissing attachment. This pattern is also overrepresented in violent or antisocial individuals. Both child maltreatment and violence may involve lack of empathy. Fonagy et al. (1997) suggests that poor attachment experiences in childhood may result in a failure to develop a capacity for empathy.

Insecurity of attachment is not synonymous with poor parenting or a risk for child maltreatment. The role of early attachment security or insecurity is best regarded as a significant protective or risk factor respectively in the development of psychopathology (Glaser, 2001). In abusive parent–child relationships the attachment person (parent) is also the source of threat for the dependent person (child). This is an important part of the negative impact on children and reinforces low self-esteem, anxiety and confusion.

Attachment theory, like any other theoretical framework, provides a particular perspective and PD development or child maltreatment both require additional explanatory frameworks, e.g. an ecological perspective (Belsky, 1993). Its chief advantage is that it offers an account of the psychological capacity to care for others, and to effectively seek care for the self.

Case example 3

Susie first attacked her baby son James when he was 3 weeks old. She continued to attack him intermittently; when he was 5 months old, she assaulted him so badly that he sustained a serious head injury. She took him to hospital, and claimed to have no idea how he had got hurt. During the subsequent child-care proceedings, she continued to deny that she had ever harmed him. James was placed in care and subsequently adopted. Four years later, Susie is pregnant again, and a psychiatric opinion about the risk to her new baby is requested. She wants to keep the baby. Two previous reports state that Susie has 'an untreatable personality disorder'.

Not surprisingly, Susie herself had a disturbed upbringing with disrupted attachments. Her mother died of a drug overdose when Susie was 3, and the children remained with their alcoholic and physically abusive father. Susie was taken into care aged 7, exhibiting behavioural difficulties and difficulties at school. She had several different foster placements; some of which broke down because of her behaviour. Susie was physically and sexually abused in the children's home, and by foster carers. Susie was 19 when she had James following three terminations. She had been ambivalent about this pregnancy too. She had been treated for depression, took three overdoses, and cut herself recurrently. James' father has been violent to her.

A parent, like Susie, with a traumatizing or abusive childhood, may internalize a relationship pattern with an abusing carer that leaves her with the identity of 'victim'. In subsequent dependency relationships (i.e. with partners, children or carers), she may experience herself as victim, and behave in ways that make that role 'fit'. Others are seen as powerful, demanding and controlling. Susie may have experienced James as cruel and demanding. She is likely to have experienced all those involved in the child protection services as a source of threat; there was some reality to this perception, reinforced by the adversarial legal process. Cultural constructions of the female gender role may encourage passivity and silent suffering, discouraging expressions of discontent, especially with being a child-carer.

The more abusive a child's experience, the wider the gap between them and a socially encountered 'normal' family. The child's daily experience of her family reality reinforces a sense of hopelessness and helplessness because of the other, 'normal' reality, which appears as both unattainable, and the ideal solution to all the child's problems. This 'ideal' may be developed as a defence against intolerable affects of pain, grief, rage and a wish to hurt in revenge.

One of the professional risks in assessing a parent with a significant history of trauma and abuse is to identify too closely with Susie as a victim who has not set out to harm her children and who has herself experienced multiple adversity through no fault of her own. Her needs must not outweigh the needs and safety of her unborn child.

Assessment and PD in parents: formulations

In cases like Susie's the diagnosis of personality disorder is often made solely on the basis of her anger and violence to the child. Susie's PD then explains her violence, which in turn increases the chance of her being violent, in professionals' minds. Such circularity of argument can make simple diagnostic statements about PD almost useless for the purposes of assessing the capacity to parent. A good formulation needs to provide hypotheses regarding Susie's original episode of harming James, and her wishes to have another baby. It must also take into account the various risk factors associated with parental inability to meet a child's needs safely and appropriately. The risks and strengths must be evaluated and lead to clear and decisive decisions to avoid unnecessary delays and exposure of a child to undue risk. A therapeutic trial of parenting must take place in a suitable setting with the necessary expertise to evaluate parenting and parent–child relationships whilst ensuring that children remain safe. This may require intense therapeutic support on a 24-hour basis, 7 days per week, usually provided in a residential setting. If a decision is made for the child to be fostered or adopted then again the arrangements must not be delayed and support must also be provided for Susie who will be experiencing yet another loss.

Human interactions can be analysed and understood as role enactments, a person's best attempt at achieving adequate relationships at the time. 'Suboptimal' enactments are likely to be too rigid or too unstable; and in relation to children will not meet their needs. In this case, Susie took up a hostile role in relation to James, experiencing him as a threat and unable to 'see' his dependence and vulnerability. Alternatively, his neediness has triggered huge feelings of anxiety and cruelty; as if she needed to destroy some aspect of him, or herself, as she perceived herself in him. A 'role-relationship' model addresses the dependence and power relationships between parents and children; an attachment theory-based model postulates that Susie's internal representations of carers and needy children are highly insecure, and do not provide her with psychological containment of her fears or distress, thus highlighting the difficulties she is likely to have in meeting the needs of her child, including ensuring emotional as well as physical safety.

Experiences in childhood can lead to patterns of relating in adulthood that are predetermined and repetitive, based on past rather than current experiences. Fixed repetition of reciprocal role patterns are usually unhelpful, reflecting a history of unresolved trauma and deprivation (Ryle & Kerr, 2002). In attachment terms they are seen as 'unresolved' experiences. Role patterns 'learned' with abusive or neglectful parents may be enacted in adult relationships, including relationships with professionals.

Research on girls raised in care suggests that they are likely to have babies at an early age, as an attempt to achieve the 'ideal' that they missed out on, and which helps to defend against intolerable distress. Of course, pregnancy and care for very small infants does not resemble the 'ideal' that many deprived children have fantasized about; nor does it fit the socially constructed ideal of feminine motherhood which suggests that pregnancy and child-care are utterly blissful. Many women like Susie lack supportive relationships which provide support with parenting difficulties. Babies, like James, are seen as ideal solutions to unconscious grief and fear; they also crucially act as affect regulators for the mother, so that Susie needed James to make her feel good about herself. This meant that James' needs were seriously compromised.

From such an idealized position, the baby can easily turn into a bad, all-powerful person, who (like the abusive parent of the previous generation) wants to make Susie feel small and helpless. James 'fails' to make her feel good, but instead makes her feel 'bad'. She does not 'see' James as a helpless baby; only as a persecutor, and she as a victim: an angry, vengeful victim. She identifies with the abusive parental representation in her mind, and projects the victim representation onto James. When James was taken from her, she lost her means of regulating her own affect, and the urgent need to manage her internal world with an external attachment solution begins again.

Susie might have easily killed James. In her mind, she did not attack her beloved child, but the monster which persecuted her. Similar formulations can be helpful in situations of multiple family murders or parental suicide (Lovrin, 1999; Ward, 1995).

Assessment and personality disorder in parents: process and problems

Generally, no single model or approach can address all the concerns about parenting capacity in parents with PD. However, there are a number of principles which underpin good practice (Department of Health, 2000) (see Falkov, Chapter 27, Göpfert et al., Chapter 7 and Asen & Schuff, Chapter 10). It is important to take a broad contextual approach, looking at both current family dynamics and the experience of the parent in their family of origin. The assessment for mental illness in the parent is important, although this must not be confused with risk assessment to the child. The nature of any assessment needs to be clear: is it a mental state assessment; a psychiatric diagnosis/prognosis; risk of suicide/homicide; parenting capacity/viability of parent–child relationship; a child's emotional well-being; evidence of significant harm to a child. This will determine who should undertake an assessment. Case example 1 demonstrates the difficulties encountered when adult psychiatrists without an appropriate training in assessing parenting make judgements about parenting ability. Importantly, absence of a psychiatric diagnosis does not equal absence of risk to children

Some specific points may be particularly important in the assessment of parents with PD. It can be difficult to engage a parent with PD in assessment because of their high levels of arousal and distress in the face of what they perceive as a threat. Perception of others as persecutors may make parents with PD uncooperative and deceitful. It is therefore often necessary to interview a parent more than once, and with some reasonable time lapse. This is especially so if the assessor has felt very hostile towards the parent. Information then becomes essential; general practice and other caring agency records are informative regarding the individual's relationship with professional caregivers, as well as past psychiatric notes.

Timing is important: a residential assessment of parenting over a 6-month period will have different implications for a 6-month-old child as compared with a 6-year-old child. Timescales for change in a parent may not meet the child's needs.

The inclination to withdraw all treatment and support once a personality disorder is suspected is inappropriate, especially if there are dependent children. Diagnostic uncertainty is an indication for referral to specialist mental health services and to children's services for assessment of parenting. Attempting to help a person who has difficulty in forming relationships may be hampered by that very difficulty. If a parent's and child's needs are seen as competing, confusion of roles and fragmented provision result and needs are not appropriately met. Consequently, children may be exposed to acute (physical) dangers or longer-term emotional harm (see Falkov, Chapter 27).

Individuals with personality disorders have a propensity for casting professionals into extreme positions – idealizing them as 'perfect' or denigrating them as 'useless'. Their complex needs may be perceived as in direct competition with the needs of their children. Professionals may then be drawn into overzealous advocacy on behalf of 'their' patient/client (adult or child), creating polarized views. It therefore cannot be overemphasized that collaboration and dialogue between professionals is vital, which makes reflection on the splitting of views more possible. The parental role by definition means that the needs of the child have to be considered paramount. Therefore, if adult mental health professionals can appropriately consider the role of parent for their patients, there should be less room for 'conflict' because their task would be to enable the parent to primarily consider the needs of the child, before the patient's own needs. This position can be difficult to hold in the face of seductive or psychopathic parents who may manipulate professional systems and services without any real regard for their children. It may also be difficult for adult-focused and child-focused professionals in the mental health field to achieve a proper understanding of their respective positions in spite of their best intentions and efforts.

Parenting capacity

Parents with a diagnosis of ASPD or BPD are more likely than other parents to exhibit hostile and irritable behaviour towards their children. They may have similar difficulties in relating to their children as they do to peers, or may find it particularly difficult to relate to a child in age-appropriate ways. This may be due to difficulty in distinguishing their own needs from those of their child or lack of an understanding of children's needs compared with adults. Impulsivity may lead to ill-considered physical discipline (smacking/assault) rather than verbal negotiation. The following issues should be borne in mind when assessing a parent with PD (Royal College of Psychiatrists, 2002*b*).

Personal history

- Their own history of being parented, especially any experience of abuse and neglect.
- Any childhood history of illness or prolonged separation from parents.
- Any history of physical harm either to self or others: age of onset, arrest or convictions, response of others to their violence.
- Suicidal or homicidal feelings: how do they manage them?
- Dissociative experiences: feeling 'out of one's head', or unreal.
- Other mental health problems, especially substance misuse.
- Can they form relationships with others? If so, are they violent ones? Are they the victim or the perpetrator?
- Relationship patterns with professional caregivers in the past and treatment compliance.

Parent–child relationship

- Was this a wanted child? How did they feel when they or their partner became pregnant? How did they imagine the child would be?
- Has the child been exposed to violence and hostility? Does the parent have any insight into this? Do they take responsibility for any or all harm to the child? Accepting responsibility is often a process which takes time, and rarely fits in with the schedules of family courts. It may also not fit in with the advice of legal advocates.

Interparental relationship

The parenting couple needs to be assessed in its own right. A partner is important as a potential source of:

- Alternative care and support.
- Additional burden because they may also show evidence of mental illness/PD.
- Direct harm for children if the partner has maltreated children and PD/mental illness prevents a parent from adequately protecting children.
- Indirect harm for children, for example if domestic violence is witnessed – a woman who is unable to adequately protect herself will struggle to ensure her children are adequately protected (Austin, 2001; Royal College of Psychiatrists, 2002a)

Special problems associated with personality disorder in parents

Parental alienation syndrome

The Parental alienation syndrome, when a child is thoroughly 'alienated' from a parent (Zirogiannis, 2001), may be an issue of relevance when working with PD parents. The personality of the parent seems to be an important variable in such relationships and why they go wrong (Kelly & Johnston, 2001; Lee & Olesen, 2001), but it also raises the question when and how children should be allowed to 'divorce' their parents (Williams, 2001; Zirogiannis, 2001).

Factitious illness by proxy (Munchausen's syndrome by Proxy)

Factitious illness by Proxy (FIP) or Munchausen's syndrome by Proxy is a form of abnormal illness behaviour where a parent (usually but not exclusively the mother) presents the child as ill to healthcare professionals. The behaviour can take many forms from fabricating accounts of symptoms to actively inducing symptoms in children in a way that is life threatening. It is likely that FIP represents a behavioural manifestation of personality disorder (Bools *et al.*, 1994), which is expressed most prominently in relation to professional carers, using dependent children as a means in the process (Schreier & Libow, 1993).

Treatability and parental PD

Treatability depends on motivation, ability to engage and confront relationship patterns and the capacity to endure negative experiences with sufficient support without leaving treatment. Even if a patient is found to be treatable, treatability also requires the availability of an adequate treatment resource (Adshead, 2001). Few services offer nonresidential treatment for PD parents. Even fewer specialist centres offer residential assessment and treatment of maltreating parents. Individuals like Susie are rarely offered any intervention at all because the prognosis is poor (Jones, 1987). A positive decision that someone is treatable can only be made on the basis of a realistic trial, and usually only after all the statutory decisions are made. There are some exceptions to this (see Göpfert *et al.*, Chapter 7).

The therapeutic task of helping someone become a parent must be to:

(1) Establish a therapeutic relationship that is based on competence rather than insufficiency and problems. This should validate the parent's experiences as reasonable under the circumstances whilst linking it to the task of responsibly caring for a child.

(2) Identify and challenge insecure attachment patterns and fixed role enactments in a carefully balanced context of positive reinforcements and genuine appreciation.

(3) Increase awareness of how these patterns and roles manifest themselves, and encourage the capacity to monitor one's own mental states. Encourage 'improvisation' of new and untried behaviours and roles.

(4) Examine how role reversal with the child takes place, and in what context, relating this to own experience.

(5) Relate the capacity to manage one's own distress to the capacity for concern for a child's distress.

(6) Understand any hostility and other negative countertransference of professionals as part of the parent's clinical formulation.

Interventions for the parent with PD may need to address a number of different psychological domains. Often parents are defeated by the realization that they have recreated their own childhood conditions for their children against all their best intentions. Fathers may experience intense shame (Lansky, 1992) whereas mothers are more likely persecuted by guilt. There may be a need for psychological interventions which aim to help the person manage anger and/or arousal better, and to understand their reactions to their child's distress. Other family members and the family with a PD parent may need interventions in their own right to help change and develop.

Assessment suggested that Susie had a dismissing model of attachment, in which she avoided any consideration of her own neediness, emphasizing the value of being 'strong' and independent. First steps in therapy for Susie would include helping her to begin to think about, and not attack, her own sense of neediness. Recent work on the neurobiology of attachment indicates that the capacity to manage negative feelings is crucial to the delivery of good enough care-giving (Schore, 2001). Attachment theory is widely used in the assessment of and intervention with maltreating parents (Howe *et al.*, 1999; Levy & Orlans, 1998), however, there is a considerable need for further progress across all methods of intervention.

Some personality disorders can be successfully treated in therapeutic communities, which may be residential or day facilities (Lees *et al.*, 1999). Unfortunately, to date, only a few of these communities can take PD parents with their children, or offer specific help in relation to failed parenting. Cognitive-analytic therapy (CAT) with its emphasis on reciprocal roles may be useful for parents with PD. There are no longer grounds for categorical statements like 'personality disorder is untreatable'; rather some types of PD are treatable in some settings, given the right expertise (Adshead, 2001; Roth & Fonagy, 1996).

Currently, the capacity of professional systems to contain risk is limited if managing risk means managing a person. That person might have strong feelings about being 'managed' if this is experienced as coercion. The limited success of the democratic therapeutic community model may be associated with the requirement that residents themselves take responsibility for managing their own risk; by doing so parents and families extend the range of treatability.

However, not all cases of PD will be treatable, especially severe cases. Assessment may conclude that no intervention is possible. Jones (1987) suggests that multiple comorbidity, denial of problems and aggression to staff are contraindications to treatment for parents who have abused their children. It is likely that these will also apply to some parents with PD. Other negative prognostic factors include:

- Persistent rejection of the child.
- Failure to recognize or be curious about the child's needs.
- Persistent blame or criticism of the child for current problems.
- Delusions about the child, or other cognitive distortions.
- Inappropriate expectations of the child.
- Ongoing emotional unavailability, unresponsiveness and neglect.
- Lack of praise and encouragement.
- Lack of comfort and love.
- Lack of age-appropriate stimulation.

Where therapy is not an option, interventions will focus on risk management. This can be usefully informed by a clinical formulation but the details are beyond the scope of this chapter.

Conclusions

This chapter has emphasized the need for all professionals to improve practice, so that children will be better protected and their parents better supported. Whilst not all parents with PD will be unable to meet their children's needs and ensure their safety, amongst this group will be found some of the most difficult to manage and dangerous parents who are a severe risk to children's safety. This requires high levels of cooperation, communication and effective joint working to ensure that such children are protected and that parents receive appropriate support.

Within the high-risk environment of the 'PD' family unit lies a substantial proportion of the next generation of parents with PD. There are therefore compelling reasons for better identification, assessment and management of such parents and their children. Improved collaboration between adult and child services could reduce the proportion of children who will go on to develop PD in adulthood and who struggle in the transition to parenthood.

REFERENCES

Adshead, G. (2001). Murmurs of discontent: treatment and treatability of personality disorder. *Advances in Psychiatric Treatment, 7*, 407–15.

Adshead, G. & Bluglass, K. (2001). Attachment representations and Factitious illness by Proxy: relevance for assessment of parenting capacity in child maltreatment. *Child Abuse Review, 10*, 398–410.

Ahnert, L., Meischner, T. & Schmidt, A. (2000). Maternal sensitivity and attachment in East German and Russian family networks. In *The Organization of Attachment Relationships: Maturation, Culture, and Context*, ed. P. M. Crittenden & A. H. Clausen, pp. 61–74. Cambridge: Cambridge University Press.

Appleby, L. & Lewis, G. (1988). Personality disorder: the patients psychiatrists dislike. *British Journal of Psychiatry, 153*, 44–9.

American Psychiatric Association (1994). *Diagnostic and Statistical Manual of Mental Disorders*, 4th revision (DSM–IV). Washington, DC: APA.

Austin, W. G. (2001). Partner violence and risk assessment in child custody evaluations. *Family Court Review, 39*, 483–96.

Belsky, J. (1993). Etiology of child maltreatment: a developmental-ecological analysis. *Psychological Bulletin, 114*, 413–34.

Benjamin, L. S. (1993). *The Interpersonal Diagnosis and Treatment of Personality Disorders.* New York: Guilford Press.

Bernstein, D. P., Cohen, P., Skodol, A., Bezirganian, S. & Brook, J. (1996). Childhood antecedents of adolescent personality disorder. *American Journal of Psychiatry, 153*, 907–13.

Bools, C., Neale, B. & Meadow, R. (1994). Munchausen's Syndrome by Proxy: a study of psychopathology. *Child Abuse and Neglect, 18*, 773–88.

Bowlby, J. (1969). *Attachment and Loss, Vol. 1. Attachment.* London: Hogarth Press.

Bugental, D. B. & Lewis, J. C. (1998). Interpersonal power repair in response to threats to control from dependent others. In *Personal Control in Action: Cognitive and Motivational Mechanisms*, ed. M. Kofta & G. Weary, pp. 341–62. New York: Plenum Press.

Byng-Hall, J. (1995). *Rewriting Family Scripts.* New York: Guilford Press.

Campling, P. (1997). Maintaining the therapeutic alliance with personality-disordered patients. *Journal of Forensic Psychiatry, 793*, 535–50.

Casey, P. & Tyrer, P. (1990). Personality disorder and psychiatric illness in general practice. *British Journal of Psychiatry*, *156*, 261–5.

Chase, N. D. (ed.) (1999). *Burdened Children: Theory, Research and Treatment of Parentification.* Thousand Oaks: Sage.

Craik, K. (1943). *The Nature of Explanation.* Cambridge: Cambridge University Press.

Crittenden, P., Partridge, M. & Claussen, A. (1991). Family patterns of relationship in normative and dysfunctional families. *Development and Psychopathology*, *3*, 491–512.

Davison, S. (2002). Principles of managing patients with personality disorder. *Advances in Psychiatric Treatment*, *8*, 1–9.

DeLozier, P. (1982). Attachment theory and child abuse. In *The Place of Attachment in Human Behaviour*, ed. C. M. Parkes & J. Stevenson-Hinde, pp. 95–117. London: Tavistock.

Department of Health (2000). *Framework for the Assessment of Children in Need and their Families.* London: The Stationery office.

Dinwiddie, S. & Bucholz, K. (1993). Psychiatric diagnoses of self-reported child abusers. *Child Abuse and Neglect*, *17*, 465–76.

Earley, L. & Cushway, D. (2002). The parentified child. *Clinical Child Psychology and Psychiatry*, *7*, 163–78.

Falkov, A. (1997). Adult psychiatry – a missing link in child protection. *Child Abuse Review*, *6*, 41–5.

Famularo, R., Kinscherff, R. & Fenton, T. (1992). Psychiatric diagnoses of abusive mothers: a preliminary report. *Journal of Nervous and Mental Disease*, *180*, 658–61.

Flynn, A., Matthews, H. & Hollins, S. (2002). Validity of the diagnosis of personality disorder in adults with learning disability and severe behaviour problems. *British Journal of Psychiatry*, *180*, 543–6.

Fonagy, P., Leigh, T., Steele, M. et al. (1996). The relationship of attachment status, psychiatric classification and response to psychotherapy. *Journal of Consulting and Clinical Psychology*, *64*, 23–31.

Fonagy, P., Target, M., Steele, M. et al. (1997). Morality, disruptive behaviour, borderline personality disorder, crime and their relationship to attachment. In *Attachment and Psychopathology*, ed. L. Atkinson & K. Zucker, pp. 233–74. New York: Guilford Press.

George, C. & Solomon, J. (1996). Representational models of relationships: links between care giving and attachment. *Infant Mental Health Journal*, *17*, 198–216.

George, C., Kaplan, N. & Main, M. (1994). *Adult Attachment Interview protocol*, 4th edn. Unpublished. Berkeley, CA: University of California at Berkeley, Dept. of Psychology.

Gergen, K. J., Hoffman, L. & Anderson, H. (1996). Is diagnosis a disaster? A constructionist trialogue. In *Handbook of Relational Diagnosis and Dysfunctional Family Patterns*, ed. F. W. Kaslow, pp. 102–118. New York: John Wiley & Sons.

Glaser, D. (2001). Attachment and child protection. *Child Abuse Review*, *10*, 371–5.

Göpfert, M. (1991). *Families with a Schizophrenic Parent. A Preliminary Enquiry.* Unpublished dissertation. Toronto: University of Toronto.

Hadden, Y. & Haigh, R. (2001/2002). Personality disorder – how much more stigmatising could a label be? Dialogue, Issues No. 9 (2001) and 10 (2002). Published as part of the Virtual

Institute of Severe Personality Disorder by the Henderson Hospital (South-West London and St. George's Mental Health Trust). Also on http://www. doh.gov.uk/hspsch/visped.

Horowitz, M. J., Eells, T., Singer, J. & Salovey, P. (1995). Role-relationship models for case formulation. *Archives of General Psychiatry, 52,* 625–32.

Howe, D., Brandon, M., Hinings, D. & Schofield, G. (1999). *Attachment Theory, Child Maltreatment and Family Support.* London: Macmillan.

Johnson, J., Cohen, P. & Brown, J. et al. (1999). Childhood maltreatment increases the risk for personality disorders in early adulthood. *Archives of General Psychiatry, 56,* 600–6.

Jones, D. (1987). The untreatable family. *Child Abuse and Neglect, 11,* 409–20.

Kelly, G. A. (1955). *The Psychology of Personal Constructs.* New York: Norton.

Kelly, J. B. & Johnston, J. R. (2001). The alienated child: a reformulation of the parental alienation syndrome. *Family Court Review, 39,* 249–66.

Kendell, R. E. (2002). The distinction between personality disorder and mental illness. *British Journal of Psychiatry, 180,* 110–15.

Kraemer, G. (1992). A psychobiological theory of attachment. *Behavioural and Brain Sciences, 15,* 493–511.

Lansky, M. R. (1992). *Fathers who Fail: Shame and Psychopathology in the Family System.* Hillsdale, NJ: The Analytic Press.

Lee, M. S. & Olesen, N. W. (2001). Assessing for alienation in child custody and access evaluations. *Family Court Review, 39,* 282–98.

Lees, J., Manning, N. & Rawlings, B. (1999). *Therapeutic Community Effectiveness.* NHS Centre Reviews and Dissemination Report, No. 17. York: University of York.

Levey, T. & Orlans, M. (1998). *Attachment Trauma and Healing: Understanding and Treating Attachment Disorder in Children and Families.* Washington, DC: Child Welfare League of America.

Livesley, W. J., Jang, K. L., Jackson, D. N. & Vernon, P. A. (1993). Genetic and environmental contributions to dimensions of personality disorder. *American Journal of Psychiatry, 150,* 1826–31.

Lovrin, M. (1999). Parental murder and suicide: post-traumatic stress disorder in children. *Journal of Child and Adolescent Psychiatric Nursing, 12,* 110–17.

Mitchell, M. (1990). Attachment antecedents and sociocultural factors in Hispanic mothers' physical abuse of their children. In *Research Explorations in Adult Attachment,* ed. K. Pottharst, pp. 129–97. New York: Peter Lang.

Modestin, J., Oberson, B. & Erni, T. (1998). Possible antecedents of DSM–III–R personality disorders. *Acta Psychiatrica Scandinavica, 97,* 260–6.

Norton, K. & Dolan, B. (1996). Personality disorder and parenting. In *Parental Psychiatric Disorder: Distressed Parents and Their Families,* ed. M. Göpfert, J. Webster & M. V. Seeman, pp. 219–232. Cambridge: Cambridge University Press.

Pryce, C. R. (1995). Determinants of motherhood in human and non-human primates. In *Motherhood in Human and Non-human Primates,* ed. C. R. Pryce, R. Martin & D. Skuse, pp. 1–15. Basel: Karger.

Raczek, S. (1992). Childhood abuse and personality disorders. *Journal of Personality Disorders, 6,* 109–16.

Radke-Yarrow, M. (1998). *Children of Depressed Mothers.* Cambridge: Cambridge University Press.

Reiss, D., Pedersen, N. L., Cederblad, M. et al. (2001). Genetic probes of three theories of maternal adjustment: I. Recent evidence and a model. *Family Process, 40*, 247–59.

Roth, A. & Fonagy, P. (1996). *What Works for Whom? A Critical Review of Psychotherapy Research.* New York: Guilford Press.

Royal College of Psychiatrists (2002*a*). *Domestic Violence.* Council Report CR 102. London: Royal College of Psychiatrists.

Royal College of Psychiatrists (2002*b*). *Patients as Parents.* Council Report CR 105. London: Royal College of Psychiatrists.

Ryle, A. (1998). *Cognitive-analytic Therapy and Borderline Personality Disorder.* Chichester: John Wiley & Sons.

Ryle, A. & Kerr, I. (2002). *Introducing Cognitive-analytic Therapy: Principles and Practice.* Chichester: John Wiley & Sons.

Sabo, A. N. (1997). The etiological significance of associations between childhood trauma and borderline personality disorders: conceptual and clinical implications. *Journal of Personality Disorders, 11*, 50–70.

Sack, A., Sperling, M. M., Fagen, G. & Foelsch, P. (1996). Attachment styles, histories and behavioural contrasts for a borderline and normal sample. *Journal of Personality Disorders, 10*, 88–101.

Samuels, J., Eaton, W. W., Bienvenu III, O. J., Brown, C. H., Costa Jr, P. T. & Nestadt, G. (2002). Prevalence and correlates of personality disorder in a community sample. *British Journal of Psychiatry, 180*, 536–42.

Schore, A. (2001). Minds in the making: attachment, the self-organising brain, and developmentally oriented psychoanalytic psychotherapy. *British Journal of Psychotherapy, 17*, 299–328.

Schreier, H. A. & Libow, J. A. (1993). *Hurting for Love: Munchausen by Proxy Syndrome.* New York: Guilford Press.

Stanley, N. & Penhale, B. (1999). The mental health problems of mothers experiencing the child protection system. *Child Abuse Review, 8*, 34–45.

Taylor, J. Spencer, N. & Baldwin, N. (2000). Social, economic and political context of parenting. *Archives of Disease in Childhood, 82*, 113–17.

Van Ijzendoorn, M. (1995). Adult attachment representations, predictive responsiveness and infant attachment: a meta-analysis of the predictive validity of the Adult Attachment Interview. *Psychological Bulletin, 117*, 387–403.

Van Ijzendoorn, M., Feldbruggen, J., Derks, F. C. H. et al. (1997). Attachment representations of personality disordered criminal offenders. *American Journal of Orthopsychiatry, 67*, 449–59.

Ward, A. (1995). The impact of parental suicide on children and staff in residential care: a case study in the function of containment. *Journal of Social Work Practice, 9*, 23–32.

Westen, D. (1997). Divergences between clinical and research methods for assessing personality disorders: Implications for research and the evolution of Axis II. *American Journal of Psychiatry, 154*, 895–903.

Westen, D. & Harnden-Fischer, J. (2001). Personality profiles in eating disorders: rethinking the distinction between axis I and axis II. *American Journal of Psychiatry*, *158*, 547–62.

Williams, J. R. (2001). Should judges close the gate on PAS and PA? *Family Court Review*, *39*, 267–81.

Zanarini, M. C., Frankenburg, F. R., Reich, D. B. et al. (2000). Biparental failure in the childhood experiences of borderline patients. *Journal of Personality Disorder*, *14*, 264–73.

Zirogiannis, L. (2001). Evidentiary issues with parental alienation syndrome. *Family Court Review*, *39*, 334–43.

Part IV

Specific treatments and service needs

16

Psychopharmacology and motherhood

Mary V. Seeman[1] and Neil Seeman[2]

[1]Centre for Addiction and Mental Health, Toronto, Canada; and [2]CANSTATTS, A Division of the Fraser Institute, Toronto, Canada

One of the most difficult decisions for women suffering from a chronic or recurrent illness is whether or not to continue taking maintenance medications during pregnancy. Women know that they should not smoke, drink alcohol or take street drugs when they are pregnant. But they are unsure about prescribed medication. The dilemma is particularly difficult for women who are unclear about their need for medication. This predicament is well captured in a Canadian study of focus group discussions among women diagnosed with schizophrenia (Chisholm, 1999). In this group of women, pregnancies were reported as largely unplanned. The question they faced at the time of the pregnancy was whether to stop antipsychotic medication or, by continuing, to harm (perhaps) their developing child. These women related mixed experience with respect to the help they received from their doctors. Some found their doctors' advice helpful; others not. More than one woman in the focus groups expressed serious regret at having opted for abortion because of the impossibility of resolving this issue. The dilemma is expressed succinctly by one of the women:

One of the biggest things I had to contend with when I thought I wanted to have a baby is you can't go off your medication just like that and this medication is potentially very, extremely damaging to a fetus.

The ideal pregnancy is one that is preplanned, with the mother-to-be taking prenatal vitamins containing folic acid a full 6 weeks prior to conception. The perfect mother is within 15% of her ideal body weight at the time of conception. She does not smoke, drink coffee or alcohol, or take drugs or herbal products and she is under the care of a physician at the outset of her pregnancy (Collaborative Group on Drug Use in Pregnancy, 1992). The ideal is, however, rare. Approximately half of all pregnancies are unplanned. Most drug-related problems occur between week 3 and week 8 of gestation, before many women realize they are pregnant (Table 16.1). The baseline fetal malformation rate is 2–4% (Baugh & Stowe, 1999) and not very much is known with certainty about how much drugs contribute to this rate

Table 16.1. General principles of drug use during pregnancy

Folic acid prior to pregnancy

Supplemental vitamins during pregnancy

2000–2800 calorie balanced diet

No smoking

Less than 300 mg/day caffeine intake

When there is a choice, known drugs are safer than new alternatives

Use lowest possible doses; drug metabolism changes over the course of pregnancy

Discourage use of over-the-counter drugs and herbal medicines

Drugs may pose different risks at different times during pregnancy

Consider risks not only for congenital anomalies but also for short-term perinatal
   problems and for possible long-term neurobehavioural effects

Use nondrug treatments (ECT, light therapy, psychotherapy) when possible

(Austin & Mitchell, 1998). What happens in animals during drug testing does not necessarily predict what will take place in humans (Koren *et al.*, 1998). Although most women stop or decrease consumption of over-the-counter drugs when they learn that they are pregnant, up to 80% of pregnant women are prescribed drugs by their physicians. One third of pregnant women in North America take psychotropic medication during pregnancy (Cohen & Rosenbaum, 1998). In order to alleviate undue worry, prospective mothers need to know that two-thirds of birth defects arise from unknown causes. Of the remaining one third, about 30% are due to genetic disease, 2% occur as a result of infections and other illnesses during pregnancy, leaving approximately 2% attributable to drug and chemical exposure during pregnancy.

As with nonpsychiatric disorders, pregnancy may either ameliorate or worsen pre-existing symptoms of illness. For instance, the rate and severity of depression appear to be similar in pregnant and nonpregnant women (about 10%) (Kumar & Robson, 1984) (see Seneviratne & Conroy, Chapter 9) but panic disorder improves in pregnancy (Klein *et al.*, 1995). Obsessive compulsive disorder, on the other hand, may be triggered at this time (Neziroglu *et al.*, 1992). Schizophrenia and bipolar illness tends to improve during pregnancy but at least 50% of women with schizophrenia need to continue psychiatric medication during pregnancy in order to avoid hospitalization (Miller, 1994).

While psychiatric medications, which all cross the placental membrane (but probably to different degrees), may pose a risk to the developing infant, untreated illness may do so as well (Baugh & Stowe, 1999), perhaps because of the adverse effects on the fetal brain of stress-induced glucocorticoids in the mother (Roughton *et al.*, 1998).

Proper randomized, double-blind controlled studies of the various psychiatric medications during pregnancy (or during breast-feeding) have not been done and cannot be done, since no psychotropic drug has been approved for use during pregnancy. Any such study would need to take many variables into account: mother's medical history, type and severity of mother's symptoms, timing and duration of drug exposure, mother's age, concomitant use of tobacco, alcohol and other drugs, as well as exposure to environmental toxins and infectious agents.

As the treatment of psychiatric disease improves, more women with psychiatric conditions will become pregnant. With respect to women diagnosed with psychotic conditions, the newer antipsychotic agents do not, as did the earlier ones, impair conception, so fertility rates in women with psychosis now approximate those of the general population.

Some drugs routinely used in psychiatric conditions have been convincingly linked with teratogenicity: lithium has been associated with a cardiac abnormality called Ebstein's anomaly; carbamazepine and valproic acid in the first trimester are held responsible for neural tube defects (Koren *et al.*, 1998). On the other hand, concern about diazepam inducing oral clefts, and oral contraceptives and salicylates causing harm during pregnancy has now largely been laid to rest (Koren *et al.*, 1998). The cardiac risk for lithium is confined to the first trimester and can be monitored with echocardiography and ultrasonography. Valproic acid may be used once the fetal neural tube is complete but antiepileptic drugs in general still pose a significant risk during pregnancy (Samren *et al.*, 1999). Antidepressants are considered safe, as are the older antipsychotic agents (Table 16.2). Little is known about the newer ones (Goldstein *et al.*, 2000).

Adverse neonatal effects have been reported after exposure to benzodiazepines during the last trimester or at the time of labour. Exposed infants are at higher than normal risk for hypotonicity, failure to feed, impaired temperature regulation, apnoea and low Apgar scores (Altshuler *et al.*, 1996). Anticholinergic drugs (used to counter the adverse effects of antipsychotic medication) have been associated with neonatal meconium ileus. A 'floppy baby' syndrome has been reported after third-trimester use of lithium and also of clozapine. Animal (but not human; Austin & Mitchell, 1998) data suggest the possibility of long-term behavioural abnormalities after fetal exposure to antipsychotic medication (Altshuler *et al.*, 1996).

Breast-feeding

The pros and cons of psychotropic drugs in breast-feeding women with mental illness is complicated by the fact that essentially all psychiatric disorders worsen in the postpartum period. Effective treatment at this vulnerable time is essential.

Table 16.2. Drugs and their risks during pregnancy

Drug	Risk during pregnancy and advice
Alcohol	Deformities and mental retardation, proportional to amount and frequency
Amphetamines or other stimulants (e.g. methylphenidate, weight reduction pills, ingredients in cold medicines)	Increased risk of miscarriage, premature delivery, low birth weight
Antacids	Safe in occasional single doses
Antianxiety medications or sleeping pills (e.g. lorazepam, diazepam, clonazepam, zopiclone)	If used close to delivery date, baby may be born with depressed breathing or experience withdrawal symptoms. Do not stop use without consulting doctor and obtain help in tapering
Antidepressants	Safe. Do not stop prescribed antidepressants
Antipsychotics	Ask doctor about safest antipsychotic and about dose requirements during different trimesters. Do not stop on own
Antihistamines	Probably safe, but may interact with other medications
Caffeine (coffee, tea, chocolate, colas, ingredient in some pain tablets)	Over 300 mg/day is unsafe for the fetus (average mug of coffee = 100 mg)
Cannabis (marijuana, hashish, pot)	Risk of abnormalities in development of fetus, undersize baby and later behaviour problems
Cocaine (crack)	Risk of miscarriage, premature delivery; possible malformations of fetus
Herbal remedies	Do not use unless ingredients are specified and then check with doctor
Household chemicals, paints, cleaning solvents, lacquers, fertilizers	Accidental breathing in of fumes may harm fetus. Use these products with caution, and in well ventilated areas
Mood stabilizers	Most mood stabilizers pose a risk to the fetus in the first trimester but do not stop without consultation with doctor
Nausea (morning sickness) remedies	Antinausea drugs vary in risk to fetus. Consult doctor before taking any medication for this purpose
Pain medications	
Non-narcotic, nonprescription, containing ASA (e.g. aspirin) or acetaminophen/ paracetamol or anti-inflammatory pills (e.g. Ibuprofen)	Safe for occasional use but check with doctor before using regularly. Do not use ASA preparations or anti-inflammatory pills during last 3 months of pregnancy because they increase the risk of bleeding. Opiates may pose risk for depressed breathing or withdrawal symptoms, slow mental and physical development if used close to delivery.
Opiate-containing codeine, morphine, demerol	Check with doctor
Tobacco	The more you smoke, the greater the risk of miscarriage, premature delivery, undersize baby, stillbirth and crib death, sudden infant death syndrome (SIDS)

Untreated illness in new mothers could lead to hospitalization and mother–child separation, deleterious for both.

The benefits of breast-feeding are well known. Breast-feeding leads to a reduction in infant morbidity and mortality. It enhances cognitive development and prevents some immunologically mediated disorders later in life. Current recommendations are that, if possible, women breast-feed their infants for at least 12 months (Ito, 2000) and these recommendations are all the more pertinent in populations of the seriously mentally ill, who are very often single mothers living in poverty and relative ill health.

Do these recommendations apply to women on psychotropic drugs? The exposure index of the infant to drugs in breast milk depends on how much milk is ingested and, as a result, how much drug concentrates in the infant's plasma. The arbitrary definition of a safe concentration is one that is less than 10% of the infant's weight-adjusted therapeutic dose (Ito, 2000). The lower the drug's rate of clearance by the infant and the higher the milk-to-maternal plasma ratio (relatively high in fat-soluble drugs like most psychotropics), the higher the exposure index. Given what we know to date, most therapeutic drugs have been judged to be relatively safe, so that mothers being treated with psychiatric drugs should not be discouraged from breast-feeding.

The exposure index of infants to antidepressant drugs (tricyclics and SSRIs) rarely reaches 10% of an infant's putative therapeutic dose, but drugs such as fluoxetine can accumulate over time and infant concentrations should be monitored. Lithium can reach high concentrations in infants' serum and adverse reactions have been reported. The American Academy of Pediatrics (1994) does not recommend its use in breast-feeding women. The use of other mood stabilizers, such as carbamazepine and valproic acid, is acceptable; the exposure index does not exceed 5% of a potential therapeutic dose. The exposure index of the newer mood stabilizers is not known but, for lamotrigine, it can apparently reach 10%, perhaps because this drug is metabolized mainly through a metabolic route called glucuronidation, a relatively slow process in the neonate (Rambeck & Wolf, 1997; Rambeck et al., 1997). Anxiolytic drugs with a long half-life (diazepam, alprazolam, clonazepam) are best avoided. Infant monitoring for potential adverse effects is advisable when the mother is taking long-acting benzodiazepines, barbiturates, gabapentin, lamotrigine, oxcarbazepine or vigabatrin. At the time of writing, there is not sufficient information about other mood stabilizers such as felbamate, tiagabine and topiramate (Bar-Oz et al., 2000). Propranolol is judged safer than other ß-blockers and, when pain alleviation is required, acetaminophen and nonsteroidal anti-inflammatory drugs are the drugs of choice during lactation. Clozapine is contraindicated both during pregnancy and lactation because of the theoretical risk of seizures and agranulocytosis in the fetus or the infant. Drugs used by the mother can also have a direct

Table 16.3. Considerations regarding drugs and lactation

Drug's entry into breast milk
Animal data regarding safety
Age of the infant
Health and hydration status of the infant
Mother's milk production
Conclusions of human studies and case reports
Changes in milk composition over time
Frequency of feedings
Frequency and timing of drug ingestion
Drug dose
Drug's half-life and other properties
Feasibility of close monitoring

effect on the production, volume, composition and ejection of milk, and may be problematic for that reason (Table 16.3) (Liston, 1998).

The main message is: it is much safer for the baby when mothers are treated for their psychiatric problems. Babies need healthy mothers. Most antidepressants, antipsychotics and antianxiety pills are safe. Breast-feeding schedules can be adjusted to minimize infant exposure to a drug (Burt *et al.*, 2001).

There are no absolutely risk-free treatment strategies for the effective treatment of psychiatric illness during pregnancy and lactation (Llwellyn *et al.*, 1998). Since over half of all pregnancies are unplanned, treatment decisions have to be made prior to pregnancy. Discussion about birth control and what will be done in case of pregnancy needs to be started early in the course of treatment. Risks/benefits of maintenance pharmacotherapy need to be thoroughly considered. If the woman intends to become pregnant, consideration should be given to avoiding novel medications whose safety in pregnancy and breast-feeding is still undetermined. All women should be prescribed extra vitamins and encouraged to eat well, to exercise and to avoid tobacco, alcohol and excessive caffeine. Herbs and natural remedies whose safety is unknown are contraindicated. All medications the woman is taking need to be considered for possible interaction effects. Personal and family history is important with respect to pregnancy and postpartum psychiatric difficulties. Premenstrual exacerbation of symptoms may foreshadow such problems. Women may need contraceptive advice and sexual counselling. To aid their decision-making, they should also be aware of the latest data on inheritance of psychiatric problems.

For women who are planning conception and who have decided to stop medication, tapering should begin 7–10 days before planned conception. Maternal drugs begin to enter the fetal circulation on day 13 postconception. Thereafter,

Table 16.4. Pregnancy treatment planning with psychiatrically ill women

Assume all women of reproductive age can become pregnant

Document birth control methods

Offer sex education programmes and discuss contraceptive options

Discourage use of tobacco, street drugs, herbal remedies, alcohol, caffeine

Check folate levels

Consider daily vitamins

Discuss pregnancy plans

Consider prepregnancy drug-risk consultation

If pregnancy has occurred and the decision is to withdraw medication, taper
gradually to prevent withdrawal reactions and start vitamins

If medication needs to be restarted because of relapse, the wisest choice may be the
original drug if it was known to be effective

Work in close collaboration with prenatal care physician

Be aware of all other medications the mother is taking

Anticipate postpartum exacerbation of symptoms

Plan for delivery of psychiatric and support services postpartum

Discuss in advance plans regarding breast-feeding, including risk/benefit of options

the pregnant mother needs to be carefully monitored and nonpharmacological treatments are to be preferred whenever possible. Table 16.4 summarizes treatment planning for psychiatric illness during pregnancy and lactation.

REFERENCES

Altshuler, L. L., Cohen, L., Szuba, M. P., Burt, V. K., Gitlin, M. & Mintz, J. (1996). Pharmacologic management of psychiatric illness during pregnancy: dilemmas and guidelines. *American Journal of Psychiatry, 153,* 592–606.

American Academy of Pediatrics, Committee on Drugs (1994). The transfer of drugs and other chemicals into human milk. *Paediatrics, 93,* 137–50.

Austin, M. P. & Mitchell, P. B. (1998). Psychotropic medications in pregnant women: treatment dilemmas. *Medical Journal of Australia, 169,* 428–31.

Bar-Oz, B., Nulman, I., Koren, G. & Ito, S. (2000). Anticonvulsants and breast-feeding: a critical review. *Paediatric Drugs, 2,* 113–26.

Baugh, C. L. & Stowe, Z. N. (1999). Treatment issues during pregnancy and lactation. *CNS Spectrums, 4,* 34–9.

Burt, V. K., Suri, R., Altschuler, L., Stowe, Z., Hendrick, V. C. & Muntean, E. (2001). The use of psychotropic medications during breast-feeding. *American Journal of Psychiatry, 158,* 1001–9.

Chisholm, F. (1999). *Women with Schizophrenia: An Assessment of Health Needs Across Life Stages.* Report to the Manitoba Schizophrenia Society.

Cohen, L. S. & Rosenbaum, J. F. (1998). Psychotropic drug use during pregnancy: weighing the risks. *Journal of Clinical Psychiatry*, *59* (Suppl. 2), 18–28.

Collaborative Group on Drug Use in Pregnancy (1992). Medication during pregnancy: an intercontinental cooperative study. *International Journal of Gynaecology and Obstetrics*, *39*, 185–96.

Goldstein, D. J., Corbin, L. A. & Fung, M. C. (2000). Olanzapine-exposed pregnancies and lactation: early experience. *Journal of Clinical Psychopharmacology*, *20*, 399–403.

Ito, S. (2000). Drug therapy for breast-feeding women. *New England Journal of Medicine*, *343*, 118–26.

Klein, D. F., Skrobala, A. M. & Garfinkel, R. S. (1995). Preliminary look at the effects of pregnancy on the course of panic disorder. *Anxiety*, *1*, 227–32.

Koren, G., Pastuszak, A. & Ito, S. (1998). Drugs in pregnancy. *New England Journal of Medicine*, *338*, 1128–37.

Kumar, R. & Robson, K. M. (1984). A prospective study of emotional disorders in childbearing women. *British Journal of Psychiatry*, *144*, 35–47.

Liston, J. (1998). Breastfeeding and the use of recreational drugs – alcohol, caffeine, nicotine and marijuana. *Breastfeeding Review*, *6*, 27–30.

Llwellyn, A., Stowe, Z. N. & Strader, J. R. (1998). The use of lithium and management of women with bipolar disorder during pregnancy and lactation. *Journal of Clinical Psychiatry*, *59*, (Suppl. 6), 57–64.

Miller, L. J. (1994). Psychiatric medication during pregnancy: understanding and minimizing the risks. *Psychiatric Annals*, *24*, 69–75.

Neziroglu, F., Anemone, R. & Yaryura, T. J. A. (1992). Onset of obsessive-compulsive disorder in pregnancy. *American Journal of Psychiatry*, *149*, 947–50.

Rambeck, B. & Wolf, P. (1997). Lamotrigine clinical pharmacokinetics. *Clinical Pharmacokinetics*, *25*, 433–43.

Rambeck, B., Kurlemann, G., Stodieck, S. R., May, T. W. & Jurgens, U. (1997). Concentrations of lamotrigine in a mother on lamotrigine treatment and her newborn child. *European Journal of Clinical Pharmacology*, *51*, 481–4.

Roughton, E. C., Schneider, M. L., Bromley, L. J. & Coe, C. L. (1998). Maternal endocrine activation during pregnancy alters neurobehavioral state in primate infants. *American Journal of Occupational Therapy*, *52*, 90–8.

Samren, E. B., van Duijn, C. M., Christiaens, G. C., Hofman, A. & Lindhout, D. (1999). Antiepileptic drug regimens and major congenital abnormalities in the offspring. *Annals of Neurology*, *46*, 739–46.

17

Social work issues

David Clodman

Centre for Addiction and Mental Health, Toronto, Canada

Introduction

This chapter is written from the perspective of a mental health social worker serving women diagnosed with schizophrenia. The Women's Clinic in which I work operates out of the Center for Addiction and Mental Health, Toronto, Canada. It offers assessment and individual and group treatment, with a special focus on women who are mothers (Seeman & Cohen, 1998).

Clinic participants come from varying backgrounds and present with a range of needs and experiences. Importantly, they vary in their awareness of the degree to which mental illness has compromised their ability to perform adequately as parents. The connection between acknowledgement of illness, adherence to a medication regime, participation in a treatment programme and maintenance of child custody is self-evident to some and not at all to others.

Some refuse to take medication because they are not convinced they are ill. Some understand that they require treatment in order to prevent recurrence of acute mental illness, but do not make the connection between illness exacerbation and the need for the child to be taken into state custody. As a social worker, I am often caught between the immediate best interests of the child and the crucial importance to the ill mother of retaining a close parental bond with her child.

In the Province of Ontario, the Family and Child Services Act provides the legal mandate for Child Welfare Agencies to either monitor or apprehend (remove) a child from parents or caregivers under specified conditions (Province of Ontario, Child and Family Services Act, 1990); the best interests of the child normally trump the rights of parents. This puts mentally ill mothers at a great disadvantage. At the time point at which Children's Aid raises questions about their ability to parent, many such mothers are in the midst of difficult personal and/or legal issues involving severed relationships with their child's father or with their family of origin or with the mental health system. They may be homeless, or on the move from one highly unstable residential situation to another, often without the financial support of a reliable disability income. As previously reported many have come to the attention of the mental health system only long after their social lives have deteriorated and they have been left without formal or informal supports, and without treatment for their mental illness. They are burdened with significant health and socioeconomic problems (Mowbray *et al.*, 1995). They may be weary and mistrustful of service providers' attempts to intervene or assist. As a social worker, my job is to enhance access to services and to help the extended family become reinvolved with the client. I try to work in collaboration with child welfare agencies but, as the following vignette illustrates, the goals of the two systems, child welfare and adult mental health, differ.

Case example: Linda
(Details in this vignette have been altered to protect client anonymity).

Linda, a mother of three, is admitted to the Women's Clinic at age 40, having first been diagnosed with schizophrenia at 25. She has a long history of noncompliance with treatment. She agrees to participation in the clinic but does not believe she has a mental illness. She believes her severe deficits in organization and functioning (which she recognizes) are caused by the stress of her three children being in foster care.

Her children's placement resulted from a child welfare social worker visiting her home and finding a significantly disorganized mother, no food in the household, and faeces throughout the house. Upon further investigation, child welfare decided to apprehend (remove) the children and requested a parenting capacity assessment for Linda. The parenting capacity assessor referred Linda to the Women's Clinic for treatment of flagrant psychotic symptoms.

Linda views the apprehending child welfare worker with suspicion and anger. She talks of killing the social worker who took her children. She cannot understand why her children were apprehended. She maintains that the smell of urine and faeces was there because washroom facilities in the apartment were not working. She tentatively agrees to treatment, hoping that it will expedite her regaining custody, but is very hesitant about providing personal information to the treatment team in case it is shared with the child welfare agency and the courts.

Linda is allowed visits with her children but is closely supervised because of concern over her potential violence. All efforts by the agency to place limits on behaviour considered inappropriate during the visits is met with verbal aggression and physical resistance. Linda does not trust the child welfare professionals. She does not believe they have the interests of the children at heart but, rather, that they are being deliberately cruel because they perceive her as mentally ill. She feels that they will never believe her capable of being a competent parent. This makes her verbally abusive which, in turn, leads the child welfare agency to view her as unable, or unwilling, to work cooperatively with them. Linda's frustration is further fuelled by her inability to obtain housing suitable for herself and her children. Housing authorities insist that she first have custody of the children before they consider her application. Linda, on the other hand, believes that the major reason why she doesn't have her children is because she does not have an appropriate place to live.

The agency requests the Women's Clinic team's assistance in supervising a visit between Linda and her children, thinking that she might be more trusting of the team than of the child welfare agency, which turns out to be so. During the visit we co-supervise, Linda presents her children with written materials which address religious questions about life and death that both clinic and agency staff consider inappropriate for children of that age. She prohibits her children from answering questions put to them. She directs the children to say that she is not mentally ill. Throughout the visit, Linda remains extremely focused on her own fears, suspicions and preoccupations and, because of this, appears unable to address her children's age-appropriate needs. For this visit, she has purchased food, gifts and materials for her children to play with. Her intent is to impress us with her love for the children, but it produces the opposite effect. Since she herself is homeless, it only demonstrates that her judgement about what to spend money on is grossly impaired.

Linda agrees to participate in a parent support group, one of the therapeutic programmes offered by the Women's Clinic (For information about other parent groups with this population please see Chapter 6 by Cowling, and Rubovitz (1996)). She brings up the confidentiality question and is told that all attempts will be made to protect her confidentiality with respect to her treatment, including what is said in the group. She is, however, warned that there are limits to confidentiality and that, if the court subpoenas the clinical record, I cannot, beyond strongly recommending against it, prevent the record being read into the court proceedings.

During the groups, Linda presents herself as a person who does not require assistance with parenting and who cannot benefit from the contributions of other members of the group. She refuses to openly acknowledge her personal vulnerable situation: her children are in the care of a child welfare agency, she is undergoing a parenting capacity assessment, and her mental functioning is unstable. It is unclear from her participation in the group whether her lack of insight prevents her from sharing experiences and fears with the other group members, or if she deliberately chooses not to because it can be used against her in court. It is never clear whether she totally trusts her treatment providers.

Linda's mother attends some of the clinic visits and plays a mediating role between Linda and the child welfare agency. We hope she can assume custody of the children, but her own circumstances prevent her from doing so. Since there appears to be no other viable option, the parental capacity assessor recommends that the custody of all three children be permanently transferred to the state. As soon as the court decision goes against her, Linda stops attending the clinic. This premature ending of the treatment contract leaves me, as her social worker, disappointed and helpless. Hope for regaining custody would have, in all likelihood, kept Linda in treatment longer and it is possible that she could have, with time, improved sufficiently to be able to parent her children effectively.

Implications of the case example

In the presence or under the scrutiny of child welfare workers, Linda denied all emotional trouble, exactly the wrong strategy if her aim was to regain child custody. She was unable, or unwilling, at those times, to recognize the close link between her untreated mental illness, her behaviour and the subsequent concerns on the part of child welfare agencies for the well-being of her children. And yet, in individual counselling, Linda often made this connection. My frustration was sympathizing with Linda's wish to regain custody, knowing that she was trying to do so in a round-about way which ended up working against her, understanding her anger and mistrust of the child welfare agency, understanding her plight vis-à-vis the housing authority, wishing that her family could come to her aid, realizing how very ill Linda was and, at the same time, knowing she could get better with treatment, treatment which she refused because she refused, most of the time, to see herself as ill.

The clinical vignette highlights Linda's priorities. Mothers whose children have been apprehended place the return of their children first on their priority list, often at the expense of their own health needs. From their point of view, the children have been wrongly taken from them. Their prime concern is to prove that they are not mentally ill. Consequently, they deny illness and refuse treatment. The more they refuse treatment, the more convinced the child welfare agency is that they are unfit parents. In this case, my role as mediator was not sufficient to overcome the fundamental misunderstanding between the mother and the child welfare agency.

As many children of a parent diagnosed with schizophrenia, one of Linda's children was developmentally delayed from birth. The relevance of this to issues of custody is that some mothers appear to be bad parents not because of their own inherent faults but because the child in question is intrinsically vulnerable. Child welfare agencies may attribute a child's difficulties solely to a mother's poor parenting. This is unfair to the 'good enough' or adequate mother. From a social work perspective, this illustrates the significant power imbalance between mother and child welfare agency. The agency view of the situation becomes the correct view even though there may be other explanations for what they observe.

Another frustration for the social worker is the misfortune of treatment offered too late. With earlier treatment and interventions that supported Linda in her role as parent, there would have been a better chance to prevent Linda's mental health from deteriorating to the point that her home became unfit for her children. An earlier referral for treatment could have been initiated by Linda's mother, by Linda's family physician or by the children's school. Earlier treatment could have provided, for instance, an opportunity for her children to be registered in a day-care programme. They would have been exposed to healthier caregivers, less bizarre behaviour and more opportunities for healthy socialization, and these would have assisted with their emotional development whether or not they were reared by their mother. With day care for her children, the burden of being a single parent struggling with a mental illness would have eased for Linda and the custody decision might have been different.

Parent and service provider perceptions of the child welfare agency

In contrast to Linda, there are mothers in the Women's Clinic who view the child welfare agency as a positive and supportive presence in their lives and in the lives of their children. They feel that the agency can assist with the challenging and sometimes overwhelming tasks of parenting, particularly when they themselves become acutely mentally ill. These mothers are able to make active use of resources and assistance offered to them by child welfare professionals. But other mothers, as illustrated by the case of Linda, have difficulty accepting the authority of the child welfare agency. The social worker, in identifying with his client, is easily persuaded by the intensity of the client's emotions and requires assistance in maintaining an objective stance. This is facilitated through team discussion and supervision.

It is often difficult to determine why some mothers in the Women's Clinic are able to trust the child welfare professionals while others are not. Like Linda, many mothers speak of their perception that simply having a mental illness makes them more vulnerable to their children being apprehended. Some are reluctant to ask child welfare professionals questions about their child's development or share their worries for fear that they will be labelled as incompetent parents and have their children taken away (Blanch *et al.*, 1994).

These mothers point to the need to educate child welfare professionals about the nature of mental illness. Their hope is that they will be given the benefit of the doubt, and that they will be able to have normal aspects of their experiences and skills validated (Nicholson *et al.*, 1996). Participating in the education of child welfare professionals is an important aspect of the social worker's role. One-to-one personal contacts provide the opportunity to enhance trust, to identify some of the issues mentioned above, and to address them at an interpersonal working level. With consent from the client, holding a joint meeting for all participating services such as child welfare, psychiatry, public health nursing, family physician, lawyers for the client and for the child, allows each service to articulate their viewpoint. Ideally, the client attends the meeting. This provides an opportunity to discuss how services for the client can be integrated. It also provides an opportunity to anticipate inter-agency problems and resolve them when they arise.

The Women's Clinic has provided training sessions and written materials with reading lists to child welfare professionals in an effort to educate workers about mental illness. Such training sessions need to be repeated as agency staff change. Inviting child welfare professionals to conferences in the mental health system and vice versa expands the knowledge and understanding discussion of both systems. Attendance and depositions of mental health professionals at child custody hearings serve a similar function.

There are several ethical questions that this work poses for the social worker. Mothers who are in psychiatric treatment and also involved with child welfare agencies are routinely asked to sign permission for the two services to communicate with one another. Are severely mentally ill mothers capable of giving informed consent for information about their treatment to be shared with the child welfare agency when the agency has taken custody of their children? Do they understand the implications of such consent or, for that matter, the implications of withholding it? They are routinely expected to cooperate with the child welfare agency and, at the same time, to engage in legal proceedings that put them in an adversarial position vis-à-vis the same agency. Do these mothers have the required skills to engage cooperatively with an agency that has taken their child, and to simultaneously be a nonwilling participant in an adversarial court system? No one educates these mothers with respect to the function of the complex systems they become involved with. Whose role is it to ensure that they understand how the child welfare and court systems function? Mentally ill mothers are stigmatized. Are current efforts to educate child welfare and mental health professionals successful at reducing the stigma? The various service systems are often working at cross purposes. When social workers from mental health and child welfare are providing service to one family, what is the best method of integrating services of the same profession across two service systems? Since each system has a different definition for a successful outcome, what implications does this have for service integration or collaboration among agencies? For relevant information and further discussion on these important topics, the reader is referred to the literature (Bailey & Koney, 1996; Bardach, 1996; Campbell, 1999; Gray, 1985; Kahn & Kamerman, 1992; Konrad, 1996; Meyers, 1993; Mulroy & Shay, 1997; O'Looney, 1994; Sandfort, 1999; Waldfogel, 1997).

Two systems at odds

Mothers such as Linda are being asked by child welfare professionals to demonstrate their ability to parent, often while they are acutely ill. It is not always an easy task for child welfare professionals to communicate expectations of exactly what mothers like Linda are required to do, if indeed there is anything they can do, in order to secure the return of their children. The child welfare professionals' activities are directed by timing guidelines as set out in child welfare legislation and policy. These society-imposed responsibilities and timing restrictions limit the mother's visits with her children and the mother's involvement in her children's care. They are not an intentional attempt by the child welfare agency to wear away at the parental identity of mothers but that is how they are experienced. Social workers attempt to assist mothers such as Linda to accept the mandate of the child welfare agency and the authority of its staff while, at the same time, permitting the healthy expression of frustration and resentment.

Treatment facilities such as the Women's Clinic see treatment for psychosis as their mandate. The time required before the mother can respond and make optimum use of treatment is often longer than the time frame within which the child welfare system operates. As in the case of Linda, the mother may not yet have attained her optimal benefit from treatment at the point when the child welfare system has rendered a final decision about the care and custody of her child.

As depicted in the case vignette, the mother may withdraw from the mental health system if she loses custody because her main, if not sole, motivation for treatment is to retain or regain custody rights. The loss of custody confirms her belief that the world is not to be trusted. When she loses custody, she is left without the support of either of the two service systems. Child welfare and mental health systems do not currently have coordinated policies or practices in place to deter mothers such as Linda from withdrawing from services at such a vulnerable and critical time in their lives.

At the front line social work level, providing services to mothers diagnosed with schizophrenia involves balancing professional responsibilities. We have a mandate to provide treatment to the mothers and to focus on their needs. We also have legal and ethical responsibilities to report children at risk and to consider our services' impact on their risk for emotional harm. We have a desire to assist mothers in coping with the stigma of mental illness, and with its frequent interference with their wish to fulfil roles of their choice, while using their capabilities to the utmost.

Schizophrenia is a disabling illness that impedes a mother's intent to improve her parenting skills. Since the obstacles that these mothers encounter on a daily basis only intensify their handicap and prevent fulfilment of their roles as mothers, it is not always easy to determine whether parenting difficulties are based on psychiatric impairment or lack of societal understanding, or a combination of both. Helping these women to navigate services, educating where knowledge of mental illness is lacking, and accepting responsibility for playing a role in the perpetuation of barriers to system collaboration is an important role for the social worker.

Conclusion

This chapter has addressed a major challenge for social workers providing mental health services to mothers with serious mental illness. When seeking access or custody of their children, these mothers are caught between two service systems with differing legal mandates, values and guidelines. Social workers are also caught between their allegiances to both systems. Recommendations for bridging the differences and integrating the systems are provided.

REFERENCES

Bailey, D. & Koney, K. M. (1996). Interorganizational community based collaboratives: A strategic response to shape the social work agenda. *Social Work, 41,* 602–11.

Bardach, E. (1996). Turf barriers to interagency collaboration. In *The State of Public Management,* ed. D. F. Kettl & M. H. Brinton, pp. 168–91. Baltimore, MD: Johns Hopkins University Press.

Blanch, A. K., Nicholson, J. & Purcell, J. (1994). Parents with severe mental illness: the need for human service integration *Journal of Mental Health Administration, 21,* 388–96.

Campbell, L. (1999). Collaboration: Building inter-agency networks for practice partnerships. In *Children of Parents with Mental Illness,* ed. V. Cowling, pp. 203–11. Melbourne: Australian Council for Educational Research.

Gray, B. (1985). Conditions facilitating interorganizational collaboration. *Human Relations, 38,* 911–36.

Kahn, A. J. & Kamerman, S. B. (1992). *Integrating Services Integration: An Overview of Initiatives, Issues and Possiblities.* Discussion paper. New York: Columbia University School of Public Health, National Center for Children in Poverty.

Konrad, E. L. (1996). A multidimensional framework for conceptualizing services integration initiatives. *New Directions for Evaluation, 69,* 5–19.

Meyers, M. K. (1993). Organizational factors in the integration of services for children. *Social Service Review, 67,* 547–75.

Mowbray, C., Oyserman, D., Zemencuk, J. & Ross, S. R. (1995). Motherhood for women with serious mental illness. *American Journal of Orthopsychiatry, 65,* 21–38.

Mulroy, E. A. & Shay, S. (1997). Non profit organizations and innovation: a model of neighbourhood- based collaboration to prevent child maltreatment. *Social Work, 42,* 515–24.

Nicholson, J., Geller, J. L. & Fisher, W. H. (1996). Sylvia Frumkin has a baby: a case study for policymakers. *Psychiatric Services, 47,* 497–501.

O'Looney, J. (1994). Modelling collaboration and social services integration: a single state's experience with developmental and non-developmental models. *Administration in Social Work, 18,* 61–86.

Province of Ontario, Child and Family Services Act, Revised Statutes of Ontario, Chapter c. 11, Amended by: 1992, c. 32, s. 3; 1993, c. 27 Sched.; 1994, c. 27, s. 43 (2); 1996, c. 2 s. 62; 1999, c. 2, ss. 1–35, 1999, c. 6, s. 6; 1999, c. 12 Sched. E, s. 1; 1999, c. 12 Sched. G, s. 16; 2001, c. 13, s. 5., Toronto, Queen's Printer, 2001.

Rubovitz, P. (1996). Project CHILD: An intervention programme for psychotic mothers and their young children. In *Parental Psychiatric Disorder: Distressed Parents and their Families,* ed. M. Göpfert, J. Webster & M. V. Seeman, pp. 161–9. Cambridge: Cambridge University Press.

Sandfort, J. (1999). The structural impediments to human service collaboration: examining welfare reform at the front lines. *Social Service Review, 73,* 314–39.

Seeman, M. & Cohen, R. (1998). A service for women with schizophrenia. *Psychiatric Services, 49,* 674–7.

Waldfogel, J. (1997). The new wave of service integration. *Social Service Review, 103,* 463–84.

18

Parental psychiatric disorder and the law: the American case

Colby C. Brunt

Washington Street, Boston, USA

Introduction

The legal rights of parents with mental illness in the United States vary from state to state. The following chapter examines the current federal and state laws in the United States regarding termination of parental rights, custody and visitation in cases involving a parent with mental illness. The final section of this chapter gives recommendations for attorneys and advocates who are working with mentally ill parents.

Recent studies have indicated that parents who are diagnosed with a mental illness too often lose custody of their children, either to another party or to the state. One study found that 70–80% of parents with mental illness lost custody of their children.[1] This added prospect of the loss of custody may also contribute to additional mental health problems for the parent. Many such parents try, unsuccessfully, to navigate a complex and confusing legal system on their own because of their inability to afford counsel. If a parent cannot afford to hire a private attorney or cannot get an attorney from their local legal aid office, typically, they must represent themselves in these very complicated and emotional hearings. It is only in termination of parental rights proceedings that parents are generally granted appointed counsel to be paid for by the state. Without effective counsel, many of these parents will certainly lose custody of their children and may even lose the right to visit their children.

Termination of parental rights

One of the most extreme infringements of individual rights is the intrusion by the state into a parent's right to raise their child. Although there is a special nature to parental rights that is recognized by law with special due process guarantees so that 'states may not lightly terminate parents' relationships with their children',[2] parents with mental illness still lose custody of their children to the state far too often. The United States Supreme Court has held that the rights to conceive and to raise one's children are essential,[3] that they are basic civil rights of man,[4] and that these rights are 'far more precious . . . than property rights'.[5] In the case of *Santosky v. Kramer*, the United States Supreme Court clarified the standard, i.e. best interests of the child, by which a determination of a parent's right to raise his or her child must be based. A court can take away that right only after establishing parental unfitness: '[u]ntil the State proves parental unfitness, the child and his parents share a vital interest in preventing erroneous termination of their natural relationship. Thus, at the fact-finding, the interests of the child and his natural parents coincide . . .'.[6] Therefore, parents and children are initially presumed to share an interest in the integrity of the family.

Federal law

In the interests of children, congress passed a federal law, the Adoption and Safe Family Act (ASFA), to provide a uniform timeline within which a state must act in cases of parental termination.[7] Under the ASFA there must be a permanency hearing within 30 days of a 'no reunification services' decision or no more than 12 months after the child has been placed in foster care.[8] Studies have shown that parents with mental illness are often unable to meet all the requirements in their reunification service plans in the time required and that the ASFA can make the process of reuniting families when a parent is mentally ill more difficult.[9] These difficulties may arise due to hospitalization, medication changes or transportation problems for the parent. While the main objective of the ASFA is to protect children and to promote their best interests, parents, especially mentally ill parents, may, in the process, be overlooked (see Göpfert *et al.*, Chapter 5; Clodman, Chapter 17; Weir, Chapter 19).

State law

Although there is federal law that addresses termination of parental rights proceedings, it is the state courts that have jurisdiction over these matters. In the United States, federal laws like the ASFA constitute baselines for state laws. This means that states cannot give lesser protections to parents than those given by federal law, and many states have provided further protections for parents either through legislative or case law. The following cases are illustrative.

'Harm to the child'

One of the key elements that the state must prove in order to terminate parental rights is harm to the child by the parent. In the case of *In the Interests of DLM*, the Appeals Court of Missouri specifically addressed the issue of harm to a child by a parent with mental illness.[10] The court stated that '[u]nlike neglect, abandonment, abuse, or nonsupport, the mental illness of a parent is not per se harmful to a child'.[11] In this case, the state initiated a proceeding to terminate the mother's parental rights due to her mental illness, failure to take medications and psychiatric hospitalizations.

The court held that 'termination of parental rights should not be granted on account of mental illness unless it is shown by clear, cogent, and convincing evidence that [the child] is harmed or is likely to be harmed in the future'.[12] Furthermore, the court held that the 'focus should be on the ability of the mother to care for [the child] and her ability to maintain a parental relationship with [the child], which would not be harmful to [the child]'.[13]

The record from the trial court reflected that the mother had worked to meet all the requirements from the state social services office and that she was prepared to seek assistance when necessary. Witnesses testified that the mother would place the child with a friend or family member whenever she had to be hospitalized, and, as well, that the mother's depression had been intensified by the ongoing litigation process involving her daughter.[14] The court further noted that there was evidence that the mother repeatedly tried to regain custody of her daughter, that she complied with the service plan,[15] and that she had a strong bond with her daughter.[16] For these reasons, the court reversed the judgement of the trial court and denied the Division of Family Services' request for a petition to terminate.

'Inability to care for the child'

Although harm is the main issue, inability to care for a child, if shown, may also constitute grounds for termination of parental rights. The New Hampshire Supreme Court case of *In re John and Jane Doe* was a termination of parental rights case where both parents suffered from a mental illness.[17] In this case, the court held that the mother's parental rights were improperly terminated based on the reliance that the mother had a personality disorder and therefore was unable to properly care for the minor children. The court referred to the governing New Hampshire statute on this issue and stated that the statute provides for 'the termination of parental rights, not because of particular parental conduct, but because of a parent's condition, i.e., mental illness or mental deficiency'.[18] The court then framed the issue before it as: "whether such mental illness renders the parents incapable of giving proper parental care and protection for a longer period of time than would be wise or prudent".[19] The court concluded that the mother's parental rights should not be terminated and that the probate court must make explicit findings, supported by the record, as to the detrimental effect of the parent's mental illness on the child.[20]

The North Carolina Court of Appeals reached a similar conclusion in the case of *In re Small*.[21] The court reversed the lower court's termination of the mother's parental rights because there was not clear and convincing evidence that the mother was unable to care for her children. The court looked to the case of *In re Scott,*[22] which held that the mother's parental rights were improperly terminated for lack of clear and convincing evidence that the mother's mental illness prevented her from properly caring for her child. In its opinion, the court in *In re Small* specifically noted that the *In re Scott* decision stated that the fact that someone carries a diagnosis of personality disorder 'does not mean that they are incapable of raising children'.[23] In reaching its final conclusion, the court examined the testimony and evidence presented at the lower level and determined that, although the mother in this case was unable to protect the children from her now-deceased husband, there was no clear and convincing evidence that she could not presently care for the children.

Ability to care may be impaired by the severity of mental illness but this should not be used to discriminate against parents with illnesses that they cannot control. In the case of *In re Neblett,* the Circuit Court of Virginia ruled that the parents had not failed to do anything that they are physically or mentally able to do.[24] In that case, the mother had cerebral palsy and mental retardation, and the father had schizophrenia and physical ailments. The court held that the parents were not at fault for their ailments and that the state had not met its burden of showing that the parents had failed to remedy the situation '*without good cause*'. The court took into account that the parents had done everything required of them by the Department of Social Services, that their illnesses were not within their control, and that a clear bond existed between the parents and their children.

'Present mental condition'

Potentially counteracting harm and inability to care, is the nature of the parent's present mental condition. The New York case of *In re Hime* gives some guidance on this issue.[25] The court stated that prediction of future harm alone could not suffice as clear and convincing evidence that the parent–child relationship should be terminated. The court stated that although, in some cases, past and present actions may be so telling as to be able to predict future inability to care for a child, these 'inferences alone cannot serve as the clear and convincing proof required for termination of the parental relationship in the present case . . .'. The court held that the testimony of the court-appointed psychiatrist could not support a termination based on possible future harm when the doctor testified that the mother may, at some point, be able to care for the child with proper therapy and medication management.

Americans with Disabilities Act

The application of the Americans with Disabilities Act (ADA) is currently one of the most heavily contested areas of United States domestic law. Many state appellate courts are being asked to consider whether the ADA is applicable to termination of parental rights cases. This issue will most likely need to be addressed by the United States Supreme Court in the future because, as the state decisions cited below will show, there is a clear divide as to the application of the ADA to these cases.

Like the ASFA, the ADA is a federal act that applies to all states. The ADA, which was enacted in 1990, is to provide 'a clear and comprehensive mandate for the elimination of discrimination against individuals with disabilities'.[26] It was the intent of the Federal Legislature to provide people with disabilities protection under the law, and allow for the ADA to act as a baseline for the state laws. The ADA specifically provides that nothing in the act shall be construed to invalidate or limit the remedies of any law of any state or jurisdiction that provides greater or equal protection for the rights of individuals with disabilities than are afforded them by the ADA.[27] It is Title II of the ADA that is at the centre of the controversy with respect to termination of parental rights proceedings. Under Title II, 'no qualified individual with a disability shall, by reason of such disability, be excluded from participation in or be denied the benefits of the services, programs, or activities of a public entity, or be subjected to discrimination by such entity ... '.[28] The question that is before many state courts is whether the ADA can be used as a defence to a termination of parental rights when one, or both of the biological parents suffers from a mental illness.

The state appellate courts have reached various conclusions as to the application of the ADA to termination of parental rights and what remedies parents have if they believe the social services agency did not comply with the ADA. The Texas Court of Appeals held that the ADA is an affirmative defence to a petition to terminate parental rights and that it must be raised at the trial level to avoid it being waived as a defence.[29] The Michigan Court of Appeals also held that the ADA requires a public agency, like a state social services agency, to make reasonable accommodations for individuals with disabilities and that the reunification services and programmes by the state agency 'must comply with the ADA'.[30] Similar to the conclusions of these above-mentioned cases, the Indiana Court of Appeals held that once an 'agency opts to provide services ... the provision of those services must be in compliance with the ADA'.[31]

Other states have held that the ADA does not apply to termination of parental rights cases because termination proceedings do not qualify as a service, programme or activity under the ADA. In the recent Massachusetts case, *Adoption of Gregory*, the court held that the ADA did not apply to termination of parental rights proceedings because they were not 'services, programs, or activities'.[32] The court further noted the state is required under the ADA and Massachusetts law to accommodate parents with special needs in its provision of services *prior* to a termination proceeding.

In addition to holding that termination of parental rights proceedings are not services, programmes or activities under the ADA, the court in *Adoption of Gregory* further remarked that to apply the ADA to these proceedings would subordinate the rights of the child to those of the parents. The case of *J. T. v. Arkansas Department of Human Services* also held that the parents' rights under the ADA must be subordinated to the protected interests of the child because the focus of all juvenile court proceedings is the 'best interests of the child'.[33] Other states have followed the same reasoning, which many would argue is in direct conflict with the United States Supreme Court decision in *Santosky v. Kramer*, which held that a parent and child are presumed to share an interest in staying together until the parent is deemed 'unfit'.[34]

Child custody disputes

One of the most difficult tasks for a Probate and Family Court judge is to determine which of the two or more disputing parties would best serve the best interests of the child with respect to physical and legal custody. Physical custody is defined as the child's primary residence. Legal custody is defined by which parent has the legal authority and responsibility for making major decisions (educational, religious, medical) for the child.[35] All states have held that it is within the trial court's discretion to allocate parental custody.

As in termination of parental rights, the standard for determining custody and visitation is the 'best interest of the child' standard. Although, in many states, there is the presumption that the primary caretaker should retain custody, in practice, this presumption does not always hold. Many times, a primary caregiver parent with a diagnosed mental illness may be asked to prove his or her fitness as a parent in order to retain custody.

The 'best interests of the child' standard

Since the 1970s, the predominate standard for determining custody and visitation has been the 'best interest of the child' standard. Currently, all states have statutes and/or case law that provides guidance on what defines the 'best interests' of a child, but many times the standard is unclear and arbitrary. In the case of *Garska v. McCoy*, the West Virginia Supreme Court held that the best interests of the child are presumptively satisfied when the primary caregiver is awarded custody of the minor child, as long as he or she is considered a 'fit parent'.[36] The ten factors to be used to determine primary caregiver status were: (1) preparing and planning of meals; (2) bathing, grooming and dressing; (3) purchasing, cleaning and care of clothes; (4) medical care; (5) arranging social interaction among peers after school; (6) arranging alternative care; (7) putting the child to bed at night, attending to child in middle of the night, waking the child in the morning; (8) disciplining; (9) educating; and (10) teaching elementary skills. The court in *Garska* adopted the primary caretaker presumption for three main reasons: (1) to prevent children from being 'pawns' in the custody battle; (2) to provide judges with a predetermined formula for deciding custody cases; and (3) to help promote settlement of these cases.[37]

Parental fitness

In addition to a 'best interests' determination, the judge must look at the fitness of the parties. Unlike the primary caregiver analysis, parental fitness, especially when mental illness may be an issue, is not as clear. Although there is case law that states that a parent is not presumptively unfit just because he or she suffers from a mental illness, in practice, the burden is often shifted to such parents who must prove their fitness. West Virginia Supreme Court Chief Justice Starcher best summarized this problem in a dissenting opinion in a case that denied custody to a mother, who was the primary caretaker of the children, but who also was alleged to suffer from a mental illness. Chief Justice Starcher stated, '[i]n my opinion, this case shows that . . . the stigma of mental illness [is] still a weakness in our court system'.[38]

In *Willey v. Willey* the issue was whether the trial was correct in denying the mother custody, and granting her visitation rights at the discretion of the father.[39] The Iowa Supreme Court ultimately ruled that the custody determination was proper, but the visitation ruling was improper. The court stated that: '[t]he appeal places before us the most difficult and perplexing problem involved in custody cases – that of whether one of the parties has a mental illness and, if so, whether it will be for the child's best interest to grant that parent custody or give him or her any visitation rights to that child'.[40]

In determining what would be in the best interest of the minor child, the court examined all the evidence presented at trial, including the expert medical testimony and the past living arrangement. Although the court decided that the mother should not be awarded custody, the court stated that this decision was not based on the mere fact that the mother may have been suffering from a mental illness.[41] The court held that '[s]light mental illness, or an arrested case in one found to be mentally ill, will not per se disqualify that person as a proper custodian of children'.[42] The court further noted that it is 'true that few persons do not at some time exhibit traits or feelings that depart from the norm, and to deny custody of a child to a good and loving parent on that basis would be unjust if not ridiculous'.[43]

Two examples of statutory law addressing this issue can be found in the Tennessee and Illinois codes. Both codes state that, in determining the best interests for a child in a custody case, the judge must look at the '*mental* and physical health' of parents,[44] or all parties involved.[45] In the case of *Lombaer v. Lombaer*, the appellate court of Illinois reversed and remanded the trial court's decision to deny custody to a mother with mental illness because of the lower court's failure to consider the statutory factors in regards to parental fitness.[46] The court also stated that the trial court primarily based its decision on the mother's failure to take medication and that on remand the trial court should take into consideration, along with the enumerated factors, which parent was the primary caregiver of the children.[47]

Effect of custodial disputes on emotional health

Some courts have made specific mention of the stress and anxiety induced by custodial conflict. In the case of *Laznovsky v. Laznovsky*, the Maryland Court of Appeals recognized the emotional level of domestic relations cases and the toll they can take by stating that '[t]he marital discord which precedes divorce and custody actions is often of such an emotional nature as to lead one or both parties to seek professional psychiatric counseling in attempting to restructure their lives'.[48] Additionally, the Maryland Court of Appeals noted that the dependent spouse, typically the wife, is the one who faces the greatest changes through the litigation process.[49] The court remarked that '[t]he desire for psychiatric consultation during this transition is understandable, and it is our feeling that such efforts should not be used against one in custody proceedings . . . '.[50] The court's holding in *Laznovsky* demonstrates the belief that parents, regardless of whether they suffer from a mental illness, should be able to seek counselling if needed without it adversely affecting the custody determination.

The case of *Severson v. Hansen* also addressed the issue of the high stress level of these proceedings and the bias against parents with mental illness in custody determinations.[51] In the *Severson* case, the North Dakota Supreme Court held that the minor child should remain in the custody of the parent who did not have a diagnosed mental illness, upholding the trial court's decision that this was in the best interest of the child. In a concurring opinion, Justice Levine wrote on the issue of gender bias and the perception of mental illness. Justice Levine noted that the trial court related the father's anger to the stress of the ongoing litigation, but related the mother's anger 'not to the tension and stress of the custody dispute or the break-up of the marriage or the fear of losing custody, but to '*hysteria*'.[52] Justice Levine also referred to the testimony of the doctor who examined the mother, who stated that 'women in child custodies [sic] will come across as disturbed. Maybe not often, but a significant amount of time and there's concern [about] what that means and how it is interpreted or misinterpreted'.[53] Justice Levine then concluded the opinion by stating that '[a] custody dispute can be a very stressful time for everyone. The anger and emotion, or repression of them, exhibited by the parties ought to be viewed and evaluated by experts in the context they are expressed'.[54]

Visitation rights

Most courts have held that visitation, or parenting time, is a right of the noncustodial parent, and should only be denied in extreme cases. The *Willey* case stated that '[t]he rule is well established in all jurisdictions that the right of access to one's child should not be denied unless the *court* is convinced such visitations are detrimental to the best interests of the child'.[55] Similar to the standard for custody determinations, the 'best interests of the child' is the controlling standard in most jurisdictions and, therefore, the burden of proving that visitation with the noncustodial parent may be harmful is placed on the custodial parent.[56]

The Tennessee Court of Appeals in *White v. White* stated that a noncustodial parent has the right to visitation 'as will enable the child and the non-custodial parent to maintain a parent–child relationship unless the court finds, after a hearing, that visitation is likely to endanger the child's physical or emotional health'.[57] The court further stated that '[t]he right to visit one's child is, for a non-custodial parent, the paramount parental right'. In the case of *Surrey v. Surrey*, the District of Columbia Court of Appeals held that the mother should not be denied the right of visitation solely on the basis of her mental illness. The court stated that '[e]ven if the mother is mentally ill, this would not ipso facto deprive her of the privilege of seeing her children'.[58] The court noted that the noncustodial parent is presumed fit for visitation and the custodial parent has the burden of proving that the contact between the noncustodial parent and the child would be detrimental and not in the child's best interests. The court held that a determination of whether visitation is in the best interests of the child must be based on the noncustodial parent's present mental condition, and not rely on past actions of the noncustodial parent.[59]

The court may also impose the burden on the mentally ill parent to prove that he or she can have visitation time *alone* with their child. In *Fine v. Fine*, the Supreme Court of Nebraska affirmed the trial court's order for supervised visits based on the mother's actions and present mental condition.[60] The court outlined some specific factors to be used in determining the structure of visitation between a child and the noncustodial parent. The court, citing the Nebraska Code, stated that the judge must consider:

[t]he relationship of the minor child to each parent prior to the commencement of the action or any subsequent hearing ... the desires and wishes of the minor child if of an age of comprehension regardless of the chronological age, when such desires and wishes are based on sound reasoning; ... the general health, welfare, and social behavior of the minor child; and ... credible evidence of abuse inflicted on any family or household member.[61]

In the *Fine* case, the court ordered supervised visitation because the mother had failed to establish a safe living environment for visiting with the child, had engaged in self-destructive behaviour, was suffering from a mental illness and was presently engaged to a man who was accused of sexual misconduct with a minor. The court stated it did not blame the mother for her mental illness, but that it 'cannot ignore the fact that the mother's living arrangements subsequent to the dissolution . . . have not provided a stable home environment free of unsettling influences which would permit safe and unsupervised visitation'.[62] The appellate court stated that the trial court was correct in ordering supervised visitation, and that this order can be modified if the situation changes.

In the case of *Lombaer v. Lombaer*, the Appeals Court of Illinois held that the trial court erred in ordering supervised visitation solely because of the mother's past hospitalization and failure to take medicine because this did not 'meet the onerous standard of serious endangerment . . . '.[63] The court, in support of its rationale, cited the Illinois Code: '[t]he court . . . shall not restrict a parent's visitation rights unless it finds that the visitation would endanger seriously the child's physical, mental, moral, or emotional health'.[64] The court concluded that failure to take medication and former hospitalizations of the parent did not meet the level of endangerment required to deny unsupervised visitation.

In *Ray v. Long*, the mother was denied unsupervised visitation and appealed the order, arguing that the trial court abused its discretion by ignoring the testimony of the previous visitation supervisor and her present doctor, both of whom supported unsupervised visitation.[65] The appeals court held that there was no abuse of discretion in ordering supervised visitation because the trial court has great latitude in ordering visitation, the court properly weighed all the evidence before it and the decision was in the best interests of the children.[66]

The court cited to the Ohio Code, in support of its decision:

[the trial court must] make a just and reasonable order or decree permitting each parent who is not the residential parent to visit the child at the time and under the conditions that the court directs, unless the court determines that it would not be in the best interest of the child to permit that parent to visit the child and includes in the journal its findings of fact and conclusions of law.[67]

The court in *Ray* held that although there was testimony as to the mother's ability to have unsupervised visitation, in light of all the evidence presented at trial, the lower court was correct in its order for continued supervised visitation.

Recommendations for attorneys

In representing mentally ill parents in termination of parental rights cases, it is important to keep in mind that, in order for a state to terminate a parent's rights, there *must* be clear and convincing evidence that a continued relationship is more likely than not to harm the child. This is a much higher standard than the one used in a custody or visitation determination because the outcomes in termination cases are final. There is no future modification of a termination order and, usually, no allowance for postadoption visitation orders. For these reasons, the state bears the burden of proof that the parent–child relationship is irreparably detrimental to the child. It is important that the attorney be aware of the following issues: (1) whether the parent has ever harmed the child; (2) whether the parent has ever lost another child to the state; (3) whether the service plan given to the parent was fair and reasonable; (4) whether the parent has cooperated with the plan as much as their illness allowed; (5) whether the mental health professionals caring for the parent support their claim; and (6) whether, with proper services in place, this parent could in the future care for the child. In the United States, attorneys should also consider whether the American with Disability Act applies to the situation before them and if raising this issue could be of benefit to the client.

In order to effectively advocate for mentally ill parents in custody disputes, attorneys need to be reminded that the controlling standard is the *best interest of the child*, and that mental illness alone does not disqualify a parent from being able to provide for children. The burden should be on the parent who is not the primary caregiver to prove why they should be given custody. Attorneys representing parents in these proceedings need to determine: (1) who was the primary caregiver; (2) which parent is better suited to meet the emotional, educational and medical needs of the child; (3) whether an effective working arrangement exists between the parents so that joint custody can be an option; (4) whether there have been any allegations of violence; (5) whether the parent seeking custody has the support of his or her therapists; and (6) whether the mentally ill parent has a realistic plan in place for the children in case he or she requires future hospitalization. In some cases, detailed affidavits from either clinicians or support agencies can assist the judge in determining whether the parent with mental illness has proper support for raising a child.

With respect to visitation, it is clear that a noncustodial parent has a right to visitation unless the court is convinced such visitation is detrimental to the child and not in their best interests. In visitation proceedings, lawyers and advocates must counsel the client to help draft a schedule which permits flexible time in a suitable venue with the parent and extended family, clarifies responsibility for picking up and dropping off the children, and spells out details of supervision if that is required. It is essential that all advocates and attorneys remember that the most important aspect of visitation is to allow for the continual growth of the parent–child relationship.

In addition to the legal standards for termination of parental rights, custody and visitation proceedings, attorneys should always be aware of the rules of their jurisdiction regarding patient–psychotherapist privilege. Many states have an exception to the privilege, either through case law or statute, when it comes to cases involving custody and/or visitation with the minor child. Attorneys, advocates and clinicians should be aware that there is a great interest in protecting the privileged medical documents of their clients. Attorneys should always seek to protect the privilege, and at the very least, seek to limit the scope of the inquiry. For many parents with mental illness, protecting their medical records is of paramount concern and both attorneys and clinicians need to work with the clients to ensure that this right is protected. The mere fact that the other side seeks the privileged documents in a custody proceeding, does not entitle them to the client's complete psychiatric history.[68]

Conclusion

When working with a parent with mental illness, it should be noted that each case is different and should be treated accordingly. It is not to anyone's advantage to make broad assumptions regarding mental illness and the ability to parent. It is only until these cases are looked at in an objective manner that parents and children will have a greater chance of sustaining a healthy, lifelong relationship with one another. Until then, one must look to the progressive states' laws and programmes for guidance on how courts should examine these cases. Practitioners must keep in mind that cases involving children are the most emotional cases, and assisting parents with maintaining contact and a continued relationship with their child is a much-needed service.

REFERENCES

1. 'Nicholson et al. *Critical Issues for Parents with Mental Illness and their Families*, 9 (quoting Joseph et al. 1999; Mowbray et al., 1995) (July 31, 2001). Unpublished paper for the Center for Mental Health Services Office of Policy, Planning and Administration. (On file with author.)
2. Popovich v. Cuyahoga County Court of Common Pleas, 2002 U.S. App. LEXIS 367, *11–12, (6th Cir. 2002).
3. Meyer v. Nebraska, 262 U.S. 390, 399 (1923).
4. Skinner v. Oklahoma, 316 U.S. 535, 541 (1942).
5. May v. Anderson, 345 U.S. 528, 533 (1953).
6. 455 U.S. 745, 760–761 (1982).
7. 42 U.S.C. § 671(a) (1997).
8. 42 U.S.C. § 675 (5)(f) (1997).
9. Nicholson, et al., *supra* note 1, at 26.
10. 31 S.W.3d 64 (Mo. Ct. App. 2000).
11. *Id.* at 69. (quoting In the Interests of C.P.B., 641 S.W.2d 456, 460 (Mo. Ct. App. 1982)).

12. *Id.* at 70.

13. *Id.*

14. *Id.*

15. A "service plan" is typically a plan that the social services agency puts in place that has various requirements for the parent to meet. Some examples are: following the medical advice of treating clinicians, attending parenting support meetings, taking parenting classes, and meeting on a regular basis with the social services case manager.

16. *Id.* at 71.

17. 465 A.2d 924 (N.H. 1983).

18. *Id.* at 929–930.

19. *Id.* at 930.

20. *Id.*

21. 530 S.E.2d 104 (N.C. Ct. App. 2000).

22. 383 S.E.2d 690 (N.C. Ct. App. 1989).

23. In re Small, at 106 (quoting In re Scott, at 691).

24. 50 Va. Cir. 457 (Va. Cir. 1999).

25. 418 N.E.2d 1305 (N.Y. App. Div. 1981).

26. 42 U.S.C. §12101(b)(1)(1990).

27. *Id.*

28. 42 U.S.C. §12132 (1990).

29. In the Interest of C.M., S.M., D.M., and J.M., 996 S.W.2d 269, 270 (Tex. App. 1999).

30. Family Independence Agency v. Terry, 610 N.W.2d 563, 570 (Mich. Ct. App. 2000) (*See also* In the Matter of John D., 934 P.2d 308 (N.M. Ct. App. 1997); In re Anthony B. et. al., 735 A.2d 893 (Conn. App. Ct. 1999), both of these cases held that the ADA applies to reunification services offered by the state agency).

31. Stone v. Daviess County Division of Children and Family Services, 656 N.E.2d 824, 830 (Ind. Ct. App. 1995).

32. 747 N.E.2d 120, 125 (Mass. 2001).

33. 947 S.W.2d 761, 768 (Ark. 1997).

34. 455 U.S. 745 (1982).

35. *See* Beck v. Beck, 432 A.2d 63 (N.J. 1981).

36. 278 S.E.2d 357 (W.Va. 1981).

37. Kathryn L. Mercer, *A Content Analysis of Judicial Decision-Making: How Judges Use the Primary Caretaker Standard to Make a Custody Determination*, 5 Wm. & Mary J. of Woman & L 1, 8 (1998).

38. Kevin S.E. Sr., v. Diana M.E., 520 S.E.2d 197, 204 (W.Va. 1999).

39. 115 N.W.2d 833 (Iowa 1962).

40. Id. at 835.

41. *Id.* (The issue of the mother's mental illness was greatly debated at the trial court level. The father produced two medical experts who testified that the mother was suffering from schizophrenia with marked paranoid tendencies. The mother had a medical expert who testified that she did not suffer from mental illness. The Court stated that their duty is to decide the case de novo and to take the facts as recorded in the trial court record which found the mother to be suffering from a mental illness.)

42. *Id.* at 837.

43. *Id.*

44. *See* Tenn. Code Ann. §36-6-106 (2001) (emphasis added).

45. *See* 750 Ill. Comp. Stat. Ann. 5/602 (2001).

46. 558 N.E.2d 388 (Ill. App. 1990).

47. *Id.* at 394 (*See* In re Marriage of Slavenas; 487 N.E.2d 739, 741 (Ill.App. 1985)).

48. 745 A.2d 1054, 1060 (Md. App. 2000).

49. *Id.*

50. *Id.*

51. 529 N.W.2d 167 (N.D. 1995).

52. *Id.* at 170 (emphasis added).

53. *Id.*

54. *Id.*

55. Willey v. Willey, 115 N.W.2d 833, 838 (Iowa 1962).

56. *Id.*

57. 2000 Tenn.App. LEXIS 259, 5 (Tenn. Ct. App. 2000) (quoting Tenn. Code Ann. §36-6-301 (1999)).

58. 144 A.2d 421, 423 (App. D.C. 1958).

59. *Id.* (emphasis added).

60. 626 N.W.2d 526 (Neb. 2001).

61. *Id.* at 532 (quoting Neb. Rev. Stat. §42-364(2)).

62. *Id.* at 533.

63. 558 N.E.2d 338, 395 (Ill. 1990).

64. *Id.* (quoting Ill.Rev.Stat. 1989, ch. 40, par. 607(c)(1989)).

65. 1997 Ohio App. LEXIS 5591, 5–6 (Ohio App. 1997).

66. *Id.* (The trial court issued a journal entry finding the following: (1) the past supervisor thought that unsupervised visitation should begin; (2) the mother provider evaluated the mother, found no mental illness, but did not consult any previous medical records or evaluations; (3) the children's counsellor testified that the children indicated that they did not want to visit with the mother unsupervised, and (4) the mother had failed to obey a previous order to undergo psychiatric counselling and submit monthly progress reports to the court.)

67. *Id.* at 4-5 (quoting Ohio Rev. Code Ann. §3109.051(A) (1997)).

68. Clark v. Clark, 371 N.W.2d 749, 753 (Neb. 1985).

19

Parenting and mental illness. Legal frameworks and issues – some international comparisons

Amy Weir

Children and Family Services, London Borough of Harrow, London, UK

Introduction

This chapter explores the legal frameworks which may apply to families affected by mental illness from a UK and an international perspective. In most countries legal frameworks have been established to regulate the relationship between the individual, the family and the state. In particular, the safeguarding of children's welfare is covered by legal provision to ensure that children's needs are met and that they are safely cared for. In the UK and elsewhere, there is also provision to support families and parents to care for their children, whenever this is possible. As far as mentally ill parents are concerned, there is also separate legal provision to safeguard and support their needs.

The issues

Mental illness is likely to affect, and even to impair, the capacity to parent. There is substantial evidence about the possible adverse effects of a parent's mental illness on their child. (Henry & Kumar, 1999; Reder *et al.*, 2000) (see Hall, Chapter 3). However, the degree to which parenting capacity is affected by the parent's condition is subject to a wide range of variables, some relating to the parent, some to the child and some to the overall circumstances in which the child is being cared for (Falkov *et al.*, 1998).

Given that the capacity to parent may be impaired in families affected by mental illness (Cleaver *et al.*, 1999; Howarth, 2001), both the supportive and the safeguarding role of the state's legal provision may apply. The law provides that the state may intervene when parents are experiencing difficulties. This may be to offer voluntary support to the family or it may be to offer, and sometimes to impose, assistance and alternative care for the child. If the mental health of the parent is sufficiently concerning, then mental health legislation may provide support, care, treatment or even hospitalization. This assistance may be provided by agreement or it may be imposed if this is in the interests of the mentally ill parent and/or their family.

There is a balance to be struck between supporting the mentally ill parent in their own right and as a parent and promoting the welfare of and safeguarding their child. This is a complex equation to manage and requires close working together by both children's and mental health professionals (Weir, 1994) (see Göpfert *et al.*, Chapter 5).

There is some variation between the different legal frameworks of different countries in relation to safeguarding the welfare of children and indeed, the treatment of mentally ill adults. There are also significant similarities about the fundamental principles that children should be safeguarded to achieve their full potential and that families should be supported to provide the care required by children, whenever this is possible.

The role of legal intervention in families affected by parental mental illness

There are no reliable data on how many children are now being cared for at home by parents or carers with mental health problems. It is clear that various developments in legal provisions and policy for mentally ill adults, are likely to have increased the number of children living with an affected parent. From the research evidence in the UK, it is likely that a significant proportion (at least 20%, probably 30% and perhaps more) of adults known to mental health services have children (Falkov *et al.*, 1998). All adults in the UK have a 1 in 4 chance of experiencing a period of mental illness (covering the wide range of severity) during their lifetime; 5.7 million (12.6%) of the adult population are suffering from a mental illness at any one time (Falkov *et al.*, 1998).

It is likely that the number of children living in the same household as a mentally ill parent has increased over recent decades. Legal and policy changes have led to the development of community-based services for the mentally ill instead of hospital-based care for those with significant or chronic mental health problems. Policy changes and new treatment options for mentally ill adults in Europe and elsewhere mean that there is a greater likelihood of mentally ill adults living in the community, rather than in hospital, and of them spending more time at home with their children than was previously the case.

Why are legal frameworks required?

Some parents affected by mental health problems manage the care of their children with support of their family and others, and do not come to the attention of child welfare agencies.

Most mentally ill mothers don't abuse children and most abusive mothers are not considered mentally ill. (Kumar, pers. comm.)

Some parents cope and manage the care of their children most of the time but may need some support at times to do so. A study of the views and needs of parents who attended day mental health centres, showed how vulnerable many parents felt. They described how much they tried to ensure that their children were always safe particularly when they knew their mental health was deteriorating. Many of the parents wanted more not less support and intervention from social workers to enable them to care as well as possible for their children. This is how one of the parents described her own efforts to make sure her children were safe:

If you've a mental health need, you make sure the children are safe because, you know, you are on guard all the time, so you make sure your children are safe all the time. Mine have phone numbers for all over . . . if I didn't have my phone I'd be stuck really . . . because it's like a safety barrier. (Hugman & Phillips, 1993).

Göpfert & Mahoney's findings (2000) confirm this.

Unfortunately, the behaviour of some mentally ill parents and the symptoms which they experience are more concerning and they are unable to care safely for their children, sometimes permanently but sometimes for brief periods only (Falkov, 1996).

The children of parents with mental health problems are generally at greater risk compared with the general population of experiencing a range of problems. Emotional difficulties, cognitive delays, psychiatric disorders, academic underachievement and poor peer and family relationships are some of the problems which have been identified in surveys of the children. There is also significant representation of the children on child protection registers and in fatal abuse.

Potential conflict of interest?

The legal frameworks which apply for the adult with mental health problems and for their child are quite distinct and separate areas of legal provision. There may be an inherent tension between the needs of a growing and developing child and those of their mentally ill parent.

Attitudes have changed generally towards mental illness and the rights of mentally ill people over the last few decades. As Sayce, in Weir & Douglas (1999), indicated, in some countries, up until the mid twentieth century, sterilization was enforced on mentally ill patients. The parent's need to parent – sometimes regarded as part of meeting their therapeutic needs – may be articulated by the professionals supporting the adult. Oates (1984) (as quoted in Reder & Lucey, 1995) described how adult psychiatrists may consider the issues in terms of 'the therapeutic usefulness' to the parent of having a parenting role.

Legislative frameworks also increasingly support the right to parent generally. The overarching European Convention on Human Rights, which is reflected in the UK Human Rights Act 1998, stipulates in Article 12, that there is a right to marry and to found a family. Article 8 provides that there is a right to respect for private and family life, home and correspondence.

However, legal provision also exists to safeguard the welfare and safety of children. In the Human Rights Convention, at Article 3, there is prohibition of torture (and inhuman and degrading treatment). This article has already been used to suggest that children had been failed by local child protection systems from abuse by their parents. The UN Convention on the Rights of the Child has established internationally the primacy of children's needs.

There are powerful tensions between the rights of children to be cared for and protected and the needs of parents, who themselves are under stress resulting from their mental ill-health. It is not easy to ensure that a safe balance is struck between meeting the needs of children and their parents. Depending on how people construe such difficulties, there may well be a conflict of interest between the needs of parents and their children (see Göpfert *et al.*, Chapters 5 and 7; also Falkov, Chapter 27). This may result in a balancing act between the needs and circumstances of the child and those of the parent. In legal terms, this will require a weighing up of strengths and concerns in relation to the respective rights and responsibilities of children and parents, as follows:

- Parents have responsibility for their children.
- Children have rights and needs.
- Within this context, there are both opportunities and risks.

At the same time, there may also be difficulty in balancing the different perspectives of the different professionals and agencies involved with the family. Some professionals may regard themselves as having a primary responsibility for the child whilst others – particularly in adult psychiatry – may see themselves as attending primarily to the needs of the ill parent. There may, therefore, be a conflict of perspective between the different professionals.

There may be a clear conflict of interest between the interests of the parent and those of the child and this conflict is reflected in the different legislative frameworks with their different priorities and raison d'être. For the mental health professionals working with families, there may also be a conflict of loyalty if they believe they should report concerns about the care of children.

Professionals engaged with families where a dependent child is living with an adult member who has a serious mental illness may find themselves at the confluence of a complex range of competing and, at times, conflicting demands which will expose them to many professional dilemmas and some of the most difficult practice challenges.

Searching for a balance in the law

The legal frameworks for child welfare start from the principle that children are generally best cared for within their own families whenever this is possible. When intervention is indicated, to support parents and to ensure children are being adequately and safely cared for, usually the policy adopted is that the intervention should be as minimal as possible. Although such low-key involvement may be laudable, it may lead to a tendency to intervene too late and not to provide sufficient early preventive services. This may be particularly significant for families affected by mental illness where parents and children may need regular and continuing support. A study by Falkov (pers. comm) of the children of adults attending a psychiatric outpatients clinic showed that, even when their parents appeared to be 'well', their children still showed significant levels of stress; since their parents were well, this was exactly the time when the families were receiving least intervention and support.

At various times, law-makers have sought to acknowledge and to manage the potential conflict of interests which may also exist between state intervention in family life when the needs of children and the capacity of parents to carry out their parenting capacities may be in question.. The Children Act 1989 covering England and Wales was drafted in an attempt to balance the rights of children and the responsibilities of parents:

> . . . we have high ambitions for this Bill. We hope and believe that it will bring order, integration, relevance and a better balance to the law – a better balance not just between the rights and responsibilities of individuals and agencies but most vitally, between the need to protect children and the need to enable parents to challenge intervention in the upbringing of their children. (David Mellor, House of commons speech, reprinted in Hansard, HOC, 27 April 1989)

The Children Act 1989 (UK) took the welfare of the child as its overriding principle. It was also predicated on an essentially adversarial model of clarifying individual rights through due legal process to establish whether the threshold of significant harm is met. The role of the law and the court process is to weigh the evidence and to act as the arbiter about whether a child's welfare is being impaired. *Working Together* (Department of Health, 1989), a complementary set of regulations, also signposted and reinforced the checks and balances approach:

> . . . Public confidence in the child protection system can only be maintained if a proper balance is struck avoiding unnecessary intrusion in families while protecting children at risk of significant harm.

For families affected by mental illness, professionals have to consider and judge whether a child's needs are being met effectively and, if necessary, provide additional support and resources working in partnership to support the parent. There will also be circumstances when the parent is not able to promote their child's welfare and safety adequately and when legal action may be required in the child's interest.

Comparing legal frameworks

The UN Convention on the Rights of the Child provides an international perspective for child welfare and the legal frameworks of many countries reflect its principles. Across the European Community, including the UK, the Human Rights legislation, as mentioned above, is also affecting how domestic legislation to safeguard children is being applied.

A recent study (Hetherington *et al.*, 2002) compared legal and service delivery frameworks across Europe and Australia. The project was to consider variations in responses and uses of legal and procedural frameworks between countries in relation to a particular set of case vignettes. The vignette described three different scenarios involving the effects of the mental health difficulties of a mother on her capacity to parent. Using this vignette with professionals from the participating countries – which covered much of continental Europe, Scandinavia, the UK and Australia (Victoria), they were able to review, contrast and compare the legal and service delivery structures and systems which were in place in several different countries (Baistow & Hetherington, 1998).

Reasons for legal intervention

Although there are similarities between the legislation in different countries, there is also variation between the various states about the reasons and thresholds for state intervention and the type and level of service delivery which exist.

All the countries in Hetherington *et al.*'s study (2002) provided that there should be intervention, compulsory if necessary, when children were not being safely or appropriately cared for or when their parent was not available to care for them.

Variation in legal requirements for intervention

Supporting families

- In Scandinavia, the law allows for high levels of support services to be provided and a wide range are provided including family centres and health visitors; in Denmark, the Social Welfare Act 1992 applies and states that "it is an obligation for the authority to offer parents guidance when a child or adolescent has problems with his/her surroundings . . ."; in Sweden, it is the Social Services Act 1980 which stipulates that services must "act in close collaboration with families to promote the comprehensive personal development and the favourable physical and social development of children and young people".

- In France, Italy and Luxembourg, social work and child health services provide support to families.
- In Germany, child and youth services have a duty to support families in looking after their children including practical problems; various voluntary organisations are also funded to give more intensive support to families.
- In Victoria, Australia, there is legislative provision for child health and family support services.
- In the different parts of the UK, legislation – Children Act 1989, Social Services (Scotland) Act 1968 and Children Act (Scotland) 1995 – requires that child health social work services for children and families are provided; in Scotland, the 1968 Act states that social work departments must "promote social welfare by making available advice, guidance and assistance".

Protection of children

- In Scandinavia, there is mandatory reporting of child abuse by professionals and citizens.
- In Australia (Victoria), professionals have to notify the child protection service of suspicions of abuse.
- In France and Luxembourg, the civil code requires all citizens to report ill-treatment of children to the authorities.
- In English-speaking countries, generally, greater use is made of the courts and legal system to protect children and they tend to adopt a much more adversarial approach as opposed to a much more inquisitorial approach elsewhere.
- In Australia and Ireland, the grounds for intervention relate to the child being likely to suffer significant harm or being abandoned; the Children and Young Persons' Act (Victoria) 1989, requires designated professionals to notify Protective Services if they believe a child has or is likely to suffer significant harm as a result of abuse.
- In the UK (England and Wales) Children Act 1989, grounds for intervention are significant harm to child attributable to the care given not being what it would be reasonable to expect a parent to give.
- In Scotland, under the Children Act (Scotland) 1995, grounds are that the child is thought to be in need of care and protection.
- The availability of family support resources, in France for example, tended to influence the extent to which compulsory powers were used.

The legal framework and the resulting service delivery options available mean that in practice, families living in the different countries surveyed are likely to receive quite different responses from country to country. It is clear that the legal basis for, and assumptions about, intervention in family life lead to considerably different outcomes across countries. However, Hetherington concluded that the difference in responses to families was much more complex than just the consequence of there being differences in legal powers and service delivery systems across the different countries. In their view, the differences appear:

To have reflected a complex distillate of resource availability, professional culture and the national conceptualisation of the appropriate relationship between citizens, families and the state. (Hetherington *et al.*, 2002)

The differences appeared to relate to the difference in significance which professionals from each country afforded to some specific factors and issues. Some of the key issues which seemed to affect how the law was applied and the service was delivered were:

- The use of compulsory psychiatric intervention, including hospitalization; in Italy, for example, there are very few mental health beds and most mentally ill adults are treated at home.
- Expectations about and use of extended family to support the family; in Italy and France, there is a much higher expectation that the extended family will be involved actively.
- The availability and role of family support services generally; in England, there are relatively few family support services.
- The provision of dedicated service to the children themselves.
- The views adopted about risk.

The brief descriptions above about the grounds for legal provision in relation to families in difficulty such as those affected by parental mental illness show a remarkable similarity as far as child welfare is concerned. However, the policy and systems in place across the different countries seem to show considerably more variation in actual practice.

The operation of child welfare and child protection services is very much affected by the context in which they are set and it is important how the circumstances of the individual child and family are 'socially constructed':

Child abuse . . . . is an inter-subjective phenomenon whose meaning and import can only be understood in the cultural and organisational contexts within which it is, not simply constructed, but negotiated and constituted. (Parton *et al.*, 1997)

A whole range of different factors could be seen to influence and affect the application of the legal process. In cases where legal intervention occurs about the parenting of a mentally ill parent, there is a particular complexity. The issues are about the vulnerability of a child whose parent is also vulnerable. There is a dynamic interplay between the legal basis for intervention in family life and those involved in the whole process. The legal framework itself is also a reflection of the society and culture from which it is derived.

Even when the statutory basis for child welfare services is really quite similar, the service provided to and experienced by families is actually quite different. For example, in the UK, there is a legal requirement to promote the upbringing of children by parents through the provision of a range of supportive services as set out in Part Two of the Children Act 1989. However, there is far more expenditure on services other than prevention – most local authorities spend a third or less of their total children's services budgets on family support. In Scandinavia, far more resources are generally dedicated to supporting families to care for their children. Programmes in the UK such as Sure Start and the Children's Fund were established in the late 1990s to increase the level of preventive funding available to support vulnerable families; however, this new programme funding is directed to areas of high resource and environmental deprivation rather than at meeting the needs of families rendered vulnerable by parental circumstance – such as mental health problems. It is likely that many families affected by parental mental illness will not therefore benefit from these programmes.

Decisions about how the law is applied in particular countries is much more driven by economic, political and cultural norms and values as well as the historical circumstances of the particular country than would necessarily be presumed to be the case. The law provides overarching frameworks for the priorities for and direction of state intervention but the service delivery outcomes are much less possible to predict.

Family support or child protection. What works?
Striking the balance in legal intervention

In the countries mentioned above, the need to prevent difficulties by early action as well as to respond to immediate problems is endorsed in their child welfare legislation. However, in many countries, and certainly in the UK, there is a tendency to provide a reactive and crisis intervention service to children and families. If in practice, as well as in statute, services to support families and to protect children were more proactive and were provided earlier, this would greatly benefit families affected by mental illness. A major research programme about children's social work in the early 1990s, Messages from Research (Department of Health, 1995) identified the need for social workers to respond more sensitively and less reactively to concerns about the welfare of children.

In the context of identifying and meeting the needs of children affected by parental mental illness, a shift of emphasis from investigating whether children are at risk of abuse from the parenting of their mentally ill parents, towards a

starting point of considering whether the parents have problems in parenting arising from their mental ill health, would be much more appropriate in most cases.
Hugman & Phillips' (1993) study made clear what parents thought would make a
difference:

> The key theme is the wish by parents with mental health problems to have their parenting, and
> their mental health needs acknowledged and responded to in such a way that neither obscures
> or dominates the other. (Hugman & Phillips, 1993)

There may be a perception of a conflict of interest between the needs of the child
and of the parent but an automatic assumption that this is the case is likely to
be regarded as unhelpful and unjustified by all concerned. Of course, there are
occasions when the needs of the child cannot be safely or appropriately met by
their parent. However, many children do live with their mentally ill parent and
appear to cope reasonably well. Several studies have asked parents to identify
what assistance would enable them to cope with their illness, for themselves and
for their children. The findings can help us further appreciate the need to work
together.

We need to remember that most children with a parent who is mentally ill do not
suffer extreme outcomes and many live at home successfully and without apparent
serious effects on their development.

For many years, I worked with a family with two children whose mother, June,
had suffered several periods of severe depression culminating in her attempted
suicide at home; in a 10-year period, June had four hospital admissions but she
always responded well to treatment and managed, with the support of her husband,
the care of her two sons who are now smart young men in their late teens. June has
recently been involved in a working party in her local borough looking at the needs
of families affected by mental illness.

For another client, Jo, who has depressive mental illness but who is well most of
the time, her main goal is always to get well again and to get back to her children.
The significance of her ill-health to the whole family was always clear to her:

> What I wanted more than anything, was to get well enough to be the parent I had always wanted
> to be [and] a parent's mental illness is not only happening to them, it's happening to the child
> as well.

A study by Cowling in Australia in 1995 (Australian Infant, Child, Adolescent and
Family Health Association, 2001) gives some indication about what legislative and
policy frameworks for service delivery are required to provide the most effective
service possible to families affected by mental illness. The study was set up to try and
gain a better understanding of what services could best meet the needs of mentally

ill parents and their children. Cowling interviewed 57 parents to ask them what support they needed; they identified the following service needs:
- Help in explaining their mental illness to their children on a regular basis.
- Respite care for their children on a regular basis.
- Parent support groups to include reassurance about their parenting when they are unwell.
- Supportive and practical in-home care which is consistent and dependable when they are unwell.

Cowling (1999) also sought the views of service providers about what could improve the service for families affected by mental illness and produced a five-point checklist for professionals when they are responding to parents who have a mental illness. They need:
- Awareness of the impact of the illness and its treatment on the children.
- Sensitivity and responsiveness to the needs of these children, the ill parent, partners, and support people for parents with a mental illness.
- Flexibility to provide what is needed when it is needed.
- Affirmation of the rights and roles of the parent despite temporary or long-term incapacity to fulfil certain parenting roles.

One theme which stands out from both these lists is the emphasis on the need for continuing, flexible support to families on a regular basis. This is not always delivered by child welfare systems which prioritize need according to the level of immediate priority and risk. Identifying risks in any given situation is useful but it may become problematic when it is applied as the main criterion for resource allocation.

As suggested by the studies outlined above, some families will need longer-term strategies of support and a variety of different services to enable parents to care appropriately for their children. These families need a flexible range of resources in the community to support families – family aides, home care, home visiting schemes, family resource centres, groups for children and parents and respite care. The services need to be accessible and flexible in their approach. By these means, the intervention by the state as required by law can be more directed to supporting children and their families rather than to undermining the capacity which they have.

The circumstances of families affected by mental illness pose a considerable challenge to ensuring that the legislative intention to support and protect families is to be met as fully as possible. There is very much a balancing of needs required by those professionals who are charged with putting the legal frameworks into practice – they have to consider the interests and needs of children against the background of their parent's illness. There is a responsibility, under human rights and separate national country legislation, to support families in the care and upbringing of their children and this is particularly important when a parent has mental health problems.

In most of the countries considered, there is a requirement to forge effective partnerships with parents, children and with other professionals in the area. Positive attempts to support families and to work in partnership with them are, in most situations, more likely to succeed. Children whose parents are mentally ill have to cope not only with the illness of their parents but also with a growing realisation that they may have an increased likelihood of being affected by a similar illness. There is much still to learn about how children cope in such families but in the meantime we have to learn to juggle the interests of children and the interests of parents. If vulnerable families can be supported to care for their children, then those children will experience far less dislocation and they will maintain an integrity of identity within their own family. Of course, it will not always be safe to keep children at home.

Maya Angelou has put very poignantly the major dilemmas of intervening in family life, in this case to the point of removing the child:

How is it possible to convince a child of his own worth after removing him from a family which is said to be unworthy, but with whom he identifies? (Maya Angelou quoted in The International Initiative, 1996)

Summary and conclusions

Meeting the needs within families which may arise from parental mental illness, is a complex and demanding challenge. The evidence from comparing the legal frameworks in several different countries shows how similarities in legal provision mean that families will experience the same level of, or nature of, service to support them.

- The law provides the essential underpinning required to ensure support for parents and the protection of children.
- Legal frameworks give direction and steer but the actual services delivered in response to them are driven by a complex range of variables (NISW, 2000) – including resource availability and the political and professional priority given to particular needs , historical structures and systems, and the prevailing culture of the society in which the needs exist.
- For state intervention in family life, balanced models of intervention which promote the capacity to parent through proactive, flexible services from an early stage are more effective than a reactive, crisis-intervention driven approach.

- Inquisitorial rather than adversarial approaches to understanding the problems parents have are more likely to be effective in meeting the needs of children and in ensuring that they are safely cared for.
- More emphasis is required in many places on the need to promote early intervention approaches which enable parents to be supported to care safely for their children, whenever possible.
- Supporting families affected by mental illness to ensure that children are parented appropriately and safely is very challenging; if the legislative intentions are to be carried out, those implementing them require knowledge and experience of both adult mental health and children's development.

REFERENCES

Australian Infant, Child, Adolescent and Family Health Association (2001). *Children of Parents Affected by a Mental Illness – Scoping Project.*

Baistow, K. & Hetherington, R. (1998). Parents' views of child welfare interventions: an Anglo-French comparison. *Children and Society, 14,* 343–54.

Cleaver, H. Unell, I. & Aldgate, J. (1999). *Children's Needs – Parenting Capacity.* London: The Stationery Office.

Cowling, V. (1999). *Children of Parents with Mental Illness.* ACER Press.

Department of Health (1989). *Working Together to Safeguard Children.* London: HMSO.

Department of Health (1995). Child Protection – Messages from Research. London: HMSO.

Falkov, A. (1996). *Study of Working Together Part 8 Reports – Fatal Child Abuse and Parental Psychiatric Disorder.* London: Department of Health.

Falkov, A. et al. (1998). *Crossing Bridges Training Manual and Reader for Working with Mentally Ill Parents and their Children.* London: Department of Health.

Göpfert, M. & Mahoney, C. (2000). Participative research with users of mental health services who are parents. *Clinical Psychology Forum, 140.*

Henry, L. A. & Kumar, R. C. (1999). Risk assessments of infants born to parents with a mental health or learning disability. In *Child Protection and Adult Mental Health – Conflict of Interest?* ed. A. Weir & A. Douglas, pp. 49–63. Oxford: Butterworth Heinemann.

Hetherington, R., Baistow, K., Katz, I., Mesie, J. & Trowell, J. (2002). *The Welfare of Children with Mentally Ill Parents – Learning from Inter-Country Comparisons.* Chichester: John Wiley & Sons.

Howarth, J. (2001). *The Child's World – Assessing Children in Need.* London: Jessica Kingsley.

Hugman, R. & Phillips, N. (1993). 'Like bees round the Honeypot'. *Practice, 6,* 193–205.

NISW (2000). *Working at the Interfaces within and between Services – Appropriate Care for the Children of Mentally Ill and Substance Abusing Parents.*

Parton, N., Thorpe, D. & Wattam, C. (1997). *Child Protection – Risk and the Moral Order.* London: Macmillan.

Reder, P. & Lucey, C. (ed.) (1995). *Assessment of Parenting – Pychiatric and Psychological Contributions.* London: Routledge.

Reder, P., McClure, M. & Jolley, A. (ed.) (2000). *Family Matters: Interfaces between Child and Adult Mental Health.* London: Routledge.

The International Initiative (1996). *Preserving Families* (leaflet). Leicester: The International Initiative.

Weir, A. (1994). *Split Decisions – Issues in Child Protection and Mental Health. Community Care,* December.

Weir, A. & Douglas, A. (ed.) (1999). *Child Protection and Adult Mental Health – Conflict of Interest?* Oxford: Butterworth Heinemann.

Part V

Child-sensitive therapeutic interventions

20

The child grown up: 'on being and becoming mindless': a personal account

Denise Roberts*

It has been a struggle to know how to write this chapter so that it might convey some meaning towards my experience of growing up within a disturbed family. The chapter title describes it in a nutshell. What does it mean, this word 'mindless'? As a way of finding a place to begin, I looked up the definition in my copy of Chambers Twentieth Century Dictionary: 'mindless, without mind: stupid: unmindful', 'unmindful, not keeping in mind, regardless (of)'.

The most powerful and pervasive feeling I have about my mother's illness is the sense of 'not knowing'. In telling my story I have felt attacked by guilt, as if I am telling tales and seeking attention and will not be believed. I can't remember exactly when it started, although I can remember an incident that places all three of us at primary-school age. All three of us being my older sister, my brother and myself. If there is such a strong sense of not knowing, then perhaps it is fair to ask what is there that I think I know?

I know that my mother repeatedly took overdoses. I remember violent fights in my parents' bedroom. My father trying to console or calm my mother. The violence came from my mother. She would scream that she could not go on any more, that she was fed up, that she'd had enough. She would go into a rage and throw objects around the bedroom, completely clear the entire surface of the dressing table with one sweep of her arm. My father would try to hold her and she would fight. She tried to throw herself from the bedroom window. As a child I believed it was possible. As an adult, I realise that she probably would have struggled to get out. As a child I was neither able to comprehend nor to rationalise this behaviour. My memory is that I felt frightened because I did not know when it would stop or what would happen next. There might be mornings when things would go wrong and I would leave the house and go to school, preoccupied and startled with the chaos in our home and wondering if it would be safe. Not telling anyone about what was happening, just performing as if it were not happening. I feel as though the act of performing

*Pseudonym.

is one of the ways in which I managed my life. It feels as if the terror became encapsulated and stored inside, hidden and not addressed. This left me with a sense of floating on the outside, interacting but not really feeling part of things. I have a clear recollection that I never felt happy to return to our home. I always experienced a sinking feeling in my stomach as we approached the house.

My mother was hospitalized over a period of 18 months to two years. I remember the name of the hospital, and the doctors who were treating her. I understand that she was admitted on a compulsory order. It feels hard to know because I don't recall any explanations that led to a sense of understanding. One of the behaviours I developed was to search through my mother's wardrobe and dressing table. Looking for something, trying to find something. Some time after her discharge from hospital I remember rooting through her things and finding a document that said that my mother was certified as 'being of sound mind and body', or words to that effect.

I believe that my sister had started senior school around the time that my mother was taken to hospital, so she was about 11 years of age. She accompanied my father to the hospital on evening visits. I remember trying to locate the place on the map of our local area. I became excited on finding it, next to 'Mental Hospital'. My sister quickly took the map away from me saying 'it's a mistake'. I had fantasies about where my mother was staying. I had a picture of a very old mansion with a large staircase. I have recollections of visualizing her on this staircase surrounded by rooms where wild and crazy women were kept. It all felt dangerous that my mother was exposed to all of this. The family never talked about this. My sister is someone whom everyone described as a child who was grown before her time. She seemed to lose her childhood by having to take on adult responsibility. Perhaps this was her way of adapting to the situation as well as being placed in it by others.

Dr Brown, one of the psychiatrists, came to our house one evening when my mother was home and she had relapsed. She had overdosed and she had fought with my father and Erica, our au pair. Erica had come to look after us when I was about nine years old. I had seen the struggle taking place. At one point my mother was in such a rage that she was about to upturn a triple wardrobe. I really wasn't sure if my father and Erica would manage to contain her. I don't recall the precise sequence of events that followed. My father and mother were upstairs while Dr Brown waited downstairs to see my mother. It was night-time, because I recall being dressed in a baby doll nightsuit and going into the lounge where Dr Brown was seated. I sat opposite him on the arm of the sofa. I recall feeling quite obvious, if not exposed, in my nightwear. I hoped he would speak to me. I remember feeling that he might at least think that I looked nice enough to talk to. I waited and waited. I thought to myself that he might ask me something, about me, how I was, what did I think? 'If I sit here for long enough and look pretty he might notice and ask about me'. He never asked me anything. He sat in the chair in silence with a pleasant enough smile on his face. My mother was taken back to hospital that night.

During her hospitalizations my mother would come home for visits. These were graded introductions into our home. She was escorted by a nurse, Sister Margaret, who would stay for the duration of the visit. At first my mother came home for part of the day; it was then increased to full days, and eventually full weekends. Sister Margaret did not sleep at our house, but stayed during the days and evenings. It felt safer to me when Sister Margaret was around. It was like a guest, someone from outside coming in. She talked more with my parents and sister than with my brother and myself. My mother also made friends with other patients, and they would visit. It seemed that we were surrounded by the hospital culture, as if our family life was caught up with people and conversations to do with people 'having nervous breakdowns', as my mother described it. Even our house was named 'Wits End' – my mother having made a name plaque in a pottery session at the hospital.

I began to get into difficulties at primary school during this time. My friendships with peers seemed to be more fragile, I was argumentative and I was being tormented by children who had previously been my friends but were now going around saying that my mother was 'mental'. I began to steal money from home and from my class teacher. I stole pennies and sixpences from home and hoarded them in my blazer pockets. I was discovered at school because my two side pockets were so heavily filled that they were weighing down the sides of my blazer. I picture it in my mind as being like a hamster with bulging pouches of food in its mouth. I know now what the stealing was about, but at the time it was dealt with punitively by school and my parents. I was not to be trusted. I began to feel isolated, like a misfit and somehow contaminated by all this madness and badness.

My mother returned home to live with us permanently. She was placed on Librium and Mogadon, which she has taken regularly since this time. Vials of Valium were kept in the medicine cupboard in case of need. In our day-to-day life I still perceived my mother as having lost her capacity to tolerate any demands placed upon her at home. She seemed always to be on the brink of fury. Anything might tip her over the edge. It might be that one used the wrong word. One evening I was being spoken to by her and I used the word 'what' instead of 'pardon'. It was enough to cause a bowl of Russian salad to be picked up and thrown at the ceiling, leaving a purple beetroot stain above her head. Now it would be my turn. I can't remember what she was shouting, but I knew that I should run. I ran from the kitchen to the lounge where she chased me around the table. Eventually I was caught and she banged my head against the sofa arm as she held my hair in her hand. I was not the only child exposed to these incomprehensible outbursts. I vividly remember difficulties one morning when my brother, who was about five, could not find his vest. My mother instructed him on how to find it but he couldn't. My sister and

I were thrown out of the bedroom, leaving my mother and my brother together. All I could hear was my mother screaming at my brother and smacking him. My brother was crying. My father tried to go into the room but my mother insisted that he stay out of the way. Sadly my father waited until my mother stopped of her own accord. My next memory is that my mother was seated on the edge of the bed crying desperately, apologising to my father. I remember being next to her and feeling that I should console her to make her feel better. What occurs to me now with great pain is that I can't remember who was taking care of my brother.

Part of my mother's problems were to do with her physical pain due to orthopaedic problems. Her pain was such that she was prescribed Fortral injections. She became dependent on these and my father chose to manage this by hiding the Fortral. He had told us where they were kept. My mother would ask us for them and we would tell her as it was far safer to do that than to face her rage. We still faced my father's blame and anger. He would not speak to us for a week. It was like living in a vacuum. The GP managed this situation by prescribing Fortral to be taken orally. My mother felt she could only benefit if she injected herself. She would dissolve the contents of the capsules in tap water in the bathroom and inject it into her veins in her arms and ankles. My sister and I were used as lookouts, keeping guard of the bathroom door in case my father or Erica came in. We also helped with holding the tourniquet around her upper arm. It made me feel sick. I really felt I had been pulled into unbearable madness. The local chemist would provide my mother with vials of Fortral when she could provide prescriptions scripted for other medicines that came to the same cost. My sister and I were used as carriers.

My father was ignorant of all this. He was tired and had sought his comfort by getting into my sister's bed and my bed. I felt trapped and overwhelmed by the emotional weight of both my parents and my father clinging to me, too physically close. My answer to all of this, as a teenager, was to overdose. The two overdoses that I took were serious, and as I look at it now, I was lucky to survive. I wanted to be out of the terrorizing world that I felt I was living in and I also felt tremendous feelings of responsibility and guilt. As an adult I can understand the origins of these feelings and I can think about the dynamics involved. I don't think I had a real concept of death but a sense of wanting to stop dead, to go no further. I was then to meet the first professional who asked about me – a social worker who met me regularly over about 16 months. She sat with me when I confronted my parents about my mother's abuse of drugs. My mother's response was 'and tell me when did you imagine all of this?'. I felt she was taking my mind away from me. The social worker saw me on neutral territory when my parents opposed any interventions. This felt like the beginning of something different. I was able to take a different path and at 17 I left home and school.

With the help of long-term psychotherapy I am beginning to find myself and to feel for myself. Being denied the necessary adult attention left me with the feeling that I did not deserve it, as if I had no right to ask to be cared for. I feel let down by the adults who might have noticed us when we were children. I now work with disturbed children and their families, where we still meet children who have been struggling unnoticed with one or both parents suffering from a mental illness.

21

Talking with children and their understanding of mental illness

Alan Cooklin

The Family Project, Camden & Islington Mental Health & Social Care Trust, London, UK

Introduction

The title of this chapter highlights an important starting point for what follows. All children with mentally ill parents construct some form of understanding about changes they observe in their parents' behaviour. If professionals are to talk helpfully to a child about his parent's illness, the talk needs to be a dialogue or dialectic between the different knowledge and understanding of the child on one hand and the professional on the other. In other words, it is no use just 'telling' the child – the professional needs to try to find out how the child understands what has happened to his mother, father, brother or sister, to talk about how he has worked it out, and then to fit the professional's knowledge into the discussion.

What to talk to children about

In a study of 11–15-year-olds living with a depressed parent, Garley *et al.* (1997) found that the children particularly wanted discussions about the following four topics:

(1) Understanding the illness. This would include their own concerns, ideas about the cause of the illness in their parent, and access to information.
(2) How to recognize the signs of an impending illness.
(3) Issues to do with hospitalization.
(4) Advice about management of the illness. This would include ideas about coping with the effect of illness on themselves as well as on their parent, suggestions about what is helpful to the parent and recommendations for other children whose parents are suffering from similar problems.

Does it help to talk?

Falkov's work (1997, 1999) suggested that the degree to which a child can be helped to develop a 'good' (reasonably accurate) explanation of a parent's mental illness correlates with a reduction in the child's confusion and self-blame, and with a rise in the child's self-esteem. It is also associated with lower levels of 'caseness' and has the potential to lessen the child's own level of psychiatric disturbance.

What do we need to do?

A presentation by children or 'young carers' of mentally ill parents in Liverpool (see Bilsborough, Chapter 1) reported both a general lack of explanation of their parent's disorder on the part of professionals and a consequent sense that the children were both responsible and to blame for the illness. Children also complained that some of their worst experiences with professionals occurred when the mental health services finally became involved in their parent's care. They described being 'ignored . . . no-one asking our opinion . . . not interested in what we had done or how we had looked after her'.

There is a prevalent social belief that 'ignoring' the problem will lead to the child 'forgetting about it'. Even if this were possible – which would fly in the face of the studies cited above – many children will live with the ongoing experience of a disturbed parent, so that 'forgetting' is not an option. A study by Yule & Williams (1990) demonstrates that parents commonly underestimate the consequences of 'critical events' on children, and the degree to which children think of what has happened and are preoccupied with it.

It seems that the assumption that 'out of sight . . . (means) . . . out of mind' continues to predominate. On the contrary, evidence shows that someone needs to be available to the child, needs to understand the mental illness, and needs to help the child understand the illness, to challenge self-blame and fears about the future, and also to help the child bring the experience down to manageable proportions (Rutter, 1990). This does not mean demanding that the child 'expose' all his feelings; it does not mean a mini-psychoanalysis of the child or even a 'detective' job to 'find' the child's worries. Some studies of the effects of various forms of trauma on children (Jones & Ramchandani, 1999) have suggested that repeated 'exploration' of the child's experience and presumed 'inner meanings' is often not helpful. Debriefing of the experience, on the other hand, and gaining a clear understanding of what happened to the parent, why it has happened (within the limits of what is known), as well as discussion of the future possible impact on the child himself, and how this can be managed, is almost always useful.

Who should do the talking?

As discussed at the end of this chapter, not only are all the professional groups somewhat wary of talking to children, but all seem to believe it is the responsibility of some other group. It is the mental health worker who is most likely to meet the child in an informal way during visits. It is the mental health worker who should have the clearest understanding of the parent's illness. But many mental health workers are overanxious about their lack of experience in talking to children, and may believe there is some mystical skill that all the other professionals possess. If the professional is friendly, warm, and talks to the child as a 'thinking' person, in a respectful manner, these are the most important qualifications. It will help if the professional has been given some training in what kinds of language children at different levels of maturity can manage, and teams need to provide this. It is also important to be reasonably firm if a child responds in a chaotic manner. Some children will respond to discussion of fearful or painful issues with erratic or uncontrolled behaviour. While it is important not to force discussion in an intrusive way, it is also necessary to prevent chaotic behaviour from getting out of control. If not controlled, such behaviour will itself make a child more anxious.

What do children require and what can they understand?

Article 12 of the United Nations Convention on the Rights of the Child enshrines the principle that children have a right to have their opinions heard and taken seriously in all matters that directly affect their well-being.

A child's capacity to understand, and, if allowed, to make appropriate decisions, was brought to the fore in the UK by the Gillick case. From this the term 'Gillick Competence' was coined to represent the ability in a child to understand the consequences of treatment, and this in turn depends on the child and the nature of the decision under consideration. As Alderson (1993) has pointed out, on the basis of an 'in depth' series of studies on children's perceptions of their 'consent' (or the lack of it) to surgery, the ability of quite young children to understand the complexities of relationships and events in such television programmes as 'Neighbours' or 'EastEnders' far outstrips what might be anticipated from many schema of child development. Alderson's book offers a compelling description of how different children, often as young as 5 years old, can be helped to understand and positively participate in decisions about their own fates, and this capacity can also be applied to decisions affecting their parents if they have been the primary carer.

Detailed descriptions of conversational modes with young children are rare, at least in the clinical field. One of the most detailed (Aldridge & Wood, 1998) comes from a surprising source: a manual to assist police and social workers in carrying out statutory joint forensic interviews of children who it is suspected may have been sexually abused.

Engaging a child in an 'active' conversation about his parent's illness and treatment

All of the above assumes that doctors, guardians or others who need to access children's perspectives are able to engage in a conversation with a child which will elicit that child's actual thinking and opinions, rather than those sought and/or expected by the professional. Among other factors the child's view of what he can discuss with a professional may be influenced by:

(1) The age and maturity of the child.
(2) The nature of, and the degree of anxiety associated with, the parent's illness.
(3) The cultural traditions of the family, and the degree to which the child would expect to participate in any decisions about his or her own life.

A child's previous experience of being, or not being, invited to participate in giving consent about matters relating to himself is likely to be one strong influence on how the child perceives the relationship with a professional. Most children, in nearly all cultures, will have had the experience of adults who expect them to 'agree' with, or at least to acquiesce to, the 'wisdom' of those adults. The child is therefore likely to perceive any attempt at 'discussion' by a professional as a demand for compliance. Real participation requires not only that a child is invited to speak, but also that the child has been given reason to believe that his or her opinion matters. To elicit a child's active participation a professional will have to find ways to combat the child's expectation that he should comply with adults in general, and with doctors, therapists and others in particular. This is a potential problem for any therapist, regardless of age or gender, but for me as a white (and white-haired) male psychiatrist it is particularly critical to find a way to free myself from the traditional expectations of others about my role. I am personally most grateful to my 10 grandchildren for their help in overcoming this obstacle.

A child, particularly one who is not used to having his opinions even considered or heard, will therefore have to discover that the context in which a professional offers to discuss his parent's mental illness is a different one. He will need to develop trust based on evidence that this adult not only wants to know how he is thinking about the issues under discussion, but that this will have relevance for the possible solutions which are considered. The professional will have to demonstrate that a different kind of conversation is both possible and sought after. The conversation as it develops needs to convey the message that 'compliance' of opinion is not required, and that different points of view are welcome.

What will facilitate this process? Factors in both child and professional will determine whether or not a child becomes able to 'switch on' his mind when the offer to discuss his parent's mental illness is made. One impediment will be the level of the child's anxiety. In order to begin to help the child lower his anxiety a shared

Table 21.1. Thinking versus passively responding child: what makes a difference in achieving the former?

The child's degree of anxiety needs to be at a level that he or she can manage

Child needs information on which to base an opinion or a choice

Information needs to be understandable and 'imaginable'

Professional needs to ensure that child's 'image' of the 'words' is close enough to that being used professionally

Relationship with professional, and his way of defining questions and giving information, needs to challenge the expectation of compliance

Help child construct a 'pros' and 'cons' list about any decisions which are open to the child to take – however small

forum for discussion and banter will need to be established. It will mean finding out what this child enjoys, is good at, and his opinions about some aspects of his life.

The professional may then need to find out in detail how this child understands his parent's illness and its treatment, how he learnt what he 'knows', and from whom. The professional may have to put considerable effort into distinguishing what is known from what is believed and/or hoped for, and to help the child organize this into a form which fits both his developmental stage as well as the metaphors commonly used by the child. So, for example, a child who understands computers may easily be able to understand some forms of psychiatric disorder in terms of '. . . the RAM (or the hard drive) being overloaded'.

Aspects of the professional's 'stance', which may encourage a child to be 'thinking' and active in the conversation, are summarized in Table 21.1.

The last of the points in Table 21.1 – helping the child to construct a 'pros and cons' list with regard to a particular decision – can be particularly helpful. Not only does it allow the child to distance himself from the painful nature of the choice to be made, but it also provides a nonthreatening avenue through which the professional can offer advice by suggesting factors for one or other side of the list.

Didactic and dialectical approaches to talking with children

Traditional forms of discussion between adults and children can frequently be defined as didactic. The ultimate goal never strays from that of ensuring that the child acknowledges the adult's wisdom. The worst examples can even include rhetorical questions masquerading as invitations to the child to express a point of view . . .

'so what did I say when you said you were scared . . . (to which the child is required to explain why he was afraid) . . . I said you can tell me why . . . ' (so that the child's perspective can be demolished). A dialectic conversation on the other hand invites expression of real difference. The Shorter Oxford Dictionary's (1973) definition of dialectical is: The process of thought by which such contradictions are seen to merge themselves in a higher truth that comprehends them. In a dialectical relationship differences are juxtaposed as a valid subject for comment, debate and argument (Cooklin, 1998, 2001). It may of course lead to an argument or debate, but the essential ingredient of a dialectic relationship is that differences can be juxtaposed and considered. The problem for a professional is less likely to be the intelligence or maturity of the child, although these are important factors, but whether the child's 'thinking participation' is 'switched on' or not.

Principles of a dialectical approach can be summarised as follows.

Avoid 'problem-focused' talk

To achieve any level of trust a child needs to experience the adult as genuinely interested in his positive attributes and life, not only in his worries and anxieties. This means avoiding a common temptation to talk about what the professional assumes are the child's sources of distress. Most professionals are most familiar with 'helping clients with problems'. A child, however, may have been struggling to protect himself from being overwhelmed by the 'constant problems' which he has perceived as the mark of the parent's world. If the child is going to begin to trust a professional he needs some evidence that this adult is genuinely interested in him as a person and in the things that are interesting to him.

Stress the child's competence

A discussion should start with genuine interest in some aspect of the child that is apparent to the professional – a particular toy, or book the child is carrying, or even a particular T-shirt logo. It is important to be beware of forced jocularity and assumptions about the child. Do not – as has been common with some police child protection interviews – start with 'So which football team do you support . . . '. It might be better to say something like 'So what kinds of things do you like to do when you haven't got to think about these grown-ups?'

Also, rather than 'presuming' empathy or sympathy which the child might not have invited, it is better to adopt a stance of congratulating the child for his achievements in a nonpatronizing way. So rather than saying 'You must have been very worried about your dad being ill, it might be preferable to say 'How did you find a way to manage all these situations so well?' (McKay & Pollard, 1996).

Presume nothing . . . be 'behind' rather than 'ahead' of the child

Resist a common professional tendency to try and guess at, or even 'suggest' what the child is thinking or feeling. It is preferable to ask a child to explain, and if necessary to acknowledge that one does not understand something a child is trying to express, and then to ask him or her to help you. So, rather than saying 'You must have been very sad/worried/frightened to see your mum looking so low/upset/frightened', it might be preferable to say 'So when you saw mum like that what was it like?' – and if the child says 'I don't know . . .', or 'Nothing really', a question that is 'easier to answer than to not answer' may be useful, such as 'Well, was it the sort of thing that might make a son more cross, more sad, or more worried?'.

Ask questions that are easier to answer than to not answer

A child who is anxious or frightened may respond to 'open' questions by trying to, or fearing a failure to, find the answer the adult is 'seeking'. A child can often respond to binary choice, or multiple-choice questions more freely, because he can either select one of the choices, reject all of them or make a different point. So rather than 'So what did you think (or worse still 'What did you feel') about your mum not getting up to make your breakfast?', it might be easier for the child to answer 'When your mum didn't get up to make your breakfast do you think you were more worried about her, more cross or just very hungry?'. Such a multiple-choice question may be easier to answer, and more difficult to avoid, than an open question. Also, if the question is not forcibly personalized, it may be easier for a child to both think about and answer. So rather than saying 'You must feel very responsible for your mum's upset' it may be preferable to say 'Did you know that many kids in this situation seem to feel as though they are responsible for caring for their parents, rather than the other way round – it's strange isn't it . . . (perhaps adding) . . . of course that may not have happened to you, but it does to lots of kids'.

Make no interpretations or presumptions about a child's experience . . . but ask

The other headings have already highlighted the importance of not playing 'guessing games' with children and young people. Given time, patience and a demonstration that the professional is prepared to wait for the child to think and speak, rather than 'thinking for' him, children of all ages will attempt to articulate even their most complex ideas. Professionals who suggest the meaning of what the child is trying to say may destroy the child's attempts to clarify his own thoughts. On the other hand, if a child consistently talks with, or draws, some repetitive images that he seems stuck with, one might suggest to the child that these images have given one a 'funny' idea, and ask if he wants to hear about it. Occasionally a child will say firmly 'no', in which case this should be respected. If the child says 'yes', then one might say 'You keep drawing these pictures of what look to me like a mum or someone getting hurt . . . so it does make me think some things . . . do you want to know what I thought?'. If the child says 'yes', one may need to say 'Well it made me think maybe Bill (the child) thinks this could happen to his mum or is worried that it might'. If the child says 'No! I just drew them because . . .', one should probably say 'Oh . . . right . . .', but sometimes a child may say 'Well it has happened to my mum'. Then it is important that the professional does not react with surprise or shock, but might say 'Would that be something we could talk about together or do you want to keep it private?'. If the child does insist it should be private – despite having 'slipped out' the statement – then one might need to say 'OK, that's for you to decide, but imagine you did tell me about it, what do you think might happen then . . . ?'.

Challenge the child's expectation of compliance to adults

This is the most difficult, because it goes against not only all adult's habits of the way they think about children's ideas, but also against children's expectations of how they will be expected to behave. It requires not only a change of tone in the conversation with a child, but often a change in one's expectations and one's whole way of thinking about children and their ideas. One of the most useful ways to approach this is to seriously encourage a child to tell one about some area of expertise about which he or she is more competent than oneself, and then both question and respectfully debate his or her point of view. It could be something as simple as how some girls think boys are a disruptive influence in the class. One can then discuss why this might be, does she think she will never want boys in the same class, and has she noticed how some girls seem to change their opinion about this when they get older.

Allow a language of contest (but not combat), and talk which may appear as 'silly' and playful at the same time as being serious, but avoid insincere 'forced' jocularity

This really follows from the need to demonstrate to the child that he can disagree with you – as noted above – by gently and good-humouredly encouraging debate with the child. It requires that the professional is not fazed when the child does disagree. It is also important that the professional resists the temptations to either try to win an argument or to humour the child in a manner that could then become patronizing.

The goal is to help the child think, not to elicit feelings – a child will show what he feels as and when he chooses

If a child can begin to think about and reflect on the topics talked about with a professional, he often will have achieved the first step in mastering his worries about whatever this issue is. If the child is contemplative: ' . . . so maybe my dad just thinks everyone is against him because he always thinks the worst will happen . . . 'it may help to encourage the child's internal debate, for example with' . . . could be . . . or I suppose maybe there could have been some times in his life when he did feel got at . . . but then did you know that some illnesses in the mind can make people feel that everyone is against them?'.

What will often not help the child is for the professional to become a kind of 'detective' trying to 'get to the bottom of' what the child feels about it all. He will show rather than tell what he feels as and when he chooses.

Draw or use other visual aids with a child and young person, both to explain illness and to understand the child's perspective

Most children and young people will need to gain some visual image of what is being explained – of the brain and nerves, a diagram to link the body, the mind and the feelings, etc. – in order for them to gain sufficient mastery over the idea for them to be able to consider it.

Finding their own voices

The goal is to help the young person find his voice, and to articulate this voice. In situations of high stress a child may be struggling with multiple, inconsistent or ambiguous voices inside himself. Reconciling these internal different voices makes it difficult for all children and young people to respond to key dilemmas that they may face in the course of treatment, but this is exacerbated if there are significantly different voices within the family, such as between the parents. In these situations children and young people may often protect themselves by sticking steadfastly to one particular story, even although they may in fact often feel invaded by the multiplicity of the pressures from adults (Cooklin, 1998).

Some elements of the above are apparent in the following example.

Case example

Geoff was aged 9. During the previous year his mother, who was a lone parent, had been hospitalized on two occasions, and Geoff had witnessed two suicide attempts. After he had described these and other events to me I asked him about his social workers.

[This extract has been edited into a number of short sequences because of limitations on space. However, periods of apparently irrelevant 'chat' are important in order to allow the child to remain engaged with the professional. The conversation may then need to be brought back to the topic of concern on repeated occasions.]

A C: So how many social workers did you have?
GEOFF: Two.

AC: Did you think that was a good idea to have to change them, or would you prefer to have the same one?

GEOFF: I wanted to change.

AC: Oh. Why was that?... Did you not like Sue?

GEOFF: No...she didn't explain things right.

AC: Didn't explain things right...Do you mean she muddled you up?

GEOFF: Yeh...

AC: And then you changed to somebody else...?

GEOFF: ...Called Keith...

AC: ...Keith.

GEOFF: He was nice.

AC: And did he explain things properly?...(Geoff nods)...So what was different in the way Keith explained things and the way Sue explained things? Suppose I heard Keith and Sue explaining, what would I hear that was different between the two? Do you see what I mean? (nods)

GEOFF: Well Sue didn't really understand what was happening.

AC: What did she think was happening?

GEOFF: I don't know...I'm not her.

AC: Yeh...but when you say she didn't understand...what kind of things did she actually say?

GEOFF: She said everything would be ok...and...she also said it doesn't matter if your mother's drunk...(shrugs)...then she played games with me...(shrugs again) and stuff like that...

AC: Right...but Keith said something different? (nods)....What did he say?

GEOFF: He explains more clearly...and...

AC: What did he explain?

GEOFF: Well he understands what's happening...more...

AC: So what would he have said that was different from what Sue said?

GEOFF: Like um...he would say we'll try our best to get you at home.

AC: But didn't Sue say that?

GEOFF: No...

AC: But she said everything was going to be alright...Did he say everything was going to be alright or did he say...?

GEOFF: Well...Sue didn't understand anything.

AC: Supposing Sue had asked you to help her understand things...

GEOFF: Yes...

[There followed a confusing debate and conversation about Sue and Keith, which was probably important in itself. It culminated as follows.]

AC: What would you have had to explain to make her understand better...What was it you think she didn't understand that she should have understood?

GEOFF: That things are not OK in life...

AC: Right...

GEOFF: ...and we need a little bit of help in life ...

AC: Right ...

GEOFF: ...and that my Mum is going to be alright, but she just needs a little bit more work ...

AC: So do you mean that she didn't sort of take you seriously?

GEOFF: No.

AC: ...treated you like you didn't need to understand ...

GEOFF: Yeh.

AC: I see ... whereas Keith thought you should understand ...

GEOFF: Yes.

AC: ...but in fact what's funny is that what he told you was worse than what she told you ...

GEOFF: Yes.

AC: ...but was more honest?

GEOFF: ...Yes ...more honest.

AC: ...and you were in care for about 7 months ...?

GEOFF: ...I wanted to come home sooner.

AC: So do you think they made a mistake?

GEOFF: Well ...[thoughtfully and then with a hint of a mischievous grin] at the end ...2 months I thought that that was good ...

AC: Yes.

GEOFF: ...but then when I heard that they changed their mind to 7 months ...

AC: Do you know why they changed their minds ...?

GEOFF: Um Hmm ...

AC: Why was that?

GEOFF: ...to keep a track on things ...

AC: ...or did they think that mum wasn't well yet or wasn't safe yet ...

GEOFF: No ...

AC: ...They didn't think she was safe?

GEOFF: Well ...they thought she was safe ...but ...just in case.

AC: But do you think they were wrong ...do you think it was really alright, and they thought it wasn't alright?

GEOFF: Yep.

AC: You think it was alright?

GEOFF: [nods]

AC: Now I'm getting a bit muddled ...I'll tell you why [Geoff begins to grin] ...because you thought Sue said everything was going to be alright before it was really alright ...[Geoff grins broadly and nods] ...whereas Keith was more honest ... right?

GEOFF: [nods]

AC: ...and was it Keith who said you should stay longer?

GEOFF: Yeah.

AC: ... and yet you disagreed ... you thought it was wrong to make you stay longer ...

GEOFF: Yeah [giggles].

AC: You see how I'm getting muddled up here?

GEOFF: Yeah.

AC: So can you help me unmuddle myself ... ?

GEOFF: Well they said that I had to be there for 2 months.

AC: Yes.

GEOFF: And then they changed their mind.

AC: Oh I see ... but do you think they were right to change their mind?

GEOFF: Kind of ... but it felt a little bit weird.

AC: You mean it felt bad ... but the question is did they still make the right decision?

GEOFF: Yeah.

AC: You think they did?

GEOFF: Yeah.

Geoff, however, is articulate and able to not only crystallize his thoughts, but also – remarkably in the course of the discussion – to distinguish his feelings and wishes from his thinking opinions. Younger children may require other media to help them articulate their experiences and dilemmas. Within the Camden and Islington Mental Health NHS Trust the Family Project – a dedicated training and implementation service for the development of family work throughout the trust – has initiated workshops for groups of children and parents, where the parent has suffered a mental illness. A group of 5- and 6-year-olds constructed and acted a play in which a mother said she was too ill to get up and make her son's breakfast. He asked what he should do, in response to which she told him he must have 'the blue and red tablets'. The child telephoned first 'the doctor', then 'the Nurse', then at the nurse's suggestion 'a friend', all of whom were 'too busy' to attend his mother. Eventually the mother gave him the prescription, which he took to the chemist. The chemist questioned so young a child collecting the tablets, but eventually agreed to give him them 'just this once ... as I know you'. When the child returned home the mother had died.

The adults – which included parents – watching this play were understandably shocked. However, in the ensuing discussion it was clear that the children had been repeatedly told 'your mum is ill' without further discussion or elaboration. Although many constructions could be put on the play, it is not surprising that the children construed failure to treat the illness as leading to death. In a subsequent workshop they decided they wanted to repeat the play so that the mother could stay alive. She did get her tablets, but still did not make the breakfast '... because it's too late now'. Thus through the play these young children became less anxious, and could be said to have resolved some of their fear through changing the ending of the play. They nevertheless retained their 'statement' that when a parent is mentally ill the child's needs may be forgotten.

Who will do it?

In the United Kingdom – as well as in other European countries – this remains a problem. Child mental health services will generally not see these children unless they present with problems themselves which would meet the criteria for 'caseness'. Children and families social services are severely under-resourced, and often can only respond to cases where there is severe overt abuse or a need for child protection. This leaves the adult mental health teams. In the past they have not seen this as their remit, partly because of workloads and a sense of inadequate training, as well as at times rigid attachment to ideas about 'confidentiality' for the parents. In the above the word 'professional' is used to denote the need without defining who should do it. In the UK government directives do now require that the above three services should 'work together'. Probably all three need to be ready to respond to a child's needs as they encounter these. However, in the UK the key responsibility is likely to fall on the shoulders of mental health workers. This has serious implications for the training of nurses, social workers, psychiatrists and others, although the Royal College of Psychiatrists has at least made a start in considering a curriculum review.

REFERENCES

Alderson, P. (1993). *Children's Consent to Surgery*. Buckingham: Open University Press.

Aldridge, M. & Wood, J. (1998). *Interviewing Children: A Guide for Child Care and Forensic Practitioners*. Chichester: John Wiley & Sons.

Cooklin, A. (1998). From the return of the repressed to dialectics: making connections through talking with children. *Journal of Family Therapy*, 20, 153–64.

Cooklin, A. (2001). Eliciting children's thinking in families and family therapy. *Family Process*, 40, 293–312.

Falkov, A. (1997). Solutions on the ground: A family mental health service. Proceedings of Michael Sieff (1997) Conference, Cumberland Lodge. Woking: Michael Sieff Foundation.

Falkov, A. (1999). Addressing family needs when a parent is mentally ill. In *Approaches to the Assessment of Need in Children's Services*, ed. H. Wood & W. Rose. London: Jessica Kingsley.

Garley, D., Gallop, R., Johnstone, N. & Pipitone, J. (1997). Children of the mentally ill: a qualitative focus group approach. *Journal of Psychiatry and Mental Health Nursing*, 4, 97–103.

Jones, D. P. H. & Ramchandani, P. (1999). *Child Sexual Abuse – Informing Practice from Research*. Abingdon: Radcliffe Medical Press and Department of Health.

McKay, D. & Pollard, J. (1996). Community support networks in education and care settings. In *Parental Psychiatric Disorder: Distressed Parents and their Families*, ed. M. Göpfert, J. Webster & M. V. Seeman, pp. 152–60. Cambridge: Cambridge University Press.

Oxford University Press (1973). Shorter Oxford Dictionary. Oxford: Oxford University Press.

Rutter, M. (1990). Psychosocial resilience and protective mechanisms. In *Risk and Protective Factors in the Development of Psychopathology*, ed. J. Rolf, A. S. Masten, D. Cicchetti, K. H. Nuechterlein & S. Weintraub, pp. 181–214. Cambridge: Cambridge University Press.

Yule, W. & Williams, R. M. (1990). Post-traumatic stress reactions in children. *Journal of Traumatic Stress*, 3, 279–95.

22

Family therapy when a parent suffers from psychiatric disorder

Alan Cooklin[1] and Gill Gorell Barnes[2]

[1] Family Project, Camden & Islington Mental Health & Social Care Trust, London, UK
[2] Tavistock Clinic, London, UK

Introduction

This chapter considers the following questions:
(1) Why work with the family?
(2) Who is the family to be worked with?
(3) What are relevant approaches to treatment?
(4) What are the goals of treatment?

Why work with the family?

Family therapy with patients with mental illness has progressed from an assumption and/or hope that a change in the relationship patterns of the individuals in the family could 'cure', for example schizophrenia, to an evidence- based model in which family members are helped, in a collaborative manner, to develop more effective and less intrusive problem-solving techniques. These techniques focus on positive ways to respond to the illness associated with the behaviour of the patient.

The important differences in these two approaches are discussed below. Neither approach has specifically considered the need to help patients in their role of parent. Also, to our knowledge, neither the outcome studies aimed at lowering relapse rates of patients with schizophrenia or bipolar disorders, nor studies targeting family burden (Magliano *et al.*, 1999; Perlick *et al.*, 2001) have addressed the adverse effects of illness on dependent children nor how parents with mental illness can be helped to mitigate such effects.

Whilst being mentally ill is both painful and lonely for the sufferer, involving, as it does, a 'loss of mind' as well as a reliable sense of 'self', living with such a person may be extremely traumatic for a vulnerable child (Moltz, 1993; Pearlmutter, 1996). It can mean intensely confusing uncertainty about when a parent can be relied upon and when the child has to care for the parent. As many of the contributors to this volume report, the child's experience includes intense guilt and self-blame, exacerbated by the fact that the parent is ill and, therefore, absolved of responsibility for his actions. As a result, children will often feel responsible for the illness whether or not they are explicitly blamed.

It has been shown that the ways in which a child construes the parent's illness can have a significant effect on the child's own psychological health (see Cooklin, Chapter 21). This chapter, therefore, is concerned with how to help the child and parents develop a more positive working understanding of the parent's illness. This includes helping the parents to re-establish some working authority, so that a more 'parental' voice of the parent can be heard – as illustrated in the examples of Irma and Chrysoulla below.

The range of ways in which a family or systemic model have so far made contributions to this area include the following.

(1) As with any family, through an understanding of, and positive intervention in, the interactional patterns between a parent with mental illness and his family members. A focus on interactional patterns should not be confused with an interactional aetiology – which often referred exclusively to the emotional interaction between intimate family members, rather than to the whole range of sociobiological factors which impact on a vulnerable individual. In the past, the latter was interpreted as blaming the parents, or depriving the patient of necessary medication. In the USA, this kind of thinking and practice led to litigation against family therapists who failed to ensure that patients with major mental illness received appropriate medication, and for a time to a virtual ban on all family approaches for this group of patients. For a long time, family therapy was seen as irrelevant or even negative (Anderson *et al.*, 1980).

(2) Through helping the family to devise and implement strategies for the management of the patient with the illness, and to adapt the pattern of family life in ways which allow the expression of the needs of all members – not only the patient's. This has partially been the goal of the range of methods included under the headings of 'Psycho-education' and 'Family management approaches' (Anderson *et al.*, 1980; Falloon, 2000; Hogarty *et al.*, 1986; Randolph *et al.*, 1994; Strachan, 1986). These approaches include 'problem-solving techniques', which in turn means that the therapist offers a structured method of 'brainstorming', selecting and trying out different solutions to practical problems which different family members (including the patient) have identified. The fact that no solution is imposed, and even silly or absurd solutions are given a fair hearing, and then rated by all family members, means that conflict *can* still be addressed, but in a playful, noncritical and not excessively emotional manner. This has been found to be particularly therapeutic for both patients with schizophrenia and their families, as it allows the patient's point of view to be taken seriously without subjecting him to excessive emotional stimulation.

(3) Through addressing the social context in which the patient and family experience the illness and its consequences, particularly social isolation, stigma, shame, self-blame and mutual recriminations. This has been the focus of most of the multifamily approaches devised for this group of patients and their families (Bishop *et al.*, 2002; McFarlane, 1990; McFarlane *et al.*, 1995) as well as network approaches which can bridge the gap between social and professional networks involved in a patient's life (Speck & Attneave, 1973).

(4) Through devising interventions which address parent–child interactions:

Attention to the children's anger with a parent who is ill.

Helping a parent assess when they can be called to account by their children for irrational or inappropriate behaviour.

Helping children know what they can continue to count on when a parent is ill (such as having their breakfast made before going to school).

Helping a parent to explicitly exonerate the child of any responsibility for the illness.

Family therapy has much to offer to the treatment of the adult mentally ill, although it has perhaps a wider use where the point of referral is a child or adolescent. This chapter draws on approaches developed within both adult- and child-oriented services. A multifamily project, the Mental Health Matters Workshops (Asen *et al.*, 2001; Bishop *et al.*, 2002), together with a series of multifamily workshops specifically for the children of mentally ill parents – the 'What Shall We Tell the Children' Workshops – will also be outlined.

Who is the family to be worked with?

A family approach includes children, partners and parents, and possibly extended family members, as well as 'substitute' extended family members, such as carers and health professionals known to the family over time. Changes can be instigated and maintained, and relapse rates reduced, through a focus on relationships. The children of adults who are ill can also be helped to develop protective mechanisms against illness themselves. Features of the parent's illness requiring the child's attention and care can be prevented from getting in the way of the child's social and emotional development (see Cooklin, Chapter 21).

Transitions and fractures in family life change the family's shape and structure, and as potent stressors, can be a factor in the manifestation of later illness in a child. For many families, pathways involving separation, divorce, re-parenting and migration (chosen or enforced) all interact. Differences in the ensuing family structures have implications for the complex management arrangements that can develop between patients and their carers, especially when the carers are children.

Relevant approaches to treatment – dominant contextual influences

The culture of mental health services

British adult psychiatry has, in the main, developed within a belief system that mental illness can be diagnosed and treated as a discrete entity, relatively independent of the social context or culture in which it occurs. In the UK, general psychiatry has paid lip service to the use of family interventions to lower relapse rates, and even to 'getting a proper family history'. However, the current training of junior psychiatrists leads, in fact, to little or no real family, and even less cultural, history being elicited from patients admitted to acute psychiatric wards (Cottrell, 1989). The dominant culture has relied almost totally on individual nosology in diagnosis and on psychopharmacological treatments. In contrast to the marked lack of development of systemic practice within the adult field, a family approach has been the fastest growing treatment approach within the field of child and adolescent psychiatry. In the last decade, a combination of family work and multifamily groups has also developed in some settings (Asen *et al.*, 2001; Bishop *et al.*, 2002).

The impact of expressed emotion research on the shape of adult mental health services

Recent family approaches in adult psychiatry draw on expressed emotion (EE) research (Leff & Vaughn, 1985; Leff *et al.*, 1982, 1987, 1990; Wig *et al.*, 1987), which highlights factors amenable to family treatment that leave patients with schizophrenia more vulnerable to relapse. Anderson examined similar dimensions of family interaction in the USA (Anderson *et al.*, 1980). Whilst there is some controversy about what 'expressed emotion' measures (Jenkins & Karno, 1992), there has been little debate about the strength of the findings: high levels of negative expressed emotion, including overinvolvement, criticism or hostility in a key relative (usually a carer) are associated with significantly increased relapse rates.

However, as already noted in the introduction to this chapter, the question of how children may be significantly affected by, and have an effect on, the mental illness of a parent has largely been neglected in the reported work to date.

Protection and stress in families

Apart from the effect of expressed emotions in family life, another key research finding is the observation that intimacy and warmth in relationships may protect against stressful life events (Brown, 1991; Brown *et al.*, 1986). As a group, families with a mentally ill parent may be more vulnerable to life events presumably because intimate relationships are strongly affected, either for better or for worse, by mental illness in a parent (Sampson *et al.*, 1964).

Goals and models of family treatment

Family work in the context of major mental illness draws on a number of sources (Gorell Barnes, 2003). The focus is on the positive development of a helpful and clear communication style, and on the development of problem-solving skills. Our work has been strongly influenced by the approach at the Marlborough Family Day Unit (Schuff & Asen 1996) (see Asen & Schuff, Chapter 10) which is in turn heavily influenced by structural family therapy theory (Minuchin, 1974; Minuchin & Fishman, 1981). This approach offers:

(1) A model of working with the family which is optimistic and does not focus on pathology, or search unrealistically for causes. It is based on the organization and development of family life rather than focusing on an individual's deficiencies. This is of particular importance with families who feel highly stigmatized by the disorder.

(2) An approach which respects the natural hierarchy and structure of the family and supports this in the development of new solutions, rather than undermining the structure by implying that the therapist knows better.

(3) A model which provides for the resolution of day-to-day practical problems through its attention to the detailed interactions between people who live together for prolonged periods.

Structural family therapy also has the advantage that it can address unhelpful interactional patterns in a way which can be mutually respectful of both parents and their children. It is a particularly useful approach for intervention with enmeshment (Minuchin, 1974; Minuchin & Fishman, 1981), a concept that has many similarities with 'overinvolvement' in EE research (Leff & Vaughn, 1985). Enmeshment/overinvolvement is remarkably resistant to influence in many of the intervention studies reported to date, although it has proven amenable to change in families with heterogeneous diagnoses, using a structural approach (Asen *et al.*, 1991).

The Family Project at University College Hospital, London (Camden and Islington Mental Health Trust)

The Family Project originated some 16 years ago and has been through many forms of development and training within the changing structures of the NHS. It has recently focused on training two pairs of linked inpatient and community teams. The family approach adopted by the Project aims to help families develop improved management strategies, but within an overall systemic framework that respects the family's beliefs about illness, and observes and processes the consequences of each practitioner's intervention. Burbach (1996) described a similar approach. Thus, whilst the project aims to reduce the factors which correlate with relapse (EE), particularly in schizophrenia and more recently in bipolar disorder, it requires skills and training in understanding development, family interaction and in self-monitoring of the professional.

In the Family Project team's view, families with a member who has suffered from schizophrenia have certain special needs. These can be summarized as:

(1) Overcoming stigma. This is more than simply convincing families, for example, that the problem is not their 'fault', or helping the family to feel 'normal'. There is often a close relationship between the isolation of the family and overinvolvement of relationships within the family. Thus, efforts to improve either factor can be beneficial to the other.

(2) Encouraging 'purposeful' interactions, counteracting the tendency to respond automatically with unqualified affection or anger. Whilst such responses can be seen as reactions to guilt or helplessness, they are counterproductive to the goal of increasing the competence of the patient. This factor is closely linked to the need to improve communication.

(3) Improving communication by:

(a) Improving the clarity and congruence between verbal and nonverbal modes, and between different contexts of time and place, and between the intent of the 'sender' of a communication and the actual communication 'received'. A simple intervention could be to encourage the family to allow one person to speak at a time, and insisting that the type of, and focus of, communications remains constant for increased periods. This would include ensuring that discussion of practical issues (work, accommodation), do not become diffused by intrusion of metaphorical or irrelevant discourse.

(b) Ensuring that statements are completed, and encouraging the person who speaks to ensure and check that he or she has been heard, and to check how he or she has been understood.

(c) Ensuring that all family members' contributions are acknowledged, and that all have an opportunity to be heard, including for example the withdrawn patient (without forcing the issue).

(d) Increasing the informational content of statements between family members. Habitual responses may be low on information content – such as statements which everyone has heard many times before and no longer take literally. The goal is to increase the proportion of statements which are either clear requests, commands or offers.

(e) Respecting the need for privacy and emotional distance. Patients often need protection from any sense of intrusiveness in their thoughts, as well as from interactions which lead to overstimulation or overarousal (Leff & Vaughn, 1985; Sturgeon et al., 1981, 1984).

Family structure, diagnosis and therapist's choices

We have already stressed the importance of the therapist monitoring his own behaviour. This is in order to ensure that the therapist aims to use his emotional responses as a positive aid to the family, rather than just as a random event. However, what the therapist does in an attempt to achieve a therapeutic result, and the way that he does it, needs also to be mediated by two other factors.

The structure of the family

The fact that the UK – in common with most other European countries – contains people with an increasingly heterogeneous set of cultural values, together with the concurrent changing patterns of marriage, cohabitation and lone-parent childrearing, means that therapists must adapt their approaches to families in ways that make them culturally congruent with the needs of each different family. The adaptations which therapists may need to make have been highlighted by Gorell Barnes (2003). Obvious examples are that a lone parent who has been ill may need to be encouraged to rediscover and exert her authority, or a father who has become very withdrawn may need to be helped to establish small periods of focused helpful contact with his children.

The diagnosis of the ill member of the family

The therapist's approach also needs to be adapted to the particular needs resulting from the diagnosis, as well as the constraints imposed by the particular illness. For example, during the recovery phase of schizophrenia – and there is evidence that this phase may last much longer than previously thought, as much as 2 years – it is very important that the patient is not put under pressure to achieve more than he is comfortable with. The ill individual may need to be helped to build his own positive privacy as a substitute for more negative isolation, and may need to be helped to protect himself from excessive intimacy which can be experienced as overstimulating and intrusive. On the other hand, a patient who has been depressed may crave greater intimacy and see this as a crucial reinforcement of his worth. Other disorders, such as phobic states and obsessive–compulsive disorder, may require a particular mixture of respect for the patient's experience coupled with an appropriate challenge to the 'reverence' often imposed by the symptoms.

Case example 1

A young lone parent, Irma, was disadvantaged by problems of immigration, social class and mental illness. She had three recent admissions to psychiatric hospital, during which the children were placed with foster carers. Following each discharge from hospital the children were returned to her care. A 'honeymoon period' of relief and intimacy was usually then followed by increasing anxiety on the children's part, manifested by increasingly demanding and provocative behaviour. Irma tended to protect herself from these 'onslaughts' by with-drawal, which in turn exacerbated the children's behaviour and was followed by further withdrawal of herself – the vicious cycle ultimately ending in a relapse of Irma's illness.

During a first meeting with the family the psychiatrist asked the children what had been explained to them about why they were attending the Marlborough Family Service and were now meeting him. Initially the children responded with much giggling, swearing and gen-erally vacant-minded behaviour, during which the mother sat passively waiting to see who would be in charge. Eventually the psychiatrist, frustrated by the children's antics, turned to her and said 'OK Irma, how would you like to deal with this, as I'm not sure what to do'. Although apparently surprised that she should in any way be considered as an 'authority', she replied with calm authority which then led to a different sequence of behaviour devel-oping within the room.

AC: ... OK ... How do you want to deal with this? ...

IRMA: [quietly but firmly] Sean!

AC: You take over because ...

IRMA: Sean! ... Billy! ... Sean will you sit down please ... [the two boys immediately sit and calm down, and start paying attention].

AC: Oh! ... If I'd had that kind of authority there wouldn't have been a problem. [The older son, Sean then decides to join the doctor in a more thoughtful discussion] What did you think that Mummy said? ...

SEAN: Because we need people to come here ... [giggles a bit nervously] ... because we're going to play here and it's for controllable children ...

AC: Why is that necessary ... ?

SEAN: Because ... because we need children to be good in that ... in our things.

AC: 'We need' meaning everybody needs that or Mummy needs it?

SEAN: Mummy needs it.

AC: I see ... Do you think the children need it too?

SEAN: Yeah ...

AC: Why do the children need it?

SEAN: Because they think they *want* it ...

AC: [Musing] ... They want some control ... ?

SEAN: Yeah they do ...

AC: ... So you think that Mummy might need some help to get the children to be more controlled?

SEAN: Yes.

Sean is then able to identify a need for control at bath time. Thus Sean has differentiated himself from the more chaotic and oppositional behaviour of his younger brother, by siding with the 'need for control'. Billy has meanwhile become very quiet, sucking his thumb, and at the same time looking intently at Sean. Irma has also been watching and closely listening to Sean, apparently surprised by what she is hearing. Sean starts to be perceived by his mother as no longer 'just trouble', but as a thinking child. This seems to help her to take charge of the chaotic 'bath-time' scenes, which had in the past led to complaints from neighbours about water coming through the ceiling.

Development of alternative modes for the resolution of conflicts

Preventing conflict avoidance can lead to an alternative to the common diffusion of, and nonresolution of, problems. One way for achieving conflict resolution is through questioning the participants in a family dialogue closely about their understanding of what is being said or implied by another, and then encouraging clarification, explanation or further dialogue with that person.

Case example 2

Chrysoulla was a 36-year-old woman with two children, Alexei (16) and Doulla (13). She had been the only daughter in a family of older sons and always acquiesced to her father's wishes. She married a man of her father's choice but this proved disastrous. She returned home to live with her father on the top floor of a large terraced house in north London. She did not complain. However, she withdrew increasingly into her room, keeping the curtains drawn, and would not go out of the house or even leave the top floor. She said nothing and eventually as she was neither speaking, nor at one point eating, she was hospitalized to the local psychiatric unit. Staff there believed that she was probably experiencing hallucinations, but as she rarely spoke, they had no direct evidence of these. A cycle of admission, discharge and readmission went on for 2 years. Whilst her son, Alexei, had begun to make more friends outside the family, and soon found work, Doulla seemed to feel increasingly caught between her grandparent's expectations and her mother's world.

In this section of an interview with Doulla, her elder brother, her mother, her uncle and the aunt who had referred her, the psychiatrist is exploring the issue of whether her mother Chrysoulla is able to have a voice in the upbringing of Doulla.

AC: So, how do you work it in your house? Supposing your mum tells you one thing and your granddad tells you another? Does that ever happen?

ALEXEI: Well you told me that sometimes granddad says you've got to be in at 5 and Mum says it doesn't matter?

DOULLA: Yes, well that does happen sometimes.

AC: So when it happens, which one do you listen to?

DOULLA: [grins] Well, it depends which one I agree with.

AC: Oh I see. That's the system. You choose which one fits what you want and you agree do what that one says.

DOULLA: Yeah.

AC TO CHRYSOULLA: So which one do you think Doulla should listen to, you or your father?

There is a silence. The therapist is not sure if Chrysoulla will answer, as she often does not. The tension begins to mount in the room.

CHRYSOULLA [EVENTUALLY ANSWERS]: Both of us.

AC: Well that sounds good. Providing you both agree. But Chrysoulla who do you think she should obey if you and your father say something different?

CHRYSOULLA [SURPRISES EVERYONE BY ANSWERING IMMEDIATELY]: She should listen to me.

Doulla has meanwhile become silently tearful, which at first appears not to be noticed by any of the family. The therapist pursues this with difficulty but eventually achieves some clarification with the daughter:

DOULLA: I didn't expect her to say anything because she doesn't.

AC: But she did just now, didn't you hear her?

DOULLA: Yes.

AC: In fact she was quite clear, she said that when my father and I say something different I want Doulla to do what I say. So how did that grab you?

DOULLA: Well that's fine, but she never says it to my granddad.

This interchange led to other members of the family supporting Doulla in getting some clarification of to whom she was to be answerable, and in fact seemed to have the effect that Chrysoulla became more vocal, at least where her daughter's welfare was concerned.

Family 'Mental Health Matters' workshops

The Family Project team experienced frustration in achieving a genuine 'climate-change' in the attitudes of the staff (some 1200 in all). Following the publication of McFarlane's outcome trials in New York and Maine (1990; McFarlane *et al.*, 1995), which compared multifamily with 'singlefamily' group work, for families in which one member had suffered a psychotic episode, the team decided to try to replicate the approach within a limited budget framework. The Family Project team, together with two senior nurses, started running single-day workshops for families which included a member who had suffered an episode of major mental illness.

The workshops were explicitly *not* a form of treatment. Soon renamed 'Mental Health Matters' workshops, they were presented as one-off educational events, available to patients and their families, carers and friends. The form and focus of the education included broader issues related to family relationships; the need for reciprocity in those relationships; advocacy in dealing with the frustrations associated with the mental health and other services, as well as more 'formal' information about the meaning of diagnoses, the effects of both prescribed and nonprescribed drugs, the effects of alcohol etc. Although each workshop was designed as a one-off event, they were repeated on average every 6 weeks. A regular clientele developed with a steering group which included both patients and relatives.

Outcome of groups

A most interesting and rather unexpected finding to the increasing staff group was that the explicit definition of the groups as nontherapeutic seemed to be associated with a view expressed by both patients and relatives that the groups had been 'the most helpful thing' that they had experienced during their involvement with the services. Descriptions included reports of a 'new understanding' about the illness; 'the first help I have ever had with medication'; 'the first time my family has had any help'. Both patients and relatives emphasized the broader benefits of 'feeling less alone'. They also had a powerful impact on the staff who were encouraged to attend with the patients for whom they are responsible.

Format of groups

Each workshop is designed with a particular theme, such as diagnosis, drug treatment, alternative therapies, 'voices' groups, the impact of mental illness and hospital admissions on children. It typically starts with a brief lecture, followed by a chaired question and discussion session, and then by small group discussions. A 'reflections' plenary follows, concluding with a structured 'feedback' ritual. Feedback comes from participants who are asked to write on a card on any aspect of the workshop which they would like 'more of' and 'less of', as well as making 'new suggestions'. Staff and participants then share lunch, usually provided by an outside sponsor. Further lectures/demonstration/small group discussions take place in the afternoon, followed by a closing plenary with a discussion of future workshops or future suggested events.

Patients and their relatives are encouraged to join different small groups in order to foster the potential for 'cross-family' and 'cross-generational' relationships. The workshops have developed both energy and a culture of their own which far exceed their rather modest original goals (Cooklin, 2001). Out of these have developed other related workshops, for example for children and their parents, in families in which one or more of the adults has suffered a major mental illness.

Children's workshops

Originally titled 'What Shall We Tell The Children', these workshops last about 4 hours each, and include children and young people of different ages, together with their parents. They start with a short individual family meeting, and a discussion with a worker in order to establish the limits of the areas of discussion tolerable to each family. There is then a short joint group, followed by separate groups for adults and children. The children's group activities include discussion, warm-up exercises and games, followed by the creation of a play. During the break they have pizzas. They then rehearse the play, which is performed by the children for the adults. A discussion follows when ideas for future events are raised. The plays usually represent the children's perceptions of parental mental illness, sometimes surprising and shocking adults (see Cooklin, Chapter 21). However, the capacity to dramatize the experience of mental illness, particularly in a way which is not a literal representation of their own situations, and then be able to change the outcomes, has proved to be both highly therapeutic to the children, as well as acceptable, and even a source of pride, to their parents.

While it was only in the last 4 years that the project introduced multifamily day workshops for families, many family members have asked why this was not always available within the health services!

Working from a child-centred service: additional approaches

In work with a family where a parent is also a patient but the point of referral is a child, it is essential to understand the family processes that are contributing to maintaining the parent's illness, and undermining his capacity to act as a parent. A study of 6 years of clinical work in one centre (Dowling & Gorell Barnes, 1999) found that a number of referrals showed a link between mental health problems and parental separation, with a particular feature of violence from a partner connected to symptoms of illness in mothers. In families where violence between a man and the mother of his children has been a regular feature, sons may also imitate their father's behaviour and take on the 'mantle' of the 'controlling male' after a father has left, or been ejected from the home.

An Eastern European mother, presenting with anxious depression, panic attacks and severe agoraphobia described for example how her husband would control her by threatening her with a knife, and how both she and 5-year-old son would repeat aspects of the pattern of violent behaviour when he (her son) wanted to get her to do something:

> I don't remember anything...how he shut me up...but I say things sometimes...I say 'don't do that I'm going to kill you' [to her son] and he [her son] says 'I'm going to kill you'...'yes' he says to me 'you're my wife, I'm your husband'...he's my husband! I say...'you're not my husband, you're my son, do as you're told'...he kick me and he throw his toys everywhere'...

Disentangling such processes, which bind women and male children in violent ways, involves detailed work with both parties at a pace that can be understood by small children. The sense of regaining parental control is usually accompanied by a diminution of the symptoms of panic – in a situation where the violence has stopped between the adult partners. Other pathological experience underlying mental illness in a parent, usually but not always in mothers, includes sexual abuse, both in childhood and within marital relationships. This needs careful attention in relation to parental concerns about and protection of their own children.

Where a mother has herself been sexually abused as a child, individual therapeutic work is usually of value, and may be essential. However, where a mother is using her own experience to highlight a concern about her children, work with her as a parent should be focused always with a mind to her parental strengths and capacity to look after her children, rather than her abuse being dwelt on as something from which she cannot herself recover. Where a family approach is not borne in mind, a woman can find herself additionally pathologized by professional concern that keeps her in the 'abused' role, rather than balancing this with her own parental concern to protect her children.

Developing alternative descriptions of a parent who is also a patient

An important influence on processes of illness and wellness may also be what the person who is in the patient position is saying to himself about the illness. In particular, do they see the illness as an overall description of themselves, or within a range of alternative descriptions of themselves and their own functioning they have been able to keep open, both in the family and within their own minds.

People can be invited to bring in photographs of 'the parent who is a patient' in different relationship contexts, within and outside the family, so that several images then become available for description and discussion. For example, one of us (GGB) encouraged a young woman whose overriding image of her mother was as a 'mad person' to find photographs of her mother when she was the same age as she, Isobel is now, as a late teenager, as a young married woman, and as an active mother with her children. Teenagers or young adults can be encouraged to write letters to other family members such as aunts, uncles and grandparents to elicit new descriptions of their ill parent. This leads both to clearer expression of anger with the *effects* of the illness, rather than with the person as a whole, as well as helping to mourn the parent who was once well-functioning in many social contexts. Thus, it also creates the freedom to relate to the parent in more than one way in their minds.

Working with mothers who have had their mental frailty exacerbated by oppressive behaviour from men, it may be useful to explore with them the different contexts in which they have felt disqualified. This may help them to think of the actual words used that have 'put them down' and the therapist may help them to think about what they would actually say the next time, and what other female relatives or friends (who do not feel threatened by this man) might say. In rehearsing these small sequences, the goal is to harness the positive ideas derived from others who the parent is close to, as well as to identify a direction the client wants to take in order that she can feel more effective the next time she encounters similar situations. This is particularly powerful where a parent is feeling disempowered to a point where they no longer trust their own voice (Gorell Barnes, 2003). Where a parent is in charge of their own young children, eliciting from the children the things a parent does well can also be empowering. The testimony of a son who can say 'you're a good mum, you've brought up two sons who love you, and you make great pancakes as well' carries a lot of weight, as does that of a daughter who can say 'I know when you go down that it's only because it's January, and you'll be going shopping again when the daffs are out'.

Frameworks for working with the families of patients with psychiatric disorders

In this chapter we have built on the proven value of the various family management approaches, to add two particular aspects:

(1) To carry out the work in a more dialectic than didactic mode, relating closely to the beliefs and cultural values of the different family members. This also means understanding and starting from their beliefs about the illness and its possible methods of treatment.

(2) To include as essential a focus on the needs of children of the ill parent – their understanding of the illness, their self-blame and adoption of excess responsibility, their fears etc.

We have expanded the frame of reference of this work to include primary care and child mental health settings, whilst also focusing on ward and community mental health teams. We have also considered the cross-reference points of common family stresses and traumata: particularly migration, separation and divorce, and violence and domination.

We have also included reports of two initiatives which can very usefully and easily be implemented by any mental health service provider: The Mental Health Matters workshops, and the equivalent workshops for families with children.

REFERENCES

Anderson, C. M., Hogarty, G. E. & Reiss, D. J. (1980). Family treatment of adult schizophrenic patients: a psycho-educational approach. *Schizophrenia Bulletin*, 6, 490–505.

Anderson, C. M., Reiss, D. J. & Hogarty, G. E. (1986). *Schizophrenia and the Family*. New York: Guilford Press.

Asen, K., Berkowitz, R., Cooklin, A., Leff, J., Loader, P., Piper, R. & Rein, L. (1991). Family therapy outcome research: a trial for families, therapists and researchers. *Family Process*, 30, 3–20.

Asen, E., Dawson, N. & McHugh, B. (2001). *Multiple Family Therapy: The Marlborough Model and its Wider Applications*. London: Karnac.

Bishop, P., Clilverd, A., Cooklin, A. & Hunt, U. (2002). Mental health matters: a multi-family framework for mental health intervention. *Journal of Family Therapy*, 24, 31–46.

Brown, G. (1991). Life events and clinical depression. *Practical Reviews in Psychiatry, Series 3, No. 2, Education in Practice*, 4–6A.

Brown, G., Harris, T. & Bifulco, A. (1986). Long term effects of early loss of a parent. In *Depression in Young People: Developmental and Clinical perspectives*, ed. M. Rutter, C. Izard & P. Read, pp. 251–96. New York: Guilford Press.

Burbach, F. (1996). Family based interventions in psychosis. An overview of, and comparison between, family therapy and family management approaches. *Journal of Mental Health, 5*, 111–34.

Cooklin, A. (2001). Eliciting children's thinking in families and family therapy. *Family Process, 40*, 293–311.

Cooklin, A., McHugh, B. & Miller, A. (1983). An institution for change: experience of the development of a family day unit. *Family Process, 22*, 453–68.

Cottrell, D. (1989). Family therapy influences on general adult psychiatry. *British Journal of Psychiatry, 154*, 473–7.

Dowling, E. & Gorell Barnes, G. (1999). *Working with Children and Parents through Separation and Divorce*. Basingstoke: Macmillan.

Falloon, I. R. (2000). Problem solving as a core strategy in the prevention of schizophrenia and other mental disorders. *Australian and New Zealand Journal of Psychiatry, 34 (Suppl.) S 185–90*.

Gorell Barnes, G. (2003). *Family Therapy in Changing Times* (2nd Edition). Basingstoke: Macmillan.

Hogarty, C. E., Anderson, C. M. & Reiss, D. J. (1986). Family psychoeducation, social skills training and maintenance chemotherapy in the aftercare treatment of schizophrenia, I: One-year effects of a controlled study of relapse and expressed emotion. *Archives of General Psychiatry, 43*, 633–42.

Jenkins, J. H. & Karno, M. (1992). The meaning of expressed emotion: theoretical issues raised by cross-cultural research. *American Journal of Psychiatry, 149*, 9–21.

Kliman, J. & Trimble, D. W. (1983). Network therapy. In *Handbook of Family and Marital Therapy*, ed. B. B. Wolman & G. Stricker. London: Plenum Press.

Leff, J. & Vaughn, C. (1985). *Expressed Emotion in Families*. London: Guilford Press.

Leff, J. P., Kuipers, I., Berkowitz, R., Liberlein-Fries, R. & Sturgeon, D. (1982). A controlled trial of social intervention in the families of schizophrenic patients. *British Journal of Psychiatry, 141*, 121–34.

Leff, J., Wig, N. N., Ghosh, A. et al. (1987). Expressed emotion and schizophrenia in North India, III: Influence of relatives' expressed emotion on the course of schizophrenia in Chandigarh. *British Journal of Psychiatry, 151*, 166–73.

Leff, J. P., Berkowitz, R., Shavit, N., Strachan, A., Glass, I. & Vaughn, C. (1990). A trial of family therapy v. a relatives' group for schizophrenia. Two-year follow-up. *British Journal of Psychiatry, 150*, 571–7.

Magliano, L., Fadden, G., Fiorillo, A. et al. (1999). Family burden and coping strategies in schizophrenia: are key relatives really different to other relatives? *Acta Psychiatrica Scandinavica, 99*, 10–15.

McFarlane, W. R. (1990). Multiple family groups and the treatment of schizophrenia. In *Handbook of Schizophrenia, Vol. 4: Psychosocial Treatment of Schizophrenia*, ed. M. I. Hertz, S. J. Keith & J. P. Docherty. Oxford: Elsevier Science Publishers.

McFarlane, W. R., Link, B., Dushay, R., Marchal, J. & Crilly, J. (1995). Psychoeducational multiple family groups: four-year relapse outcome in schizophrenia. *Family Process, 34*, 127–44.

Minuchin, S. (1974). *Families and Family Therapy*. London: Tavistock.

Minuchin, S. & Fishman, C. (1981). *Family Therapy Techniques*. Cambridge, MA: Harvard University Press.

Moltz, D. A. (1993). Bipolar disorder and the family: an integrative model. *Family Process, 32*, 409–23.

Pearlmutter, R. A. (1996). *A Family Approach to Psychiatric Disorder*. Washington, DC: American Psychiatric Press.

Perlick, D. A., Rosenheck, R. R., Clarkin, J. F., Raue, P. & Sirey, J. (2001). Impact of family burden and patient symptom status on clinical outcome in bipolar affective disorder. *Journal of Nervous and Mental Disease, 189*, 31–7.

Randolph, E. T., Eta, S., Glynn S. M. et al. (1994). Behavioural family management: outcome of a clinical-based intervention. *British Journal of Psychiatry, 164*, 601–6.

Sampson, H., Messinger, S. L. & Towne, R. D. (1964). *Schizophrenic Women: Studies in Marital Crisis*. New York: Atherton Press.

Schuff, G. H. & Asen, K. E. (1996). The disturbed parent and the disturbed family. In *Parental Psychiatric Disorder: Distressed Parents and their Families*, ed. M. Göpfert, J. Webster & M. V. Seeman, pp. 135–51. Cambridge: Cambridge University Press.

Speck, R. & Attneave, C. (1973). *Family Networks*. New York: Pantheon.

Strachan, A. M. (1986). Family intervention for the rehabilitation of schizophrenia: toward protection and coping. *Schizophrenia Bulletin, 12*, 678–98.

Sturgeon, D. A., Kuipers, L., Berkowitz, R., Turpin, G. & Leff, J. (1981). Psychophysiological responses of schizophrenic patients to high and low expressed emotion relatives. *British Journal of Psychiatry, 133*, 40–5.

Sturgeon, D. A., Turpin, G., Kuipers, L., Berkowitz, R. & Leff, J. (1984). Psychosocial responses of schizophrenic patients to high and low expressed emotion relatives: a follow-up study. *British Journal of Psychiatry, 145*, 62–9.

Wig, N. N., Menon, D. K., Bedi, H. et al. (1987). Expressed emotion and schizophrenia in North India, II: Distribution of expressed emotion components among relatives of schizophrenic patients in Aarhus and Chandigarh. *British Journal of Psychiatry, 151*, 160–5 (correction 870).

Part VI

Models for collaborative services and staff training

23

Keeping the family in mind: setting a local agenda for change

Clare Mahoney

National Institute for Mental Health (North-West Team), UK

Without changes in culture and practice within health and social care organizations, there can be little improvement to provision for children and families affected by mental distress. A strategic combination of actions are needed, but the cornerstone of all change must be the participation of children and families themselves. This chapter is an account of how organizations in Liverpool, UK, are working with children and families to implement the recommendations of a recent consultation with service users (Göpfert *et al.*, 1999). A small development project called 'Keeping the family in mind' (KFIM) and run by Barnardos Action with Young Carers (see Bilsborough, Chapter 1) has been set up to facilitate and coordinate the change agenda.

Why change is necessary

Adult and child services do not habitually connect and communicate. The following situation illustrates how this separateness can sometimes result in disservice to families. A children's social worker asked the Action with Young Carers project if they would explain to two children why they had been fostered to Liverpool relatives some 100 miles' distance from their home town. One of the children's parents had serious mental health problems, to the extent that the parents were unable to care for their children. The children were already fostered without any of the professionals involved having had this important conversation with the children. Why this omission? The ill parent had a social worker who knew about mental health, but not about children. The children's social workers felt they did not know enough about mental health to undertake the explanation. Along the way, it is certain that other professionals also came into contact with the children's mother. These workers felt unable to cross their 'professional' boundaries in order to explain to the children why their lives were being turned upside down.

Contributors to the "Keeping the Family in Mind" (KFIM) consultation (Göpfert *et al.*, 1999) highlighted similar experiences:

When I was taken to hospital when I had a breakdown, my eldest child was 14. I had four children then. No-one took the time to say to them 'Are you all right? Do you understand what is happening?' . . .

This quotation cries out for solutions which need not require sophisticated training. Ensuring these children's needs are attended to needs empathy and willingness, basic communication skills and a better use of resources than currently exists. Why then are these situations neither rare nor unique? And if the problem is clear, why is the solution so difficult?

The policy context

Conventional health and social care services seem unable to moderate some of the consequences of mental distress on children and families, even where services have the capability and resources. More disturbingly, it would appear that services can sometimes perpetuate and exacerbate distress.

Macdonald describes this as the 'fatal inappropriateness' of a service planning and delivery system dominated by the medical model (Macdonald, 1993, p. 19). The antidote is an approach to planning health and social care systems termed 'primary health care' (World Health Organization/UNICEF, 1978). The three pillars of primary health care are participation, equity and working with other sectors. Recent policies for health and social care in the UK reflect the currency of this approach, typically aiming for social inclusion, equality of access, integration, prevention and participation (Department of Health, 2000; North West Regional Office/Department of Health, 2002). The policy incentive to reduce the impact of poverty on health, and increase access to health services by using these approaches, is stronger than it has ever been (Acheson, 1998).

Nevertheless, even where policy and guidance is explicit in requiring that services work with the whole family (Department of Health, 1998), it tends to be diluted by service planning systems which continue to reflect the divisions between child and adult services. The evidence that this policy is helping to ensure that services deliver appropriate and useful support to families affected by mental health problems is not yet there.

Does this matter? Perhaps not to a crucial extent. Policy is not, in itself, the key driver for change. 'The notion that policy makers exercise – or ought to exercise – some kind of direct and determinant control over policy implementation might be called the 'noble lie' of conventional public administration and policy analysis' (Elmore, 1979–80, p. 603) (see Göpfert *et al.*, Chapter 5). While policy can be helpful, other change agents are effective. Of the three primary health care pillars, participation, equity and joint-working, the greatest of these is participation.

Building for participation

Knowledge of current policy or community development theory was not necessary to identify problems and issues requiring action. The participants of the KFIM consultation told their stories of how services, as well as mental health problems, affected them and their families. The starting point was to listen to these families and to identify the problems as they experienced them. The next step was to find ways of involving them in the development of solutions. This bottom-up form of policy development and implementation is described by Elmore (1979–80) as 'backward mapping'. It begins with understanding what happens at the point when service users come into contact with services. 'The closer one is to the source of the problem, the greater is one's ability to influence it' (Elmore, 1979–80, p. 605).

Participation means gathering together, sharing ideas and planning action (Martin, 1983; Traitler, 1974). Its collective nature is one of its most effective attributes, particularly in relation to health. The examples already given show how addressing the needs of an adult with mental health problems can result in the creation of problems for other family members. Collective action aims to bring about better health for everyone, without impairing the health of anyone.

Consultation can be a first step to participation, though if the process stops there, it can be perceived as tokenism (Arnstein, 1971). Without follow-up action, it does not necessarily help develop group structures for the 'higher' forms of participation, those of decision-making and evaluation (Macdonald, 1993). These are the aspects of participation most likely to bring about change. Since participation is about the redistribution of power, it 'is rarely going to be a totally smooth process, not anywhere, and not in health care systems either' (Macdonald, 1993, p. 98). For services, the investment in working relationships with service users is not primarily about process, but in learning about how to become more effective.

The work in Liverpool began with a consultation for two main reasons: there was little awareness of the health needs of the whole family in any parts of the service planning and delivery systems; and it was hard to access the perspectives of parents, carers and children through existing structures.

Parents and carers will be under-represented in user-led groups unless their exclusion by default is addressed. Parents are often women who have little access to services because they have caring responsibilities. The combined jeopardy of caring responsibilities and mental ill health is sufficient to militate against a parent's recourse to mechanisms for user-involvement. The impact of racism, disability, stigma and poverty adds further impediment (Bird, 1999; Webb, 1998; Wilkinson, 1996). Children and young people are less likely than adults to be listened to and have their views taken seriously, either within the family or by service providers (James & Prout, 1997).

To reduce the effects of this marginalization, the KFIM development project was established within a children's organization. Barnardos Action with Young Carers had a track record of involving children and young people in decision-making and evaluation, and was linked into national initiatives researching the experiences of children and young people (Aldridge *et al.*, 2001). It was also one of the few organizations in Liverpool that had developed work practices to bridge the divide between child and adult services. The project began initially by strengthening its links with parents and carers via local service-user and stakeholder organizations. Its capacity to facilitate change continues to depend on its ability to maintain and develop these relationships with children and families.

Learning to listen and listening to learn

In this section, learning from the KFIM consultation and its follow-up development project is used to illustrate how service users identify key problems in the existing service regime and point to those areas of work that would benefit from change. All quotations are from the KFIM report.

The importance of strengthening parents and families

The least little thing starts me off worrying over something, over the children, whether they're all right and that starts me off . . . It upsets me a lot, you see why I'm frightened is that because I had the other two took off (me) and I'm frightened of losing these two . . .

One woman saw me at the office . . . and spoke to me for about half an hour, maybe an hour . . . Then she came up and saw me in the garden with my son, playing with him and because he wouldn't do what I was asking him to do she wrote the report for the courts as if she's known me all my life . . . What annoyed me, the one that did the report on me came out into the garden and saw me with M, but she didn't see before she came, that I was playing with M in the car, but she didn't see that part. She came 10 minutes later . . . and she said I'd only played with him for a few minutes and M wouldn't listen to me. M wouldn't listen to me because he was too excited.

The detrimental consequences of assessing parents badly or wrongly, as sometimes happens, can be far-reaching for both the parents and the children.

Trust and continuity of staff

It is not that parents do not want help from services. Those elements and attributes of services seen as helpful were appreciated and applauded. The importance of developing long-term and trusting relationships with staff was often highlighted as a factor for effectiveness, but the benefits of continuity are largely ignored by service planners, as shown by any organizational restructuring.

I don't want a person who'll say yes, no, three bags full and then put in a bad report on me . . . She got to know me as an individual person and she's been up to my flat and she said it's nice but you could do with wiping the table down and I said OK I'll do it. At least someone was on my side for a change, someone who knows the real me.

. . . I asked her would she be as straightforward with me in the best way possible. I said I won't take an overdose or cut my wrists, but I want someone to be frank with me . . .

Opportunities for prevention

Parents recognized that services had the potential to help during episodes of mental distress and they pinpointed opportunities for preventative work.

If social workers would have just looked in and made sure that those kids were OK, seeing was there anything they needed . . . That stopped me from getting better, all that extra worry, it stopped me from getting properly better, quicker.

Those parents who were consulted recognized and were fearful of a service emphasis on child protection and risk assessment. As one parent summed up, 'they assess the risk to the child, they don't assess the impact'.

Better joint working between child and adult services

A focus on risk assessment is one consequence of the increase in specialized services. Many staff are expert in child protection, or mental health, or parenting support and assessment, but it is rare to find these areas of knowledge combined (Kearney *et al.*, 2000). This restricts the effectiveness of service provision (Blanch *et al.*, 1994) (see Falkov, Chapter 27). Support which might be found in the primary care, education, community and voluntary sectors, can remain untapped and uncoordinated.

The following example describes the centrality of child care, points to the importance of making better use of existing resources, and contributes to understanding of the need to work across professional boundaries.

During all these problems, I was stuck in. I used to go to the day centre, thank God for that place. Luckily it's the only day centre I actually know that allows you to take kids with you . . . We have had a lot of help from the day centre, more than from anywhere else really. There's always someone there you can have a chat to . . . [Having children in day centres] . . . that causes problems, because there's some people there that can't cope with kids, especially little ones. Fortunately mine were 11 and 9 so they were able to be told to sit down and do that and be quiet. There are a lot of people who can't stand the noise of kids . . . they don't have the facilities for a crèche.

Coordination of care and facilities for children

During the consultation, we came across only two mental health day centres, both in the voluntary sector, which allowed children on the premises. One of them ran a crèche, though keeping it funded was a persistent problem. The other, described above, was inclusive and welcoming to children, even though it did not provide a service for children per se. A third day centre had a close working relationship with a local nursery, so that if the child did not attend, day centre staff would be called and asked to check on the parent. These are examples of working across agencies and outside professional boundaries. Parents highlighted this as important, while many staff emphasized this as difficult, citing barriers such as public liability and child protection requirements.

One of the early activities of the KFIM development project was to work with a hospital to design a family room in one of its psychiatric wards. Children and young people played a major role in its design and promotion. The cost implications have been small and a preliminary evaluation suggests that it is well used. Initiatives such as this are almost unique despite the fact that all adult psychiatric hospitals in the UK are required to have developed protocols for children visiting their parents (Department of Health, 1999).

Stigma and labelling

Nearly every participant, including the children consulted, described how the prejudice and stigma attached to mental distress had affected their access to facilities that helped with the task of raising children. These facilities included day centres and clinics, as well as school, nurseries, play and social activities. Every parent needs family and social networks to raise children and the capacity of distressed parents to maintain these tends to be reduced even before the impact of stigma is taken into account (Booth & Booth, 1997; McKay & Pollard, 1996). Two users described how neighbours had falsely accused them of prostitution and child abuse, which had a subsequent devastating impact on their access to support systems.

Conclusion

The inclination in service-providing systems to focus on barriers and limitations to change can be regulated by service user involvement which has an emphasis on problem solving. The challenge to services is fundamentally one of listening actively to the stories and experiences of all family members including children and young people. Increased participation of parents, carers and their children is needed in the planning and design of services in order to evaluate whether services help in the way they are supposed to. Without this, services risk adding to families' existing difficulties and missing opportunities to be helpful.

For copies of the Keeping the Family in Mind report, or more information about the project, contact Keeping the Family in Mind, c/o Young Carers, 24 Colquitt Street, Liverpool, England, UK, L1 4DE

REFERENCES

Acheson, D. (1998). *Independent Inquiry into Inequalities in Health*. London: The Stationery Office.

Aldridge, J., Becker, S. & Dearden, C. (2001). Children caring for family members with severe and enduring mental health problems. *YCRG Bulletin: The Bulletin of the Young Carer Research Group, Issue* 2. Loughborough: Loughborough University.

Arnstein, S. R. (1971). Eight rungs on the ladder of citizen participation. In *Citizen Participation: Effecting Community Change*, ed. E. S. Cahn & B. A. Posset, pp. 69–91. New York: Praeger.

Bird, L. (1999). *The Fundamental Facts . . . All the Latest Facts and Figures on Mental Illness*. London: The Mental Health Foundation.

Blanch, A. K., Nicholson, J. & Purcell, J. (1994). Parents with severe mental illness and their children: the need for human service integration. *Journal of Mental Health Administration, 21*, 388–96.

Booth, T. & Booth, W. (1997). *Exceptional Childhoods, Unexceptional Children – Growing up with Parents who have Learning Difficulties*. London: Family Policy Studies Centre.

Department of Health (1998). *Supporting Families: A Consultation Document*. London: The Stationery Office.

Department of Health (1999). HSC 1999/222: LAC (99)32. *Mental Health Act 1983 Code of Practice: Guidance on the Visiting of Psychiatric Patients by Children*. London: Department of Health.

Department of Health (2000). *The NHS Plan*. London: The Stationery Office.

Elmore, R. (1979–80). Backward mapping: implementation research and policy decisions. *Political Science Quarterly, 94*, 601–16.

Göpfert, M., Harrison, P. & Mahoney, C. (1999). *Keeping the Family in Mind: Participative Research into Mental Ill-health and how it Affects the Whole Family*. Liverpool: Save the Children, Barnardos, Imagine and North Mersey Community Trust.

James, A. & Prout, A. (1997). *Constructing and Reconstructing Childhood*. London: Falmer Press.

Kearney, P., Levin, E. & Rosen. G. (2000). *Alcohol, Drug and Mental Health Problems: Working with Families*. London: National Institute for Social Work.

Macdonald, J. (1993). *Primary Health Care: Medicine in its Place*. London: Earthscan.

Martin, P. (1983). Community participation in primary health care. *Primary Health Care Issues, 1*, 5. Washington, DC: American Public Health Association.

Mayes, K., Diggins, M. & Falkov, A. (1998). *Crossing Bridges – Training Resources for Working with Mentally ill Parents and their Children*. Liverpool: Department of Health.

McKay, D. & Pollard, J. (1996). Community support networks in education and care settings. In *Parental psychiatric disorder: Distressed Parents and their Families*, ed. M. Göpfert, J. Webster & M. V. Seeman, pp. 152–60. Cambridge: Cambridge University Press.

North West Regional Office, Department of Health (2002). *Supporting Children and Young People: The Work of the North West Children's Task Force.* Liverpool: NWRO/DOH.

Traitler, R. (1974). *People's Participation in Development. A Reflection on the Debate.* CCPPD, Document 4. Geneva: World Council of Churches.

Webb, E. (1998). Children and the Inverse Care Law. *British Medical Journal, 316,* 1588–91.

Wilkinson, R. (1996). *Unhealthy Societies.* London: Routledge.

World Health Organization/UNICEF (1978). *Primary Health Care: the Alma Ata Conference.* Geneva: WHO.

24

Are services for families with a mentally ill parent adequate?

Duncan McLean, Jennifer Hearle and John McGrath

Queensland Centre for Schizophrenia Research, Wacol, Australia

Introduction

Parenthood is a valued social role. People with mental illness have the same aspirations for parenthood and face the same challenges associated with this role as do other community members (Sand, 1995). The parenting experience varies enormously from person to person; for those parents with the added dimension of mental illness this remains true. For some it results in improved social networks, a greater sense of identity, a meaningful work role and reduced stigma (Schwab *et al.*, 1991). For others, the parenting experience may be associated with grief, loss and frustration (Human Rights and Equal Opportunity Commission, 1993). For many people with a mental illness, particularly women, the parenting role preceded the onset of mental illness.

In this chapter we will provide a brief overview of the literature about the needs of parents with a psychotic disorder. A case example will be used to illustrate some of the practical issues in delivering services to these families. Based on two recent surveys undertaken by the authors, we will summarize our findings regarding the needs of parents with psychotic disorders, from the perspective of both the consumer and of the service provider. Finally, we will address the challenge of closing the gap between optimal and current services.

First, what is the scope of the problem? Parenthood has not always been seen as an option for many people with psychotic disorders. Many individuals with psychosis were ostracized from mainstream society, kept hidden by families who were ashamed of them or locked away in asylums or other institutions, giving them little opportunity to form relationships. When forced segregation failed, or when sexual exploitation occurred, the resultant offspring were either terminated, adopted out or raised by the extended family. More recently, many factors have conspired to change this pattern. In Australia, as in many other countries, the availability of more effective medications in the 1950s, the civil rights movement of the 1960s and the progress towards deinstitutionalization and community care all had a significant impact on the likelihood of a person with mental illness not only becoming a parent, but also being able to fulfill that role to some extent. A recent national survey of psychosis in Australia interviewed a representative sample of individuals with psychotic disorders. Of the 980 interviewed, 33.1% were parents, and based on the total group, 8.1% had dependent children (Jablensky *et al.*, 1999).

Background

A review of the literature shows a relative lack of empirical data related to the needs of parents with psychotic disorders. In the past, research about parents with mental illness tended to focus on genetics, and the ongoing search for the elusive 'cause' of mental illness. Studies would examine the parent–child relationship, either in an attempt to attribute poor parenting or communication skills as the cause of the illness or in an attempt to identify risk factors that may predict later onset of illness. In general, the picture of mentally ill parents painted by the literature has been a negative one, with a tendency to focus on the toxic or dangerous impact of parental mental illness on children (Oates, 1997).

In more recent years, however, there have been attempts to identify parents with mental illness and to consider the service implications for this client group. Most studies in this area have been qualitative in design. Studies from both the UK (Bassett *et al.*, 1999) and the US (Nicholson *et al.*, 1998a) identify the difficulties of dealing with general, day-to-day parenting and the fear of losing contact with children as central issues for parents with a mental illness. A recent study by Wang & Goldschmidt (1994, 1996) was based on interviews with mentally ill parents with dependent children (n = 50: 33 women, 17 men). This study revealed that 25% of the families had offspring placed in institutions or foster care and 40% had never received professional help related to their children. In addition, 33% of the parents expressed a need for support which was not received, and many stated they did not know where to go for help or would not be comfortable doing so. There has been a marked lack of data on the experiences and needs of fathers with mental illness. One study (Nicholson *et al.*, 1999) compared fathers and mothers with mental illness. Fathers were shown to have the same resource and service needs as mothers.

The literature shows that service providers have been slow to recognize this population. One study (DeChillo *et al.*, 1987) reviewed hospital charts and found that the presence of children was frequently not acknowledged. Only 20% of charts recorded the presence of children, and even then there was no information concerning the whereabouts and placement circumstances of these children (see Falkov, Chapter 27).

Community and service providers have been found to have negative perceptions when interviewed about families with a psychotic parent (S. Wragg, personal communication). These include: that children are irrevocably harmed by remaining in the care of parents who may be psychotic; that parents with a mental illness are incapable of caring for children; and that parents with a mental illness have no right to have children.

Several studies (Cogan, 1998; Cowling, 1996; Wang & Goldschmidt, 1996) have examined the experiences of mentally ill parents with professional help and intervention in relation to their children. They all found that there is significant contact between parents and both government and nongovernment agencies, although parents do not always perceive this contact as helpful (Wang & Goldschmidt, 1996). Parents report that they would rather manage alone (Cowling, 1996). They also fear that asking for help will result in them losing custody of their children (Cogan, 1998).

The following case example illustrates the complexities of situations involving parents with a mental illness, and highlights the urgency of service integration and greater collaboration.

Case example: John and his family vs. the system

John developed schizophrenia in adolescence. He met his wife (Tracey) at a social club for people with disabilities. Initially his family viewed his relationship positively and was supportive of the newlyweds, especially Tracey who had a moderate intellectual disability. With the birth of their grandson, however, extended family members from both sides were called upon to provide increasing levels of support to John, Tracey and their son Ben.

Child health staff monitored the physical health of the baby and trained Tracey in infant care. As Ben grew older, however, both parents had increasing difficulty in meeting Ben's developmental needs and responding to his sometimes difficult behaviour. School staff became concerned, as Ben was often late, unkempt in appearance and without lunch. They raised these issues with John and Tracey who were unable to respond. John became increasingly paranoid, refusing to leave the house and increasingly resentful of the extended family's attempts to assist. After months of near total isolation John was hospitalized under the Mental Health Act. This occurred with police assistance and was so traumatizing to Tracey that she became mute and totally unable to respond to the situation – she too was hospitalized and child welfare officers placed Ben with members of the extended family.

John's mental state was stabilized, however he remained without insight in regard to his illness, angry at being admitted and suspicious of family and service providers. He cancelled his appointments with the mental health service and now sees a general practitioner. Ben returned home and initially was monitored by child protection services. There has also been continuing support from his extended family.

Both Ben's parents love him dearly but are unable to adequately meet his needs, resulting in him having learning and behavioural problems at school. Mental health services are unable to assist the family, as John will not consent to their involvement. Child protection services identify Ben as neglected but assess the family situation as not warranting removal of Ben. Tracey's intellectual disability precludes her from participating in generic parent and family support programmes. This situation is exacerbated by John's reluctance to acknowledge any problem or cooperate with any voluntary support services. He sees any attempts at support and intervention as threatening. Disability services do not see the family as a priority for service, as the main identified problem is in regard to adequacy of parenting, which they see as a child protection matter. The extended family is unable to provide the level of support needed and are reluctant to be involved. It is likely that this family will continue to struggle on until John's mental state deteriorates to the extent of mandatory treatment, or until Ben's behaviour deteriorates to a point that brings him to the attention of the juvenile justice system. By this time irreparable harm is likely to have occurred to all members of this family.

This case is far from isolated and illustrates issues familiar to practitioners from child welfare, mental health, education and disability services. Because the needs of this family are complex they are unlikely to be adequately met by a single service – however, they also are not within the core business of any one service. In times of increasing demand for services, competition for funding and inadequate community resources, it is easy for such situations to continue until a crisis develops. Such circumstances are traumatic for all family members and unlikely to result in good outcomes for anyone.

This case also demonstrates the need for good collaboration between agencies and partnerships between services and family members. For many families the only experience they have of service delivery is when they are in crisis and have little or no choice about what happens. This may mean involvement with workers they have never met before and result in decisions being made in which they are unable to participate. When multiple agencies are involved communication frequently breaks down and can be exacerbated by services using different practice frameworks and sometimes working towards conflicting goals.

In the above case example, mental health workers were in favour of Ben remaining with his parents as they saw that as a motivating factor for John to remain on medication. They saw John as their client and were therefore working towards his identified goal of fatherhood. School staff advocated for Ben, seeing placement elsewhere as his best chance for optimal education where his developmental needs would be met. Non mental-health staff involved had limited understanding of or training in mental illness and treatment. They were fearful of John and had difficulty in understanding his behaviour. It is easy to see how parents can get conflicting messages from different services and how this can lead to decreasing trust in workers. Links between mental health, child protection and welfare agencies are often inadequate and frequently informal. The differing agendas of services often mean poor collaboration and a failure to deal with the needs of the whole family adequately, if at all.

A survey of the needs of parents with psychotic disorders

A survey was conducted to gain insight into the characteristics and needs of parents with psychotic disorders. Full details of the methods and the findings can be found elsewhere (Hearle *et al.*, 1999; McGrath *et al.*, 1999). In brief, participants were systematically drawn from two community mental health services and an extended-care psychiatric hospital. A structured questionnaire was used to elicit a wide range of relevant demographic, illness and child-care related information. This study included only people who were diagnosed with a psychotic illness, although the issues raised are certainly relevant to a much wider population, including people with other types of psychiatric disorder.

Three hundred and forty-two individuals with a psychotic disorder participated in the study. The diagnoses included schizophrenia, schizophreniform psychosis, delusional disorder, bipolar affective disorder, depression with psychotic features, schizoaffective disorder and atypical psychosis. Over a third of participants (36.3%) were parents. These 124 parents had a total of 323 children. Most women (59.1%) with psychoses were mothers, while only a quarter of men (25.4%) with psychoses were fathers. Of the parents, 11 (8.9%) had a partner with a serious mental illness.

Of the 124 parents, 27 fathers and 21 mothers had children less than 16 years of age, and 20 of these parents (41.7%) had their children living with them. In total, there were 75 offspring who were aged less than 16. Of these, 34 children resided with the parent taking part in this study, 24 resided with the other parent (often the well parent after separation), four resided with other relatives of their parents and five were in permanent foster care or adoption. The whereabouts of three children was unknown to the parent, and data were missing for five offspring.

Concerning child-care, the majority of parents (87%) had relied on relatives for assistance, while 24% relied on friends. Other forms of child-care included: foster care (14%), crèche (4%), day-care (3%) and emergency respite care (5%). Five children had been placed in permanent adoption (5%). Parents were asked what type of agencies organized child-care assistance or interventions. The most commonly identified were state-government statutory child protection agencies (18%), followed by mental health clinics (13%) and church groups (10%). Of the parents, 11% stated that they had received intervention relating to care of their child against their will.

Parents were also asked if certain prespecified factors had impeded access to ideal child-care assistance. The following factors were noted, in decreasing order of frequency: a desire to manage alone (49%), an inability to pay for help (40%), hadn't thought of seeking help (37%), not knowing where to get help (36%), a fear that children would be removed from the parent (30%), being too embarrassed to ask for help (22%), no services available in the subject's vicinity (21%) and having asked for but not received help (12%).

The study provides insight into the pattern of child-care utilization for parents with a psychotic disorder. Clearly, family and friends are often relied upon for support. Providing timely and practical support related to child-care for these carers may serve to keep such support networks intact. Other researchers have also commented on the important role that a supportive social support network can play in keeping children within the family system (Miller, 1997; Nicholson *et al.*, 1998*b*; Wang & Goldschmidt, 1996).

This study also found that many parents with psychoses did identify that they needed support, but were unable to access this for various reasons. Those involved in service planning need to address barriers such as lack of affordable, local services in order to improve outcome for the current generation of parents with psychotic disorders. Other factors that impede access to optimal child-care (e. g. embarrassment, fear of loss of child) require consumer education and practical demonstrations that services respect the needs of parents with psychotic illnesses.

The needs and desires of parents with a mental illness who do not have their children living with them require special attention. Although more than half the parents in the study did not live with their children, this population has been widely neglected. Losing custody of a child does not invalidate a person's role as a parent. Services need to recognize this fact, and to deal effectively with the issues that stem from this. For noncustodial parents, interventions should target areas such as access visits, grief and loss counselling and role validation and empowerment of the parent (see Göpfert *et al.*, Chapters 5 and 7).

The needs of parents with psychotic disorders – the perspective of the health-care provider

In addition to surveying parents with psychotic disorders directly, we conducted a separate survey of health providers (Byrne *et al.*, 2000). A questionnaire was mailed to key agencies involved in providing input and support to parents with a history of serious mental illness. These included State Mental Health services, the Department for Families, Youth and Community Care, and the Education Department. In addition, nongovernment agencies that provided services such as family support, child-care and respite and disability services were also approached.

We received completed forms from 77 individuals. While the majority of services did routinely record whether their clients had dependent children, 70% of the respondents reported that they did not have written guidelines for the case management of these families. Eighty per cent of respondents reported collaborating with other agencies in the management of their clients. Where it was reported that collaboration did not take place, most said it was because of confidentiality concerns.

Overwhelmingly the service providers reported that current services for this population are inadequate (88%). Most of the respondents (73%) felt that these parents can adequately care for their children, although it is clear that their coping abilities would improve given more appropriate services. Respondents were divided in their opinion (52% agree vs. 48% disagree) as to whether government agencies should monitor the children of mentally ill parents as a matter of course. The majority (69%) believed that working with these families was often difficult and complex.

Service providers identified a range of issues related to the needs of the children in these families. These include issues related to (a) the children 'parenting their parent', (b) the children's concern about their own risk of future mental illness, (c) a lack of knowledge and understanding about their parent's mental illness, (d) isolation from peers and other adults, (e) unmet developmental needs and (f) a range of psychological issues related to feelings of grief, loss, anger and depression.

Service providers nominated a range of services that, based on their own past experience, had been effective services for these families. Coordinated service provision and professional development programmes were viewed as being the most important resources. Hands-on resources such as workbooks and games that explain mental illness were considered to be relatively helpful. Support groups for parents, educational videos, support groups for children and written clinical practice guidelines were seen as being less important.

Respondents were presented with four statements regarding perceived barriers to effective service delivery. Lack of knowledge and expertise was perceived as a significant barrier by slightly less than half (46%) of service providers. Eighty-two per cent of respondents reported that lack of liaison between service agencies was the number one barrier to effective service delivery. Lack of appropriate community resources was another major factor identified (80%). High workloads and lack of time is also a significant barrier to providing the quality and quantity of service required by families that include a parent with a psychotic disorder (66%).

Results from surveys such as this need to be interpreted with caution. However, based on the sample of service providers, families with psychotic parents are perceived to be challenging. Not only is it acknowledged that services are lacking, the quality of service to these clients is further compromised by the lack of coordination between existing services. Service providers acknowledged difficulties and problems specific to parents with a serious mental illness and their offspring. This has implications for service provision, indicating a need for specialized programmes. It would be difficult to address such specific needs by generic family support or parent education programmes. Parent-based support seemed to be the most favoured method of assisting these families. This includes respite services and help at the time of hospitalization. Consumer-based research has identified these types of interventions as being useful for parents (Cogan, 1998).

Despite an awareness of the overall problem in working with parents with mental illness, very few agencies have written policy guidelines for the management of these clients. A significant proportion of services do not identify these clients as a group, since details regarding whether children are present are not recorded. Unless this client group is identified and their needs for a range of services recognized, coordinated delivery will not occur. Once again this has direct implications for the likelihood of achieving adequate funding.

It is evident that the needs of parents with a history of serious mental illness present many challenges for service providers. These clients need a variety of services, and, as no single agency has specific responsibility for this group, effective collaboration is essential. Further work is needed on integration of service delivery and appropriate policy development. In order to redress the disadvantages being suffered by these parents and their children, these issues must be addressed. This is an area where service providers have the ability to make a difference by reviewing their own practice and lobbying for a better deal for these families.

How can we improve services for parents with a psychotic disorder?

As part of the Second National Mental Health Plan, the Australian Commonwealth Government has recently released a report specifically focusing on the needs of children with mentally ill parents (Australian Infant, Child, Adolescent and Family Association, 2001). The recommendations are divided into three areas: mental health services, intersectoral collaboration and research and education. Within the mental health services recommendations, the report proposed that an expert, multi-disciplinary group be set up to develop national guidelines for service providers on appropriate responses to families with a mentally ill parent. Furthermore, it was recommended that a communication strategy be developed to ensure the thorough dissemination of these guidelines. The state governments were encouraged to implement programmes that adhere to these guidelines. In the past, the Commonwealth Government has tied funds to state governments to specific programmes, although such strategies were not detailed in this report.

The report recommended that mental health services should take a leadership role in developing protocols for collaboration across all sectors involved with children. Information and education for workers on the needs of families with a mentally ill parent should be widely disseminated. Barriers to collaboration need to be clearly identified, and practical strategies implemented to overcome them.

With regard to research and education, states and territories were encouraged to provide expert research assistance to mental health professionals, to help them document and analyse the effectiveness of newly adopted strategies. In general, previous research should be examined and adapted, and successful programmes should be promoted and shared. The report also recommends that a central resource should be set up that provides access to, and analyses current research regarding the needs of families with a parent with a mental illness.

If a central resource is to be set up to centralize a knowledge base on issues concerning families with a mentally ill parent, it needs to be well funded, monitored and updated. Its auspicing body must be clearly defined, as anecdotal evidence suggests that central knowledge bases tend to be difficult to maintain and update, and are frequently seen as ineffective.

Most of these recommendations are common sense, and tend to be based on coordinated change at all organizational levels, and across a wide range of service providers. Prevention, promotion and early intervention are central to this strategy.

In addition to policy development at the national and state level, our group (the Queensland Centre for Schizophrenia Research) has developed an information kit based on the research studies outlined in this chapter. The purpose of this kit is to provide service providers with a starting point to assist them in working with their clients. The aim is to raise levels of awareness regarding the issues faced by families with a mentally ill parent. The information kit consists of fact sheets covering topics such as: barriers to service utilization faced by parents; general tips for service providers; family planning; antenatal care; and accessing available resources. Tip sheets for parents with a mental illness are included. Copies of this kit are available on the QCSR website.

Conclusions

For most people with children, the parenting experience is central to their identity and is a fundamental life role. It is a very personal experience, but it is also a social role that is undertaken within an everchanging family, social and community context. The way in which a person carries out their parenting role is influenced by many factors, including their own experience of being parented, the expectations they have of this role and of their children, the extent and nature of support to which they have access and the culture to which they belong. External factors such as income, adequate housing and access to resources also have a major impact.

Service systems must, therefore, be able to respond to a myriad of individuals' needs for assistance, and must be flexible enough to adapt to the changing environmental circumstances of their clients. There is ongoing debate about the best method of assisting families with a parent who has a mental illness. Some have argued that there is a need for specialized services, a 'one-stop shop' where these families can get a wide range of needs met. One drawback of this approach is that specialized services are less cost-effective than more general services (given a similar level of service) because they are targeted at a very limited population. Yet, supporters argue that it is not possible for existing services to provide a level of service similar to a specialized service.

It is important that services take a strengths perspective in working with mentally ill parents. All people have strengths, and a person's difficulties do not necessarily stem from their mental illness or incompetence as parents, but often arise from environmental problems. This approach allows for planning to be undertaken that can build on a parent's abilities, strengthen supports and take into account their individual needs and identified goals.

Service providers must take care not to create additional stresses for parents who may already be struggling. It is likely that parents with a mental illness will, at times, face problems in coping with their illness and its treatment and this will impact on their parental functioning. They may also have need of services to assist them with environmental problems such as reduced income, insecure housing, relationship difficulties and social isolation resulting in a lack of support. They are likely to require assistance from many different services. Yet service systems are often fragmented, difficult to access and often have rigid inclusion/exclusion criteria, particularly when funding is scarce. Given that mentally ill parents are frequently reluctant to ask for assistance for fear of losing custody of their children, it is important that the service system does not put extra barriers in place that may discourage people from using the services that are available.

The current lack of collaboration between agencies has been constantly raised as the single most important barrier to effective service delivery for families with a parent who has a mental illness. Too many people in need of assistance 'fall through the gaps' because many service providers believe other agencies are primarily responsible for the needs of these families.

Collaboration between existing agencies is a crucial component of effective service integration, which can 'close the gaps' and address the needs of parents with a mental illness. The fundamental keys to effective collaboration between agencies are the responsibility of all service providers. Change is required at all organizational levels. Collaborative strategies must be adopted at a policy level in order to minimize conflicting interagency goals and agendas. In addition, issues involving privacy/confidentiality of clients and information-sharing agreements between agencies must be legislated in order for collaboration to work in practice. Regular meetings between relevant stakeholders can be invaluable in addressing operational inadequacies, conflicts and overlaps. Effective strategies need to be sustainable, and not vulnerable to attrition resulting from staff turnover at the agencies involved.

Finally, collaboration must also be embraced at the case-manager level, since it is there that services are actually provided to the public, and it is there that the day-to-day decisions that affect how families are dealt with are made. It is very important for workers to have a clear understanding of the services that are available to their clients, and to develop a good working relationship with those services that their clients use most frequently.

Parents with a psychotic disorder clearly have many unmet needs. The challenge for service providers is to reduce the gap between currently available services and optimal services. The eventual total cost of our current neglect will be substantial, with immediate adverse outcomes for the parents and long-term adverse outcomes for the children.

REFERENCES

Australian Infant, Child, Adolescent and Family Association (2001). *Children of Parents Affected By a Mental Illness: Scoping Project.* Canberra: Commonwealth of Australia.

Bassett, H., Lampe, J. & Lloyd, C. (1999). Parenting experiences and feelings of parents with a mental illness. *Journal of Mental Health, 8,* 597–604.

Byrne, L., Hearle, J., Plant, K., Barkla, J. & McGrath, J. (2000). Working with parents with a serious mental illness: what do service providers think? *Australian Social Work, 53,* 21–6.

Cogan, J. C. (1998). The consumer as expert: women with serious mental illness and their relationship-based needs. *Psychiatric Rehabilitation Journal, 22,* 142–54.

Cowling, V. (1996). Meeting the support needs of families with dependent children where the parent has a mental illness. *Family Matters, 45,* 22–5.

DeChillo, N., Matorin, S. & Hallahan, C. (1987). Children of psychiatric patients: rarely seen or heard. *Health and Social Work, 12,* 296–302.

Hearle, J., Plant, K., Jenner, L., Barkla, J. & McGrath, J. (1999). A survey of contact with offspring and assistance with child care among parents with psychotic disorders. *Psychiatric Services, 50,* 1354–6.

Human Rights and Equal Opportunity Commission (1993). *Human Rights and Mental Illness.* Canberra: Australian Government Publishing Service.

Jablensky, A., McGrath, J., Herrman, H. et al. (1999). *People Living with Psychotic Illness: An Australian Study 1997–98.* Canberra: Commonwealth of Australia.

McGrath, J. J., Hearle, J., Jenner, L., Plant, K., Drummond, A. & Barkla, J. M. (1999). The fertility and fecundity of patients with psychoses. *Acta Psychiatrica Scandinavica, 99,* 441–6.

Miller, L. J. (1997). Sexuality, reproduction, and family planning in women with schizophrenia. *Schizophrenia Bulletin, 23,* 623–35.

Nicholson, J., Sweeney, E. M. & Geller, J. L. (1998*a*). Mothers with mental illness: I. The competing demands of parenting and living with mental illness. *Psychiatric Services, 49,* 635–42.

Nicholson, J., Sweeney, E. M. & Geller, J. L. (1998*b*). Mothers with mental illness: II. Family relationships and the context of parenting. *Psychiatric Services, 49,* 643–9.

Nicholson, J., Nason, M. W., Calabresi, A. O. & Yando, R. (1999). Fathers with severe mental illness: characteristics and comparisons. *American Journal of Orthopsychiatry, 69*, 134–41.

Oates, M. (1997). Patients as parents: the risk to children. *British Journal of Psychiatry, 170*, 22–7.

Sand, S. (1995). The parenting experience of low-income single women with serious mental disorders. *Families in Society: The Journal of Contemporary Human Services, 2*, 86–96.

Schwab, B., Clark, R. & Drake, R. (1991). An ethnographic note on clients as parents. *Psychosocial Rehabilitation Journal, 15*, 95–9.

Wang, A. R. & Goldschmidt, V. V. (1994). Interviews of psychiatric inpatients about their family situation and young children. *Acta Psychiatrica Scandinavica, 90*, 459–65.

Wang, A. R. & Goldschmidt, V. V. (1996). Interviews with psychiatric inpatients about professional intervention with regard to their children. *Acta Psychiatrica Scandinavica, 93*, 57–61.

25

Models of service provision in three countries: Marlboro, New Haven, Sydney, Melbourne and Lewisham

Vicki Cowling

Maroondah Hospital CAMHS, Victoria, Australia

With Toni Wolf, Cheryl Burack-Lynch, Carlie Dean and Coralie McMillan, Rose Cuff and Helen Mildred, Ann Daniel and Marie Diggins

Introduction

> Collaboration among various services is essential for success. (Barnett, 1999, p. xi)

There is much diversity in the models of services for parents who have a mental illness, but a visit to programmes in several countries shows that all service models share a unity of purpose. They arise from a perceived local need, and they all emphasize collaboration among several agencies and disciplines. The theme of *working together* stands out as central in each of these programmes. This chapter describes five such programmes in three countries.

Massachusetts Clubhouse Family Legal Support Project, Marlboro, Massachusetts, USA

Problem and need

There was an early recognition in this part of Massachusetts that parents diagnosed with mental illness were at high risk, not only of losing custody of their children but of losing complete contact with them. This was happening because they were assumed to be unfit to parent, an assumption, grounded in stereotype, that appeared to be empirically unfounded. A person's ability to be a successful parent had been shown to have less to do with the fact of mental ability and more to do with parenting resources and support. Factors enhancing the ability of a parent with severe mental illness to raise children had been studied and results showed that they included respite care, education on childrearing and child development, an early intervention programme, paediatric support with extra awareness to support positive maternal development and guidance, primary care for the mother with special attention paid to her reproductive health and needs for training, vocational training, psychother-apy and psychopharmacology, and legal counsel, adequate housing arrangements and financial support (Apfel & Handel, 1993).

What services existed

Employment Options, a comprehensive clubhouse model, was already in existence in Marlboro. It provided job training, housing assistance, education, counselling, peer supports and a range of parenting supports. Parent supports included 24-hour staff availability, housing, family support meetings, special events and supervised visitation.

Legal representation was missing

While all these supports were helpful, they were not enough to ensure that par-ents maintained contact with children whom they had lost to child protection agencies. These parents often lost visitation rights *and* custody of their children without the benefit of counsel or judicial process. In Massachusetts parents are entitled to effective assistance in cases of termination of parenting rights or con-tested care and protection cases. However, those parents who become involved with the Department of Social Services (a child-protection state agency) as a result of voluntary agreements or reports of suspected abuse and neglect, lose the right to court-appointed counsel. Parents with mental illness are often involved in care and custody disputes with family members where there is no right to appointed counsel. Furthermore, low-income parents with mental illness rarely receive representation from privately practising legal practitioners. Attorneys are reluctant to represent clients in these cases because they lack specialized training in mental health law, clinical understanding and knowledge about available parenting support services. Lacking counsel and under pressure from state agencies, parents with mental illness often relinquish rights that they never knew they had.

Effective legal advice, counselling and representation early on in the process are necessary to preserve the family. It became evident that, if they wanted to truly serve parents, Employment Options needed to seek legal expertise. Employment Options began to work collaboratively with the Mental Heath Legal Advisors Com-mittee, a state group of the Massachusetts Supreme Judicial Court comprised of judges and attorneys with mental health law expertise. For 25 years, in addition to direct representation of persons with mental illness, Mental Health Legal Advisors Committee has engaged in systematic advocacy through education and training of clients, attorneys and judges, litigation and legislative efforts. This linkage helped but was insufficient.

To better address the needs of clients, the Clubhouse Family Legal Support Project was created. The project was funded jointly by the Massachusetts Bar Foundation and the National Association of Public Interest Law, and co-led by Employment Options and the Mental Health Legal Advisors Committee. This Project provides effective legal representation to low-income parents with mental illness who are at risk of losing custody and contact with their children. Legal assistance has included legal advice, referral, establishment or enforcement of visitation rights and negotiation of service plans with state agencies. In addition, the Project also educates and trains the Department of Mental Health, the courts and legal services providers by dispelling misconceptions about parents with mental illness.

The Clubhouse Family Legal Support Project has utilized the innovative approach of integrating legal and human service resources to enhance the quantity and quality of legal representation for a greatly underserved population – low-income parents with mental illness (see also Brunt, Chapter 18).

Client profile

Ms A is a 41-year-old mother of a 12-year-old boy. Ms A is diagnosed with schizoaffective disorder. She has been hospitalized in the past as a result of her illness, but now she is involved in an area clubhouse, and regularly sees both her treating therapist and psychiatrist.

Ms A has been divorced from her husband for over 5 years. In the divorce, her ex-husband was given sole physical and legal custody of their son. After the divorce, the client was found at her child's school with a substantial amount of money and both her and her child's passports. As a result of this, her ex-husband was able to obtain an abuse prevention order, which did not permit any contact between the client and her son. The client was subsequently hospitalized as a result of this action. The client was unable to see her son for over 2 years.

Ms A was released from the hospital over 2 years ago and with the assistance of the Clubhouse Family Legal Support Project, has been able to resume contact with her son. With legal counsel, the abuse prevention order was dismissed and a Complaint for Modification asking for visitation was allowed. Over time, Ms A gained unlimited mail and telephone contact and an increase in the amount of supervised visitation. Ms A is now managing daily living confidently, working as a volunteer in computer processing at the clubhouse and walks daily to stay in shape. Over the last year, due to this Project, Ms A was awarded unsupervised visitation. Ms A now hopes to reach her ultimate goal: to be able to have her son visit with her overnight.

The Family Support Collaborative, New Haven, Connecticut, USA

Two private, nonprofit agencies in New Haven have partnered to create the Family Support Collaborative (FSC). The programme works to reduce homelessness and strengthen family functioning for parents with a psychiatric disability, addiction or cognitive limitation by providing supportive housing, intensive case management and home-based parenting education. Specifically, the goals are to:

(1) Help the family find and establish permanent, stable housing. This includes assistance with housing costs and material needs.

(2) Develop an integrated plan for comprehensive, wrap-around services for the parent. This includes the direct delivery of assertive, one-to-one case management.

(3) Provide parenting education and child-care skills development to prevent child abuse and neglect and to enhance parent effectiveness.

(4) Assess the risk factors and the need for special services to the children in the home and refer for services when such needs are identified.

In creating the programme, the two agencies – Coordinating Council for Children in Crisis Inc. and ALSO/Cornerstone Inc. – recognized an underserved area relating to each organization's speciality. The collaborative was intended to build a new programme upon the existing skills and strengths of each agency in a cost-effective manner.

ALSO/Cornerstone Inc. has provided housing and support services to mentally ill adults in the Greater New Haven, Connecticut, community for 30 years, but had almost always worked exclusively with single adults. Coordinating Council for Children in Crisis Inc. has a mission to prevent child abuse, neglect and victimization across the life span but had neither housing resources nor specialized expertise in working with the mentally ill.

New programme services

Each family is now screened through an assessment process that explores the family's history, needs, strengths, resources, mental health, substance abuse, domestic violence and concerns about the children. Parents and any other involved service providers participate in the development of a treatment plan, which is reviewed every 3 months. Services are individualized and home-based. Parents are asked to agree to weekly visits with the case manager and parent educator, to participate in weekly group activities, to enter needed clinical treatment, to maintain a drug-free lifestyle and to create a plan for repayment of security loans.

The case manager's job is to provide assistance in obtaining safe and affordable housing, entitlements, vocational training, employment support services and educational services, to provide financial and living skills training, to develop a natural social support network, to provide medication supervision and to help with transportation. The parent educator makes regularly scheduled home visits, educates parents about child development, child-care, child safety, limit setting, behaviour management and other aspects of positive parenting, teaches family strengthening activities, acts as a role model and mentor, works to increase parental esteem and self-confidence, provides support to decrease isolation and link families to other needed services. All families participate in parent support groups and social, cultural and recreational activities.

The 'B' family

Sue B is a 48-year-old separated African-American mother of seven children, including five adult children and two younger daughters, Sabrina (12) and Linda (10). She is a cancer survivor with a history of alcohol and cocaine dependence and a psychiatric diagnosis of depression and borderline personality disorder. Her child protective services worker referred Sue to the Family Support Collaborative when she and Sabrina were living in a shelter and Sue was in the early stages of recovery. Linda was in a foster home and the foster parents were considering adoption.

A parent educator and case manager worked with Sue B to develop a treatment plan. Goals included finding permanent housing, maintaining her sobriety by continuing substance-abuse treatment, developing household management skills, linking Sabrina to a paediatrician and registering her for school. They also helped Sue to reconnect and develop a relationship with her youngest daughter.

The foster family's plans for adoption did not come to fruition and Linda was returned to Sue. Child protective services recognized that by now, Sue had successfully engaged in treatment, had maintained a stable living environment for herself and Sabrina and was actively involved in the FSC programme.

Today, Sue and her children continue to live together. Both children are medically up to date and are doing well in school. Linda has been diagnosed with attention deficit hyperactivity disorder (ADHD), is on medication and meets weekly with a child therapist.

Sue is alcohol- and drug-free and now works as a mentor at her substance-abuse treatment facility. She is an active member of her church and works part-time at a free clothing distribution centre. Although her cancer has reoccurred, she is now in remission. She meets with her parent educator and case manager every 2 weeks. Goals now focus on budgeting, limit setting and discipline, stress management and understanding the characteristics of ADHD. Sue attends support groups and family activities sponsored by the two agencies and is preparing for her upcoming graduation from the programme. She relates that every time she moves up a level in the programme she is scared that she will not succeed, and would like an aftercare group and warm line to answer her questions after she leaves the programme. She still grieves for the older daughters she was not able to raise, but is grateful that her two youngest girls are with her today. She has expressed a strong desire to volunteer and help create a peer mentor support group for other families in the programme.

Programme partnership

The partnership of these two agencies has gone smoothly with few turf issues. This has probably been due to the clear delineation of expertise and roles and the commitment of all involved. Policies regarding confidentiality, referral, intake, assessment and programme expectations were developed during administrative meetings between the agency directors, assistant directors and assigned staff. These meetings continue to take place monthly to discuss programme policy and development, management, funding and other related issues. A weekly case conference with the front line staff and assistant directors is used to review cases, seek solutions for problems and make recommendations. The parent educator and case manager continue to work out of their own agencies but communicate on a daily basis and often make home visits together.

Although all the staff involved in the project were seasoned workers in their own agencies, they needed to cross-train each other, particularly in the identification and response to child abuse and domestic violence, and the clinical and advocacy issues involved in case management. Since then, the two agencies continue to open their ongoing in-service training programmes to each other.

Initial results

At the time of evaluation, the programme had served 27 families since it began in 1998. Four families were discharged after failing to participate in the programme as required. Fourteen of the remaining 23 families entered the programme without their children and have since been reunified. All 23 families are still together and in permanent housing. Two families had planned discharges, or graduations and three more were in the planning stage.

Since its inception, the programme capacity doubled from 6 to 12 families and is currently providing services to a third organization working with women returning to the community after residential treatment. The partnership of the two agencies has fostered the provision of family-focused services, giving the staff of both agencies the opportunity to learn from each other and expand their perspectives and has provided a model within the larger service system for effective interagency cooperation and collaborative programme development.

The Sutherland Children in Families Affected by Mental Illness Project, Sydney, Australia

Introduction and project aims

The Division of Mental Health, Sutherland, which serves adults who are mentally ill in a metropolitan region of southern Sydney, Australia, has conducted a project to address the needs of the children of their adult clients. Over the last 2 years, the project introduced a systematic approach to such children. This meant identifying consumers with dependent children and determining whether the children required services.

A number of barriers were encountered, but mechanisms have now been introduced to incorporate children's issues into the routine practice of adult mental health services, and these have been implemented with reasonable success. The project has expanded the intervention options available for these children to include telephone support groups and school consultation.

Barriers encountered

One of the initial barriers was the separation of adult mental health services from those for children and adolescents. Collaboration across organizational boundaries presented particular challenges.

There were barriers from within the adult mental health services. The dominance of a medical model of treatment and a focus on the seriously mentally ill contributed to the view that the adult should be the main focus of treatment rather than the whole family, especially when resources were constrained. Adult workers had little understanding of children's issues and did not know how to talk to children. They did not know how to assess parenting capacity beyond looking for obvious indicators of abuse and neglect. The adult workers felt that their loyalties were to the parent and that a separate worker was needed to work with and advocate for the child. There was the view that the children would not receive help even when identified, due to lack of suitable services or because the family would put up 'road blocks'.

There were also some attitudinal barriers from within child-focused services: 'These families require more resources than we can give', 'We don't understand psychotic mental illness sufficiently to know how to help these families', 'We only see people at the clinic on an appointment basis and if they can't get here and at the correct time we can't help', 'The parent has to want help about the child and we work with what the parent sees as the problem'.

In addition, there were barriers from the families themselves: denial of illness, fear of the child being removed, fear of stigma. Family situations were often chaotic and plans made for children were not followed.

What has been implemented

In the adult mental health services a standard intake form was introduced which included the following questions: 'Are there children under 18 years in the household?' and 'Where are the children now and who are they with?'. The form included an assessment of risk and of the support available to the client and family, with prompts to consider the children in assessing these factors, and an action plan to identify plans for children's care.

A standard comprehensive assessment form was introduced into the adult mental health service with a page for information on the family and children. A genogram is now required, showing the family structure and the ages of the children.

The Child Risk Checklist (Table 25.1) covers current emotional, behavioural and learning problems for the child, risk factors arising from the parental mental illness

Table 25.1. The Child Risk Checklist

Is the child/children exhibiting a behavioural/emotional/learning problem?

If yes, is the problem persistent and severe? If yes, please give details.

Is the child/children receiving help? If yes, where?

Is the mental illness of the family member both severe and long-term?

Is there a reliable caregiver during periods of acute parental mental illness?

Is there or has there been abuse/neglect/contact with the Department of Community
   Services (that is, the state-mandated children protection service)?

Is the child/children involved in the family member/s delusions?

Do you as a clinician have any other concerns pertinent to the child/children? e.g. severe
   ongoing conflict in the family. If yes, please give details.

Is there immediate safety risk for this child/children?

itself, the availability of an alternative, reliable caregiver and safety issues. When any concern emerges from this screening, the worker develops a management plan for the child as well as for the adult client, including referrals to child mental health and community agencies. Adult mental health staff have had training to increase their understanding of the needs of the children and the impact of the parental mental illness on them. The training includes the use of the screening instruments, knowledge of child and adolescent mental health services and of other community resources for children and families, child protection issues and case studies focusing on a collaborative approach between adult and child mental health services.

The Project Coordinator works closely with the child and adolescent mental health services to increase the flexibility of their response to these families and to promote a model of joint case management. In the same way, work has been undertaken with a range of community agencies outside health, in order to achieve better cooperation and to develop collaborative ventures that meet the recreational, respite and support needs of the children. These agencies have included schools, government child protection services, and nongovernment organizations. such as family support services and consumer groups.

Specific interventions

An innovative approach to providing these children with increased support, peer contact and positive coping skills has been the use of telephone support groups. These are conducted for small groups of children connected by a telephone conference link-up, with two staff acting as facilitators. The group is scheduled at a set time each week and is conducted over 7 weeks. One advantage of telephone groups over face-to-face services is that they reduce access difficulties. So far, these telephone groups have been held with groups of children between 8 and 12 years of age. Despite the convenience of the service, there still have been some difficulties recruiting children to the group. Evaluation has been limited to qualitative feedback from the children and parents, which has been very positive. Training in running teleGroup counselling is provided by Carers New South Wales Inc.

Another approach to assist these children has been the school consultation model, used in some cases when the family will not accept a referral to child and family mental health services. Consultation is provided to school personnel to support the child. The school might request assistance for a child who is not attending school, or who is having serious difficulties in coping, and parental mental illness is a contributing factor. School personnel can play a very important role in supporting the child to manage their difficulties but they need also some understanding of the parental mental illness and how to help the child and family.

The consultation model is one where a worker from the child and adolescent mental health service, and sometimes from the adult mental health service, attends a case conference at the school. Others at the case conference can be the teachers, the principal and school counsellor, the home–school liaison officer (if attendance is an issue) and in some cases a child protection officer. If possible, one or both parents are also involved in part of the meeting. Confidentiality of health information and consent to have health workers involved must be negotiated.

Evidence of the impact of the project

A file audit was undertaken to examine 50 files of adults assessed by the mental health service where there were dependent children.

It was found that, since the introduction of the reforms, all adults are now asked at intake if there are dependent children under 18 years in the household. Family genograms are completed in about 80% of cases. The Child Risk Checklist is being used in only one-third of cases. However, staff are documenting child protection concerns, and sometimes problems with parenting, in other parts of their assessment. There was evidence that for 80% of the adults assessed, the worker had specifically asked questions about risk factors for the children. The adult workers were making reports to child protection authorities where needed. In fact, in about 40% of the cases examined, child protection concerns were noted and acted upon. The file audit also showed that children were being referred to a variety of health and community agencies for services. Follow-up of these agencies showed that these referrals were accepted and acted upon.

Conclusions

This project has increased the capacity of the adult mental health services to address the needs of their clients who are parents, and of their children. It has also achieved closer collaboration between the mental health services for adults and for children and adolescents, and between health services and other community agencies, such as schools.

Parents in Partnerships: The Parents' Project, Melbourne, Australia

Background

Currently, in Australia, adult mental health services do not routinely consider or provide for the needs of clients as parents, and the general health and welfare services do not cater well for clients of mental health services or their children. As elsewhere, parents are anxious about seeking services regarding parenting help for fear of intervention by child protection and loss of custody of their children. The negative consequences on the social, psychological and physical health of these parents and their children have been well documented, and addressing this has been identified as a priority area for the development of mental health service provision. (Blanch *et al.*, 1994; Cowling *et al.*, 1995; Department of Health and Community Services, 1995; Department of Human Services, 1997; Human Rights and Equal Opportunity Commission, 1993; Pietsch & Cuff, 1995; Pietsch & Short, 1996; Sands, 1995; E. Short, pers. comm.; Zemencuk *et al.*, 1995).

Mothers who have a serious mental illness had identified parenting support programmes as a priority need (Cogan, 1993; Cowling, 1996; Nicholson & Blanch 1994; Oyserman *et al.*, 1992; Pacers, 1994; Pietsch & Cuff 1995; Pietsch & Short 1996; E. Short, pers. comm.; Silverman, 1989; Wallace, 1992; S. Wragg, pers. comm.).

The project

The Parent's Project (Parents in Partnerships) commenced in the Outer East of Melbourne in September 1997, initially for a 12-month period. The aims of the project were:

1. To improve the mental health, parenting skills and confidence of parents who have a mental illness.

    This was achieved through developing parent support groups run on a school term basis. The programs are designed by the consumers and cofacilitated by a mental health and a family support worker. They provide forums for participants to discuss issues of isolation, parenting, mental illness and identity.

2. To improve mental health workers' awareness of, and competency in working with parents who have a mental illness.

    This was achieved through case-based consultation and topic-based education to mental health workers about the issues affecting parents with a mental illness.

The project today

The two initiatives have been evaluated very positively by participants and remain key components of the project. At the completion of the first 12 months, the project worker has continued to be employed, due to demonstrated positive outcomes for both consumers and carers. The scope of the project has broadened significantly to embrace direct and indirect service to workers, to the children as well as to parents with a mental illness. The project has also developed a number of collaborative programmes to better meet the needs of families. These include the Eastern Network for Family Mental Health, support groups for children and parents, primary, secondary and tertiary consultation for service providers and government organizations, and resource development. Consumer and carer involvement is fundamental to the development and implementation of all of these project initiatives.

- The Eastern Network for Family Mental Health is an information-sharing, advocacy and fund-raising group consisting of parents who are consumers, carers and representatives from a broad range of community-based agencies including adult, child and adolescent mental health.
- Support groups and activities for children provide a blend of recreation, respite and psycho-education using a model of peer support. The programmes have targeted children aged 8–12. The programmes have been named CHAMPS (children and mentally ill parents) and activities include:
    CHAMPS 4-day school holiday programmes for children aged 8–12.
    CHAMPS camps are weekends away, cofacilitated by mental health and community workers, consumers and carers. They provide fun, physical challenge and opportunities for discussion and making friends.
    CHAMPS after-school programme meets every 2 weeks and provides children with the opportunity to meet and discuss ideas and issues with other young people.
- Primary, secondary and tertiary consultation. A direct referral service is available for the project worker to meet with families, with the aim of facilitating discussion and understanding of a parent's mental illness and how it may be impacting on family members, particularly children.
- Resource development. The project worker has helped to develop information resources: 'Kidz Kit' for children aged 8–12; the Families and Mental Health Resource Kit (with the Victorian State Government Department of Human Services); a brochure aimed at providing information to families, particularly children, where a parent is self-harming in the context of a borderline personality disorder; and a resource manual to guide people wanting to provide CHAMPS camps for the children.
- Consumer and carer participation has been an important feature of the project. Consumers and carers are actively involved in the network and in the actual delivery of programmes. The CHAMPS Chronicle Newsletter is a quarterly production and is prepared by a consumer.

Evaluation of the CHAMPS programmes suggests that the two most important outcomes for children are the sense of reduced isolation and an increase in coping abilities. A positive outcome of CHAMPS for the parents of the children is that they feel more confident about discussing their illness with their children. Evaluation of the parent support groups indicates that the parents feel recognized and supported both as parents and as people with a mental illness.

The Building Bridges Project for parent-users of mental health services and their children, Lewisham, UK

A factor which influenced the development of the Building Bridges Project was the recognition that social services departments in the UK were concentrating on child protection procedures and providing few services to families where there were concerns about parenting. It seemed as if many families were receiving services that were intrusive and unhelpful. A report to the Department of Health examined 100 enquiries into child deaths and found a high rate of parental mental illness and very poor interagency coordination. This report provided another call to action (Falkov, 1996).

In the Lewisham area, specific communities were overrepresented within the mental health and child welfare systems, such as black people of Caribbean origin, which led to the Building Bridges Project.

A respite adventure weekend for a group of children of parents with mental illness was the first step. This initiative, in 1995, won an Enterprise Award. The additional funds enabled more weekends and the boost to take the work forward.

A research project was undertaken to examine how Lewisham Social Services could facilitate effective joint agency and intra-agency work with families where the parents have mental health problems. The research focused on four main areas: social work skills, working together (inter and intra-agency), training and resources.

Parties involved included the Family Welfare Association, the Lewisham User Forum (a group for users of mental health services) and the Lewisham and Guy's Mental Health NHS Trust (now South London and Maudsley NHS Trust). Funds were provided by the Department of Health and Lewisham Joint Consultative Committee. The current project employs six part-time staff including a project manager, social worker, project workers, development worker and administrator.

The aim in setting up Building Bridges was to develop an innovative service that could respond flexibly to parents with mental illness and their children. The objectives of Building Bridges are:

(1) To work with families where the parent has or is at serious risk of developing mental illness.
(2) To provide practical and therapeutic resources to meet the needs of the target group.
(3) To promote awareness, encourage collaborative and integrated models of assessment and treatment.
(4) To monitor and evaluate outcomes of the project's work.

Services provided by Building Bridges

The Building Bridges objectives are achieved through the provision of home-support services and group work.

The home-support service includes assessment of the needs of both children and adults in the family, assisting parents to establish or re-establish daily routines, and improve parenting skills, to assist the children to voice their own views and needs and to encourage and enable parents and children to access appropriate services including the group work programme.

The group work programme provides a weekly confidence-building programme for women, combined with an open discussion forum, a regular children's group to discuss issues arising from living with mental illness, school holiday activities, and specific groups and activities which address issues such as managing children's difficult behaviour, returning to work and domestic violence.

Review and evaluation

Building Bridges has been taking referrals since mid 1998. Review and evaluation was completed after the first 12 months. In this period the Project provided a service to families from a wide range of racial and cultural backgrounds, accepting 93 new referrals. Fifty-four per cent of service users had depression, with 22% having schizophrenia. The average time invested in a case was around 6 months, with some continuing for 11 months. Most referrals are made by health visitors, with community mental health teams and child and family social workers following on. Some families self-refer.

After 6 months, the project introduced research questionnaires to be completed by new clients at the time of assessment, and again when clients are to be discharged. The Strengths and Difficulties Questionnaire (SDQ) is a behavioural screening questionnaire for children and young people and was completed for five young people. Just under half the children had emotional symptoms, peer difficulties and conduct problems. The General Health Questionnaire (GHQ) was completed by eight service users. They were having problems with carrying out normal daily activities due to sleeplessness, unhappiness, lack of confidence and a general feeling of despair.

The Parental Stress Inventory (PSI) measures stress in the parent–child system. Eight parents completed the PSI and their responses reflected stress derived from their interactions with their children and from aspects of their child's behaviour. Some of the mothers showed low self-esteem and have difficulties independent of child issues.

Group activities such as day trips have been generally well received. Many of the women in violent relationships were able to speak about their experiences for the first time in the group. A drop-in group provides a safe forum for women to meet for emotional support, to gain access to information and raise self-esteem. The structure is informal with activities such as exercises or a talk by a solicitor. Parents and children have lunch together, with women bringing meals from their particular culture. This group experience is the only opportunity many of the children have to mix with others, as most do not attend child-care or nursery. The women reported that the best thing about the group was having other women to talk to, to listen to them without judging them. A number of the women stated that it was the only place that they felt normal and respected.

General feedback from service users (n = 16) about Building Bridges was the benefit derived from learning to be assertive, having someone to talk to and feeling 'normal'. All of the women reporting back said their stress levels had decreased, they enjoyed the continuity of staff and were pleased to receive a range of services from the same location. Unmet needs include more practical help in getting children to school, shopping trips and services in the evenings and weekends.

Feedback from referring professionals (n = 12) stated that Building Bridges was an essential service, and supported the parents in saying that practical services and weekend support would be welcome additions. A valuable element of the project was identified as the flexibility to respond to a range of circumstances in a positive and practical way. A number of professionals stated that without Building Bridges their clients would have deteriorated and required hospitalization.

Conclusion

These innovative programmes in three countries all arose from a perceived local need and an emphasis on interagency collaboration. The Family Legal Support Project in Marlboro, Massachusetts addresses the need that parents with a mental illness have in negotiating a complex legal system. In New Haven, Connecticut, a fruitful partnership has developed between two organizations who had previously served their own specific community groups for many years. The Family Support Collaborative now uses the existing strengths and expertise of each agency to support families in which parents suffer from a mental illness.

The Children in Families Affected by Mental Illness Project in Sydney, Australia, overcame initial barriers existing between adult mental health and child mental health services. The project has been successful in changing the way people work. The Parents in Partnership Project in Melbourne illustrates the process of building step by step. A research thesis led to a 1-year project which was so effective in the locality it served that it has continued. The Building Bridges Project in Lewisham, UK illustrates how serendipity works. Building Bridges began as an adventure weekend to give children and their parents time out. Persistence, interagency teamwork and ingenuity have permitted Building Bridges to develop a flexible service to families, both preventive and supportive. These five programmes offer encouragement to other practitioners.

REFERENCES

Apfel, R. J. & Handel, M. H. (1993). *Madness and Loss of Motherhood*. Washington, DC: American Psychiatric Press.

Barnett, B. E. W. (1999). Finding answers, making changes. In *Children of Parents with Mental Illness*, ed. V. Cowling, pp. xi–xii. Melbourne: Australian Council for Educational Research.

Blanch, A. , Nicholson, J. & Purcell, J. (1994). Parents with severe mental illness and their children: the need for human services integration. *Journal of Mental Health Administration, 21*, 388–96.

Cogan, J. (1993). *Accessing the Community Support Service Needs which Women with Psychiatric Disabilities May Have Regarding Relationships*. Vermont: Trinity College, The Centre for Community Change through Housing and Support.

Cowling, V. (1996). *Report on Eight Focus Group Interviews with Parents*. Melbourne: Early Psychosis Research Centre.

Cowling, V., McGorry, P. & Hay, D. (1995). Children of parents with psychotic disorders. *Medical Journal of Australia, 163*, 119–20.

Department of Health and Community Services (1995). *Victoria's Child and Adolescent Mental Health Services: Future Directions for Service Delivery*. Melbourne: Department of Health and Community Services.

Department of Human Services (1997). *Victoria's Mental Health Services: Tailoring Services to Meet the Needs of Women*. Melbourne: Department of Human Services.

Falkov, A. (1996). *Study of Working Together: Part 8 Reports*. London: Department of Health.

Human Rights and Equal Opportunity Commission (1993). *Human Rights and Mental Illness: Report of National Enquiry into the Rights of People with Mental Illness*, pp. 493–506. Canberra: Australian Government Publishing Service.

Nicholson, J. & Blanch, A. (1994). Rehabilitation for parenting roles for people with serious mental illness. *Psychosocial Rehabilitation Journal, 18*, 109–19.

Oyserman, D., Mowbray, C. & Zemencuk, J. (1992). Resources and supports for mothers with a severe mental illness. *Health and Social Work, 19*, 132–42.

Pacers, M. (1994). *Clara House Review: Needs Analysis and Future Directions of a Mother's Psychiatric Disability Support Program*. Melbourne: Prahran Mission.

Pietsch, J. & Cuff, R. (1995). *Hidden Children: Families Caught Between Two Systems*. Melbourne: Mental Health Research Institute.

Pietsch, J. & Short, E. (1996). *Working Together: Developing Best Practice for Service Provision and Interagency Collaboration with Families where a Parent Has a Mental Illness*. Melbourne: Mental Health Research Institute and Broadmeadows Community Mental Health Service.

Sands, R. (1995). The parenting experience of low-income single women with serious mental disorders. *Journal of Contemporary Human Services*, February, 87–97.

Silverman, M. (1989). Children of psychiatrically ill parents: a prevention perspective. *Hospital and Community Psychiatry, 40,* 1257–65.

Wallace, A. (1992). *Mothers with Mental Illness: Unheard Voices, Unmet Needs.* Vermont: Trinity College, The Centre for Community Change Through Housing and Support.

Yarborough, G. (1997). quoting Dr Joanne Nicholson, Associate Professor at the University of Massachusetts Medical School. *The Myths and Realities of Parents with Mental Illness,* 46 ADVISOR 7.

Zemencuk, J., Rogosch, F. & Mowbray, C. (1995). The seriously mentally ill woman in the role of parent: characteristics, parenting sensitivity, and needs. *Psychosocial Rehabilitation Journal, 18,* 77–82.

26

Overcoming obstacles to interagency support: learning from Europe

Karen Baistow[1] and Rachael Hetherington

[1] Kings College, London, UK

The 'problem' for families and service providers

When mentally ill people are parents as well as patients, a range of psychological, emotional and social problems are faced by them and their children, as the chapters in this book clearly demonstrate. Negotiating everyday life as well as longer-term concerns can at times be fraught for these families. Whatever their clinical problems, mentally ill parents and their families live in social, economic and legal contexts that contribute to their well-being, or lack of it. Responding appropriately to these families' problems poses difficulties for service providers in health, welfare and social care, who have responsibilities to ensure that needs are met. The concerns that surround these families, which range from those connected to the parent as patient to those of the patient as parent, mean that a number of professionals and agencies are likely to be involved. These problems are not only experienced in the UK. Regardless of differences in structures of service delivery, the problems of cooperation between services and agencies are experienced in some form and to some degree throughout Europe.

Parents with a mental health problem face difficulties in caring for their children that stem from their illness, from social responses to their illness and from a generalized social exclusion. Unemployment, housing problems, poverty and the stigma attached to mental illness increase the pressure on parents whose mental health is fragile. They often struggle financially and they are likely to live in social isolation. Support for these families therefore needs to be sensitive both to the nature of the parents' illness and to the social factors which are associated with mental ill health more generally. Mental illness can be chronic but in the families where children are living at home, it is frequently episodic. Their support needs make different demands on welfare systems from those of other disabled parents. The welfare and protection of the children, the parents' mental health problems, parenting assessment and support, all require specialized services which can also act in a combined approach to minimize potential conflicts of interest. Mentally ill parents are often very well aware of their problems in parenting but their fear that their children will be taken away from them can make it hard for them to ask for help (O'Hagan, 1993; Phillips & Hugman, 1999).

The impact of parental mental illness on child health, welfare and development is well documented. The difficulties faced by these children and their families are very complex, depending on such factors as the nature and severity of the parental illness, psychosocial risk factors, resources of the wider family and available services (Reder *et al.*, 2000; Rutter, 1989; Weir & Douglas 1999) (see Hall, Chapter 3; Göpfert *et al.*, Chapter 5). All children with a mentally ill parent are likely, at the very least, to experience disruption of their lives and anxieties about their own future mental health. In the most acute cases their lives are at risk (Falkov, 1996; Ramsay *et al.*, 1998; Reder & Duncan, 1999; Stroud, 1997). Research studies have reported a range of possible effects of parental mental ill-health on children including the risk of emotional and physical harm, lack of stimulation, developmental delay, neglect, isolation and subsequent disturbances in the child, both in the short term, and longer term into adolescence and adulthood (Cummings & Davies, 1994; Downey & Coyne, 1990; Henry & Kumar, 1999; Oates, 1997; Reder *et al.*, 2000; Rutter & Quinton, 1984). In addition, these children may have to take on practical and emotional responsibilities for the care of their parents and siblings which can place emotional and social strains on normal developmental processes, often unnoticed by service providers (Dearden & Becker, 2000; Frank, 1995).

It is clear, therefore, that parental mental ill-health is often associated with a range of problems within the family, of which some may result in child protection concerns. The question of how to achieve a workable balance in meeting the respective needs of these parents and their children has come under increased scrutiny in recent years (Cleaver *et al.*, 1999; Göpfert *et al.*, 1996; Hetherington *et al.*, 2001; Reder *et al.*, 2000; Weir & Douglas, 1999) and it is an active area of concern for the UK Department of Health, which has published training materials (Mayes *et al.*, 1998; Falkov, 1998) (see Falkov, Chapter 27). There is widespread agreement that interagency collaboration is essential if these families are to be supported effectively, however, the realities of practice suggest that working together is easier said than done.

The European dimension

In the last 20 years other European countries too have undergone changes in the pattern of psychiatric treatment and care, the development of care in the community and shifts in child-care policy towards keeping children, as far as possible, in the care of their parents. As a result they also recognize the necessity for new types of service delivery which bring together the various agencies responsible for mental health and child-care. However, as in the UK, the recognition that interagency collaboration and coordination are essential, does not necessarily mean that their implementation is straightforward.

The Icarus Project

The Icarus Project was set up in 1998 by the Centre for Social Work Studies (CC-SWS), Brunel University with the aim of studying interagency cooperation between mental health and child welfare agencies in a range of European countries. Our research partners were located in Norway, Sweden, Denmark, Scotland, Northern Ireland, England, Ireland, France, Germany, Luxembourg, Italy and Greece. The representation was broadened internationally by researchers in Australia, who carried out the study in the state of Victoria (Hetherington *et al.*, 2001). Our objective was to identify principles, approaches and practices that could underpin the development of better services for these families. By working with professionals practising in both fields, the project aimed to generate knowledge that was grounded in a realistic appraisal of what is possible and practicable.

Comparison can be a useful source of new ideas and new ways of thinking about problems. Although care has to be taken in the process of transplanting policies and practices from one culture and system to another, learning about the services and interventions of another country can offer inspiration and serve as a stimulus to thinking and action (Baistow, 2000; Hetherington, 1998). Learning about how and why they do things elsewhere can increase our knowledge and broaden our horizons. Exposing ourselves to different ideas and ways of doing things extends our ideas about what is possible. It can also help us to think more creatively. The process of comparison enables us to scrutinize our own policies and practices, which have often become taken for granted. Comparative research can also enable us to learn from others more specifically, through identifying examples of good practice which it may be possible to borrow or transfer. Practices are closely tied in with social, historical, political and economic contexts and therefore cannot be easily imported in isolation from these, but it is possible to identify principles and approaches that we can make use of in our own context.

Our research methodology uses a ground-level approach because experience tells us that there can be significant differences between a policy, its intentions and its effects. The perspectives and experiences of practitioners and service users can tell us what it is like to be on the receiving end of policies and directives. They know what works and does not work, and the difficulties that can arise in implementing policies.

The research methodology

In each country groups of mental health professionals and child welfare professionals were given a three-stage case vignette which told the story of a mother, her

7-year-old daughter Anna and her husband (Anna's stepfather). At each stage the participating professionals were asked to discuss what they thought would happen within their system. At the beginning of the story, the mother has just returned home after giving birth to her second child. She is presented as being in a state of acute anxiety, possibly psychotic. At the second stage, three years later, the mother is anxious and tired. She is again pregnant, and the new baby is due in four months. Anna's behaviour is severely disturbed and the father unemployed. The mother finds her second child difficult, but she is not willing to accept help for Anna, and seems to be afraid of involvement with services. At the final stage, a month after the birth of the third child, the mother is clearly severely mentally ill. The children are very distressed and the father is drinking heavily. He has not been seen for several days and the family has no money. At each stage the participants were asked what they would expect to happen in their locality. Where would the family go for help, what services would be involved, what kinds of interventions would take place and what resources would be available? They were also asked about their explanations, concerns and expectations. At a second meeting the groups heard about the responses of other countries and discussed these in relation to their own. At a third meeting an international group of researchers and representative participants identified key themes for concern and examples of good practice. Background information was collected from each country on the organization of health and welfare services and on relevant legislation (see Hetherington *et al.*, 2001).

Barriers to interagency collaboration

Perhaps not surprisingly, all countries in the Icarus Project viewed interagency collaboration as the mainstay of effective support for families with a mentally ill parent. At the same time, in many countries, this collaboration was experienced as difficult and frustrating. In some, there was an optimism, in spite of the problems; in others, although it remained an ideal there was a prevailing pessimism about the possibility of interagency collaboration taking place.

Our analysis indicated that a number of factors affected the ways in which agencies, and the professionals within them, worked together. The effects of these factors were often mutually reinforcing, and they applied to participating countries to different degrees and in different ways. The barriers to interagency working were structural, organizational, geographic and economic. If there was a lack of shared knowledge and a 'cultural' separation of services, these barriers were reinforced. Professional confidence and optimism interacted with these factors, both shaping and being shaped by them.

Organization of services

The way in which the delivery of health and social care is organized creates a range of connected conditions which make collaboration more, or less, possible. It demarcates the territory of service delivery through the allocation of roles, responsibilities and accountability and it also encompasses resources, budgets, communication channels and knowledge bases. Our findings suggest that the division of services into free-standing units, with specialized terms of reference, as in England, tends to reinforce a fragmented approach to the problem, described by Douglas as 'formalised fragmentation' (Douglas, 1999, p. 188). The possibilities of interagency collaboration are greatly enhanced where there are more integrated service structures, as for example in Denmark; where health and social care are organized under the same broad umbrella either nationally or locally (like the health and social services joint boards and trusts in Ireland and Northern Ireland) or where multidisciplinary teams exist within child welfare services (such as the French CISS).

Specialization and separation of services can denote clearly defined boundaries, which in other contexts of care may be an advantage. However, comparisons with alternative ways of organizing services suggests that, for a number of reasons, in this area they may be counterproductive to a 'whole family' approach. Where precisely specified territorial service divisions are accompanied by strong budgetary boundaries, as in England, there are implications for financial, managerial and professional accountability. In the cost-aware culture of the purchaser–provider model found in England, questions regarding the resourcing of interagency work frequently focus on 'who is paying?'. With the necessity to demonstrate effectiveness there is an additional reluctance to spend without a tangible agency-related outcome. Moreover, unlike many other European countries, access to resources in England is governed by a strict adherence to procedures and legislation which constrains interagency work (Cooper *et al.*, 1995; Hetherington *et al.*, 1997). This adherence can militate against flexible targeting of resources within an agency; it also means that innovative interagency work, especially where it falls outside the scope of existing procedures, will be more difficult to fund and manage.

Organizational separation may also be mirrored in geographical separation, with agencies being located not merely in different buildings but on different sites. Geographical separation makes it more difficult for agencies, and the professionals within them, to set up formal meetings for collaboration and the sharing of information. In the experience of our participants this often proved to be unsatisfactory for reasons of time and conflicting commitments. However, they considered that even where there were formalized opportunities for joint working, informal contact could promote more effective communications between professionals and could set the scene for working together. Participants from Northern Ireland, for example, stressed the important part played, in their view, by the physical proximity of colleagues from different agencies. Working in the same building did not just mean having access to shared information and shared social space; informal contact opened up real possibilities for practitioners to get to know more about one another's work. When agencies are geographically separated (which participants in England typically reported) informal contact or chance meetings thus became even more vital but much less likely to happen. As a result knowledge sharing, and the kind of human contact that facilitates cooperation, suffered.

It was not only geography that could separate agencies from one another. In some countries, participants displayed a professional territorialism which relied on a firm, sometimes rigid, demarcation of knowledge, roles and responsibilities towards different family members in the case vignette. In England, this was manifested less in a desire to guard one's own professional territory but more in an unwillingness to trespass on that of another, particularly where there was an assumption that another service was 'responsible'. Furthermore, in some countries the principle of professional confidentiality meant that sharing knowledge and information with colleagues from another profession was viewed with suspicion and mistrust. Where there are specialist monodisciplinary child welfare teams, as in England, issues of confidentiality posed more uncertainties than in other countries. Under these circumstances, a lack of clarity about confidentiality, as Douglas (1999, p. 188) points out, can result in important information not being passed on. By comparison, in France, where the multidisciplinary PMI team has child health and welfare responsibilities, information sharing was not seen to be limited by the need for confidentiality to the same extent.

One factor which interacted, in some countries, with attitudes and practices concerning confidentiality was mandatory reporting – the legal obligation on professionals to declare knowledge of child maltreatment. In the Scandinavian countries, where professionals have to report abuse and suspicion of abuse, the participants had clear views about the value of information sharing and the means to put it into practice. Sharing information enabled them to offer help at an earlier stage, increasing the possibilities of prevention. In their view mandatory reporting existed to counteract a strong service culture of confidentiality – it was needed as an explicit stimulus to teamwork between sectors.

Accompanying these concerns about information sharing, was a general uncertainty (and sometimes ignorance) on the part of child welfare professionals about mental illness and, equally, on the part of mental health professionals uncertainties about child development, and a wariness of working with children. In some countries, including England, both groups of professionals, in general, showed a lack of knowledge of the other's services and occasionally were as misinformed as the general public. With these professional divisions of labour and knowledge, the possibilities of establishing a 'whole-family' approach seemed unlikely.

Shared knowledge and training

Underpinning the cultural separation of child welfare and mental health professionals was a broad-based lack of shared knowledge. This included the lack of shared knowledge bases regarding mental illness, child welfare and development and information about the family itself. On the whole, and perhaps predictably, in countries where there were specialized services with few generic roles, participating practitioners felt most unfamiliar with knowledge relating to the other field. As a consequence they also felt uncertain about making assessments and professional judgements that might call upon this knowledge, though some did venture opinions. These also tended to be the groups who knew little about the structure and functioning of other agencies and the services they could provide.

A lack of such shared knowledge not only reinforces territorial divisions but also tends to fragment the problem and solutions to it. This kind of compartmentalized knowledge is associated with a lack of shared discourse about the family which can have repercussions beyond professional roles and sensitivities. Given the reflexive relationship between discourse and practice, divided services and separate discourses not only create the conditions for mutual suspicion and possible conflicts of interest between professionals and between agencies, they can also influence the way that family members think about and experience the family's problems and their own relationships with one another and with practitioners. These views in turn can affect those of practitioners; but professional relationships do not have to replicate familial ones. Shared aims and objectives, which denote 'a common sense of purpose', rather than oppositional ones, as Douglas (1999, p. 187) suggests, can only come from considering needs of the family as a whole – even when they may appear to be in conflict. In the Icarus study it was noticeable, for example, that there was a high degree of consensus between the adult mental health and child welfare teams in Germany and Italy, and also in Northern Ireland. In these countries both teams showed a balance of concern between the mother's mental health and the welfare of the children and, importantly, they saw both issues as interlinked.

Whilst it is unrealistic to expect that specialist professionals should have detailed knowledge of another field, it became clear during the course of the research that families with parental mental health problems would greatly benefit from a broader common knowledge base and information sharing among the professionals concerned. In all the countries studied, professionals in child welfare and mental health (particularly social workers and community nurses) operated at the interface between institutions and the community, or between agencies with different remits. It was therefore particularly important for them to have an extensive generic knowledge base and wide-ranging information about resources.

The best time for this to be acquired is during prequalifying training, both in order that it can be built on subsequently but also so that its existence can be taken for granted, as a routine basis of good practice and thus part of the 'cultural' expectations of all professionals. There are a number of ways that this can take place. Generic training, particularly for community nurses and social workers, can most obviously offer a wide, shared knowledge base but even specialized training can initially provide shared knowledge, before specific pathways are followed. In the UK in recent years there has been a number of national and local initiatives to provide shared postqualifying training to overcome the problems caused by early specialization, and as part of strategies for increasing interagency collaboration (Reder *et al.*, 2000; Weir & Douglas, 1999). In other European countries and in Australia, prequalifying social work training is at least 3 years and in most European countries this is a generic training. In this international context, specialization in social work training is highly unusual, and in this research its disadvantages were apparent.

However, the nature of professional training, whether specialized or broad, does not exist in isolation but needs to be understood in relation to changing social, political and economic contexts; it reflects, and feeds back into, policies of welfare delivery and associated professional remits. In France (and in Luxembourg) for example, the *assistante sociale du secteur*, who is the generic social worker of the local authority social service, has a patch-based responsibility for children and adults whatever the nature of their problems and a generic training which provides the wide knowledge base that is necessary for the work. By contrast, in England, the absence of a professional role for generalist community social workers negates the need for broad-based training. Apart from those trained before the reorganization of social care and welfare during the 1980s and 90s, a shared knowledge of mental health and child welfare issues is rare and implicitly unnecessary.

Resources

A consistent theme, which was noticeable at every stage in the discussions of the case vignette and in subsequent discussions, was the role that resources played in professional responses and decision making. In some countries (Germany, France and Scandinavia) resources were noticeable because of their absence in discussion, while in others (England, Greece and Italy) they were noticeable by their frequent presence. In the latter group, the main allusion to 'resources' was as a critical factor inhibiting professional responses and interagency working. The professionals in England were envious of the higher resource levels of other countries and of the flexibility which good resources offered. They were also more likely explicitly to take resource levels into account when considering their own responses to the vignette. They made a point of differentiating between what would be desirable and what was possible.

A key perceived difference between countries lay not just in the availability of resources that could be offered to the family, but also in their accessibility. With some notable exceptions, in most of the participating countries there existed a basic similarity in the range of possible resources that could be offered to the family members; what differed was the ease with which these could be obtained. In England, access to resources was governed both by organizational and budgetary boundaries and by a necessity to follow procedures. For the professionals concerned, these requirements constrained flexibility and creative resource targeting and hampered joint working. For our hypothetical family, the effects were profound.

The shortfall in resources in England was associated with rationing, such that professionals made intervention decisions according to a hierarchy of severity. Only in the most serious cases, where there was extreme concern for the children's safety and the mother's mental health, was the 'spending' of resources warranted. For the child welfare groups in England, it was not until Stage 3 of the vignette, when the mother is acutely ill, her husband has left home and the children are unfed, that our case fell into this category. Thus assessments were made with resources in mind. As one participant pointed out, a chronic shortage of resources not only affects responses to need but also the way in which it is conceptualized. By the time the groups in England felt it was appropriate and necessary to intervene, their counterparts in other countries, most notably Germany and Scandinavia, could not recognize the case as presenting a realistic scenario. According to their groups, what was all too familiar in England would have been unlikely to develop in these countries, because intensive resources would have been deployed in Stage 1. Thus lower thresholds meant earlier interventions. In dealing early on with the relatively minor problems of the family, especially those of the mother, these interventions were intended to deal with current problems and to minimize or prevent later ones. Early action, in other countries, also tended to be accompanied by more expensive interventions in the shape of qualified expert practitioners with time to spend in the family home and a more confident, optimistic approach on the part of professionals that something positive could be achieved. By contrast, in England and Northern Ireland resources, including professional time, were hoarded. When the mother was first ill, the family's difficulties were well below the threshold for intervention in England. Support to the family might be offered at Stage 2 on a limited basis and even then would be generally undertaken by a family support worker, the least qualified and therefore 'cheapest' member of the children and families team.

Time, communication and trust

During the course of the research, professional time emerged as a key resource, which differed significantly between countries. Participants were clear that practitioners and their managers needed to have enough time if cooperative working was to be developed and, importantly, sustained. Establishing and maintaining good communications between colleagues and building relationships of trust and confidence with family members all depended on professional availability.

A shortage of time reduces professional availability to meet with colleagues. As well as enabling nonurgent and unscheduled meetings to take place, time is needed to 'network', to make and develop contacts and to carry out preventative groundwork. It is also necessary in building and consolidating relationships with clients and with colleagues. At each stage of the case, the participants from all countries agreed on the vital role played by the quality of communications between professionals and the family and between different groups of professionals; regular communication made cooperation possible. It also helped in building up trust. Whilst formal channels of communication were one important pathway, for example through regular meetings, it also became clear that informal contacts, even opportunistic ones, were more useful in exchanging information about the family. This type of contact also helped in developing a shared understanding of the family's needs and a shared sense of responsibility in meeting them. Thus in Sweden and in Italy, for example, where existing structures were seen as conducive to cooperative working, practitioners nonetheless saw an important role for individual, informal contacts. Even though taking advantage of informal contacts might give rise to inconsistent levels of collaboration, it increased the chances of working together.

Participants across different countries agreed that informal contact was more likely to happen if practitioners already had a history of working together or, as we saw earlier, if their offices were located in the same building. However, in the experience of participants in some countries, including in England, there were few opportunities for informal contact. The structural division and geographical separation of different agencies meant that there was little or no chance of meeting outside formal, prearranged settings. Moreover, formal meetings, such as the child protection conference, did not provide the best opportunity for building up collaborative practice because they were essentially reactive, crisis-driven and case-specific. Across the public sector, the overriding factor which made it very difficult to set up extra interagency meetings was lack of time. There was little or no flexibility in any one's daily or weekly schedule to fit in another meeting. Thus while professionals in England recognized the benefits of meeting each other, they were pessimistic about this happening, either by chance or by arrangement.

In parallel with this, though there was a consensus that professional flexibility, responsiveness and availability to talk and to listen are essential to the formation of trusting relationships with clients, for some this was an ideal rather than a reality. One of the clearest differences in time as a resource, was in terms of the amount of time that professionals in different countries could 'afford' to devote to their clients.

Previous comparative research with service users in England, France and Germany suggested that being able to form relationships with professionals who they felt they could trust, was highly valued by clients and seen as an important ingredient in the perceived success of the intervention (Baistow & Hetherington, 1998; Baistow & Wilford, 2000). A key feature of trustworthy professionals was their accessibility; they made time to listen and gave time to their clients who felt that they were being taken seriously. In the current study, though practitioners in all countries saw the short- and long-term value of spending time with clients, in some, notably Greece and England, there were low expectations of this happening; the time of qualified, expert practitioners was a resource in very short supply. They had much less professional time than elsewhere to spend with family members and the time that was available had to be saved until it was most needed. As we have seen this had repercussions for assessment and for the timing and nature of interventions, which were likely to be left until there was no alternative. In contrast to this situation, participants from France, Germany, Norway and Sweden envisaged the extensive use of professional time, working on a number of aspects of personal and family life from early on in the case. This could mean intensive support at home by qualified social workers on a daily basis, including, in Germany and Sweden, support for the family if the mother was hospitalized. In the view of practitioners from these countries, this kind of early expenditure of professional time would have prevented the later, more serious developments and would have provided a longer-term basis for trust to be established.

Shortage of time and shortage of resources do not in themselves prevent creativity. For example, a Greek participant pointed out that a shortage of resources led them to be imaginative in their responses. In many respects practitioners in England and Greece were faced with similar shortages. The key difference lay in the constraining bureaucracy in England. In offering professionals protection, the procedures and guidelines left little time for inventive responses. They also discouraged the kind of creative problem solving that could be found elsewhere. While the Italian social workers talked about taking risks, the practitioners in England talked about avoiding risk.

Translating findings into action

This chapter has examined some of the factors affecting interagency support for families with a mentally ill parent across Europe. One of the most important of these is the key part played by resources in the provision of early, expert interventions. Recent research from Sweden reinforces the notion that proper resourcing has the potential to make a significant difference to the lives of the children concerned (and indirectly to the lives of their parents). In spite of the difficulties that children with a mentally ill parent face, this research suggests that extensive supportive services in health, welfare and education can help them to overcome their disadvantages (Ruppert & Bågedahl-Strindlund, 2001).

However, though the problems of working together would benefit from increased funding, reductions in welfare spending across Europe mean that these services may be under threat in many places. This is particularly the case in England, which in comparison with other European countries is particularly poorly resourced for the kind of supportive interventions that these families need. Given these circumstances, which are unlikely to improve in the foreseeable future, we need to find other ways of resolving the difficulties of working together. This means developing new ways of thinking about the issues and asking ourselves how we can make the most of what we have, building on existing strengths. There are structural strengths, for example, our active and developing primary care system, including the universal provision offered by health visiting. Health visitors at national and local level not only recognize the difficulties faced by these families but also are keen to work with others in supporting them. Multidisciplinary community mental health teams, by their interprofessional constituency, are well-placed to support patients in a range of social as well as clinical contexts, including the context of family life. But, these strengths in themselves are not enough. We learned from this comparative research that there is an interaction of factors that facilitate or hinder interagency cooperation.

From European practitioners working under different conditions and systems, from Scandinavia to the Mediterranean, we also found out that a shared sense of responsibility can enable professionals to work flexibly to circumvent potential obstacles. The next stage is to consider how this information can be translated into the context of English service delivery. We believe that action in the following areas could significantly enhance interagency working and encourage a culture of collaboration.

- Raising knowledge levels concerning mental illness and psychiatric services amongst child welfare professionals and raising knowledge levels about child development and family welfare services amongst mental health professionals. This would need changes to qualifying training and the development of postqualifying training and multidisciplinary training.
- The consultative use of child and adolescent psychiatry services as a source of information and understanding of adult mental health and children's needs.
- A shift in managerial approaches towards encouraging and providing opportunities for formal and informal interagency and interprofessional contact.
- Establishing financial conditions which are conducive to joint working. This could include the creation of joint budgets and the loosening of boundaries between budgets such that interagency work could be funded in a more straightforward way.

• The active promotion of 'whole-family' approaches through the above measures and through joint training.

In our view these areas of action can (and should) be implemented at the level of national policy making. However, in our experience, presenting these findings to practitioners and managers is also a fruitful way of stimulating new ideas and approaches. In a professional world which has been characterized by uncertainty and pessimism, this offers them encouragement and evidence that positive, practicable strategies can be implemented at the local level. In turn this can enhance professional confidence and the will to work together, helping in the evolution of a culture in which there is an expectation that collaborative practice is not just desirable but possible, even in the face of obstacles.

REFERENCES

Baistow, K. (2000). Cross-national research: learning from comparisons. *Social Work in Europe*, 7, 8–13.

Baistow, K. & Hetherington, R. (1998). Parents' experiences of child welfare interventions: an Anglo-French comparison. *Children and Society*, 22, 113–24.

Baistow, K. & Wilford, G. (2000). Helping parents, protecting children: ideas from Germany. *Children and Society*, 14, 343–54.

Cleaver, H., Unell, I. & Aldgate, J. (1999). *Children's Needs – Parenting Capacity. The Impact of Parental Mental Illness, Problem Alcohol and Drug Abuse, and Domestic Violence on Children's Development.* London: The Stationery Office.

Cooper, A., Hetherington, R., Baistow, K., Pitts, J. & Spriggs, A. (1995). *Positive Child Protection: A View from Abroad.* Lyme Regis: Russell House Press.

Cummings, M. & Davies, P. (1994). Maternal depression and child development. *Journal of Child Psychology and Psychiatry*, 35, 73–112.

Dearden, C. & Becker, S. (2000). *Growing up Caring: Vulnerability and Transition to Adulthood – Young Carers' Experiences.* Leicester: The National Youth Agency.

Douglas, A. (1999). Building bridges: lessons for the future. In *Child Protection and Adult Mental Health. Conflict of Interest?*, ed. A. Weir & A. Douglas, pp. 182–8. Oxford: Butterworth-Heinemann.

Downey, G. & Coyne, J. C. (1990). Children of depressed parents: an integrative review. *Psychological Bulletin*, 108, 50–76.

Falkov, A. (1996). *A Study of Working Together "Part 8" Reports: Fatal Child Abuse and Parental Psychiatric Disorder.* London: Department of Health.

Falkov, A. (ed.) (1998). *Crossing Bridges. Training Resources for Working with Mentally Ill Parents and their Children. A Reader for Managers, Practitioners and Trainers.* Brighton: Department of Health and Pavilion Publishing.

Frank, J. (1995). *Couldn't Care More – A study of Young Carers and their Needs.* London: The Children's Society.

Göpfert, M., Webster, J. & Seeman, M. V. (ed.) (1996). *Parental Psychiatric Disorder: Distressed Parents and their Families*. Cambridge: Cambridge University Press.

Henry, L. A. & Kumar, R. C. (1999). Risk assessments of infants born to parents with a mental health or a learning disability. In *Child Protection and Adult Mental Health. Conflict of Interest?*, ed. A. Weir & A. Douglas, pp. 49–62. Oxford: Butterworth Heinemann.

Hetherington, R. (1998). Issues in European child protection research. *European Journal of Social Work*, *1*, 71–82.

Hetherington, R., Cooper, A., Smith, P. & Wilford, W. (1997). *Protecting Children: Messages from Europe*. Lyme Regis: Russell House Publishing.

Hetherington, R., Baistow, K., Katz, I., Mesie, J. & Trowell, J. (2001). *The Welfare of Children with Mentally Ill Parents: Learning from Inter-country Comparisons*. Chichester: John Wiley & Sons.

Mayes, K., Diggins, M. & Falkov, A. (1998). *Crossing Bridges. Training Resources for Working with Mentally Ill Parents and their Children: Trainer*. Brighton: Department of Health and Pavilion Press.

Oates, M. (1997). Patients as parents: the risk to children. *British Journal of Psychiatry*, *170* (Suppl. 32), 22–7.

O'Hagan, K. (1993). *Emotional and Psychological Abuse of Children*. Buckingham: Open University Press.

Phillips, N. & Hugman, R. (1999). The user's perspective: the experience of being a parent with a mental health problem. In *Child Protection and Adult Mental Health. Conflict of Interest?* ed. A. Weir & A. Douglas, pp. 96–108. Oxford: Butterworth Heinemann.

Ramsay, R., Howard, M. & Kumar, C. (1998). Schizophrenia and the safety of infants: a report on a UK mother and baby service. *International Journal of Social Psychiatry*, *44*, 127–34.

Reder, P. & Duncan, S. (1999). *Lost Innocence. A Follow Up Study of Fatal Child Abuse*. London: Routledge.

Reder, P., McClure, M. & Jolley, A. (ed.) (2000). *Family Matters: Interfaces between Child and Adult Mental Health*. London: Routledge.

Ruppert, S. & Bågedahl-Strindlund, M. (2001). Children of parapartum mentally ill mothers: a follow-up study. *Psychopathology*, *34*, 174–8.

Rutter, M. (1989). Psychiatric disorder in parents as a risk factor for children. In *Prevention of Mental Disorder, Alcohol and Drug Use in Children and Adolescents*, ed. D. Schaffer. Rockville, MD: Office for Substance Abuse, USDHHS.

Rutter, M. & Quinton, D. (1984). Parental psychiatric disorder: effects on children. *Psychological Medicine*, *14*, 853–80.

Sayce, L. (1999). Parenting as a civil right: supporting service users who choose to have children. In *Child Protection and Adult Mental Health. Conflict of Interest?* ed. A. Weir & A. Douglas, pp. 28–48. Oxford: Butterworth Heinemann.

Stroud, J. (1997). Mental disorder and the homicide of children: a review. *Social Work and Social Sciences Review*, *6*, 149–62.

Weir, A. & Douglas, A. (ed.) (1999). *Child Protection and Adult Mental Health. Conflict of Interest?* Oxford: Butterworth Heinemann.

27

Training and practice protocols

Adrian Falkov

Children's Hospital, Westmead, Australia

Introduction

At any point in time one adult in six suffers from a form of mental illness (Department of Health, 1999). The majority of these individuals will live in families and many will have responsibility for looking after children. In turn, those children whose parents experience mental ill-health are at particular risk for a wide range of difficulties in adjustment throughout childhood and adolescence (Cleaver *et al.*, 1999; Downey & Coyne, 1990; Laucht *et al.*, 1994; Rutter, 1966; Watt *et al.*, 1984) (see Hall, Chapter 3). The nature and quality of experiences in earlier years is known to be an important predictor of adult susceptibility to mental ill-health, relationship difficulties and life-long underachievement (Andrews *et al.*, 1990; Bifulco & Moran, 1998; Harris *et al.*, 1987; Landerman *et al.*, 1991; Oliver, 1985; Quinton *et al.*, 1990).

This is a substantial public health issue for all mental health, social and primary care services implicating earlier intervention, mental health promotion and more effective cross-service and interagency collaboration (Meltzer *et al.*, 1995, 2000; Oates, 1997). Yet, despite the increasing awareness of need, there are very few mental health and social care services explicitly configured to address the needs of *both* mentally ill parents and their children (Reder *et al.*, 2000).

This chapter will describe the development of a training programme commissioned by the Department of Health (UK) in 1998. This is followed by examples of its use and ongoing challenges to implementation and evaluation. Risks for staff and costs to families are presented to highlight the need for improving practice through the use of service protocols. The chapter emphasizes the need to integrate training and protocols in order to achieve better outcomes for children and their mentally ill parents.

Background and context

In the UK, the absence of a national strategy for mentally ill parents and their children is compounded by various other barriers which continue to impede service development. In particular, stigma and discrimination are amongst the most deep-rooted and pervasive negative influences which continue to fuel unhelpful, media-driven stereotypes involving mental illness, gender, ethnicity, parenting and child-hood (see Mahoney, Chapter 23).

An era of increasing specialization in health and social sciences has brought with it a more focused approach to undergraduate core curricula. Whilst this undoubtedly has provided some benefits in terms of in-depth training in one particular area, it has also limited the breadth of view of the same professionals, an important clinical skill crucial in enabling functional solutions for patients and their families. For example, workers in adult services attend to the needs of the client/patient as an individual whilst being unable to see the 'patient as parent' and her dependent children. Or at best they can only conceptualize this as an issue that needs to be dealt with by someone else who does have the necessary skills. In turn, staff in children's services work with children and their parents/carers directly but with insufficient emphasis on the mental health needs of parents and the adverse impact on children. Whilst adult services staff fail to 'see' the child and do not 'think family', in children's social services Sheppard (1997) has demonstrated that social workers both fail to identify maternal depression and wrongly diagnose it (Community Practitioners and Health Visitors Association, 2001) (see Seneviratne & Conroy, Chapter 9).

Children and young people are therefore at significant risk because their very existence is hidden/unacknowledged, the capacity to identify and recognize mental ill-health in their parents is poor and the requisite expertise to ascertain the impact of this adversity on their development and well-being is missing.

An almost universal accompaniment to research, audit and service development initiatives in this field is the recommendation for additional training for staff across all services and agencies (Department of Health, 2001). Issues of risk raise anxiety amongst clinicians, managers and policy makers and increasing effort is being devoted to the role of service protocols to lower anxiety in service providers and facilitate appropriate services for this group of families (Kearney *et al.*, 2000; NSPCC, 2001; Royal College of Psychiatrists, 2002; Weir & Douglas, 1999) (see Göpfert *et al.*, Chapter 5).

An education and training strategy in conjunction with a service protocol is one of the ways in which clinicians and managers across all services can be helped to develop an approach to practice that facilitates recognition of the needs of parents experiencing mental ill-health and their children. Such a strategy can facilitate earlier intervention and prevention.

Crossing Bridges – The Department of Health (UK) training programme

The mental health and well-being of children and adults within families in which an adult carer is mentally ill, are intimately linked in at least four ways:

(1) Parental mental illness can adversely affect the development and in some cases the safety of children (a parent to child influence).

(2) Growing up with a mentally ill parent can have a negative influence on the quality of that person's adjustment in adulthood, including their transition to parenthood (a childhood to adulthood (lifespan) influence).

(3) Children, particularly those with emotional, behavioural or chronic physical difficulties, can precipitate or exacerbate mental ill-health in their parents/carers (a child to parent influence).

(4) Adverse circumstances (poverty, single parenthood, isolation, stigma) can negatively influence both parent and child mental health (an environment to person influence).

These principles highlight the key areas of relevance and the interconnections between mental illness, parenting and children. They also demonstrate the links over time (childhood to adulthood) and across generations. Mental illness has profound implications for the affected individual and for that individual's network of family and social relationships. Given the prevalence of mental illness, major implications ensue, not only for individuals and families, but also for society as a whole.

In recognition of growing awareness of need and the increasing emphasis on earlier intervention and mental health promotion, the Department of Health (UK) commissioned the development of training materials on 'The Impact of Parental Mental Illness on Children'. The pack, entitled Crossing Bridges, consists of a comprehensive set of training materials designed to enhance practice and improve services for families in which mentally ill parents/carers live with dependent children (Box 27.1). The pack is intended specifically for use by trainers across *all* agencies to promote good practice (raising awareness, knowledge and skills) amongst staff in adult mental health and children's services, as well as within primary care and the voluntary sector.

A multidisciplinary, multicentre team consisting of child and adult specialists in mental health, social care, research, policy and training produced the materials. The team was assisted by active involvement of service users. The materials were based on literature reviews, focus groups of practitioners working in a variety of adult and children's services across health and social care, and were piloted using multidisciplinary, multiagency groups.

Requirements for the programme

Adequate and appropriate training for practitioners lies at the heart of any attempt to improve practice and develop services better able to respond to the needs of individuals as family members. But such comprehensive training faces many challenges. A good training programme to address the needs of *both* children and their parents requires an approach which will support staff of varying experience, with

---

Box 27.1. Crossing Bridges – key messages

Crossing Bridges – a broader approach linking traditional divisions of language, culture, geography and training across organizations and services by promoting:

An inclusive approach ('something for everyone')
　Children *and* parents (families)
　Mental health *and* social care
　Professionals working with adults *and* children
　Support *and* protection
A balanced approach (Mental illness *and* parenting)
　The presence of a mental illness does not automatically preclude an ability to parent. But some parents do struggle and with appropriate support can be helped to meet their children's needs. However, some parents are unable to ensure their children's safety, even with support and alternative care arrangements will be necessary.
Dialogue and partnership ('It's good to talk')
　Children, even very young children, can understand and, given the right (safe) circumstances, will talk. Explanation for them is important. But for parents to provide explanations they need to know about their own difficulties and disorder.
　Dialogue must involve:
　　Professionals with each other
　　Professionals with parents and children
　　Parents and children
　　Statutory and voluntary sectors
　　Primary care and specialist sectors and education.
Good practice:
　Comprehensive needs assessment based on key conceptual models
　　(1) The family model – developmental trajectories and intergenerational pathways (Mayes *et al.*, 1998)
　　(2) 'Framework for children in need' (Department of Health, 2000)
　　(3) Continuum of parent–child–professional interactions (Falkov, 2002)
　Partnerships in intervention within and across services and agencies
　Respectful inclusion of service users and carers
　Training and protocol development
　Best use of existing resources and sound arguments for additional investment
　Prevention

---

differing professional backgrounds, working in diverse settings and within a context of insufficient resources and stigma regarding mental illness(Box 27.2).

Initially, when considering the requirements for a training programme, there was no shortage of existing training materials for each of the key areas: adult mental

---

Box 27.2. Training – necessary but not sufficient. A programme for staff working with children and their mentally ill parents

Training must be:

Flexible, relevant, understandable, easily deliverable, effective and efficient
Grounded in appropriate theoretical (ecological) approaches
Underpinned by coherent conceptual models which promote a family and systems
   approach
Informed by experiences of both service users and deliverers
Able to enhance awareness, knowledge and skills
Evaluated

---

health; parenting; child protection; risk management; child development and mental health. There was no programme, however, that drew together the key elements from each domain into a coherent, integrated approach sufficiently flexible for delivery to practitioners with very different needs and efficient enough in terms of time to be supported by service and senior managers.

Key conceptual frameworks

A broader approach was required to link the traditional divisions between hospital and community; adult and child; health and social care. This approach was necessary to tackle one of the unhelpful consequences of specialization, namely the overfocused and therefore blinkered learning experiences in new generations of students. A shift in learning culture was required away from exclusive single-model approaches to broader (and more sophisticated) approaches better able to integrate health and social sciences.

The materials were therefore based on the biopsychosocial model which could more adequately represent the true complexity of the multiple systems in which individuals exist. By drawing on the strengths of biogenetic and psychosocial models (nature *and* nurture), a richer, more integrated understanding could be used to underpin an approach in which mental health, human development, family relationships and parenting are better integrated.

A systems attitude was also required. This model was well suited to complement the biopsychosocial approach by linking the various domains relevant to mentally ill individuals within a family and social context (see Göpfert *et al.*, Chapter 5; Cooklin & Gorell Barnes, Chapter 22). The emphasis here was on harnessing the method and its applicability for training staff of varying experience and professional background working in diverse settings across different agencies. This can incorporate the proximal influences and interactions of an individual within the family as well as more distal relationships such as neighbourhood and religious networks, as well as schools, cultural and societal values and aspirations.

Both the biopsychosocial and systems approaches needed to incorporate a developmental perspective. This was essential to promote a better understanding about the influences and interplay between the developing child and his various contexts over time (a lifespan approach). This included knowledge about normal child development as well as the rapidly evolving field of developmental psychopathology (Rolf *et al.*, 1990).

Involving clinicians and managers

In producing a comprehensive programme, the intention was to ensure explicit, early involvement of senior managers to address top-down and bottom-up tensions within any organization, support for frontline staff and feedback for managers. A balance was sought between the historically overfocused child protection agenda in the UK and the broader continuum of need in families (Department of Health, 1995, 2000) including opportunities for early intervention (Falkov, 2002).

Harnessing specialist expertise in joint working

There was no attempt to create experts in all fields. Instead, the team endeavoured to create an approach which would facilitate sufficient baseline understanding and familiarity with roles, language and responsibilities across different services to enable practitioners to talk to each other, to collaborate and to cross bridges. This would help practitioners to harness a range of expertise from various services according to the diverse needs of individuals within families.

Aims

The broad aim was to provide a systemic conceptual framework which incorporated developmental, family, social and mental health domains together with an approach for considering the range of parent–child–professional interactions. The intention was also to assist practitioners and managers in translating broad national guidelines and priorities into locally deliverable and sustainable initiatives to improve the quality of life for all families in which mentally ill parents/carers live with their dependent children. Specific aims were to:

(1) Improve individual practice whilst encouraging interagency collaboration across key services. This was based on the premise that children and their mentally ill parents are better supported and protected if agencies coordinate services and interventions

(2) Ensure that training was linked and integrated into individual practice and service provision by involving managers and service users as well as frontline staff. This included the development and implementation of service protocols.

(3) Reduce the impact of mental illness on parents and children by facilitating earlier intervention and provision of both practical support and treatment for all family members. This included assessments of need to ensure appropriate support for parents and protection of children.

The training package thus provides an opportunity to implement frequently rehearsed recommendations from various child abuse and homicide inquiries about the need for better communication, coordination and collaboration (Department of Health, 2001; Falkov, 1996).

Content

Crossing Bridges consists of a Reader and a Trainer, which have been designed to complement each other. The Reader (Falkov, 1998) provides selective reviews of key topics covering adult mental health, child-care and implications for practice, including child protection. It also provides essential background information for trainers and is a further reference for participants. The Reader can stand alone and will help those who have been unable to participate in training. There are:

References and recommendations for further reading.

Examples of good practice (including work involving users, parents and children).

Conceptual frameworks and suggested models and protocols to improve understanding and practice.

The Trainer (Mayes *et al.*, 1998) consists of four modules:

(1) Module for managers – ensures involvement of senior managers.

(2) Foundation knowledge – facilitates acquisition of a shared understanding of different language, culture and organizational systems without requiring practitioners to be experts in all fields.

(3) Working together – assists practitioners to develop common approaches and closer collaboration.

(4) Assessment, intervention and care planning – provides opportunities to acquire experience in risk management and earlier intervention.

It provides:

A detailed guide for trainers on the use of materials, including how to involve users and how to ensure that managers at all levels are an integral part of the training.

A menu of options to suit local training requirements.

A guide on individual sessions within each of the modules, together with learning objectives and outcomes.

Materials to support training including exercises, case studies, overhead transparencies and handouts.

The training is sufficiently flexible to provide focused basic training in specialist areas as well as encompassing differing levels of staff experience in all agencies.

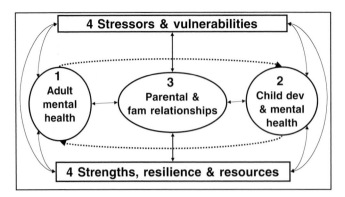

Figure 27.1   Family model.

Conceptual underpinnings – the family model

The family model (Fig. 27.1) illustrates the core components of the conceptual framework which includes relevant aspects of:

- Adult mental health (1).
- Child development and mental health (2).
- Parent–child relationships and parenting (3).
- Risk factors and stressors as well as protective factors including available resources (4).

All components must be considered if there is to be effective assessment and treatment when there is a parent with mental illness. The aim of the model is to facilitate an understanding of the processes that underlie and influence how:

- Parental mental illness affects children (1 → 2).
- Mental illness can affect parenting and the parent–child relationship (1 → 3).
- Parenthood can precipitate and influence mental illness (3 → 1).
- Children's mental health and developmental needs have an impact on parental mental health (2 → 1) and on parenting and the parent–child relationship (2 → 3).
- Risk and protective factors interact with parental mental illness, child development and mental health, parenting and the parent–child relationship in a bi-directional manner (4 ↔ 1; 4 ↔ 2; 4 ↔ 3).

The interactions between each of these components are illustrated by the arrows. They highlight the relevance of a systems approach to assessment and intervention. Each component affects and is affected by every other component. Such an approach requires consideration of:

- The tasks and responsibilities of parenthood and an individual's coping resources. This includes family of origin and childhood experiences as well as susceptibility to difficulties in the transition to parenthood.

- Unique aspects of the relationship between a parent and child.
- The nature of the mental illness experienced by the adult.
- The child's own needs according to their developmental stage and ability, as well as temperament, physical and mental/emotional health.
- The family, social and environmental context in which these interactions take place, and the impact of this context on those interactions.

How these core components interact and influence each other determines the quality of an individual's adjustment within his or her family, as well as the adequacy of the whole family's adaptation to living with a mentally ill member.

Use of the materials

Trainers in a variety of settings and contexts within the mental health, local authority and voluntary sectors have used the materials and feedback over the past 2 years has been positive. Training has included single and multi-agency approaches varying in scope and scale. Most participants have favoured locality-specific interagency events as part of an ongoing rolling programme, using experience gained from the 'foundation' module to maximize understanding and utilization of the 'working together' and 'assessment and care planning' modules. Staff who work within a common geographic area serving a similar catchment population use the time to get to know each other and to exchange details about their respective services and contact information. Where senior managers are actively involved this time has been used to plan baseline audits, to map services and to put together proposals for additional resources. In some instances service innovations have been planned such as secondments, 'named' members of staff to contact in teams and work on referral prioritization. In some cases the training has formed the basis for the launch of a protocol whilst in other services the training has served as a forum to initiate the process of protocol development.

Training has worked best when those responsible for its delivery have sought (and secured) the interest and support of senior managers and where training has been part of a process of awareness raising and service improvement, not a one-off event. Seeking the views of participants prior to and after training has been a helpful way of ensuring that frontline concerns can be incorporated into training and fed back to senior managers. Frontline staff have been far more motivated when senior managers have been visibly and actively involved.

Involving service users in delivery of training has been much more variable. Inevitably this requires more detailed planning and participants can be faced with greater anxieties. Where they have been involved, participants have been more challenged, moved and motivated.

In terms of time, training has varied from one-off single day/half-day events to carefully planned and coordinated annual rolling programmes consisting of 1–3 day programmes. Materials have been readily adaptable for local usage and the use of two trainers – one with a mental health background and one with child-care and protection experience – has worked best.

Two examples of use in different settings are provided.

Collaboration in Europe

The materials have demonstrated crosscultural relevance following successful piloting over a 12-month period in Thessaloniki, Greece. The project was funded via the European Union (Daphne Programme) to explore the use of the materials in raising awareness and improving services for mentally ill parents and their children within a linguistically, culturally and organizationally different setting. A core group consisting of clinical psychologist, adult psychiatrist, social worker and child mental health worker established a successful training programme for 30 practitioners from mental health, child welfare, police, education and various nongovernment organizations. The core group found the materials easy to understand and readily adaptable to local requirements. Analysis of the training process and outcomes for a group of 30 local families is in progress.

Training the trainers – A county-wide implementation of Crossing Bridges

In Bedfordshire, England, a programme of training will assist trainers with experience in both child-care/development/protection and adult mental health to establish a county-wide programme of locality-specific interagency training. Trainers will target mental health, social care and primary care practitioners (e.g. school nurses and health visitors) in the first instance. User involvement will be incorporated and implementation will be independently evaluated.

There will be intended benefits for practitioners, their managers and for parents and children. For example:

- All practitioners will be helped to acquire a shared understanding of roles and responsibilities across services.
- Child-care practitioners will be helped to gain better knowledge of mental health issues and to overcome anxieties and uncertainties about dealing with mentally ill parents.
- Adult mental health staff will be helped to gain confidence in recognizing how mental illness can impact on parenting and vice versa. They will be helped to feel more able to talk with children directly.
- Managers will be helped to find ways of supporting front-line practitioners in the achievement of best practice despite inevitable resource constraints.
- Through improved joint working children will be helped to acquire a better understanding of their parents' problems and to be able to ask questions and express confusion or uncertainty.

- Parents will be helped to recognize ways in which their difficulties may impact on their children and to feel more able to talk directly with their children and to respond in developmentally appropriate ways.

Challenges to systematic implementation and evaluation of training

One of the weaknesses in the development of the Crossing Bridges programme is the absence of a centrally coordinated implementation and evaluation strategy. This has resulted in great variation in the manner and extent to which local implementation has occurred across the country. Furthermore, whilst individual (anecdotal) feedback from trainers, frontline staff and managers has been uniformly positive, there is little in the way of formal evaluation of the extent of uptake (usage of the materials), changes in practice and service developments as a consequence of training.

The need for broad-based (national) approaches to raise standards and improve outcomes for individuals and families is highlighted in the UK by the increasing number of national strategies and frameworks. For example, there are a National Service Framework for Children, a National Service Framework for Mental Health and a Framework for the Assessment of Children in Need. Whilst this reflects growing importance being attached to both mental health and children in general, the proposals do not explicitly address the needs of these particular families. It requires translation of the standards and approaches to practice and therefore does not have the essential 'must do' (and compelling) quality for clinicians and managers responsible for implementation.

The needs of families can be considered within 'Standard One' of the National Service Framework for Mental Health (early intervention/mental health promotion). But this is vague, there are many competing priorities regarding mental health prevention and the existing focus on the mental health needs of adults as individuals does not readily promote the needs of patients as parents. 'Standard Six' addresses carer issues. Whilst young (dependent, child) carers are recognized, individuals affected by mental ill-health who are carers (i.e. parents) are not. The emphasis from the highest level continues to focus on the mental health of individuals. Parents, their children and their mental health do not feature in an integrated and coherent way.

Within children's (social) services the Framework for Assessment of Children in Need (Department of Health, 2000) is a helpful tool in assisting practitioners to undertake systematic assessments of the needs of all family members. It will therefore help to identify gaps in provision and provide opportunities for establishing better links with mental health service practitioners. However, whilst there is some reference to mentally ill parents, the approach is a generic one to raise standards and it does not directly address the issue of parents with mental health problems and the impact on children. In particular the absence of high level, joint agreement on implementation means that (yet again) a single agency is left to grapple with trying to engage staff in other services without jointly agreed priorities for collaboration. Good practice with regard to joint work remains a well-intentioned aspiration – 'we should' rather than 'we must'.

Combined efforts which effectively harness mental health and child-care assessment skills will ensure much richer, comprehensive service provision focused on need rather than either approach in isolation. In their current form these significant high-level approaches continue to perpetuate existing barriers. These barriers (see Göpfert et al., Chapter 5) are not unique to the UK. Similar difficulties have been documented in Europe, Australia and the USA (Hetherington, 2000; Nicholson et al., 1993) (see Baistow & Hetherington, Chapter 26).

Developing protocols to integrate training and practice

Improvements in both mental health and parenting not only provide opportunities for more rewarding family life, but can also have an important preventive element by reducing the proportion of parents who are unable to meet their children's needs and ensure their safety. Earlier intervention will also help to reduce the number of children with emotional and behavioural problems who will require specialist children's services as well as the proportion who will need mental health and other services in adulthood, thereby reducing costs in the long term.

One of the ways in which risk can be reduced is to ensure systematic identification of relevant families – knowing which patients are parents and which parents have mental health problems. Having ensured a mechanism for identifying families, a set of procedures with clear questions and actions will assist staff in appropriately and safely assessing need, specifying gaps or uncertainties and taking steps to ensure prompt intervention (Box 27.3). This will include knowing which colleagues in other services to contact as well as being confident that their communication and/or questions will be appropriately prioritized. This is the basis for effective collaboration and joint working.

The amount and quality of communication between staff working across numerous interfaces is therefore a vital determinant of joint working. If a referrer provides the sort of information recommended in training and if the recipient service places priority on referrals of mentally ill parents and their children, then the likelihood of traditional barriers – the thresholds 'clash' – being triggered, is lessened. Staff in adult mental health services may be less inclined to invoke the severe mental illness threshold as an immediate/automatic response to a referral from a children's social worker. Staff in children's services may be more amenable to considering a

Box 27.3. Protocols – necessary but not sufficient. A programme for staff working with children and their mentally ill parents

A protocol is a set of principles, procedures, questions and instructions to raise awareness and guide practice. It should be brief, clear and understandable as well as practical and specific, with timescales and flow charts. The purpose is to raise standards by ensuring:

A standardized, systematic approach to addressing a particular problem or issue

Better coverage (all who are eligible are included)

Consistency in provision of support and intervention

A mechanism for review and audit – evaluation of the protocol itself (adherence, usability, understandability etc.) and of influence on practice for individual staff and services as a whole

It should:

Promote partnership between practitioners, mentally ill parents and their children

Demonstrate to staff that this an important issue and provide them with a guide to procedures about how to identify relevant families (what questions to ask) and the steps to take having done so (what to do, who to contact and when)

Provide the support (bridge) to enable practitioners in different services/agencies to communicate more effectively and at an earlier stage in a family's contact with services

Raise (and maintain) awareness about the needs of these families amongst managers and service planners regarding annual priorities and resource allocation

To accomplish the above, the protocol must be:

Acknowledged and supported by key agencies/services (collective stakeholder ownership)

Backed by senior managers to ensure routine incorporation into practice, including support for training staff who will have responsibility for implementation

Linked to a clear implementation plan with mechanisms for evaluating individual adherence and service-wide impacts

Linked to a programme of training which ensures appropriate awareness and familiarity, understanding, confidence and competence in its use. Training also ensures understanding about the aims, purpose and target groups for the protocol as well as awareness of unmet need and best ways to support families. Training can therefore enhance staff cooperation and skill in using the protocol and in raising standards

Distinct from but appropriately linked to policy, legislation, relevant research and evidence-based practice

Accurate and kept up to date

broader range of supports for children whose parents are known to adult mental health services, rather than considering only those referrals which require urgent intervention for children at risk of serious harm.

A good protocol can help staff to implement new awareness and learning from training into practice. It therefore complements the use of training to improve practice by ensuring that individual practitioners can be helped to achieve a set of standards consistent with aims and aspirations of the service. Training targets individuals and a protocol helps with consistency of approach to a high standard across the service. A protocol can help to reduce risk by:

- Ensuring systematic identification of relevant family members and their needs. For example, parenting needs of mentally ill adults, mental health needs of parents and the development and safety needs of children of mentally ill parents.
- Guiding communication across various service and agency interfaces.
- Supporting comprehensive assessment of need by practitioners with appropriate experience.
- Facilitating appropriate support and intervention.

Protocols can therefore help frontline staff to incorporate new learning into practice, which is consistent with service standards, to review caseloads and receive appropriate support and supervision. Frontline managers can use protocols to review individual practice and to evaluate whether a team is achieving service targets and outcomes. Regular audit can demonstrate areas of concern, the need for additional resources and evidence of the implementation of good practice (are individuals within families receiving a level and type of support consistent with their assessed needs?). Senior managers can use aggregated information derived from the use of protocols to review the implementation of strategy, the adherence to good practice, to justify the use of and need for additional resources and to initiate and maintain active dialogue and collaboration with senior colleagues in other agencies.

In developing and implementing a protocol, the process of establishing shared ownership is crucial. This requires the support of agencies to develop, share and support a common agenda with core principles, practical steps and agreed pathways. All too often a well-intentioned (but single) service attempts to champion the issue by distributing their (not *our*) protocol with the naive expectation that other services will accept and adopt the proposals. This can frequently result in frustration, delays and tensions (them vs. us), which blocks collaborative opportunities. Developing joint ownership and trust is inevitably time consuming and it requires sustained commitment from all parties.

The availability and deployment of resources to support implementation of a protocol is also crucial. To this end senior managers will have to emulate frontline collaboration by considering various options and models for high level pooling of resources and budgets. Exhorting frontline staff to collaborate is not enough.

Part of good risk management will be the recognition by managers about the potential opportunities associated with prioritizing the needs of these families. For example, child fatalities attract such intense and adverse media exposure that the presence of a clear protocol, with appropriate training and support can be used to demonstrate both individual and service-wide good practice amidst the inevitable media frenzy. However, training and protocols cannot guarantee the absence of fatalities. A child's death can highlight poor practice and, as with adult homicide enquiries, the importance of lesson-learning lies less in the prevention of rare but tragic and sensationalized individual deaths and more in the positive impact on procedures and practices. Improving awareness, knowledge and skills can help the much larger group of children who are abused, but not killed and constitute the at-risk population from which many child fatalities arise (Falkov, 1996; Reder & Duncan, 1999).

A basic template for protocol development is provided in the Crossing Bridges Reader (Falkov, 1998, p. 142) (see Appendix 7.1 for a sample interagency protocol).

Conclusion

The Department of Health (UK) has demonstrated a commitment to raising standards and improving outcomes for mentally ill parents and their children by commissioning a comprehensive training programme specifically for all staff in contact with members of this group of families. To date the programme has demonstrated success in terms of utility and deliverability as well as awareness raising and knowledge improvement. However, whilst it has clear potential for national implementation, there has, as yet, been insufficient evaluation of the impact on practice and service development. Challenges to national implementation have been outlined together with the costs to children and their parents and opportunities for better risk management and early intervention.

For training to occur successfully the full support of all tiers of management is a critical requirement to initiate, implement, sustain and evaluate training initiatives. This combination of top-down and bottom-up approaches is essential to ensure that frontline staff are supported in their efforts to implement the good practice obtained from training. Similarly, senior managers have the authority to ensure that the needs of such families are included in their strategic plans and annual reviews, that they are able to match frontline innovation and good practice with funding and that they are able to talk with their colleagues across agencies to establish necessary pathways and supports to promote joint working at the point of contact.

Unless and until all practitioners know which patients/clients are parents and which parents have mental health problems, children, their parents and practitioners will continue to be at risk.

Furthermore, training is a necessary but insufficient requirement for service development which promotes best practice. A service protocol can usefully complement a training programme. The needs of families are therefore best met when mentally ill parents and their children's support and safety needs are systematically acknowledged, assessed, facilitated and regularly reviewed. A training programme which raises awareness, knowledge and skills in conjunction with a well-designed, jointly agreed and systematically implemented protocol can facilitate this.

It is the process of securing jointly agreed and explicitly supported prioritization of the needs of children and their mentally ill parents which is vital. A programme of training and a clear, fully supported protocol must be the minimum necessary requirements to ensure implementation of best practice. The opportunities for prevention and early intervention would be well supported by adherence to a protocol which promoted timely referrals and an appropriate network of relevant professionals to assess, support, treat and review needs.

Early intervention is good risk management and good risk management requires early intervention.

REFERENCES

Andrews, B., Brown, G. & Creasey, L. (1990). Intergenerational links between psychiatric disorder in mothers and daughters: the role of parenting experiences. *Journal of Child Psychology and Psychiatry*, *31*, 1115–29.

Bifulco, A. & Moran, P. (1998). *Wednesday's Child: Research into Women's Experience of Neglect and Abuse in Childhood and Adult Depression*. London: Routledge.

Cleaver, H., Unell, I. & Aldgate, J. (1999). *Childrens' Needs – Parenting Capacity: The Impact of Parental Mental Illness, Problem Alcohol and Drug Use, and Domestic Violence on Children's Development*. London: The Stationery Office.

Community Practitioners and Health Visitors Association (2001). *Conference Proceedings Post-natal Depression and Maternal Mental Health: A Public Health Priority*. Quoted in CPHVA (2002) *Strategy for Postnatal Depression and Maternal Mental Health*. London: CPHVA. (www.msfcphva.org)

Department of Health (1995). *Child Protection: Messages from Research*. London: HMSO.

Department of Health (1999). *A National Service Framework for Mental Health: Modern Standards & Service Models*. London: The Stationery Office.

Department of Health, Department for Education and Employment, Home Office (2000). *Framework for the Assessment of Children in Need and Their Families*. London: The Stationery Office.

Department of Health (2001). *Safety First – Five-Year Report of the National Confidential Inquiry into Suicide and Homicide by People with Mental Illness*. London: Department of Health. Crown Copyright.

Downey, G. & Coyne, J. C. (1990). Children of depressed parents: an integrative review. *Psychological Bulletin*, *108*, 50–76.

Falkov, A. (1996). *Department of Health Study of Working Together 'Part 8' Reports: Fatal Child Abuse and Parental Psychiatric Disorder.* ACPC Series Report No. 1. London: Department of Health.

Falkov, A. (ed.) (1998). *Crossing Bridges: Training Resources for Working with Mentally Ill Parents and their Children – An Evidence-based Reader.* Brighton: Department of Health and Pavilion Publishing.

Falkov, A. (2002). Addressing family needs when a parent is mentally ill. In *Approaches to Needs Assessment in Children's Services*, ed. H. Ward & W. Rose. London: Jessica Kingsley.

Harris, T., Brown, G. & Bifulco, A. (1987). Loss of parent in childhood and adult psychiatric disorder: the role of social class position and premarital pregnancy. *Psychological Medicine, 17,* 163–83.

Hetherington, R. (2000). *The Icarus Project: Professional Interventions for Mentally Ill Parents and their Children: Building a European Model.* Uxbridge: Centre for Comparative Social Work Studies, Brunel University.

Kearney, P., Levin, E. & Rosen, G. (2000). *Alcohol, Drug and Mental Health Problems: Working With Families.* London: The National Institute for Social Work.

Landerman, R., George, L. & Blazer, D. (1991). Adult vulnerability for psychiatric disorders: interactive effects of negative childhood experiences and recent stress. *Journal of Nervous and Mental Disease, 179,* 656–63.

Laucht, M., Esser, G. & Schmidt, M. (1994). Parental mental disorder and early child development. *European Child and Adolescent Psychiatry, 3,* 125–37.

Mayes, K., Diggins, M. & Falkov, A. (1998). *Crossing Bridges: Training Resources for Working with Mentally Ill Parents and their Children – Trainer.* Brighton: Department of Health and Pavilion Publishing.

Meltzer, H., Gill, B., Petticrew, N. & Hinds, K. (1995). *The Prevalence of Psychiatric Morbidity among Adults aged 16–64 Living in Private Households in Great Britain.* OPCS Surveys: Report 1. London: OPCS.

Meltzer, H., Gatward, R., Goodman, R. & Ford, T. (2000). *The Mental Health of Children and Adolescents in Great Britain.* Office for National Statistics, Social Survey Division. London: The Stationery Office.

Nicholson, J., Geller, J., Fisher, W. & Dion, G. (1993). State policies and programs that address the needs of mentally ill mothers in the public sector. *Hospital and Community Psychiatry, 44,* 484–9.

NSPCC (2001). *Out of Sight – NSPCC Report on Child Deaths from Abuse 1973–2000.* London: Elmtree Graphics Ltd.

Oates, M. (1997). Patients as parents: the risk to children. *British Journal of Psychiatry, 170* (Suppl. 32), 22–7.

Oliver, J. E. (1985). Successive generations of child maltreatment: social and medical disorders in the parents. *British Journal of Psychiatry, 147,* 484–90.

Quinton, D., Rutter, M. & Gulliver, L. (1990). Continuities in psychiatric disorders from childhood to adulthood in the children of psychiatric patients. In *Straight and Devious Pathways from Childhood to Adulthood*, ed. L. Robins & M. Rutter. New York: Cambridge University Press.

Reder, P. & Duncan, S. (1999). *Lost Innocents: A Follow-up Study of Fatal Child Abuse.* London: Routledge.

Reder, P., McClure, M. & Jolley, A. (ed.) (2000). *Family Matters: Interfaces between Child and Adult Mental Health.* London: Routledge.

Rolf, J., Masten, A. S., Cicchetti, D., Nuechterlein, K. & Weintraub, S. (ed.) (1990). *Risk and Protector Factors in the Development of Psychopathology.* Cambridge: Cambridge University Press.

Royal College of Psychiatrists (2002). *Patients as Parents,* Council Report CR 105. London: Royal College of Psychiatrists.

Rutter, M. (1966). *Children of Sick Parents: An Environmental and Psychiatric Study.* Institute of Psychiatry Maudsley Monographs No. 16. Oxford: Oxford University Press.

Sheppard, M. (1997). Double jeopardy: the link between child abuse and maternal depression in child and family social work. *Child and Family Social Work, 2,* 91–107.

Watt, N., Anthony, E. J., Wynne, L. C. & Rolf, J. E. (ed.) (1984). *Children At Risk For Schizophrenia: A Longitudinal Perspective.* Cambridge: Cambridge University Press.

Weir, A. & Douglas, A. (ed.) (1999). *Child Protection and Adult Mental Health: Conflict of Interest?* Oxford: Butterworth Heinemann.

Afterword

John Cox

Immediate Past President, Royal College of Psychiatrists

I expect some readers who have reached this afterword may already share my reflection about this important book which has underlined the need to 'Think Family' and to consider 'Patients as Parents'. In my early training at The London Hospital I was fortunate, and probably more fortunate than many contemporary postgraduate students, as Desmond Pond had established a Family Unit in his new department. I was taught dynamic psychiatry and basic psychoanalytic concepts by a child analyst, and my first psychotherapy experience was play therapy. However, this training in child psychiatry was narrowly confined to 1 day a week for no more than 6 months. Yet such was the impact of this training that almost the first questions I asked in Uganda and Great Britain about the consequences of postnatal depression was: "What is the impact of this disabling disorder on the infant?"

A further prominent question raised by this book, and surely linked to the demand for a second edition so soon after the first, is: "What is happening to our society that has provoked parents and health professionals from a wide variety of disciplines to focus now on problems for parents and parenting?"

Elsewhere I have described these massive societal changes as a "cultural revolution"; it is within family relationships that values, attitudes and beliefs are transmitted between generations. Family life *has* changed considerably over the last 30 years. Some regret this, others regard it as inevitable, but those wishing to put the clock back are, in my opinion, misguided in their recollections and incorrect in their assumptions.

Indeed the term 'marital status' with its bald descriptors is long out-moded. Certainly our terminology and approach now needs to recognize different forms of families, yet to understand that disrupted relationships following prolonged discord can be harmful to the individuals and to the children of these partnerships. The evidence, however, for increased rates of mental disorder (in particular depression), substance misuse and alcoholism, as well as attempted and completed suicide in those who are separated or divorced is overwhelming and should not be brushed under the liberal post-modern carpet without very careful thought, but rather be investigated and verified within a new contemporary circumstance.

As found in earlier studies from Nigeria, when societies are in transition there is an increase in anxiety, especially in women, and in our own society, increased unhappiness in young men. Nevertheless the increased roles of grandparents in supporting grandchildren and providing physical care and emotional support, whilst the parents are working and trying to meet the demands of society for greater autonomy and affluence, are also being documented.

I would expect the next edition of this book to include more about grandparents and grandparenting, and the literature on grandparental anxiety and depression following the birth of a grandchild will be burgeoning.

Parents and their children, as poignantly pointed out by contributors to this volume, are looking to mental health professionals to acknowledge their priorities and predicaments. These are indeed often linked to their parenting roles and their concerns about their disturbed and ill children. If we fail to acknowledge these concerns even when identifying a defined mental disorder in one parent, then we will not only lose credibility as professionals, but the parents may seek help from elsewhere and so neglect to access a contemporary evidence-based mental illness service.

Parents themselves, as well as professionals, are now looking again at the brain/mind interface as two qualities of one substance, and at the specific role of psychiatrists trained in biological and social sciences and in developmental psychology. This breadth of training can span the brain/mind contiguities and provide a coordinated approach to the recognition and treatment of mental disorders, which is truly holistic and certainly multidisciplinary.

The other demand now placed on mental health services is that we should think 'family' more frequently than we do.

This book is therefore to my way of thinking a 'cri de coeur'. At first sight it is daunting. How can mental health professionals do more than what they are doing, when what they are doing is undertaken with inadequate human and financial resources? How can adult psychiatrists struggling to meet the day to day priorities consider in detail the impact of mental disorder on children, taking into account developmental milestones, socio-cultural constraints and bringing to bear a knowledge of mental disorder in children as well as adults? To many of my colleagues this question seems academic, because the answer is linked to increased demands, and could only be coped with by a further restriction of clinical activity and eventually by a reluctant acknowledgement that these additional tasks are impossible to achieve.

Yet should we not think in more radical terms? Why is the training of child and adolescent psychiatrists and adult psychiatrists in this country (and even more so on the continent) separated almost from the moment of conception? This in my view is a mistake. To meet the needs identified in this book, all psychiatrists need to be trained in a developmental approach. They need to be familiar with the principles of psychological treatments including family therapy and systemic therapy and to have had experience of child and adolescent psychiatry and in the way in which adult mental disorder impacts on parenting skills and work roles.

One solution actively considered by the Royal College of Psychiatrists is that all future psychiatrists would have dual specialty certificates; first training for 4–5 years in adult psychiatry and then specialist training subsequently in child and adolescent psychiatry. Although this might prolong training slightly, it may take this period of time to produce the leaders of services that would enable the coordination of treatments for parents and children, and have the credibility to coordinate other health professionals and to consider the wishes of the parents and their children.

Is this utopian at the present time? Yes, probably. Could it be achieved over a 5–10 year period given the political will and revolutionized training programmes? Yes it could. Early experience as postgraduate students in our several mental health professions could then stick in the mind as clearly as the supervised play therapy I undertook over 30 years ago. The difference now being that such breadth of training and supervised experience in family work, would be a routine part of the training of all mental health professionals including consultant psychiatrists.

The next edition of this book in 10 years' time could then indicate whether this change in direction of services has happened or whether the opportunity has been lost in a welter of increased bureaucracy, the demise of family or more likely the lack of political will.

Index